Educating Managers through Real World Projects

S0-BNB-469

a volume in
Research in Management Education and Development
Series Editors: Charles Wankel and Robert DeFillippi

Research in Management Education and Development

Charles Wankel and Robert DeFillippi, Series Editors

The Cutting Edge of International Management Education (2004)
  edited by Charles Wankel and Robert DeFillippi

Educating Managers with Tomorrow's Technologies (2003)
  edited by Charles Wankel and Robert DeFillippi

Rethinking Management Education for the 21st Century (2002)
  edited by Charles Wankel and Robert DeFillippi

Educating Managers through Real World Projects

edited by

Charles Wankel
St. John's University

and

Robert DeFillippi
Suffolk University

INFORMATION AGE
PUBLISHING

Greenwich, Connecticut • www.infoagepub.com

Library of Congress Cataloging-in-Publication Data

Educating managers through real world projects / edited by Charles Wankel
and Robert DeFillippi.
    p. cm. — (Research in management education and development)
  Includes bibliographical references.
  ISBN 1-59311-370-6 (pbk.) — ISBN 1-59311-371-4 (hardcover)
  1. Management—Study and teaching. 2. Business education. I. Wankel,
Charles. II. DeFillippi, Bob. III. Series.
  HD30.4.E32 2005
  650'.071'1—dc22

                 2005017307

Printed in the United States of America

EDITORIAL REVIEW BOARD

LIST OF CONTRIBUTORS

Susan Adams	Bentley College Waltham, MA
Karen Ayas	Erasmus University Rotterdam, the Netherlands
Mark V. Cannice	University of San Francisco San Francisco, CA
Patricia Gorman Clifford	University of Pennsylvania Philadelphia, PA
Eugene Baten	Central Connecticut State University New Britain, CT
Jan Brace-Govan	Monash University Melbourne, Australia
Burton V. Dean	San Jose State University San Jose, CA
Robert DeFillippi	Suffolk University Boston, MA
Jane Hiller Farran	University of Pennsylvania Philadelphia, PA
David Fearon	Central Connecticut State University New Britain, CT
C. Patrick Fleenor	Seattle University Seattle, WA
Cheryl Harrison	Quinnipiac University Hamden, CT
Richard T. Harrison	University of Edinburgh Scotland, UK
Paula J. Hyde	Manchester Business School Manchester, England
Timothy C. Johnston	University of Tennessee at Martin Martin, TN
Claire M. Leitch	Queens University Belfast Northern Ireland, UK
Leonard Lodish	University of Pennsylvania Philadelphia, PA
Mats Lundeberg	Stockholm School of Economics Stockholm, Sweden
Pär Mårtensson	Stockholm School of Economics Stockholm, Sweden

Lucas C.P.M. Meijs	Erasmus University Rotterdam, the Netherlands
Philip Mirvis	Boston College Boston, MA
Marjolein van Noort	Hogeschool Zeeland Vlissingen, the Netherlands
Asbjorn Osland	San Jose State University San Jose, CA
K. Nadia Papamichail	Manchester Business School Manchester, England
Irene H. Powell	Monash University Melbourne, Australia
Peter V. Raven	Seattle University Seattle, WA
Jerry Ralston	Seattle University Seattle, WA
Tudor Rickards	Manchester Business School Manchester, England
Malu Roldan	San Jose State University San Jose, CA
Georges Romme	Tilburg University Tilburg, the Netherlands
Paul Shrivastava	Bucknell University Lewisburg, PA
Michael Solt	San Jose State University San Jose, CA
Oon-Seng Tan	Nanyang Technological University Singapore
Judith van der Voort	Erasmus University Rotterdam, the Netherlands
Charles Wankel	St. John's University New York, NY
Gail Whiteman	Erasmus University Rotterdam, the Netherlands
Lyle Yorks	Columbia University New York, NY

CONTENTS

ix

INTRODUCTION

REAL WORLD PROJECTS AND PROJECT-BASED LEARNING PEDAGOGIES

Robert DeFillippi and Charles Wankel

University-based management education has frequently been subject to the criticism of being out of touch with the real world (Mintzberg, 2004). Yet, management educators have created a variety of learning pedagogies based on their students working on real-world projects (Coombs & Elden, 2004). Volume four of *Research in Management Education and Development* examines some best practices for educating managers through real world projects. As you will see, the determination of what is "real world" is always in the eye of the beholder. All the pedagogical practices described in volume four require the learner to engage in project-based activities that primarily occur outside the classroom. Real world projects may thus be broadly defined as educationally directed activities involving out-of-classroom action settings complemented by student and/or instructor directed reflection on the links between theory and practice.

A variety of project-based learning theories and pedagogic practices have arisen over the years. Project-based learning refers to the theory and practice of engaging in time-limited projects to achieve pre-specified or emergent performance objectives (project deliverables) and to facilitate individual and collective learning (Smith & Dodds, 1997; DeFillippi, 2001). Project-based learning is related to the action learning writings of Reg Revans (1982) who theorized that learning resulted from the interaction between programmed instruction and the spontaneous questioning that arises from the interpretation of experience. Additionally, the project-based learning perspective owes much to pragmatic learning perspectives associated with Dewey (1933), who argued for experimenting in the real world. Raelin (2000) identifies the roots of work-based learning (a close kin of project-based learning) in experiential learning (e.g., Kolb, 1984) and in the processes of reflection employed in adult learning (Mezirow, 1991).

Another important foundational perspective for project-based learning is Lewin's (1946) action research and its underlying assumption that knowledge will be used in the service of action. These action research perspectives have been subsequently employed in the design and implementation of learning projects (e.g., Coghlan, 2001). Another action perspective sympathetic to project-based learning assumptions is action science, whose most famous theoretician and practitioner Chris Argyris (2001) asserts that knowledge that is disconnected from action is not only not useful but also dangerous. Finally, some project-based learning theorists emphasize the shared learning that arises within the community of reflective practitioners (Schön, 1983) with whom one collaborates in project-based learning activities (Ayas & Zeniuk, 2001). Students report significantly greater development of meta-adaptive skills (e.g., learning to learn) than in conventional teaching designs (Lizzio & Wilson, 2004).

To elaborate on its psychological theory foundations, project-based learning theory and practice tends to draw upon cognitive learning perspectives. Smith (2001) identifies the following relevant schools of cognitive theory for action learning interventions: distributed cognition theory (Dede, 1996), cognitive flexibility theory (Spiro et al., 1988), situated cognition theory (Perret-Clermont, 1993), and metacognition theory (Flavell, 1976). Most action learning theorists cite the experiential learning models of Kolb (1984), who in turn draws upon the developmental psychology of Piaget (1981) for inspiration. Similarly, many action learning theorist-practitioners (e.g., Raelin, 2000; Smith, 2001) cite Mezirow (1991) and his writings on reflection, which draw explicitly upon cognitive developmental psychology (e.g., Kegan, 1982). A detailed comparison of project-based learning assumptions to other psychological learning perspectives can be found in DeFillippi and Ornstein (2003).

When applied to management education, project-based learning has specific implications for instructional design. Typically, students work on a semi-structured or open-ended assignment that requires some engagement outside the classroom setting with a project client or project sponsor. The teacher acts as a facilitator, perhaps providing access to project opportunities, perhaps providing resources (technological, material, and financial) and advice (often a mix of coaching, mentoring, and consulting) to students. The students (most frequently working in small teams) assume responsibility for designing and implementing activities focused on creating a set of project deliverables for their client. Knowledge is created through student project involvement, which provides the experiential basis for student reflection and dialogue on the interrelationships between theoretical knowledge and its action implications when knowledge is put into practice. Project-based learning thus provides a learning context in which teachers can help students increase their skills and knowledge through cooperative learning and collaborative problem solving and reflection.

Project-based learning has found specific expression in a variety of academic institutional practices, such as internships, service learning, student fieldwork and consulting projects. Each of these institutionalized vehicles for project-based learning is examined in the chapters that follow. The role of project-based learning within management education varies widely across academic institutions. For some universities, project-based student learning is the exception to a heavily theoretical and classroom-based learning culture. However, project-based learning is more than a technique. In recent years, an increasing number of business schools have heeded the call for greater relevance by instituting programs of instruction that are centrally focused on the creation of more project-learning-based knowledge and skills. Several of these exemplar institutions are featured in the chapters to follow.

To facilitate the diverse project learning practices available to management educators, the volume is organized according to different types of real world projects and project-based learning approaches: consulting projects, service learning projects, action learning pedagogies, and a potpourri of project-based learning perspectives and practices, including work embedded e-learning, problem-based learning, business plan competitions, and concluding chapters on the role of the student and the role of assessment in project learning. Although these categories overlap in many of their core assumptions about learning and instructional design, we believe that each genre of real world project and project-based learning pedagogy makes a distinctive contribution to management education and thus is deserving of separate mention in the sections to follow.

CONSULTING PROJECTS

The role of consulting projects in international management education was previously addressed in volume three of our book series (see Coombs & Yost, 2004). Consulting projects have a long history in project-based teaching pedagogy and their practice appears to be increasing. Adams and Zanzi, (2001, 2004) reviewed the use of field projects in management consulting courses and found a significant increase in the number of top tier schools incorporating field consulting from 18.3% to 30.9% during the 2001-2003 time period. Widening the view to all AACSB accredited MBA programs, the use of field consulting projects in management consulting courses was 15.3% in 2003 (a significant increase over 2002), indicating that the use of consulting field projects is beginning to attract a wider audience than just the elite schools. In response to these trends, we feature four chapters on consulting project-based learning pedagogies from four schools representing a diverse range of university-based practice settings.

Patricia Gorman Clifford, Jane Hiller Farran, and Leonard Lodish's (University of Pennsylvania Wharton School of Business) chapter "Wharton's Global Consulting Practicum: Interdependence, Ambiguity and Reflection" examines how first year MBA students carrying a full course load take on team consulting assignments for public and private companies. Client organizations in GCP are all outside the United States and typically have one or more products they would like to introduce into the U.S. market. MBA students must manage and shape the consulting assignment, from initial contracting about focus and scope through to the delivery of an agreed-upon output. Their chapter highlights key three elements essential to GCP program success: First, the interdependence among GCP program components is vital to creating a learning challenge. Second, the ambiguity intentionally unresolved in the projects and processes forces the important questions about the project team and its work and promotes learning by doing. Third, the use of guided reflection exercises provides the participants with a powerful means of approaching future corporate and organizational challenges.

C. Patrick Fleenor, Peter V. Raven and Jerry Ralston (Seattle University) describe in their chapter on "Project-Based International Business Consulting" how the Global Business EDGE Program at Seattle University provides multiple opportunities for student consulting on real projects for real companies in real time. Their chapter focuses on the International Business Consulting (IBC) program, where international business projects with locally based international companies are embedded in the curriculum of Seattle University MBA, MIB (Master of International Business), and MSF (Master of Science in Finance) programs. While no two projects are exactly alike, they tend to fall into several main categories, including market opportunity analysis, country attractiveness, target market selection, laws and regulatory issues, market entry strategies, and marketing plan development. The appendices of support documents used in these projects are valuable reference materials for anyone wishing to develop similar project-based international consulting courses for their students.

Mats Lundeberg and Pär Mårtensson's (Stockholm School of Economics) chapter "*Real* Real World Projects" reflects on their school's multiyear experience with a program in which Executive MBA students are provided the following one line project assignment: n project-groups of two, achieve *a sustainable change* in an organization by the end of this course. A core assumption of the Real *Real* world project is that understanding of a context increases when you try to change it. A theoretical root to this assumption is Kurt Lewin's view that you cannot understand a human system without trying to change it (Lewin, 1947; Schein, 1987). The design of the required second year course is to teach the EMBA-students basic skills in handling change processes by letting them carry out real changes in real organizations meeting real people. This chapter richly describes such projects, the theory behind the course design, and some of the experiences of the course instructors with this highly challenging project-based learning course.

Susan Adams (Bentley College) focuses her chapter "Managing Divergent and Convergent Focus of Learning in Student Field Projects" on how the learning needs of project stakeholders (students, faculty, and project sponsors or clients) are initially divergent, converge during the course of project-based course work and diverge again at project completion. This chapter describes a continuum of types of student field projects.

Field projects can range from interviewing a manager to reporting on the use of particular course concepts in a field setting to full-blown consulting projects for client organizations. A student *field study* project is usually undertaken to focus on specific content material such as operations, marketing, or strategy, whereas a student *consulting project* focuses more on having the students learn the consulting process or organizational problem solving. Using the example of a student consulting project, the author provides a series of valuable teaching guidelines for facilitating an effective student consulting experience to meet the needs of the various parties involved.

SERVICE LEARNING PROJECTS

Service learning has received previous attention in our book series (see McCarthy, Tucker, & Dean, 2002) and included in the present volume are three chapter contributions representing quite distinctive forms of service learning project scope, purpose and practice. The first chapter (Ayas & Mirvis) examines how global multinational companies utilize service learning in executive development programs. The second chapter (Brace-Govan & Powell) examines how service learning projects may be incorporated within company sponsored student internships. The third chapter (van der Voort, Meijs, & Whiteman) focuses on relatively time and resource limited applications of service learning for undergraduate and graduate course work within a university setting. These three chapters thus represent a very wide range of applications of service learning and illustrate the distinctive practice challenges and benefits associated with each application setting.

Karen Ayas (the Ripples Group and Erasmus University) and Philip Mirvis's (Boston College) chapter "Educating Managers through Service Learning Projects" examines the purpose, design and benefits of several executive development programs that involved service learning projects. In each case (Ford Motor Co., Unilever, and Shell) service learning was integral to the executive leadership development initiative. The service learning projects described here varied from a half-day limited engagement with a community to ongoing sustained business-community partnerships, but key components of service learning—achieving the learning objectives through the service, mutual benefit for the managers and the community, and structured reflection—are enacted in all. In these programs, the top leaders of each company frequently joined in the service learning projects with their company teams. The content of the service learning project was themed to incorporate important leadership development concerns (e.g., self-knowledge, story telling, learning from others, diversity) and, where appropriate and feasible, to include strategic considerations of the business (e.g., corporate citizenship, consumer understanding, core purpose). The authors assert that service learning projects often deepen and inform self-reflection that is crucial to the leadership development agenda mostly missing from corporate training programs.

Jan Brace-Govan and Irene H. Powell (Monash University) write in "Real World Transfer of Professional Knowledge" about service learning projects conducted within the undergraduate internship program at Monash University in Australia. A feature of internships is that there is a transfer of experience and knowledge through working along side an experienced professional. Several case studies in the chapter show the value of internship projects focused on providing service to nonprofit organizations. A unique feature of the internship-based service learning project was the creation of a triadic relationship between the student intern, the nonprofit client and a business mentor serving as a reflective coach to the student. Overall, the combination of a nonprofit community service project with a "reflective coach" business mentor provides student learners with a real world experience that facilitates a range of valuable learning and professional outcomes. Such service learning internships create additional benefits for the nonprofit client organization, the business mentor and the university's relationships to its alumni and surrounding community.

Judith van der Voort, Lucas C.P.M. Meijs, and Gail Whiteman's (Erasmus University, the Netherlands) chapter "Creating Actionable Knowledge" examines how their undergraduate and graduate business programs each provide opportunities for project-based learning through civic engagement in political advocacy and nonprofit fund-raising ventures. Within the undergraduate program, students are asked to write a letter to the editor (for a major newspaper) on some political/ethical issue (CEO-compensation, good governance, fair pricing for aids-medicines, working with human rights, etc.). A major Dutch advocacy nonprofit (e.g., Amnesty International) next discusses and evaluates the letters. In the graduate program, the Dutch Red Cross provides opportunities for Master students to write business proposals for fundraising, organizing volunteers, organizing logistics and public accountability. Members of the management team of the Red Cross then help mentor the students and grade the business proposals. Both service-learning approaches illustrate project-based student learning applied for the public good. A distinctive contribution of this chapter is to examine how service learning projects are introduced in a national context where voluntary service is frequently subordinated to publicly funded and administered provision of community services.

ACTION LEARNING

Action learning originated with Reg Revans (1945), who emphasized a learning approach premised on comrades in adversity learning from and with each other through discriminating questioning, fresh experience and reflective insight (Smith, 2001, p. 35). More recently Mike Marquardt (1999) has offered a more formalized codification of the action learning process into six elements: (1) the problem in need of resolution; (2) a group of people (the action set); (3) a commitment to the use of a questioning and reflection process; (4) a commitment to taking action by one with the authority to do so; (5) a commitment to learning; and (6) a facilitator/coach to enable the process. Each of the four chapters to follow embodies all or most of the six elements that Marquardt identifies as an action learning perspective. As a set of readings, these chapters illustrate the wide range of project-based learning pedagogies within the action learning perspective.

Lyle Yorks' (Columbia University) chapter "Action Learning as a Vehicle for Management Development and Organizational Learning: Empirical Patterns from Practice and Theoretical Implications" is a tour de force of current perspectives on action learning (AL), to which Professor Yorks has been a major contributor (e.g., Yorks, O'Neil, & Marsick, 1999) The chapter's wide-ranging review of AL practice includes an overview of a typology of four schools of AL practice: the tacit or incidental school, the scientific school, the experiential school, and the critical reflection school (O'Neil, 1999). The chapter links these forms of AL practice to specific forms of learning within the learning community or action set. This chapter next draws on data from three field case studies, supplemented by insights from four other case studies. The three focal cases represent three of the four schools of AL practice (i.e., critical reflection, experiential and tacit). The chapter concludes with an in-depth evaluation of the impact of each program specific AL practice design on the types of learning (fragmented, pooled, synergistic) that results from these distinctive interventions.

Richard T. Harrison (University of Edinburgh, Scotland, UK) and Claire M. Leitch's (Queens University Belfast, Northern Ireland, UK) chapter "Action Learning for Management Development: Lessons from a Leadership Development Program" presents a summary of an action learning program to assist senior executives in both large and entrepreneurial small companies to transform their companies by providing team-based leadership through the creation and communication of vision and values. The accumulated learning from the program (both in terms of process and content) provided the basis for the completion of a final dissertation, assessed for the award of the degree of M.Sc. in Executive Leadership for program participants. An action learning as a toolbox of techniques perspective is taken in the chapter, although the overall executive program also incorporated at times views of action learning as therapy and as philosophy. The detailed case reporting and evaluative data derived from the experience of program participants in this entrepreneurial executive development program is a noteworthy contribution.

Tudor Rickards, Paula J. Hyde and K. Naida Papamichail's (Manchester Business School) chapter "The Manchester Method: A Critical Review of a Learning Experiment" examines the historical evolution of the Manchester method of action learning, whose intellectual origins derive from the Tavistock approach to organizational development (Astrachan, 1975). The method incorporates subject-based lectures with group projects in live settings. Students take increasing responsibility throughout the MBA program for project acquisition, management and delivery. The Manchester Method's bias toward experiential methods emphasizes the importance of understanding group processes and the sociotechnical system in which action arises. These influences are then linked to recent innovations in the method, such as the new business incubator and the development of e-learning networks. Participants (faculty, students, staff) involved in the Manchester Method have continued to encounter issues around personal and team development, leadership, reflectivity, and the management of ambiguity. This chapter concludes with a discussion of the tensions inherent in sustaining and evolving for the past forty years an institutionalized action learning practice within the Manchester Business School.

Eugene Baten and David Fearon (Central Connecticut State University), and Cheryl Harrison (Quinnipiac University) conclude our Action learning section with their chapter "A Management Education Model for Bridging the Academic and the Real World." They describe their own Two Worlds Learning Bridge (TWLB) system of action learning in terms of four operating assumptions: making the workplace (not just the physical building) the classroom, making the work the curriculum, letting the organization's strategic plan reveal its content, and lastly evaluating learning progress, not on what managers know but on what they can do. One element of their practice is *intelligent project management* (Cavaleri & Fearon, 2000), accomplished by integrating cycles of project management (planning, implementation, documenting lessons learned) and action learning (concrete experience, reflective observation, abstract conceptualization, and active experimentation.).

A POTPOURRI OF PROJECT-BASED PRACTICES AND PERSPECTIVES

The concluding section of Volume 4 features a heterogeneous array of specific project-based learning practices and perspectives. These include work embedded eLearning (Shrivastava), problem-based learning (Tan), business plan competitions (Roldan et al.), the role of the student in project learning (Johnston), and assessing performance in projects (Van Noort & Romme). Each of these chapters adds additional perspective to our accumulating understanding of project-based approaches to pedagogy for management education and development.

Paul Shrivastava (eSocrates and Bucknell University) addresses "Work Embedded eLearning" in terms of designing organizational tasks and embedding training for employees that provide just-in-time learning and also saves training time. The goal of work embedded learning systems is to repackage knowledge required to do work into work procedures themselves. By avoiding pulling workers out of production space and time for training purposes, work embedded learning saves setup and set down times. It may completely eliminate several setup cycles. Technologies enabling such work embedded learning are now becoming widely available. The challenge facing companies is to manage the comprehensive technological and organizational change processes that such systems entail. Embedding learning into work processes changes not only the nature of learning, but also the work. The chapter provides specific examples of work embedded eLearning applications derived from the experience of eSocrates, the eLearning company founded by Shrivastava.

Oon-Seng Tan (Nanyang Technological University) writes about "Problem-based Learning Approaches in Management Education" and defines problem-based learning (PBL) as an educational philosophy for designing curricula and an instructional method that uses problems as a context for students to acquire and apply knowledge (Gijselaers, 1996). It is an integrated system for student learning in which students are confronted with real-life problems that need to be discussed and solved. The learning process starts with the activation of the students prior knowledge. Students work in small groups (3–4 people) to discuss the problem scenario. Students use a systematic procedure to analyze the problem, to formulate learning objectives, to collect additional information and to acquire new and relevant knowledge. In a group discussion facilitated by their PBL tutor, the students refine their learning objectives into more pertinent questions that require the acquisition of deeper knowledge and insights important for their future professional practice. The effective integration of problem-based learning models and e-learning blending face-to-face with internet-enabled team work is recommended for the next phase of PBL practice.

Malu Roldan, Asbjorn Osland, Michael Solt, Burton V. Dean (San Jose State University) and Mark V. Cannice (University of San Francisco) write about "Business Plan Competition: Vehicles for Learning Entrepreneurship," based upon their respective experiences in the Silicon Valley Business Plan Competition (SVBPC) at San Jose State University (SJSU) and the well-established International Business Plan Competition at the University of San Francisco (USF). In both competitions, student teams are required to develop a business plan and a working prototype of a solution to a problem or need posed by their client. Aside from programmatic impacts and outcomes directly attributed to these competitions, their chapter provides results from the assessment of learning outcomes from an interdisciplinary set of teams that participated in SJSU competition. Their chapter persuasively argues that business plan competitions are impressive vehicles for inspiring innovation, spawning new businesses, and boosting university development.

Timothy C. Johnston (University of Tennessee at Martin) evaluates "The Role of the Student in Project Learning." The chapter reviews five student roles in project learning: (1) ready learner, (2) coachee, (3) contributor, (4) team member, and (5) academic scholar. For each of these five roles, the chapter reviews relevant literature findings interspersed with the chapter author's own insights and suggestions for fostering an active engagement by students in each of the five roles. Although based on the author's extensive experience in utilizing projects in undergraduate marketing courses, the lessons to be learned from this chapter are broadly applicable to undergraduate management education. Moreover, in presenting a comprehensive assessment of the role of the student, the chapter provides a complementary perspective on the role of the teacher in project learning instruction.

Marjolein van Noort (Hogeschool Zeeland) and Georges Romme (Tilburg University) conclude our volume with their thoughtful chapter on "Assessing Performance in Projects from Different Angles." In this chapter three design propositions for assessing authentic business projects are described: delegate part of the assessment to exploit the benefits of self and peer assessment, provide feedback from different angles, and set clear and vivid assessment criteria to create a constructive friction between the skills students have initially and those expected at the end. The next section shows how these propositions are applied to assessing performance on projects in an undergraduate program at Tilburg University. The final section discusses how students, instructors and client-organizations evaluated this assessment approach. The chapter concludes that the different angles (evaluative perspectives) taken by academic staff, students and clients can be effectively combined in assessing team and individual performance on projects.

REAL WORLD PROJECTS AND PROJECT-BASED LEARNING: FINAL THOUGHTS

After completing this summary review of project-based learning applications and pedagogic approaches, one comes away with an appreciation of just how far management education and development have brought both the real world into the classroom and the classroom into the real world. For full time undergraduate and graduate students, project-based learning applications have enabled them to inquire into real world concerns and to problem solve with each other to understand these problems and to devise practical solutions. However, for overburdened executives and employees, the use of project-based reflective learning has provided a space within which to more fully consider the larger implications for personal and organizational development of their real world projects. In the case of service learning, we find opportunities for both student and employer to participate in projects that contribute to specific aspects of community betterment while also fostering personal development and organizational goodwill. Our review also suggests that project-based learning pedagogies and practices have taken deep root in a wide variety of academic institutions worldwide and that the accumulated experience of these institutions provides a wonderful platform from which we can all draw to help develop and educate managers through real world projects.

REFERENCES

Adams, S.M., & Zanzi, A. (2001). Are we producing information age consultants?: Reflections on U.S. business schools course offerings. In A. Buono (Ed.), *Current trends in management consulting (Research in management consulting*, Vol. 1, pp. 189-206). Greenwich, CT: Information Age Publishing.

Adams, S.M., & Zanzi, A. (2004). Academic development for careers in management consulting. *Career Developmental International, 9*(6), 559-577.

Argyris, C. (2001). *Organizational Intervention with Chris Argyris.* 11-15 November 2001, Klinten, R vig Denmark. Retrieved March 14, 2005 from http://ella.hint.no/~eii/FORSKNING/argyris.html

Astrachan, B.M., (1975). The Tavistock model of laboratory training. In K.D.Benne, L.P. Bradford, J.R.Gibb, & R.O. Lippitt (Eds.), *The laboratory method of changing and learning: Theory and application*. Palo Alto, CA: Science and Behavior Books Inc.

Ayas, K., & Zeniuk, N. (2001). Project-based learning: Building communities of reflective practitioners. *Management Learning, 32*(1), 61-76.

Cavaleri, S., & Fearon, D. (2000). Integrating organizational learning and business praxis: a case for intelligent project management. *The Learning Organization, 7*(5), 251-258.

Coghlan, D. (2001). Insider action research projects: Implications for practising managers. *Management Learning, 32*(1), 49-60.

Coombs, G., & Elden, M. (2004) Introduction to the Special Issue: Problem-based learning as social inquiry--PBL and management education. *Journal of Management Education, 28*(5), 523-535.

Coombs, G., & Yost, E. (2004). Teaching international business through international student consulting projects: The GCP/JSCP at Ohio University. In C. Wankel & R. DeFillippi (Eds.), *The cutting edge of international management education* (pp.285-305). Greenwich, CT: Information Age Publishing.

Dede, C. (1996). Emerging technologies and distributed learning. *American Journal of Distance Education, 10*(2), 4-36.

DeFillippi, R.J. (2001). Project-based learning, reflective practices and learning outcomes. *Management Learning, 32*(1), 5-10.

DeFillippi, R., & Ornstein, S. (2003). Psychological perspectives underlying theories of organizational learning. In M. Easterby-Smith & M. Lyles (Eds.), *Handbook of organizational learning and knowledge* (pp. 19-37). Oxford: Blackwell Press.

Dewey, J. (1933). *How we think*. Chicago: Henry Regnery.

Flavell, J.H. (1976). Metacognitive aspects of problem solving. In L.B. Resnick (Ed.), *The nature of intelligence* (pp. 231-235). Hillsdale, NJ: Erlbaum.

Gijselaers, W.H. (1996). Connecting problem-based practices with educational theory. In L. Wilkerson & W. H. Gijselaers (Eds.), *Bringing problem-based learning to higher education: Theory and practice* (pp. 13–21). New directions for teaching and learning, No. 68. San Francisco: Jossey-Bass.

Kegan, R. (1982). *The evolving self*. Cambridge, MA: Harvard University Press.

Kolb, D.A. (1984). *Experiential learning as the source of learning and development*. Englewood Cliffs, NJ: Prentice-Hall.

Lewin, K. (1946). Action research and minority problems. *Journal of Social Issues, 2*(4), 34-46.

Lewin, K. (1947). Frontiers in group dynamics. In K. Lewin (1997). *Resolving social conflicts & field theory in social science* (pp. 301-336). Washington, DC: American Psychological Association.

Lizzio, A., & Wilson, K. (2004). Action learning in higher education: An investigation of its potential to develop professional capability. *Studies in Higher Education, 29*(4), 469-488.

Marquardt, M. J. (2004). *Optimizing the power of action learning*. Palo Alto, CA: Davis-Black.

McCarthy, A., Tucker, M. L, & Lund Dean, K. (2002). Service learning: Creating community. In C. Wankel & R. DeFillippi (Eds.), *Rethinking management education for the 21st century* (pp. 63-88). Greenwich, CT: Information Age.

Mezirow, J. (1991). *Transformative dimensions of adult learning*. San Francisco: Jossey-Bass.

Mintzberg, J. (2004). *Managers not MBAs*. San Francisco: Berrett-Koehler.

O'Neil, J. (1999). *The role of the learning adviser in action learning*. Unpublished doctoral dissertation, Teachers College, Columbia University, New York.

Perret-Clermont, A.N. (1993). What is it that develops? *Cognition and Instruction, 11*,197-205.

Piaget, J. (1981). *Intelligence and affectivity*. Palo Alto, CA: Annual Reviews.

Raelin, J.A. (2000). *Work-based learning: The new frontier of management development*. Englewood Cliffs, NJ: Prentice-Hall.

Revans, R.W. (1945). *Plans for recruitment, training and education in the mining industry*. London: Mining Associate of Great Britain.

Revans, R.W. (1982). *The origin and growth of action learning*. Brickley, UK: Chartwell-Bratt.

Schein, E.H. (1987). The clinical perspective in fieldwork. In *Qualitative research methods series* (Vol. 5). Newbury Park, CA: Sage.

Schön, D.A. (1983). *The reflective practitioner: How professionals think in action*. New York: Basic Books, HarperCollins.

Smith, P.A.C. (2001). Action learning and reflective practice in project environments that are related to leadership development. *Management Learning, 32*(1), 31-48.

Smith, B., & Dodds, R. (1997). *Developing managers through project-based learning*. Brookfield, VT: Aldershot/Gower.

Spiro, R.J., Coulson, R.L., Feltovich, P.J., & Anderson, D.K. (1988). Cognitive flexibility: Advanced knowledge acquisition in ill-structured domains. *Proceedings of the Tenth Annual Conference of the Cognitive Science Society*. Hillsdale, NJ: Erlbaum.

Yorks, L., O'Neil, J., & Marsick, V. J. (Eds.). (1999). Action learning: Theoretical bases and varieties of practice. In *Action learning: Successful strategies for individual, team, and organizational development. Advances in developing human resources* (pp. 1-18). San Francisco: The Academy of Human Resource Development and Berrett-Koehler.

PART I

CONSULTING PROJECTS

CHAPTER 1

WHARTON'S GLOBAL CONSULTING PRACTICUM

Interdependence, Ambiguity, and Reflection

Patricia Gorman Clifford, Jane Hiller Farran, and Leonard Lodish

The Global Consulting Practicum at Wharton is experiential learning embedded in corporate contexts. First year MBA students carrying a full course load take on team consulting assignments for public and private companies. Essential to its success: interdependence is vital to creating a learning challenge adequate to provoke participants; ambiguity intentionally unrelved in the projects and processes forces the articulation of questions promoting learning by doing; and the use of guided reflection generates insights. These 3 factors, along with other learning tools and teaching methods extend the received wisdom gleaned from qualitative case studies, empirical survey work and other scholarship on action learning and team dynamics in classroom teaching. This analysis of key attributes of the Global Consulting Practicum will contribute to our collective understanding of collaborative action learning and continue the tradition of scholarship around effective processes and techniques in this area.

Educating Managers through Real World Projects, 3–24

OVERVIEW

The Global Consulting Practicum (GCP) at the Wharton School of Business is a unique example of experiential learning in a complex organizational setting. First year MBA students carrying a full course load take on team consulting assignments for companies outside the United States. Through an array of both frustrating and illuminating experiences and with a good deal of analysis and hard work, they integrate and apply concepts from Marketing, Strategy, Finance, Operations, Entrepreneurship, Organization Behavior and related fields to deliver on consulting engagements in the Practicum. At the conclusion of the project, the students' work is evaluated by their clients, their faculty and their peers.

For 25 years, this constantly evolving international program has provided cross-cultural consulting experience for selected Wharton MBAs. GCP is described by its participants as "the most real-world experience you can get at business school" and is typically oversubscribed by at least 100%. This chapter highlights three elements of this established, successful action learning program that are essential to its effectiveness.

First, the interdependence among GCP's components is vital to creating a complex learning challenge adequate to provoke participants to surface their embedded assumptions and to reject overly simplistic solutions. Second, the ambiguity intentionally unresolved in the projects and processes forces the articulation of important questions about the team and its work and promotes learning by doing (Costello, Brunner, & Hasty, 2002). Third, the use of guided reflection as a learning mechanism generates immediate insights and arms the participants with a powerful means of approaching future corporate and organizational challenges (Eyler, 2001).

The action learning and experiential learning precepts of the GCP experience spring from and extend a solid tradition. Action Learning has been an effective learning methodology since Lewin's exploratory work in 1948 (Lewin, 1948, 1951.) It is based on repeated cycles of action, discovery, planning, evaluation (Lewin, 1948, 1951; Hall & Lindzey, 1978) and collective self-reflective enquiry (Kemmis & McTaggart, 1988). Experiential learning concepts are closely related to action learning and have been applied in the context of service projects (Eyler, 2001) and education (Carr & Kemmis, 1986). Processes necessary for managing intercultural relationships have been established as highly instrumental, and various approaches have been developed and proposed that emphasize the importance of reflection (Harvey & Griffith, 2002). While it is beyond the scope of this chapter, at a conceptual level it seems probable that the application of systems theory or cybernetics might also provide rich insights into the experiences we observe and describe here (Schwaninger,

2004). Social process perspectives may also illuminate the team formation issues in greater detail (Shanley & Peteraf, 2004).

The received wisdom gleaned from qualitative case studies, empirical survey work (Fiechtner & Davis, 1984-85) and other scholarship on action learning and team dynamics in classroom teaching and in business settings (Bosworth & Hamilton, 1994; Dotlich, 1998) is not inconsistent with our conclusions regarding GCP success factors. Since there has been relatively little formal exploration of learning outcomes in experiential academic business programs, however, the following analysis of key attributes of the Global Consulting Practicum is a contribution to our collective understanding of collaborative action learning and continues the tradition of scholarship around effective processes and techniques for learning in real world settings (Schein, 1995).

INTRODUCTION

The videoconference went well, but David wondered if his Chilean teammates were really supportive of the proposal under discussion, or were just being polite. As "scribe" for the day, drafting an email summary of the meeting and sending the draft to his local team for their review was all he had time to do before rushing to an afternoon class. He took with him the sketches of the client's prototype for their upcoming U.S. product launch. Maybe his Operations professor could guide them on cost estimates for distribution? As he hurried along the quad he wondered if he should send a quick note to the client to check in and build support for the proposal. Elisa was "officially" the client liaison, but she hadn't been connecting as much as David wanted her to. It seemed to him she was much too dependent on help from Chile. "They're running their piece in lock step," thought David. "We'd be out of the weeds by now if GCP had designated team leaders for us and for Chile. At least we wouldn't be wasting so much time trying to get consensus."

David is a student in the Global Consulting Practicum, and his business school experience includes both traditional classroom work and collaborative action learning in a corporate context. GCP is structured as a practicum course and couples Wharton MBA teams with MBA teams at partner schools in selected countries, including Israel, India, Peru and Chile. MBA's must apply for acceptance to the practicum and are selected based on their skills, experience and willingness to commit the time and energy necessary for this intense program. Wharton teams are composed with an eye to maximizing the diversity of resources on each team, and matching students and clients with relevant industry or market experience. Most, but not all partner teams use similar processes and criteria to select and assign teams.

GCP is a one semester course but teams begin working about eight weeks prior to the start of the semester. The work kicks off for the Wharton teams with a short teambuilding experience and inputs on the philosophy of GCP, the milestone deliverables and the resources available to teams. Each team is given a faculty-prepared brief on its client, since the students are not involved in securing client commitments. The next order of business is for the Wharton team to connect with the partner school team and to begin initial research on the client's market and issues.

At the start of the semester the combined teams visit the clients at their factory or headquarters to discuss the scope of the engagement and to review an early project plan. Following this meeting, the teams work virtually to progress the project. Each team works toward a client review after 3 months and final project recommendations after 5 months. The 5-month meeting is held at Wharton in a colloquium format and is often combined with market trips or contacts for the client elsewhere in the United States.

The combined teams are supported in their GCP work by project faculty (PF's), teaching associates (TA's) and administrators who jointly effect the complex but bounded learning environment of the Practicum. Technical inputs are available to the teams: subject matter experts and class sessions on client and project management and analytical models. In addition, teams have access to the broader Wharton faculty and to a GCP library of models, processes and templates. There is a dedicated and secure web café which offers chat capability and document storage and review, with private areas for each team as well as community areas. Microsoft Project is available to aid organization, and video, audio and web conferencing capabilities enable team and client meetings.

Consulting engagements for the GCP teams generally involve primary and secondary market research, strategic market analysis, product differentiation, and business strategy. Students have opportunities to apply and refine entrepreneurial marketing, consulting and business modeling skills. At the same time, projects require cross-cultural sensitivity, multicultural teamwork and managing the dynamics of full-time students, heavy work loads and challenging clients. Students who perform well in this Practicum demonstrate significant development in their interpersonal communication and negotiations skills (Kalem & Fer, 2003), in their process identification and intervention abilities, in their effectiveness as team members and leaders, and in their confidence in decision making under uncertainty.

Initially, students are far more conscious of their progress on the "hard" skills than on the "softer" skills this program demands. In most cases, students perceive their learning early in the program as being industry or technology focused. Often participants eagerly seize the opportunity to directly apply textbook models to reality. While it is true that the teams' work draws from many disciplines, no individual discipline is as important as the cross disciplinary synthesis and process learning that occurs as the participants live the GCP experience (Lightsey, 2000). As the project progresses, issues like power dynamics, cross-cultural communications, time pressure and/or resource constraints (the teams have limited research budgets) begin to impede progress. Individuals and teams begin to realize that identifying a winning product and a large market are not enough. The process of reaching consensus around a marketing plan that incorporates the best skills of everyone in the combined team and that is acceptable to a client is an altogether different challenge.

The challenges of complexity and ambiguity inherent in the GCP structure and experience are reflective of reality in complex organizations. The interdependence of people, resources, work streams and skills emphasizes the synthetic nature of the experience and requires students to adopt a systems view that questions fragmented or additive corporate models (Langan-Fox, Anglim, & Wilson, 2004). Sometimes the complexity and ambiguity are perceived by students as weaknesses of the Practicum. Students ask for more structure, more issue identification and more faculty intervention. However, our experience and other research strongly suggest that unresolved, bounded complexity and ambiguity are important features of powerful learning contexts (Pich, de Loch, & de Meyer, 2002). Students for whom the process is simplified and clarified tend to realize less benefit from their GCP experience, since the process of eliminating its complexity and ambiguity fundamentally changes their learning experience from active to passive. GCP student feedback over a four-year period indicates that students engage less fully, rely on their teammates more than themselves, experience less ownership of the process and its outcomes, and develop less meaningful client dialogue if they do not struggle with the challenge of defining their role in the overall group (GCP Feedback, 2000-2003; Armington & Cassano, 1996).

While the interdependent structure of the program and the challenges it presents to the students provide learning opportunities, it is the third program element, guided reflection, that ensures the internalization and transferability of this learning. Structured opportunities for guided reflection help students recognize and consider the causal chain of events, along with their own assumptions and their insights. They can then formulate new models of team process and new hypotheses about how to reach their objectives. These new models and hypotheses serve as a basis for subsequent experimentation throughout the program. In this way, the 3 core elements of GCP are exemplars of Kolb's foundational adult learning model (Kolb, 1984) as well as examples of what makes peer learning communities function effectively (Tosey, 1999; Kofman & Senge, 1993.)

Interdependence, Ambiguity and Guided Reflection are taken in turn in the next three sections of the chapter.

STRUCTURAL INTERDEPENDENCE

The Global Consulting Practicum is structured more like a complex organization than a university MBA course. Conscious choices were made to create and structure a program with multiple lines of authority, multiple constituencies and variously motivated shareholders and geographically and culturally distant clients. These factors taken together create a rich and varied learning experience. However, as each of these factors interacts with other aspects of the GCP experience, students in this course are exposed to the real frustrations and competing demands typical in complex organizations.

Multiple Lines of Authority and Multiple Constituencies: "How do Things Work?"

GCP has an executive director who is also a key academic resource, a consulting director who manages the GCP program "on the ground," administrative managers, project faculty for each team, a teaching assistant (TA) for each team, and expert resources including a process consultant, a cross-cultural expert, and various subject and industry experts. No other class in the University has a lower ratio of students to non-student participants (including faculty). No other class so closely approximates a multinational company, complete with real overseas clients and team members in remote locations with interdependent roles and tasks.

The GCP program implicitly requires students to interact with most or all of the authorities and actors mentioned above. Students must decide how and when to access each in appropriate ways and how to use each effectively. Within the GCP organizational structure, each authority or group has specific expertise, and, as is the case in most organizations, their authority is both distinct and partially overlapping.

The multiple authority roles in GCP give rise over time to typical group behaviors aimed at "splitting" the TA and the PF (dividing loyalties or instigating discord) in order to increase the ability of the teams to control their own destiny. Some teams try to annex in the TA as a member of the team, creating a single point of external "control" in the PF. Other teams make either the TA or the PF the "good guy" and the other the "bad guy," and cut off or limit communication with the "bad guy." Still other teams experience most authority ambiguity with the TA or PF of their partner team, and willingly submit to the authority of their own TA and PF in solidarity against the overseas hierarchy.

The interdependence among the players in the GCP hierarchy is discovered and explored by the students as the projects move forward (Agazarian & Gantt, 2003). For example, the students may meet with their TA regularly, and their TA meets regularly with TAs from other projects, updates the faculty assigned to that team, and periodically briefs the program's process consultant. These linkages create a potentially powerful network of resources on behalf of the student team. A team may ask their TA for leads on market information and benefit from the contributions of all TAs, faculty and others associated with the program. On the other hand, when the TA and team do not agree on a way forward, these resource network meetings and conversations may be utilized to enlist support for one point of view or another in a political fashion.

Interdependence can lead to cooperation if it is positive (Johnson & Johnson, 1995). However, discomfort with these multiple lines of authority and the struggle to sort out how to use them, what each expects, and who has what power, is often the basis for some of the earliest learning in the program. For example, early in the semester the combined teams meet overseas with their clients. This is the first in-person meeting of the two halves of each team and it is the occasion of the first major deliverable in GCP: an initial scoping document for the client and a work plan. The teams now begin in earnest to explore their assumptions about authority and causality within the program.

Most teams ask their TA's and PF's for guidance or help in preparing the scoping document and in getting connected with their partner teams. Imagine a clip from a continuous video recording of a pre-trip team meeting:

Jennifer: "We need to plan some sort of integration process with our partner team. Even thought we've talked several times, this will be different."

Sunil: "Why don't we have them do the same things we did at our opening team building meeting?"

Ian: "We don't have time for much. From what I can tell talking to people who did this last year, we're going to have to work flat out. Besides, we all know what preliminary research we've done. I still don't understand what the other team has done and they don't seem to want to get it to us until their TA gives them the go-ahead."

Jennifer:	"Why don't we divide up the planning to be done for the trip and get on with it?"
Sunil:	[in a conciliatory tone] "I don't think we've even agreed what the planning tasks are yet. Why don't we ask Rich (TA) tonight how his team did this last year?"
Ian:	"What makes us think that his way is the right way for us? Look at what we're dealing with. Besides, Laurie (PF) made it clear that we needed to get on the stick with our story board for the scoping."
Simone:	"I still don't know why she's so wedded to story boarding. There are other ways to do this."

Enter Rich, the team's TA. The team airs its questions about how his team did it last year and inquires whether they need to limit themselves to story boarding.

Rich:	"Different teams manage this visit in different ways, and some of it depends on the culture of the country/partner team/client. What research have you done into that? The work itself it pretty straightforward and yes, you'll work flat out. Story boarding is a good technique—not the only one, though. I would take that as guidance, not a directive. Bill (GCP director) uses it a lot, but you should use an approach that's appropriate and works for you."

Rich leaves after responding to these questions. He was prepared to stay at the team's request, however, their perception of his role did not lead them into further discussion.

Jennifer:	"Oh great. It's 'guidance' but Bill likes it."
Ian:	"Forget it. We're supposed to be making our own decisions. What do we want to do?"
Sunil:	"This is true, but why not use the story boarding method? Laurie likes it too."
Jennifer:	"She's new, though, so she might not know that she and we have options."

The Team starts to fight internally about the way forward. They complain that the program ought to set up a single process for the scoping deliverable. They question whether their TA was being straight with them when he said there's no best approach to use.

Multiple lines of authority and multiple constituents—TA, Faculty, team members, clients, partners—are challenges that require the participants in GCP to analyze their own roles in new ways and to explicitly define their own and others' objectives and perspectives (Agazarian,

1982). While they may prefer to consider one issue at a time and think about one audience at a time, students learn that in complex real world settings, it is necessary to consider *sets* of issues and *sets* of audiences at all times. That is, at various decision points, the combined team must consider not only their own sense of what is the right way to go, but the cultural dynamics of the decision, their PF's views, their TA's views, their client's views and the views of other GCP authorities who may be connected to the issue. Ironically, most of the students have had exposure to business tools like stakeholder analysis, but very rarely apply such tools to their projects in the early stage.

For GCP teams, the consulting challenges are amplified by the make-up of their teams and by the behavior of their clients. All GCP teams are multi-cultural, not only because half the team members are in the client country, but because the Wharton student body is multi-cultural itself. And most GCP clients, like most corporate clients, change scope, have internal disagreements about focus, and sometimes discover that what they want might not be what they need.

This layering of variables and responsibilities is often stressful for the students. Team members sometimes disagree with each other members of their teams in interpreting client messages and devising appropriate responses. Teams regularly find themselves in the awkward position of trying to form a viable team at the same time they are trying to gain clarity about their client's issues and their relationship with the client. Out of this "messy" interdependence—whether it is handled well or not handled well—comes visceral learning (Bion, 1959). Take for example this experience:

A Wharton/Israel team got through their initial research in a somewhat perfunctory manner. The two halves of the team connected fairly well, and they found some temporary coherence in being united against various inputs from their respective project faculty. They had several joint calls with their client in Israel, and they set up a schedule of weekly check-ins to keep the client updated as their thinking progressed on the project.

About a month into this schedule, they realized, through the thoughtful questioning of their TA, that there was a major flaw in the logic they were applying to the project. The team panicked. They went back through their thought process. They asked the TA how to fix it. The TA turned the question back to the team. The team began to tick through all the options they had learned in their course work. They became inwardly focused and only thought to clue-in their partner team when their liaison emailed to ask why they had missed their weekly call. Together the combined team worked feverishly to rectify the error in logic, to go back through the data, and to work up a new project approach and interim report for the client.

All told, this took three and a half weeks. In that time, they had completely forgotten their client, the person. They were focused exclusively on the work and the pressure to perform. During a videoconference with their client to go over the project interim report, the first thing he asked was where they had been for the last 3 weeks and why they failed to contact him. The team, who had been feeling elated about "rescuing" the project before the client knew it was going down, were taken aback and shocked when they realized how insular and isolated their response to the problem had been.

When they had completed their videoconference, their TA suggested that they debrief "How do you think you got here?" the TA asked the group. "What happened and what were you thinking, feeling?"

Gil, a Wharton teammate, responded first: "I think the pressure to perform blew everything else out of our minds. I know speaking for me personally I had a feeling of panic when I realized that the underlying logic didn't stand up. It was "pull out all the stops and get this baby fixed!"

Zehavit, an Israeli teammate, spoke next: "I think for us it feels bad that your first reaction was to circle the wagons. You cut us out, or more exactly, didn't think of us as in it with you or helping. So what does that say about our team?"

Yael, another Israeli team member, added: "The thing that amazes me still is how we completely forgot the client. We slipped right back into being students in a class. Shows how old habits are hard to break. I'm wondering, if this is real, you know, if this is how we might respond in a situation next year after we've graduated, how we stop ourselves. What's the early warning sign? How do we ensure against it?"

"Those would be great questions for you to talk about now," said the TA.

The interdependence of teams, issues, and client is at the heart of corporate life, and at the heart of experiential learning and action research (Brown, 1988). Telling students or employees about the tradeoffs and interrelatedness can only go so far in teaching them. Actually, grappling with the tensions across and among the interdependent features of real situations results in more visceral and lasting learning. Attacking interdependent problems sequentially is not a viable strategy in most corporate contexts, nor is it effective in the GCP setting, especially if innovative solutions are desired (Janssen, van de Vliert, & West, 2004). Complex tasks require the ability to consider multiple and changing variables, to learn, to test, to adopt a strategy but be willing to adapt approaches (Pich et al., 2002). Interdependence in the structure of GCP, particularly between tasks and roles, helps create opportunities for real learning in this area.

CHALLENGES OF AMBIGUITY

Not only are the elements of the GCP closely interrelated and structurally interdependent, they are also ill-defined—and this ambiguity is the next central learning trigger. Some significant challenges of ambiguity are inherent in any ambitious action learning program. It is impossible to specify the relevant variables and contingencies in such programs with enough detail and accuracy to leave no ambiguous "gray" areas. The GCP recognized this reality early in its institutional life and concluded that the ambiguous nature of some aspects of the program was actually quite productive.

The ambiguity of the GCP program allows its participants to identify possible futures, explore their roles as shapers of their reality, and enact strategies to achieve desired outcomes (Weick, 1979). These emergent strategies and the repeated experiments that teams knowingly and unwittingly carry out as a result of them are at the heart of the GCP learning experience. This type of learning is intensely frustrating to students who are seeking structured answers and codified "best practices," but the feedback gathered from alumni of the program indicates that this frustration is appreciated as learning once the knowledge is applied in subsequent situations (GCP feedback, 2000-2003).

Three types of ambiguity in particular are consciously left unresolved in the design of the Global Consulting Practicum: Leadership Ambiguity, Process Ambiguity and Performance Ambiguity.

Leadership Ambiguity: "Where Are We Going?"

The first ambiguity the Wharton GCP participants encounter is in the realm of leadership. The introductory "class" meeting brings together the GCP program founder, administrative leadership, faculty, teaching assistants (TAs) and non-faculty experts and introduces them to the students. No hierarchy among these players is established. Soon thereafter, the leadership issues become even more opaque as the participants quickly become aware that their partner school has its own coterie of "leaders," including a program director/founder, administrative personnel, and faculty, TAs, and non-faculty experts.

In GCP, the multiple authority roles and the absence of direction regarding team roles has the effect of requiring students to become much clearer about their own authority. In order for the teams to make effective choices about how to access and utilize the authority and the resources they require, they have to begin to sort out their own responsibility, authority and resources. Through a process of observation, participation, experimentation and intervention, the team members refine their awareness of how and when to exercise this authority. We believe this experience produces important learning for students on the individual, team and program levels.

When the teams look to their fellow students for leadership, they are usually comforted by the concept of situational team leadership (Fiedler, 1967). Internally, the application of situational leadership concepts allows the team to experiment with sequential and shared leadership roles, especially within their immediate (4-6 person) team. Typically, some tension arises throughout the program between those participants with strong needs for control or strong "telling" styles and their teammates with other styles and profiles. Valuable learning in this area occurs as the participants realize the distinction between a nominal and a de facto leader, and factor the impact of personality type and relationship strength into their pre-existing notions of leadership (Beck, 1981).

> One Wharton MBA student, a banker before coming to graduate school, was intentionally assigned to a GCP team for a financial services client. Her first instinct, implicitly supported by several of her fellow team members, was to take a position as the expert on the client's issues. This approach became problematic as soon as the Wharton team started to do research into the product/service lines and markets in which the client company was proposing to participate. The banker's experience seemed to fly in the face of the research results. Since leadership and control were still unresolved issues in this team, there was some sentiment in favor of disregarding the self-appointed expert. In fact, the team at this point seemed in search of a leader who could smooth the workload, not raise issues or exceptions. They moved to shut out the banker and to disregard her expertise and assumed leadership.
>
> After several data-driven conversations prompted by timely questions from the project faculty and TA, the banker and her fellow team members stood back to look at how the banker's prior experience might coexist with or inform the market and product/service data they had collected. They hypothesized that the banker's experience was revealing some regional niche trends that they had not yet picked up in their research. Ultimately, this hypothesis proved correct. The team members were able to apply this empirical regional knowledge to their client's situation, quite beneficially recommending against this particular regional niche as a product/service opportunity worth pursuing. The banker regained her status on the team, but another colleague tended to lead through using a facilitative style for the majority of the subsequent meetings.

The real-world setting of the GCP program, like other experiential learning venues, enables both faculty and students to gain skills, capabilities and awareness not easily replicable in the classroom (Steffes, 2004). However, as the example above implies, this real-world setting also demands of the faculty and students a style of "teaching" and "learning," an attention to structure and resources, and a willingness to allow and support complexity and ambiguity that are unusual and at times uncomfortable. The most effective GCP teams reject the notion of leadership narrowly defined as authority, distinguish between policy/administration and leadership, and become increasingly comfortable with the ambiguity in this area. The least effective teams are at times paralyzed. They await guidance and clarity; they defer decisions and spend their meeting time in unproductive debates and complaints.

In creating and tolerating ambiguity around program leadership, GCP mirrors a common feature of complex corporate settings. The idea that any given work team is managed and lead only by their immediate boss or leader is usually a gross oversimplification of the organizational reality. Administrative personnel set and enforce policies, layers of management create and communicate their vision, line and staff management identify and interpret decision moments, clients' desires and demands must be acknowledged—and many voices enter a dialogue about where the team or organization should go. In fact, most leaders regularly have the experience of managing someone who knows more about a subject than they do. The approach to leadership in GCP acknowledges this reality and implicitly asks a team to define leadership in a way that allows for the duality of leadership and followership (Berg, 1992.)

Process Ambiguity: "How Should We Proceed?"

"Management by objectives" (Carroll & Tosi, 1973) is analogous to the process at the core of the Global Consulting Practicum. Participants are given milestone targets and deadlines at various intervals, with few constraints as to how they reach them. For example, by a certain point in the program they must complete tasks such as getting to know their partner team, preparing a draft work plan for client approval, conducting market research to inform the client's situation, and presenting interim findings to the client.

The milestones themselves are relatively unambiguous, but the process for achieving the milestone is intentionally vague. Should introductions be via phone, teleconference, email or all three? Should the introductions be made with faculty or TA intervention—or by the team? There are many large and small process decisions that the team must make. Some are not consciously addressed, but instead are implemented by default.

"Class is supposed to meet once a week," asserts Raoul.

"I think that schedule is just for the bureaucrats in the Registrar's office. How often do we need to meet?" injects Janeen.

A discussion of whether to meet based on team member's schedule availability, client needs and/or strict calendars ensues. No clear model emerges as dominant, but Raoul has been increasingly taking a leadership role and now takes the floor "Let's meet once a week for the next 2 weeks. Once we have our work plan done we can just email and get together as the work demands—probably a lot less often than 3 hours/week!"

There is some side-talk, but the group moves onto another topic. Had the team queried their TA or faculty about meeting frequency, they would likely have been told, "Use your own judgment."

The students in the GCP program make their own decisions about meeting times and venues unless a mandatory program meeting is announced. The "meetings decision" *seems* simple, but because there are many interdependencies in the program structure, as discussed above, student teams come to realize that there are few truly simple decisions. The appropriate frequency of meetings, for example, is dependent upon the stage and pace of the project, the quality and frequency of team communication, the clarity of the client engagement, and the level of interaction with faculty and teaching assistants.

Some teams by "default" meet once a week for 2 hours. Others start out using this process and add meetings when crises arise or workflow surges. Best practice teams identify and discuss a process for "calling a meeting" and also anticipate the need for and purpose of meetings. At some stages in the program, these latter teams actually meet less than their counterparts and yet accomplish more over the course of the semester. The ambiguity around something as seemingly trivial as the meeting schedule thus provides huge learning potential.

In GCP, team processes are illuminated through intentional process ambiguity in ways that would be impossible if the class schedule was simply adjusted by the faculty to accommodate typical project workflows and team dynamics. When the faculty and staff solve these and other "problems" before the team has a chance to encounter them, they do a disservice to the team's learning and thus to the program (Wenger, 1999).

Performance Ambiguity: "What Is Success?"

The third locus of ambiguity in the GCP program is performance. The possible and desirable goals and rewards of this program may initially appear obvious, but they are quite difficult to define and tend to change depending on the stage of the project and the constituency under consideration. Many students first assume success is equivalent to a good grade and to leveraging the GCP experience to attain a desirable job offer for a summer or full time job. Whether the whole team attains the good grade, and whether everyone in the team or the program is well placed in the job market, may emerge later as broader measures of success. Certainly client satisfaction, team learning and meeting milestones are other possible success measures.

In GCP, students must decide with minimal guidance what their goals are and how to factor-in the objectives of various constituents (client, partners, TAs) to their concept of performance. Discomfort with multiple possible definitions of performance and the struggle to sort out how to prioritize them, what each demands, and what constitutes success or failure in each is often the basis for some deep experiential learning in the program as students strive to identify, articulate and achieve various "goals." In fact, GCP is well bounded, and a team will not be allowed to fail through ignorance or by getting themselves to a discovery or learning space from which they cannot deliver in the course time remaining. Teams are told this, but they only learn this by getting there, so although there is a safety net, it does not inhibit exploration and experimentation.

The program could unambiguously define and reward performance by grading. GCP could weight client satisfaction 20% (based on a survey), meeting milestones 40% (with further breakdown by milestone), quality of team process 20% (rated by expert/faculty) and quality of team output 20% (rated by expert/faculty). However, this approach has been consciously rejected by the program. Instead, intentional ambiguity around success measures has been designed into the program. Ultimately, grading is done by clients, faculty and peers. It is team-based and takes into account learning, experience, active exploration and team growth as factors of performance (McTaggart, 1996).

Students must self-determine and negotiate their performance metrics. Is an indicator of high performance the ability to "stick to" their work plan? If deviating from the work plan is defined as failure, then how can adjustments be accommodated throughout the project? When tradeoffs must be made between quality of analysis and timeliness or brevity of the report?

Some teams conclude that their client's long-term success in their product launch is the litmus test of the whole course's effectiveness. The team might then make the argument that using an external market research firm would provide a more comprehensive viewpoint on the client's future prospects. "Can we use our budget to buy the industry report instead of collecting the data ourselves? The results will better serve the client." This sort of question can lead to a dialogue that gets to the core of the performance issue and one that opens the door to insights for all involved (Winter, 1987). By considering the pros and cons of outsourcing to experts v. building internal expertise through hands on learning, participants expose their embedded assumptions about success and must articulate their beliefs about the purpose of the Practicum. Rather than a sterile exercise comparing costs and benefits of outsourcing, learning in GCP is a function of immersion in a complex, realistic context, where their decision is rational and emotional, reasoned and felt, conceived and tested.

PROCESSES FOR GUIDED REFLECTION

Experiential learning requires good "processing" in order to reach its potential (Kolb, 1984). Usually some confirming or out of the ordinary take-away from an experience are realized, but without guided reflection many aspects of the experience are lost. Some experiences are not consciously noticed, others are confusing and hard to interpret. Often the participant experiences too many stimuli to process in real time.

Reflective questioning extends the range of learning from an experience in at least three ways. It enables the participants to identify their roles in the cause and effect elements of the experience. It crystallizes the impacts of their actions, inactions and reactions. It encourages them to make explicit the many implicit cues, observations and feelings they have registered in the course of the experience. Guided reflection can also facilitate learning not just at the individual level, but also at the team and collective or program levels. This is an important step in embedding learning (Vygotsky, 1978; Lave & Wenger, 1990). For these reasons, we see guided reflection as the third driver of impact in GCP and guided reflection of many types is woven into the structure of the Global Consulting Practicum at Wharton.

Opening Workshop: "Why Am I Here?"

During the Opening Workshop for GCP, teams meet together for the first time. In this early piece of guided reflection, team members are asked to work individually first and make explicit for themselves the experiences, the knowledge, the expectations and the feelings they are bringing into the GCP team. Specifically, they are asked to write down the things they bring as resources to the team, the things they believe will be most difficult for them, how they hope to benefit from their GCP experience and any special pace/timing issues they have.

The individual reflection is followed by team discussion and reflection—essentially the first team meeting (see below). The agenda for this initial meeting is simple. The team is to listen to each member and to discuss how these individual inputs connect and what they mean for the team. In addition to creating an explicit dialogue that begins to form some understandings and norms in the new team, this session taps into the implicit and in some cases unrecognized thoughts and feelings of the students (Kolb, 1984). The team discussion of these individual reflections helps to ground the students with each other and establishes some of the first team realities and team learning (similar to the situated learning of Brown, Collins, & Duguid, 1989).

After the fact, students report that if they hadn't been asked to do this task, they never would have done it. They say that this initial team meeting in the Opening Workshop gives them something they can come back to, a touchstone which can help them bring up process issues, address individual needs, look at their own operation as a team and get over hurdles in the client work (GCP student feedback, 2000-2003.)

Team Meetings

Case in Point

The project faculty (PF) for an Israeli project had worked with his team over a period of weeks as they struggled with how to best make sense of the data they had collected, how to utilize the two halves of their team effectively, and how to manage their relationship with the client, who seemed to be subtly broadening the focus of the project on every conference call. This faculty was particularly adept at asking questions which would cause the group to examine why they were doing and what they were doing:

> "Think back on the focus you identified. Does this course of action take you where you said you were going to go?"

> "What do you hear your client saying? Has it changed at all from what he said last week?"

> "How are you feeling about the direction you've chosen? Are you all on board with it? Does it meet your criteria? The client's? Does it fulfill the essential elements of the analysis model we gave you?"

At times, the reflection produced by this questioning took the team right to the aspects of their work that needed changing. However, the dynamics of the team were such that they could not look at these issues and address them. The stuck doggedly to the path they had chosen. The PF, though extremely frustrated by this, made the considered decision to let the team pursue its chosen course up through the first deliverable to the client. He expected they would be pulled up short, but he believed they had time in the project to recover.

The first big client deliverable took place in a face to face meeting in the March trip to the client site. The joint team delivered their presentation by the script they had planned. It went off without a hitch, until the client's reacted:

The research you have done is useful to us, but your analysis does not incorporate the application of some of our product's most important features, ones we are very interested in promoting and marketing. We have discussed these on several calls and you have all our documentation with these outlined.

And this analysis is too restricted. It addresses just a fraction of what we see as the possibilities. We need to talk about how this goes forward and what can be done to put this project on the track we are looking for.

The team was surprised and visibly uncomfortable. They responded that the features they were focusing were the ones that they and the client had agreed to at the start of the project. The client reminded them that they had a number of conversations since that one and that the thinking had progressed. At that point the Israeli team partners suggested that the team go back, reconsider their approach, and get back to the client in two weeks with a revised plan.

As the team left the office, the PF and TA, who had sat through the meeting, suggested that they all meet for a debrief. It was the last thing the team wanted to do just then, but in terms of learning, it was good timing. The PF asked them one by one how they felt about the meeting. Then he asked them to think about what factors might have contributed to the result they got with the client. The TA asked them to think back to any "pinch points" they had experienced as a team and how—or if—they had dealt with the conflict or the disagreement that caused each. The team discussion that resulted from these questions amounted to a self diagnosis of critical incidents in their team process and in their work on the project. They surfaced factors they had all noticed but not acknowledged. And they uncovered important differences of opinion in the group.

Outcomes such as this are critical in the GCP learning experience for several reasons. They build in the team a sense of ownership for the client work. They contribute to a growing feeling of competence or mastery that is one of the specific goals of GCP. And they provide a learning and resultant knowledge that is understood viscerally, that is integrated and ready to use or apply again.

Milestone Debriefs

There are three points in a GCP semester at which guided reflection occurs in a planned way. These three debriefs serve several purposes in the learning agenda for GCP. First, they provide a means to crystallize some of the overarching concepts that are emerging in the experience. For instance, after the first in-person client meeting, some of the guided reflection questions ask the teams to think about what they are beginning to know about the nature of their relationship with their client and what frames, choices, actions and events have helped to shape that relationship.

Second, these debriefs are the formal mechanisms for guided reflection at the collective or program level. In two of these debriefs, all the Wharton teams meet together. After team discussions, they have a collective conversation about their observations, experience take-aways, and learnings. In the May Colloquium debrief at the end of the GCP course, the combined teams meet together—all Wharton and partner schools collectively. After a short period of reflection, the collective becomes the forum.

When the teams start talking to each other about their conclusions, their questions, their emerging concepts, the processes they've adopted and their client, team or project strategies, the whole group of students begins to learn together from the variety and the commonality of their experiences (McDermott in Murphy, 1999.) It becomes obvious from the discussions that two teams confronted with very similar situations often choose different courses of actions that result in varied outcomes. It is also usually evident that two teams who have similar experiences often take-away quite different learning from those experiences.

The third learning purpose served by the formal debriefs in GCP is to provide the program itself with a barometer for the course, the results of which can be roughly compared from year to year. We learn from seeing the impact or effects of various changes we make in the program, as evidenced in what learnings are emerging from students, teams and the class and how these learnings are taking shape. These data contribute to the reshaping of the program each year as part of a feedback-application loop that is a key element of experiential learning (Kolb, 1984).

SUMMARY

While it is the GCP system in its entirety that creates the GCP experience, three critical aspects of the GCP experience drive its impact and value as a learning endeavor: the structural interdependence of the program elements; the challenges engendered by intentional ambiguity around leadership, process and performance; and the support for guided reflection provided to the students individually, in their teams and across the program as a whole.

The **interdependence** of the program elements mirrors the real world environment by demonstrating how even "trivial" decisions affect and are affected by other choices and constraints in the organizational context. The **ambiguity** of the program forces exploration and question/ issue framing to become central to team process and project progress. Consequently, the learning process is primarily shaped by the interaction of learners, events, choices and resources rather than by teachers. **Reflective techniques** enable the students to crystallize and extract learnings from their experiences and to articulate these learnings within, across and beyond their teams.

As MBA students are challenged to bring more immediately relevant and applicable skills to their workplaces, learning in real world settings will continue to be attractive to students and to their future employers. However, these are difficult programs to design, coordinate and execute. The challenges at the intellectual, interpersonal and institutional levels are not fully appreciated by the participants. The learning that is possible within this "structure within a structure" is truly internal and transferable—deep learning that makes the effort worthwhile for the faculty and staff involved.

A program as ambitious and complex as the Global Consulting Practicum is not necessary to make progress in this area. Any learning program in a real world setting that captures the essence of this program can offer a learning experience that is qualitatively different from the typical MBA classroom. These essential elements may be summarized as follows:

1. *Complex Structure*:   Create a team-based structure that accurately captures the complex realities of accomplishing multiple project objectives, interfacing with several types of authority, and accessing a variety of limited resources. Bound that system. That is, be very clear about the learning boundary (the difference between mis-stepping and stumbling in the process of exploration and going into free-fall out of ignorance) and the performance boundary (the point at which a team's mode of exploration/discovery/learning is going against the philosophy of the program or will put the team into a position from which they will not be able to recover in the remaining time available.)

2. *Self-Defining Context*:   Create a context where the participants must define their roles, goals, resources and rewards themselves.

3. *Learning Comes First*:   Live by the philosophy that the first objective of the program is learning. "Teach" by asking good questions. Let experience or the learners themselves provide answers.

4. *Multiple Reflection Points*:   Be skillful and varied in designing and enacting guided reflection opportunities.

REFERENCES

Armington, R., & Cassano, S. (1996). The challenge of the member role in group problem-solving. *SCT Journal: Systems Centered Theory and Practice, 1*(1), 41-43.

Agazarian, Y.M., & Gantt, S. P. (2003). Phases of group development: systems-centered hypotheses and their implications for research and practice. *Group DynamicsTheory, Research and Practice, 7*(3), 238-252.

Agazarian, Y.M. (1982). Role as a bridge construct in understanding the relationship between the individual and the group. In M. Pines & L. Rafaelson (Eds.), *The individual and the group: Boundaries and interrelations, 1: Theory*. New York: Plenum Press.

Beck, A.P. (1981). A study of group phase development and emergent leadership. *Group: The Journal of the Eastern Group Psychotherapy Society, 5*(4) 48-54.

Berg, D.N. (1992). Resurrecting the muse: Followership in organizations. In E.B. Klein, F. Gabelnick, & P. Herr (Eds.), *The psychodynamics of leadership*. Madison, CT: Psychosocial Press.

Bion, W.R. (1959). *Experiences in groups*. London: Tavistock.

Bosworth, K., & Hamilton, J. (1994). Collaborative learning: Underlying processes and effective techniques. *New directions for teaching and learning*, No. 59. San Francisco: Jossey-Bass.

Brown, R. (1988). *Group processes—Dynamics within and between groups*. Oxford: Blackwell.

Brown, J.S., Collins, A., & Duguid, S. (1989). Situated cognition and the culture of learning. *Education Researcher, 18*(1), 32-42.

Carr, W., & Kemmis, S. (1986). *Becoming critical: Education, knowledge and action research*. Lewes: Falmer Press.

Carroll, S.J., & Tosi, H.L., Jr. (1973). *Management by objectives: Applications and research*. New York: Macmillan.

Costello, M.L., Brunner, P.W., & Hasty, K. (2002). Preparing students for the empowered workplace: The risks and rewards in a management classroom. *Active Learning in Higher Education, 3*(2), 117-127.

Dotlich, D., & Noel, J. (1998). *Action learning: How the world's top companies are re-creating their leaders and themselves*. San Francisco: Jossey Bass

Fiechtner, S.B., & Davis, E.A. (1984-85). Why some groups fail: A survey of students' experience with learning groups. *Organizational Behavior Teaching Review, 9*, 58-71.

Fiedler, F.E. (1967). *A theory of leadership effectiveness*. New York: McGraw-Hill.

GCP Feedback. (2000-2003). Unpublished annual report summary of participant evaluative inputs.

Hall, C.S., & Lindzey, G. (1978). *Theories of personality* (3rd ed.). New York: Wiley.

Harvey, M. G., & Griffith, D. A. (2002). Developing effective intercultural relationships: the importance of communication strategies. *Thunderbird International Business Review, 44*(4), 455-476.

Janssen, O., van de Vliert, E., & West, M. (2004). The bright and dark sides of individual and group innovation: A special issue introduction. *Journal of Organizational Behavior, 25*(2), 129-145.

Johnson, D.W., & Johnson, R.T. (1995). Positive interdependence: Key to effective cooperation. In R. Hertz-Lazarowitz & N. Miller (Eds.), *Interaction in cooperative groups: The theoretical anatomy of group learning* (pp.174-199). Cambridge: Cambridge University Press.

Kalem, S., & Fer, S. (2003). The effects of the active learning model on students' learning, teaching and communication. *Educationalssciences: Theory & Practice, 3*(2), 455-461.

Kemmis, S., & McTaggart, R. (1988). *The action research planner.* Geelong, Victoria: Deakin University Press.

Kofman, F., & Senge, P.M. (1993). Communities of commitment: The heart of the learning organization. *Organization Dynamics, 22*(2), 5-11.

Kolb, D.A. (1984). *Experiential learning: Experience as the source of learning and development.* Englewood Cliffs, NJ: Prentice- Hall.

Langan-Fox, J., Anglim, J., & Wilson, J.R. (2004). Mental models, team mental models, and performance: process, development and future directions. *Human Factors and Ergonomics in Manufacturing, 14*(4) 331-352.

Lave, J., & Wenger, E. (1990). *Situated learning: Legitimate peripheral participation.* Cambridge: Cambridge University Press.

Lewin, K (1948). *Resolving social conflicts: Selected papers on group dynamics.* New York: Harper & Row.

Lewin, K. (1951). *Field theory in social science: Selected theoretical papers.* New York: Harper & Row.

Lightsey, R.H. (2000). Engineering management training: Comparison of experiential vs. lecture methods of instruction. *Acquisition Review Quarterly, 7*(2), 1–17.

McTaggart, R. (1996). Issues for participatory action researchers. In O. Zuber-Skerrit (Ed.), *New directions in action research.* London: Falmer Press.

Murphy, P. (Ed.). (1999). *Learners, learning and assessment.* London: Paul Chapman.

Pich, M.T., Loch, C.H., & de Meyer, A. (2002). On uncertainty, ambiguity and complexity in project management. *Management Science, 48*(8), 1008-1015.

Schein, E. (1995). Kurt Lewin's change theory in the field and in the classroom: Notes toward a model of managed learning. *Systems Practice.* Retrieved March 14, 2005 from http://www.solonline.org/res/wp/10006.html

Schwaninger, M. (2004). Methodologies in conflict: Achieving synergies between system dynamics and organizational cybernetics. *Systems Research and Behavioral Science, 21*(4), 411-431.

Shanley, M., & Peteraf, M. (2004). Vertical group formation: A social process perspective. *Managerial and Decision Economics, 25*(6-7), 473-488.

Steffes, J. S. (2004, May/June). Creating powerful learning environments. *Change.*

Tosey, P. (1999). The peer learning community: A contextual design for learning? *Management Decision, 37*(5), 403-410.

Vygotsky, L.S. (1978). *Mind in society.* Cambridge, MA: MIT Press.

Weick, K.E. (1979). *The social psychology of organizing.* Reading, MA: Addison-Wesley Publishing.

Wenger, E. (1999). *Communities of practice: Learning, meaning and identity.* Cambridge: Cambridge University Press.

Winter, R. (1987). Action-research and the nature of social inquiry. *Professional innovation and educational work.* Aldershot: Avebury.

CHAPTER 2

PROJECT-BASED INTERNATIONAL BUSINESS CONSULTING

C. Patrick Fleenor, Peter V. Raven, and Jerry Ralston

The AACSB suggests offering business students more practical applications of business theory, especially in a global context. Exposing students to actual problems and opportunities in this dynamic field helps them integrate and apply lessons from their graduate business programs. This course helps meet that objective by helping students achieve an understanding of the international environment in which businesses must compete and managers manage. Students work closely with client firms and are involved in analyzing issues such as: global market opportunities, the economic and political forces that shape the patterns of international trade; problems of international investment and finance; market entry strategies, and communicating across cultures. Local and regional companies take advantage of the expertise of business students under faculty supervision in researching foreign market problems, reaching conclusions, and making recommendations for the organizations. Thus, a win-win situation results for both students and companies.

INTRODUCTION

Realistic business cases have long been a part of a business education, especially at the graduate level. Cases invite students to apply business

Educating Managers through Real World Projects, 25–46
Copyright © 2005 by Information Age Publishing
All rights of reproduction in any form reserved.

school theories, and from analyzing them, they learn how to apply concepts that otherwise might remain strictly academic exercises. Taking the case method a step further, we believe live cases provide opportunities for reciprocal learning. Students undertake real business projects and at the same time businesses learn how to resolve problems and explore initiatives that would otherwise not get done, be postponed, or cancelled outright. Through this process, students learn to integrate their experiences and are trained in critical thinking and project management. This chapter describes a program that meets these learning goals.

The Global Business EDGE (Education for Global Executives) Program was established to promote and facilitate strategic partnerships between Pacific Northwest (PNW) businesses and the Albers School of Business and Economics at Seattle University (SU). Its objectives are:

- To provide students with a rigorous and exciting environment that integrates outside, practical experience with classroom education.
- To make extensive research, informational, analytical and educational resources at the University available to firms entering or engaged in the global marketplace to improve their competitiveness and profitability.
- To provide resources for faculty to use in class enhancement and help them gain practical experience to aid in applying concepts.

These objectives are accomplished through a variety of interactive services described below. Participating companies range from the small to the very large, and include both product and service firms. They represent many industries whose activities touch every geographical region. Before we discuss the actual program, we review some of the pertinent literature that forms a pedagogical basis for our program.

LITERATURE REVIEW

Case Analysis

Case studies have an important role in business education. Bonoma and Kosnik (1989) describe very different pedagogical goals in using case studies and experiential learning versus traditional teaching methods, such as lectures. Some advantages of the case method are that learning is more personal and powerful and tends to be retained longer, since the learning is learner-based, rather than teacher-based. The disadvantage of case studies is that students accustomed to faculty direction must take responsibility for their own learning. The student has primary responsibility for the learning's failure or success. Some students, even at the graduate level, struggle with this learner centered approach.

Harvard University is the best-known business school with an early focus on case studies. Bongiorno (1993) described how the traditional case study method at Harvard changed to better reflect current business practice. For example, in the past, cases were analyzed and written by individuals, but today teams are more likely to be involved. This adds a dimension of complexity, and also possibilities for greater learning. Managing teams can sometimes be problematic (Siciliano, 1999; Brooks & Ammons, 2003), but students often learn a great deal from team interactions. For example, in teams that don't function ideally, students must still learn to make their teams meet a client's needs and deadlines.

The experiences and background each student brings to the team will likely differ and complement those of other students, allowing the team to view case problems from different perspectives and often provide richer solutions to problems. Mattern, Weinholtz, and Friedman (1983) observed as individual team members learn, they are better able to contribute and use contributions of others. As teams achieve cohesion, they promote additional learning among individual members. Considering recent well-known ethical and legal lapses of WorldCom, Enron, Tyco, Ahold, and other firms, some suggest that the business case method can be integrated to better understand real-life business problems by introducing casuistry methods which involve "the use of settled cases to resolve present moral problems" (Calkins, 2001). In a sense, students analyzing written or "live" cases use these techniques, at least internally, in business case analysis. Students often draw upon previous case analyses to resolve current case problems. Especially in "live" cases of company projects that have never before been analyzed, students must not only recall techniques for analysis, but also draw on past experiences and past case analyses in order to complete the task.

It is not just in management practice where the case method has been successful. Multidisciplinary skills are needed by accounting and finance students, especially in today's economy (Collett, 2000). Increasingly, business programs require relevance to real-world problems. Case studies and team projects aid in bringing reality to otherwise strictly academic studies.

Educators recognize that professional curricula must include activities that help integrate theory with the skills needed to manage unanticipated problems and policies in business. Real-life cases help bridge the gap between theory and practice and provide realistic problem solving opportunities for students (Friedman, 1995).

Case analyses provide a powerful method for reaching pedagogical objectives. Harrison-Walker (2000) integrates work from several authors to list the following learning benefits:

- Cases allow for a better understanding of reality, including problems that are not clearly defined and for which there may be several solutions;
- The focus is on students learning through their joint, cooperative efforts, rather than through a teacher;
- Cases have a strong appeal for many students turned off by traditional, lecture-type courses that focus on facts and content;
- The case method involves the development of oral communication skills as students defend their recommendations;
- Students gain confidence in themselves and in relating to their peers.

Students are more likely to internalize concepts used to solve real-world situations. These benefits to learning exist to an even greater extent with real-life problem solving cases. Here, students encounter the advantages of realism with the time constraints of corporate decision-making.

The Internet can facilitate student interactivity with case material, as well as with other students. The Web allows teachers to develop more up to date materials, provide diversity in types of cases, and rapid feedback (Henson et al., 2003). While the case method of teaching business has many advantages, it still lacks the realism and uncertainty of real-life business decision-making. Using field cases or consulting on real business projects enhances realism, complexity, and uncertainty.

In a management context, consulting is essentially "the transfer of expertise so that the client organization will be more effective after the consultant's departure" (Corey, 1990, p. 1). A consultant has some influence over an organization, but no direct power to make changes or implement programs (Block, 1999). A manager, in contrast, takes direct responsibility for an action. Consulting projects are often done by teams and require the typical management skills of planning, organizing, controlling, and leading. In addition, project teams need to be flexible and responsive as changes are likely to occur throughout a project. Project teams often benefit when members consist of students from different academic disciplines, due to the complexity of problems.

Consulting

Variously called real-life cases, fieldwork, live cases, or field cases, management-consulting projects take the classroom case a step further toward integrating theory, experience, and real managerial problems (Gundry & Buchko, 1996). Field-cases and traditional written cases are compared on

Table 2.1. A Comparison of Written and Field-based Cases

Written Cases	Field-Based Cases
Narrower approach—illustrates a few points	Holistic approach—many points and concepts are observed
Information is strategically manipulated—presented or withheld, depending on purpose	Information available may be inaccurate, distorted, or difficult to retrieve
Little or no personal contact with case characters	High degree of contact with people
Little or no intervention possible—case facts cannot be altered	High degree of intervention possible—solicit multiple perspectives
No future impact on decisions	Future impact on company decisions
No follow-up possible	Follow-up possible

Source: Based on Gundry and Buchko (1996).

several bases (see Table 2.1). The live case typically presents more complexity and more ambiguity than traditional cases for the students. The point of the case is not always evident, except that the client has a problem to be solved. The information needed to solve the problem is not usually readily available—otherwise it would have already been resolved. Often, the definition of the problem is also poorly understood—for example, symptoms of a problem may be confused with the underlying reasons causing the problem. Finally, project scope sometimes changes as client and team interact. These issues provide students with an opportunity for in-depth learning about problems firms confront. On the other hand, because a live-case is a real business problem, solving it can be much more meaningful and rewarding for students than a text-case. Students are enthusiastic about applying their academic knowledge to solving real-world problems.

Management consulting has been an increasingly important part of modern business activities and especially important has been providing international perspectives. Tapp (1997) proposed a number of reasons for this phenomenon:

- Technology facilitating globalization;
- Increased complexity of business problems;
- A growing use of outsourcing;
- Global competition.

Because fieldwork is experiential in nature, pedagogical objectives must be demonstrated. Gundry and Buchko (1996) describe a framework proposed by Kolb, Lublin, Spoth, and Baker (1987) that lists learning outcomes from fieldwork. These outcomes help students develop competencies to become better and more effective managers.

- Behavioral competence—taking the initiative to seek information and make recommendations;
- Perceptual competence—identifying the correct problems; gathering, organizing, and interpreting information; considering several perspectives;
- Affective competence—developing empathy and sensitivity to others' views and managing disagreements;
- Symbolic competence—understanding the business as a system of interrelated parts.

As businesses explore new markets globally, consultants provide advice on laws, business practices, tax systems, competition, and many other aspects of doing business globally. In many cases, the issues and problems' consultants are hired to identify and resolve are complex and have no precedence. Many firms, even very large firms, find it more efficient to hire consultants than developing the expertise in-house to solve these issues.

Consulting as Clinical Practice

EDGE consulting projects mirror important aspects of clinical teaching as practiced in medical schools and law schools. Irby (2005) observed in clinical education the process of learning is principally by doing. This form of experiential learning differs from most classroom settings. In experiential learning, information is generated through the sequence of steps themselves. Experiential learning is time-consuming and requires repeated actions in enough circumstances to allow for the development of a generalization from experience. When the consequence of action is separated in time and space, the learning process is not effective. A typical observation of those who have learned something through this process is that "they cannot verbalize it, but they can do it."

The weakest link in experiential learning is in generalizing from the particular experiences to a general principle applicable to other circumstances. Post-experience discussion is critical to the learning process to infer general principles from the experience. The strengths of this learning process include intrinsic motivation (since action occurs at the beginning, the need for learning exists from the outset) and stronger recall than learning only through information processing. Clinical education relies heavily on experiential learning, but also uses information processing for knowledge acquisition.

Consulting as Experiential Learning

The Global Business EDGE Program at Seattle University consists of three different activities: International Business Consulting (IBC), Students Acquiring Global Education (SAGE), and Overseas Research Projects (ORP). Although they differ from one another, each activity focuses on students consulting on real projects for real companies in real time. We briefly explain each element, but will then concentrate on the IBC element.

1. *International Business Consulting (IBC)*—Projects are performed in the context of the regular academic curriculum. Team results are formalized in comprehensive written reports that are prepared carefully and thoroughly. We expect the reports will be complete and convincing enough to allow the conclusions and recommendations to be utilized productively. Students make formal presentations of their findings and recommendations to each client company. Faculty feedback to student teams is voluminous and nearly constant. The faculty member meets formally with each team at least once a week, and communication by email or course management software are frequent, and sometimes occurs several times in a given day.

2. *Students Acquiring Global Education (SAGE)*—students and peers in other selected business schools worldwide work on a technology assisted team project. Working together on the same project, students are supervised by faculty from each university, bridging the geographic gap in real time with email and interactive video. The teams also write a joint report and make joint presentations to client companies through technology such as video conferencing.

3. *Overseas Research Projects (ORP)*—students on exchanges or other academic programs overseas, or who are foreign nationals returning temporarily to their home countries, undertake on-site market investigations and research projects for US firms. Projects may include conducting primary research (interviews, surveys), gathering information from data bases and publications not readily available in the United States and evaluating competitors' activities.

International Business Consulting (IBC)

The IBC course assigns students to projects proposed by client firms. Each team works on international issues, problems, or opportunities that firms are unable to initiate or complete due to constraints such as time, expertise or resources. This allows students to observe the decision-making processes in firms and provides these firms with a focused project performed by professionals. For example, many projects initiated by firms are broadly specified and too general to provide focused responses by student teams. In addition, firms may not be able initially to articulate the problems needing solutions exactly. By working closely with firms throughout the process, but especially in project definition, students learn more about the company's decision-making process and have an opportunity to focus the consulting project.

Student Teams—Students are drawn from Seattle University's MBA, MIB (Master of International Business), and MSF (Master of Science in Finance) programs, all of which are sponsored by the Albers School of Business and Economics. In addition, the Albers School conducts joint programs with the Seattle University School of Law, (leading to MBA/JD, MSF/JD and MIB/JD degrees), and a few students from these programs participate in the IBC course.

Most students are working professionals with backgrounds in engineering (e.g., Boeing employees), computer science and software development (e.g., Microsoft employees), and other backgrounds ranging from accounting to immunology. In addition, a number of international graduate students from various countries in Asia, the Middle East, and Europe take this course. The variety of student backgrounds adds to the richness of the interactions and perspectives in the final reports. Students work in two four-person teams on projects. Students choose their projects from the pool offered to the class and typically get their first or second choice. Working in teams generally requires considerable maintenance activity by members and oversight by instructors. Group dynamics create many interesting issues, some positive and some not.

Clients—Client firms represent the spectrum of companies in the Puget Sound region—from large firms such as Boeing, PACCAR, Microsoft, and Weyerhaeuser to much smaller firms in various industries from high-technology, freight forwarding and medical instruments to plant sanitation. The primary requirement for a candidate firm is a project that will be interesting, challenging, and doable in the framework of an academic term. Client firms pay a nominal fee to cover university expenses and reimburse students for out-of-pocket expenses such as overseas telephone calls, printing, etc. Contact people at the firm are typically middle managers or senior executives, depending on the nature of the firm and project.

Projects—While no two projects are exactly alike, they tend to fall into several main categories, including market opportunity analysis, country attractiveness, target market selection, laws and regulatory issues, market entry strategies, and marketing plan development. In a number of instances, student teams from one term developed projects to a stage that allows students in a subsequent term to follow up and take the project to a higher level. For example, student teams have worked with a local freight forwarder over several terms on a profitability model. In another case, projects for a life insurance firm have built on each other over four terms. Student teams present the client with both a professionally written report and a formal presentation of the results and recommendations at the client's office. This adds to the challenge and realism of the projects.

Faculty Role—Faculty have an important role in advising student teams throughout the term. Since few students have had consulting experience, faculty members share their experiences and techniques to help students develop systematic approaches to problem solving. One of the biggest challenges is to help the students focus and define the project such that it can be completed in a term and maximize the benefits for the client. To continue the metaphor of clinical teaching, one can paraphrase a landmark study by Ullian (1986) that profiled the behaviors and characteristics of excellent clinical teachers: Expert, Teacher, Supervisor, and Person.

There is considerable discrepancy between the Expert's level of experience and wisdom and that of the students. This discrepancy, after all, is the reason the expert and students are together. Sometimes it is necessary to tap other experts (faculty and/or practitioners) for their expertise. As a Teacher, the educator must be aware of the needs of students, but not assume it is possible to provide them with everything they need. As a Supervisor, the educator demonstrates critical thinking, provides practice, observes and assesses performance and provides feedback. Finally, as a Person, the educator must develop an atmosphere of sufficient trust that students are comfortable sharing ideas, feelings and thoughts. The Person should expect to provide significant personal help and support outside the formal teaching setting. IBC faculty members find the majority of their work to feature modeling of good process rather than explaining theory.

Deliverables—Each client firm receives a bound copy of the written report and often a disk of any data collected for further use. In addition, the student teams make a 45 minute presentation to executives of the firm at their headquarters or offices. Senior executives, and often the CEO, attend these presentations. Both the written report and the presentation describe the project focus, the methodology used, and quantitative and qualitative results. Teams present conclusions drawn from the data along with specific recommendations and action items for the client firm. The oral presentation is completed after a question and answer session, which is often very lively.

During the academic term, the teams make two practice presentations to the assembled class. The first presentation features the consulting/research plan and progress to date. The second presentation is much more formal and essentially represents the final product in rough form. This presentation allows the class to help colleagues in solving last minute problems, ask questions a team might expect from its client, and reinforce the requirement for a fully professional presentation.

We have found that one faculty member can reasonably handle up to six teams of three during a term. More than that reduces the time faculty can work with the teams and can reduce the value of the learning experience for students and of the final product for clients. Some projects are more demanding of faculty time than others, but all require considerable effort on the part of faculty and students both.

Process and Documentation

The IBC faculty and EDGE board members actively solicit projects. As the program matures (now in its third year), repeat clients somewhat reduce the need for active marketing. Firms that wish to sponsor a project sign a contract that illuminates major activities expected of them (Appendix A). Students and IBC faculty sign a "confidentiality agreement" assuring the client that information shared with the team will remain confidential (Appendix B).

The ten-week quarter system places serious pressure on IBC teams and faculty. Student teams must meet with their clients within days of the first class session. Before that meeting, teams must prepare a letter of engagement (Appendix C). The letter of engagement is the first step in negotiating the scope and depth of a project. The letter sometimes goes through several revisions before the parties are in agreement and is signed by students, faculty, and client. Once the parties agree on the broad tasks spelled out in the letter, the consulting team breaks the tasks down to create a quite detailed statement of work (Appendix D). The statement of work outlines the major objective of the project, questions and issues to be addressed, depth of analysis, and expected scope of recommendations.

At periodic intervals in the academic term, IBC faculty provide and discuss materials describing project guidelines, data gathering techniques, interview protocols, and guidelines for preparing the final report, and presentation. Samples of these documents are available from the authors. IBC faculty review and revise materials on a regular basis. The materials serve two crucial needs. The first is as educational tools, giving students information on procedures for structuring successful consulting projects. The second is to assure that clients and the student teams have the same expectations. Neither side appreciates surprises. The IBC materials and procedures strive to clarify expectations, catch miscommunication early on, and avoid serious misunderstanding and hard feelings.

Examples from Previous Projects

Because all of the projects are proprietary and students and faculty sign non-disclosure agreements, we are unable to provide specifics about any project. Some general examples, however, provide an idea of the extent and scope of the projects.

1. *Boeing Company*—Boeing has a well-developed ethics program and was interested in expanding it globally. The IBC team evaluated the issues in developing a global ethics program, providing specifics for a particular region of interest.

2. *Microsoft Corporation*—Intellectual property issues are of great concern to Microsoft, as piracy and counterfeits are prevalent in many markets. The IBC team used a survey of businesses in selected countries to help Microsoft understand some of the user issues to allow them to develop software piracy prevention plans.

3. *PACCAR*—This firm makes large trucks and tractors, including Peterbilt, DAF, and Kenworth brands, and others. The IBC team examined market opportunities for the various products in a large developing country.

4. *Neuvant Aerospace*—This firm manufactures parts and components for the aerospace industry. The IBC team examined sourcing opportunities, with a special focus on offset opportunities in emerging markets.

5. *Farmers Life Insurance*—The IBC team examined market opportunities in a developed country and international insurance products that may be useful in the U.S. market.

6. *Airborne Express* (now DHL)—Over several terms, IBC teams examined pricing and profit issues in their global markets using a large data set. Another IBC team examined financial synergies expected from the acquisition by DHL.

7. *Safeworks*—This firm manufactures motorized scaffolds used in washing windows of large buildings. The IBC team examined licensing opportunities in an emerging market.

8. *AquaEnergy*—This company specializes in harnessing energy from ocean waves and translating it into electric power. The IBC team examined market opportunities in several developing markets, using specific criteria required by the firm.

9. *Weyerhaeuser*—The IBC team evaluated the North American market for containerboard for a specific industry.

Post-project evaluations by clients indicate that the results were very useful and that the value far exceeded the nominal fee. In many cases, firms indicated the costs of a comparable project from a commercial consulting firm to be in excess of $10,000 to $150,000—many times the cost of the IBC team.

Community Outcomes

1. *Serving the Business Community*—The Global Business EDGE program interacts with firms that are now or want to be active global business participants. Many of our projects have been with Small and Medium-sized Enterprises (SMEs), which generally do not have the financial or technical resources to conduct research for exploring new markets. As the program has become better known in the community, the solicitation of appropriate projects should become even easier.

2. *University Outreach*—

   (a) The Global Business EDGE program helps forge ties with the business community. We have written letters of introduction about the program to a number of local firms, members of the advisory boards, mentors, and others. A number of responses, including some projects, resulted from this campaign. The program now has its own advisory board, composed of three faculty members and three executives with broad international experience. The executives include the founder and president of an engineering consulting firm with offices in several countries, the president of a bank that specializes in international lending and a recently retired executive who managed overseas operations of a Fortune 500 company. The EDGE program has conducted projects for two of the executive members' firms. Board members promote the program through their professional networks, advise on administrative processes, and monitor program quality.

(b) The Global Business EDGE program allows the University to showcase some of its top students. The presentations to client firms have all been professional and polished. Some students have secured internships, and several have been encouraged to seek employment at client firms.

(c) The Global Business EDGE program also allows the school to leverage its contacts in advisory boards, the mentor program, and others. Many business people are interested in working with the University and this program provides them with another outlet to connect with the University.

(d) The Global Business EDGE program is interesting to many international trade organizations, as well as to the AACSB, and presentations have been made to several of these organizations.

SUMMARY

Our experience with the Global Business EDGE program has been very positive. While students find the IBC course challenging and more work than expected, they also realize the benefits they are gaining—in education, experience, and contacts. From a faculty perspective, the course is also challenging, but most interesting. Applying theories and business concepts to real-world problems that have never before been solved is involving and exciting. While we keep lectures to a minimum, only providing basic information as needed, faculty members are available both in class and out of class for consultations. These consultations are often long and in-depth.

The most difficult part of the process has been the solicitation of *appropriate* projects. Some firms define their projects so broadly that they cannot be accomplished in an academic term, if at all. Others often are unable to articulate their underlying problems until some research has already been accomplished. Students, faculty, and firms need to be flexible in both defining the project and in its completion. Some projects cannot be adequately addressed in one or even two terms, but subsequent teams may continue to work on them.

While our university is set up in quarters and our graduate classes typically meet only once a week in the evening, other structures may work even better. A semester term would allow more in-depth research and reduce some of the time pressures of a quarter term, although the time pressure also adds to the realism of the project, reflecting time constraints often faced by business executives. More frequent contact periods would also be beneficial.

Students benefit by an introduction to the library facilities, especially the wealth of information on international issues and data. Our librarian has provided students a number of sources of information appropriate to their topics and a short presentation on research techniques. In addition, we have someone from the US Export Assistance Center talk to the class about the resources available from the US and state governments. Students indicate that both of these presentations are valuable in giving them a good start on their projects. Recently we added a class session early in the term featuring professional consultants who describe techniques for defining projects and communicating with clients.

The Global Business EDGE program has provided depth, understanding, and real-world experience for our students. In addition, students develop confidence in themselves and in their abilities to communicate, not only with peers, but also with business executives. Business clients have indicated they receive fresh (although sometimes naïve) perspectives of problems they have not resolved. This sometimes leads to resolutions that are innovative and enthusiastically adopted. Faculty find the consulting projects challenging and interesting. There has been some opportunity for conducting academic research, which is expected to increase. A real benefit to faculty, though, is the bringing of real-life examples to the classroom. The university has benefitted from the exposure to a large number of businesses. Since the program is self-sustaining through client fees, there is very little downside for the university. A Board of Advisors drawn largely from the local business community helps in promotion and in credibility of the program. All in all, the Global Business EDGE continues to be a successful program at Seattle University.

APPENDIX A: CLIENT PARTICIPATION AGREEMENT

I am interested in participating in the International Business Consulting program offered by The Albers School of Business and Economics at Seattle University.

I am submitting a project herewith for consideration. Should this project be approved and selected for inclusion in the program, I agree to the following terms and condition:

1. To pay a fee of XXXX upon notification that my project has been accepted and upon receipt of an invoice for this amount.

2. To schedule a briefing with the students involved in my project promptly upon notification of acceptance and to meet with the student team up to six times during the academic term (10 weeks) to

discuss the project in a free and open manner and address any questions/issues which may have arisen, to the best of my ability.

3. To provide and make freely available to the student team any and all data, information and other materials which I may have already gathered or have in my possession, or which I may acquire, pertaining to the project.

4. To establish a budget level for directly related project costs, such as online data searches, data or publication purchases, copies, communications, printing, etc., and to reimburse the students' out of pocket expenses incurred for these items during their work on this project (typical budget level = $200-300).

5. To familiarize the students with my company and its activities and capabilities by providing product, marketing, production, financial, and other relevant information insofar as this is required or useful for completion of the project and providing realistic recommendations.

I understand that submission of this agreement and project neither assures that it will be undertaken nor places the Albers School under any obligation to do so. However, if my project is not chosen for the academic quarter for which it is submitted, I understand that it will be given priority for the subsequent quarter.

I understand further that any project undertaken on my behalf will be performed under the confidentiality and ethical standards indicated in the Confidentiality Agreement, a copy of which will be executed and furnished to me prior to engagement by each member of the student team. I agree that these standards and terms are acceptable.

_____

Company Name

_____   _____

Authorized Signature   Date

APPENDIX B: CONFIDENTIALITY AGREEMENT

IN CONSIDERATION OF my being selected for and being permitted to participate in a consulting project while a student at Seattle University's Albers School of Business and Economics for the provision of advice and assistance to an established business entity and thus receive the educational experience that will result;

I AGREE AND CERTIFY as follows:

1. I will treat in strict and absolute confidence all data, information and other materials received by me, in writing, orally or by any other means, from any business firm or person requesting assistance during this project (my client company). The only exceptions to this commitment will be my faculty supervisor, project advisor (if any), and the other members of my project team.

2. I will not recommend to my client the purchase of goods or services from sources in which I or other members of my project team may be interested in any way whatsoever, nor will I accept fees, commissions, gratuities or other benefits if any such purchase should occur directly or indirectly as a result of any information I or other members of my project team may provide to my client.

3. I am not currently involved in any way in any business that competes with my client in any way whatsoever and I will not be involved in any such business during the course of this consulting project nor during the period immediately subsequent to its completion.

4. I will maintain, permanently, the confidentiality of any information or data concerning my client, and I will in no case use or discuss any such material outside the classroom environment, except with my client, or with the express permission of my client.

5. I will not accept any fees, commissions, gifts or gratuities from my client, nor serve on its advisory board, and I will avoid any other appearance of any conflict of interest.

6. Neither I nor any immediate family member has any interest in the ownership of my client's business.

GIVEN at Seattle, Washington, this ____ day of _____, 2005.

_____

Name of Student Consultant

_____

Signature

APPENDIX C: SAMPLE LETTER OF ENGAGEMENT

January 15, 2005

Mr. John Doe
Vice President of International Development
Firm
Address

Dear Mr. Doe:

This letter is to:

1. Verify that we intend to pursue the consulting project we discussed with you on our visit to your company on Tuesday, January 14, 2003
2. Explain our understanding of the tasks we are expected to accomplish
3. Advise you of the information and material we expect to need in order to accomplish our assignment, and
4. To submit our confidentiality agreements.

Based on our discussion with you, we intend to accomplish the following tasks while completing this consulting assignment:

1. Task 1
2. Task 2
3. Task 3

These tasks are more fully described in the enclosed Statement of Work. We expect to generate useful recommendations as a result of our efforts and hope that these will be of value and assistance to you in achieving your international business objectives. Whereas additional tasks may be undertaken (time allowing), our emphasis will be on completing the tasks listed. Our goal is to provide a final written report and oral briefing for you and your staff by the week of March 10, 2003.

In order to accomplish our work, we will need the following material and/or information:

1. Relevant contacts
2. Current customers
3. Current competitors
4. Etc.

Please inform us if you have any questions concerning our interpretation of the work to be accomplished. If you are in agreement with the objectives and tasks listed in our Statement of Work, please so indicate by signing and returning the copy of this letter enclosed for this purpose.

Thank you for giving us the opportunity to apply our knowledge and skills in an actual business environment. We are looking forward to this interesting and challenging assignment.

Sincerely,

(Consultant Name)	IBC Supervising Faculty Member
(Consultant Name)	Approved: Date _____
(Consultant Name)	John Doe

enclosed: Statement of Work
        Confidentiality Agreements (3)

APPENDIX D: SAMPLE STATEMENT OF WORK

OBJECTIVE

Develop best pricing strategies for small retail shippers within the primary international markets.

In light of the new segment information that **FIRM** has collected, we will be evaluating both general strategic choices (international freight with focus on small retail shippers) and tactical choices (low cost positioning, purchasing and pricing strategy, value added services).

This process will involve consideration of market factors, which may directly affect the company's services. For example:

- industry indicators such as: market structure, standards and trends, services offered
- marketing indicators such as: pricing strategy, advertising, promotions
- competitive indicators in terms of the identities, market share, strengths and weaknesses, organization, specific advantages, and other such considerations in terms of other firms in the market

Pricing Strategy Analysis

In so far as information is available, the following issues/questions will be addressed during the course of this project:

The Industry

    A. *Market Structure*

        1. Is this a concentrated industry?
        2. What is the market size?
        3. How competitive is the industry?
        4. What geographic regions comprise the market?

    B. *Trends*

        1. What was the output in terms of total shipments for the last five years?
        2. What was the consumption trend for the last five years?
        3. What have exports/imports been for the last five years?
        4. Do constraints exist?
        5. What are the projected sales for the service?
        6. What are short, long-term growth prospects?

Marketing Analysis

    A. *Media*

        1. What types of advertising are generally used?
        2. What are the advertising costs?
        3. What is the most effective channel of communication?
        4. Do general marketing support services exist (graphics, printing, etc)?

    B. *Distribution Channels*

        1. What kind of distribution channels, if any, is generally used (central warehouses, distribution centers)?
        2. What is the average delivery time?
        3. What is the average per unit/shipment costs?

    C. *Customers*

        1. Who is a typical customer?
        2. What aspect of the product influence buying decisions?
        3. Have widely recognized price points developed?
        4. What preconceptions exist about the product?
        5. Who are the potential new customers for the product?

D.   *Pricing Strategy*
1.   What is competitive pricing for this market segment?
2.   What types of discount are available?
3.   Does loss leader pricing exist? To what extent?

E.   *Value Added Services*
1.   What is the value added service offered by **FIRM**?
2.   What do customers expect when shipping international freight?
3.   What is important to them?

Competition

A.   *Basic Data*
1.   Who are the major competitors?
2.   Where are they located?
3.   What are their respective market shares?

B.   *Marketing Considerations*
1.   Describe the competitor's sales organization
2.   What is the relationship with agents/distributors?

C.   *Product*
1.   What are the individual products and services supplied by each competitor?
2.   How complete are their products and services?
3.   How do their products and services compare in quality, performance, and acceptance?
4.   How important is consolidation and customs clearance?

Conclusion/Considerations

A.   *Comparisons/Evaluations*

We will compare FIRM product and value added services as well as its pricing strategy to those of main competitors and evaluate the adequacy of the current product offer and price strategy.

Recommendations

A.   Strategy and time lines
Based on all the above findings we will give recommendations on current price strategy and optimization options.

B.   Action items
An action items list will be than provided as a tool for implement-

ing any recommendation/improvement/changes in the current price strategy

Bibliography of Sources

Will be provided as a source of reference.

Appendices

REFERENCES

Block, P. (1999). *Flawless consulting*. San Francisco: Jossey-Bass.

Bongiorno, L. (1993). A case study in change at Harvard. *Business Week*, (3346), 42.

Bonoma, T.V., & Kosnik, T. (1989). *Learning by the case method in marketing*. Boston: Harvard Business School.

Brooks, C.M., & Ammons, J.L. (2003). Free riding in group projects and the effects of timing, frequency, and specificity of criteria in peer assessments. *Journal of Education for Business, 78*(5), 268-272.

Calkins, M. (2001). Casuistry and the business case method. *Business Ethics Quarterly, 11*(2), 237-259.

Collett, N.J. (2000). Innovation or renovation: Effective project design for accounting and MBA students. *Accounting Education, 9*(1), 67-92.

Corey, E.R. (Ed.). (1990). *MBA field studies: A guide for students and faculty*. Boston: Harvard Business School Publishing Division.

Friedman, W.H. (1995). A new model for case analysis: Iterative triadic thinking. *Journal of Education for Business, 70*(4), 228-233.

Gundry, L.K., & Buchko, A.A. (1996). *Field casework*. Thousand Oaks, CA: Sage.

Harrison-Walker, L.J. (2000). A comprehensive pedagogy for dialectic team-based marketing management case analysis. *Journal of Education for Business 75*(4), 241-246.

Henson, S.W. et al. (2003). Web-based cases in strategic marketing. *Journal of Marketing Education, 25*(3), 250-350.

Irby, D.M. (2005) *Effective clinical teaching & learning: Clinical teaching and the clinical teacher*. Retrieved June 10, 2005, from http://www.med.cmu.ac.th/secret/meded/ct2.htm

Kolb, D., Lublin, S., Spoth, J., & Baker, R. (1987). Strategic management development: Using experiential learning theory to assess and develop managerial competencies. *Journal of Management Development, 5*, 13-24.

Mattern, W.D., Weinholtz, D., & Friedman, C.P. (1983). The attending physician as teacher. *New England Journal of Medicine, 308*, 1129-1132.

Siciliano, J. (1999). A template for managing teamwork in courses across the curriculum. *Journal of Education for Business, 75*, 261-264.

Tapp, L.G. (1997). Maintaining excellence in management consulting. *Ivey Business Journal, 62*(2), 15-17.

Ullian, J.A. (1986). Medical student and resident perceptions of clinical teaching. *Healthcare Chapter News (National Society for Performance and Instruction), 1*(4), 4-5.

CHAPTER 3

REAL REAL WORLD PROJECTS

Mats Lundeberg and Pär Mårtensson

At the Stockholm School of Economics (SSE), for the past 15 years, the authors have been teaching students on different levels of basic skills in handling change processes by letting them carry out *real changes* in *real business firms* meeting *real people*. This is what the authors call "*Real* Real World Projects," projects where students have the responsibility to achieve a sustainable change by carrying out a project, including implementation in reality. Working with real changes in real businesses, meeting real people, results in a qualitatively different learning experience with a number of positive effects. Students are engaged and eager to achieve good results. Students perceive the approach as valuable, useful, and fun. The knowledge needed for such teaching is more focused on handling learning processes than on specific subject area expertise. The key is to find people interested in learning issues, and especially interested in supporting learning processes.

THE SETTING

At the Stockholm School of Economics (SSE), for the past 15 years, we have been teaching students on different levels basic skills in handling change processes by letting them carry out real changes in real business firms meeting real people. This is what we call *Real* Real World Projects. The purpose of this chapter is to describe such projects, the theory behind the course design, and some of our experiences. Although we have worked with

Educating Managers through Real World Projects, 47–64
Copyright © 2005 by Information Age Publishing
All rights of reproduction in any form reserved.

students on a number of different levels (MSc, Executive MBA, and Executive In-Company Programs), in this chapter we will focus on our recent work with students on the Executive MBA (EMBA) level.

The setting for our work with Real World Projects (RWP) is a course in Change Management in the EMBA program. The course is called *Change and Integration* and is a required second year course in the 2-year EMBA-program. In this program, the EMBA students meet approximately every fifth week for sixteen sessions. The participants are normally between 30 and 40 years old. Class size is normally 40-50 participants. Most of them are from Scandinavia as a large part of this EMBA-program is taught in Swedish.

REAL REAL WORLD PROJECTS IN AN EXECUTIVE MBA PROGRAM

We have given the EMBA students the following single sentence assignment for the past six years:

> In project groups of two, achieve *a sustainable change* in a real business firm (or corresponding organization) by the end of this course.

The course takes somewhat less than a year.

This formulation raises a lot of questions, such as: Which business firm should we choose to work with? What type of change should we accomplish? What does "sustainable change" mean?

The process is of vital importance here. It starts right from the beginning when the project groups (i.e., pairs of students) try to find a business firm in which to carry out the project. As a constituent element of the project, to make it "real" the participants have to both find their business firm on their own and determine what type of change they want to accomplish. The business firm might be the organization of either of the two participants, or another business firm. The faculty supervisors can support in this process but the responsibility lies with the project groups themselves.

Before describing more details of the course, let us start with some of the background and experiences behind the course.

THE STORY BEHIND IT

Our way of working with *Real* Real World Projects has developed over the years. Here we want to give you some background regarding this development.

Background and Early Experiences

Both of the authors have a background in Information Management. In the early days of information systems and information technology, we were researchers and educators in what was called "information analysis." The purpose of information analysis was to analyze the information needs of users before building information systems. In developing theory and methods for this we used small, delimited, concrete examples to illustrate concepts and relationships. These were then used as introductory, hypothetical examples in our courses. We then let the participants apply information analysis theory and methods to actual areas from their own companies in developing examples to discuss. Thus, real examples were developed to use for educational purposes. From time to time, business firms with ongoing information analysis projects contacted us to obtain our help with them. We then organized internal company seminars where the business firms presented problems and we put forth theory and methods for solving them. The purpose was to obtain results in real world projects. Our early experiences can be used to discuss different levels of ambition when relating theory and practice.

Three Levels of Ambition When Relating Theory and Practice

The relationship between theory and practice in education is and has been a challenging relationship (e.g., Schön, 1987). Traditionally, as a researcher and educator one starts with specific hypothetical examples to illustrate theory (Figure 3.1). A possible next step is to apply theory to examples from the real world such as case studies and their associated

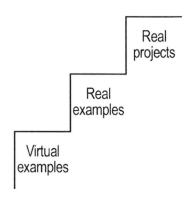

Figure 3.1.   Three levels of ambition when relating theory and practice.

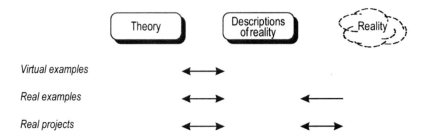

Figure 3.2.   Different types of interaction between reality, descriptions of reality, and theory.

traditional teaching methods (e.g., Christensen & Hansen, 1981). A higher level of ambition is to use theory to solve real world problems and to implement such solutions in real world projects.

Korzybski has formulated the well-known statement: "The map is not the territory" in the 1940s (Korzybski, 1941). With this formulation, he emphasizes the difference between reality and descriptions of reality. *The described real example is not the reality* just as the map is not the territory. The three levels of ambition when relating theory and practice can be analyzed with this distinction in mind. When applying theory to hypothetical situations, the relationship with reality per se is undefined (see Figure 3.2). When we work with real examples, the descriptions are developed from reality but there is no feedback to reality. When working with real projects, there is a combined interaction between reality and descriptions of it on the one hand, and between theory and such descriptions on the other hand. This allows for a richer relationship between theory and practice and in turn leads to richer learning experiences for the people who participate in real projects.

Ongoing Experiences

Based on our early positive experiences of real world projects we have continued working with alternative ways of using such projects in educational contexts. Early on we continued with courses in the area of information systems development where the participants worked with real world projects. We worked with these in two versions. In the initial version, the courses focused on producing information systems development plans. In a subsequent version, the courses were extended to include information systems implementation. It was our experience that the inclusion of implementation raised the level of quality of the results. Indeed, some projects only involving plans were rather loosely associated with reality. Participants' knowledge that they were also responsible for implementation rather than just planning strengthened the relationship between their work on this project and the real world.

A constraint in the information systems projects described above was the assumption that information systems were to be developed. The relationship to reality is strengthened if you are open as to what kind of measures you will take to solve the problems that you find. Our ongoing work has included a "Change and Integration" course whose focus was not restricted to information systems development and implementation but can range over areas such as marketing, production, and organization. We have here also worked with more planning-oriented courses (for instance business plan development) as well as courses including implementation. Our experience here is the same as before: including implementation increases the quality of the results.

Different Types of Real World Projects

We can now distinguish between different types of real world projects in educational settings. Our basic distinction is between *planning-oriented* and *implementation-oriented* projects. Our experience is that the latter provide very rewarding though quite challenging educational contexts. We also make a distinction between projects where the *subject area* is taken for granted and where it is not (Figure 3.3). In other words, according to our experiences, working with projects in categories C and D in Figure 3.3 increase the quality of the results, as compared to projects in categories A and B.

Four Levels of Ambition When Working with Real World Projects

When working with real world projects, we can distinguish between four levels of ambition, which we will describe below.

		Orientation of project	
		Planning-oriented	Implementation-oriented
Subject area	Open	B	D
	Taken for granted	A	C

Figure 3.3.   Four different types of real world projects.

The first step: The participants go out and *investigate* the real world and write a report about it. This is when you have moved to the third level in Figure 3.1 above and start using real world projects, as compared to hypothetical and real examples. The aim in the use of projects is thus to let the students to see and investigate a real situation. This first step can be useful for example in courses with inexperienced young students without work experience in order to give the students some first-hand knowledge of situations in business firms.

The second step: The participants go out, *investigate* and *analyze* the real world, and write a report about it. In this step they go further, not only investigating but also analyzing the situation. That is, it is not enough to just observe and report, rather sort of analysis must be undertaken. This second step can be useful in courses where the focus is on using certain theoretical models, in which the students go to a business firm, observe and then apply a particular model or theory, and then report about it.

The third step: The participants go out, *investigate, analyze* and *suggest actions* to initiate in the real world, and then write a report about it. In this step we have added actually recommending courses of actions. That is, moving one additional step beyond analysis to reaching a conclusion and contemplating suitable actions premised on the result of the analysis. This third step can be useful in courses where time restrictions do not allow for implementation but where you want them to go beyond analysis and link tighter to reality.

The fourth step: The participants go out, *investigate, analyze, suggest actions,* and *implement the suggested actions* in the real world. Then they write a report about it. In this fourth and final step, implementation is included. We have found this step very useful in a variety of contexts, especially in courses that can be scheduled to extend over a fairly long period.

From one perspective, we can call all four steps "real world projects." What we have found, however, is that there is a fundamental difference between the first three steps and the fourth step.

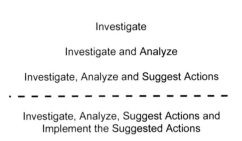

Figure 3.4. A fundamental shift.

When suggested actions are to be implemented there is a shift from being a real world project to become a *real* real world project. The plan developed by the participant meets reality—meets businesspeople in companies supporting or opposing the suggested actions etc. Here factual knowledge of a topic is not enough. Also requisite is process-oriented knowledge and to some extent tacit knowledge (cf. Polanyi, 1966).

The four levels of using real world projects can be seen in light of Bloom's taxonomy of educational objectives (Bloom, 1956). One aim of the different levels is to move beyond mere fact collection to rather situational analysis and critical evaluation and action recommendation. The fourth step is to bring this yet another step; i.e., to actually implement the actions suggested (which in some senses transcend Bloom).

REAL REAL WORLD PROJECTS: A FUNDAMENTAL DIFFERENCE

Working with real changes in real businesses, meeting real people, results in a qualitatively different learning experience. You may think that talking about *real* real world projects is only word play but we argue it is not. We argue that there is a fundamental difference, as discussed above. In our teaching we use *real* real world projects (RRWP) referring to projects where:

- students have the responsibility to achieve a sustainable change;
- students have the responsibility to carry out an implementation;
- students, depending on the type of course, either have the subject area specified or not.

Real real world projects have a number of positive effects:

- students are engaged and eager to achieve good results;
- students perceive the approach as valuable, useful, and fun;
- learning is taking place in several different dimensions:
  ◊ about the subject area (e.g., models for handling change processes);
  ◊ about the specific contents of their own and other projects;
  ◊ about group dynamics.

Successful *real* real world projects are based on several key factors:

- faculty members involved as supervisors need to have an interest and competence in supporting learning processes in a group environment;
- faculty members involved also need to trust the process, as there is no possibility to know the outcome of the process in advance;
- there needs to be sufficient time allocated for the process seminars involved in the course (described in more detail below).

WORKING WITH *REAL* REAL WORLD PROJECTS

What is working with *real* real world projects like? What are the experiences? We start by describing the course design used for the EMBA students.

The EMBA Course "Change and Integration"

The course "Change and Integration" takes place during the entire second year of the 2-year-long EMBA-program. Typically this course starts in February and ends in January the following year. There is a mix of lectures and process seminars as outlined below.

The project work in this course is presented as an invitation to the students to apply parts of the theories from the EMBA program as well as their own experiences in a *real* real world project. It is intended to give the participants training in description, analysis, and presentation of a change project. As mentioned before, the course builds on a single sentence directive:

> In project-groups of two, achieve *a sustainable change* in a real business firm (or corresponding organization) by the end of this course.

The students are asked to reflect on how they best want to make use of the opportunity that this invitation represents. Which business firm should they choose to work with? What type of change should they accomplish? Do they as students want to:

- Have fun?
- Do something which is important to them?
- Achieve interesting results?

- Learn more about specific topics?
- Specialize within a specific topic area?
- Try something new?
- Apply what they learned in the EMBA program?

One of the messages from the course is *Make use of the freedom of action that you have!* Reflecting on how to use the opportunity above can be seen as a first application of this message. Many students value such freedom of action. Some students like to have more firm guidelines.

Another basic message is *Alternate between different perspectives!* The assumption here is that the students should work with different perspectives and switch among these. This is implemented in the course in several different ways. As the students work in pairs, there will be two different perspectives in each project group. Each project group belongs to a tutoring group, with approximately five project groups in each tutoring group. This provides quite a number of new perspectives. There is also a difference between participating in a project and being outside of the project. Finally, in using theory, different theoretical perspectives are employed.

When it comes to the word "results," the course makes a basic distinction between the *deliverables* of a project and the *effects* of using these deliverables. A "sustainable change" is a change where certain sustainable effects (e.g., reduced lead times, increased market share, increased number of satisfied customers) have been achieved. Our experience is that many of the EMBA students are not trained to distinguish between deliverables and effects. Even worse, many students seem to be happy to achieve deliverables without worrying about what effects such deliverables will have. When reflecting on and choosing between different possible projects, early on we encourage the students to think of the projects in terms of deliverables and effects.

The so-called *process seminars* form a core part of the course. The process seminars are carried out in the tutoring groups with, as mentioned earlier, approximately five project groups in each tutoring group. Written drafts are sent in advance by email to all persons in the tutoring group to which you belong. Students are free to send whatever they prioritize themselves. However, they are encouraged to focus on issues that they think are important to help advancing the project. There is no point focusing on areas where the project is doing okay. All persons in the tutoring group read all the drafts sent to the group members. All projects are discussed during the process seminar. The time allotted is about one hour per project group. Every project group is a designated contributor to a specific other project group. This means that the persons in the project group are designated as responsible for helping this other project group advance their work as much as possible. The course schedule is as follows (sorted by the weeks over a year):

1.   Choice of projects.
2.   Presentation of theories and methods for handling change processes, discussion of the first short project description.
3.   Lecture and process seminars in tutoring groups.
4.   Lecture and process seminars in tutoring groups.
5.   Lecture and process seminars in tutoring groups.
6.   Presentation and discussion of change study report.
7.   Lecture and process seminars in tutoring groups.
8.   Lecture and process seminars in tutoring groups.
9.   Presentation and discussion of implementation report, presentation of all projects in a final conference day.

The project work is divided in two main parts, each resulting in a separate report:

1.   A change study where the current situation, intended future situation, needs for change and change alternatives are discussed and where an action plan is decided upon.
2.   An implementation study where the carrying out of the action plan is described and where the project is evaluated.

The reports are assessed in relation to a single page criteria list, which is distributed in advance. The reports can receive only Pass or Fail evaluations.

Underlying Assumptions and Theoretical Roots

The importance of the implementation phase illustrates one underlying assumption: *the understanding of a context increases when you try to change it*. A theoretical root to this assumption can be traced to Kurt Lewin's view that you cannot understand a human system without trying to change it (Lewin, 1947; Schein, 1991). In research this is often referred to as *the clinical research approach* where the researcher adopts a helping role in the organization and focuses on helping the client (Schein, 1987). The roots of the clinical research approach can also be traced to Roethlisberger (1977).

Another central underlying assumption is that by deliberately and consistently *alternating between different perspectives* an increased understanding of the change processes is achieved (Lundeberg, 1993). The use of different perspectives can also be described as a case of binocular vision where the differences between the different perspectives add new information and an extra dimension (Bateson, 1979).

A third assumption underlying the approach is that the learning processes need to be fostered; e.g., by using *"designated contributors"* instead of "opponents." The aim is to accomplish an open atmosphere with an air of trust, which in turn can support the learning process (cf. Schön, 1987). By focusing on contributions rather than opposition, the reflection processes taking place can also be supported (cf. Schön, 1983). The contributors can furthermore help the project-group to reframe the situation, and thereby increase their understanding of the situation at hand (cf. Watzlawick et al., 1974). This means that there are shifts between working with the concrete experiences in the projects and the reflective observations, etc. (cf. Kolb, 1984).

A fourth underlying assumption is that much of the *responsibility* in the process throughout the course is with the participants. Given the setting, with participants most often in managerial positions, the challenge is to help these persons to reflect and to learn (cf. Argyris & Schön, 1974; Schön, 1983).

Lessons Learned from a Student Perspective

In the following we will outline some typical lessons learned from a student perspective. We condensed a very long list of lessons, selecting a typical list of lessons learned expressed by the students over the years we have run the course:

Lesson # 1: The usefulness of changing between different perspectives.

Comment: This lesson can be seen from different points of view. First, the students appreciate the opportunity to switch between the academic perspective at the business school to the more practice-oriented perspective in their business firm. Second, the design of the course forces the students to switch between different perspectives when discussing the different projects, which helps the students not to be blind to defects in their own work.

Lesson # 2: The importance of taking people into consideration in projects.

Comment: This lesson may sound trivial. Given that the students often have more than 10 years of work experience, the importance of people is a well-known fact. Still it is interesting to note that there is something in this course that makes the students even more aware of this issue.

Lesson # 3: The importance of defining the actual problem.

Comment: During the process of the course the definition of the core problem often varies over time. That is, what at first appears to be the key problem may at a later stage turn out to be of less importance. When facing a real business firm with real people the students are forced to identify *the* key problem. Often this does not occur until the implementation phase is about to begin.

Lesson # 4: The difficulty to change course of direction.

Comment: This lesson is closely related to the previous one about defining the problem. Many times the students learn about the importance of being able to change their course of direction when they face difficulties in the implementation phase. If they had not faced this step, but stopped at simply suggesting actions, they would not have reached this lesson.

Lesson # 5: The usefulness of a really simple toolbox.

Comment: In the beginning of the course we introduce a number of simple conceptual models to be used during the course. At first, many students often complain that the models are overly simplistic and hardly useful. At later stages when they face the complexity in their business firms they often change their minds and comments may be heard about that one should not fool oneself by a simple model but instead make use of it in the complex real world.

Lesson # 6: The work takes longer than you think.

Comment: This is, obviously, nothing new to the students. But once again, the step to include the implementation makes the students much more aware of the importance to find suitable limits for their projects. If they were just to suggest actions and not implement them it is likely that the suggestions many times would be difficult to implement due to overly complex and comprehensive suggestions.

Lesson # 7: Time for reflection is important.

Comment: Using *real* real world projects may indicate that there is a focus only on action and implementation. We have found, however, that it is of vital importance to combine these action- and implementation-oriented projects with time for reflection, which therefore is included in the process of supporting the projects and the learning processes.

Lesson # 8: Many things you cannot learn by reading.

Comment: When using RRWP many aspects of the implementation part of the projects concern tacit knowledge, or at least types of knowledge that are not easily learned by reading a book or an article. When the challenges related to implementation are put in a real context, the understanding of the situation is much stronger than if simply read about.

Lesson # 9: "To analyze and suggest actions is simple compared to implementation."

Comment: This is a quote that we hear over and over again. The students first do not see the major difference between suggesting actions and being responsible for the implementation. When entering the implementation phase they usually become very aware of this difference.

Lesson # 10: It is demanding and fun to work with real problems.

Comment: Many students perceive this course as one of the toughest in the entire EMBA-program. They find it demanding because they have the responsibility to achieve something in a real world context and not only produce a report or presentation for the school. The course is more "for real." One should also add that most students find it fun.

Surprises

We have also asked the students to describe what they have perceived as most surprising during the course. The following is a brief summary of some of the surprises we have heard from them:

- *Simple models can be very useful!*
- *How much one can learn from other projects!*
- *Projects with different subjects still often face similar problems!*
- *How easily one gets stuck in one's own ideas!*
- *The small and specific issues in a project are often very important!*

Comment: When looking at this list, we ask ourselves how come the list looks like this. We do not find many new revolutionary items on the list. What we, on the other hand, and the students find is important is an important aspect of the subjects of the course. That is, the use of RRWP supports the learning of issues that may seem to be trivial but have proved to have dramatic effects in the realization of projects in reality.

Lessons Learned from a Faculty Perspective

Every year about 4-6 faculty members have been involved as supervisors. Two of us have been involved every year and the other members have varied. We have aimed at including faculty members from different subject areas in order to cover a broad area taken together. Now we will outline some lessons learned from a faculty perspective:

Lesson # 1: This is about supporting learning processes rather than teaching subjects.

Comment: The first lesson learned is that every faculty member involved has realized that their role is to support a process and be a facilitator, rather than being an expert teaching a subject. It is also interesting to note there is a learning process for the faculty members involved too (cf. Christensen, 1991).

Lesson # 2: The importance of trusting the process.

Comment: When teaching in this context one key is to trust the process. As a faculty member one cannot know in advance what will happen in the projects. It is not possible to have a grand plan for the course and for the different sessions. Instead one has to constantly adjust to the process. Most faculty members who have been involved have found this both fun and rewarding, although in some cases unusual (and maybe a bit scary).

Lesson # 3: It is about helping, but not being in the limelight.

Comment: The students play the major roles when using RRWP. The faculty members in facilitating roles play minor roles, although very important roles. This means that faculty members used to being in the limelight may at first find this an unfamiliar role.

Lesson # 4: It is amazing what students can achieve once they have the responsibility.

Comment: Often the students achieve far better results than we from a faculty perspective thought would be possible within given timeframes etc. When we have discussed this between faculty members we have found that one keyword is responsibility. Once the students perceive that they have the full responsibility they can sometimes achieve surprisingly good results both from a practical and a learning perspective.

Lesson # 5: Once you have started to use RRWP you are stuck there!

Comment: One lesson is that it is difficult to "step back" and use other forms of projects once you have started to use RRWP. Other types of projects tend to feel superficial and not liked to reality for real. This may be problematic as it is not always possible to work with RRWP, given the conditions needed for example regarding time and resources to invest in the course.

Preconditions and Demands Concerning Faculty

Given the discussion above about projects that are not subject specific, the question is what expertise the faculty members involved need to have? Do we need universal geniuses for running this type of course? No, instead we argue that the knowledge needed is more focused on handling learning processes than on the subject specific area(s). In our empirical use of the approach described above we have involved faculty members from a number of different subject areas but the key has been to find people interested in learning issues, and especially interested in supporting learning processes. Another key has been to find people that truly can trust the process and are not too worried about not knowing in advance what the process is going to look like.

An interesting effect that we have noticed concerning faculty is that this course has been one, out of very few, courses where faculty members from different subject areas have worked together. Here a common theme has been to facilitate the learning processes rather than conveying subject-oriented messages. This in itself is not linked to the use of RRWP, but has, at least in our case, been possible to carry through in the context of RRWP.

Some Critical Views

For natural reasons, we have in this chapter focused on the potential, the advantages, and some mainly positive experiences from working with *real* real world projects. This way of working is not without its drawbacks and negative experiences. Let us briefly mention some critical views:

Lesson # 1: Several EMBA students do not like this way of working

Comment: Most EMBA students have a lot of working experience when they come to the EMBA program. Many have extensive experience of project work in general. What more can they learn from working with *real* real world projects? Paradoxically we have found a high correlation between our estimation of student learning needs in this area and the degree to which the students dislike this way of working.

Lesson # 2: Teaching real real world projects is not for all educators

Comment: Some educators are more focused on specific subject areas and topics rather than on managing learning processes. Of course, such persons should select other ways of teaching. However, this is not a major problem in the sense that we need different kinds of educators for different parts of the EMBA program.

Lesson # 3: Using real real world projects in a program is highly resource consuming

Comment: The battles for resources within a business school are well known. Using tutoring groups with 10 students is five times as expensive as giving lectures in a class of 50 students. Administrators who only looks at the costs find it hard to justify such proportions. We argue that you need to look at an EMBA program as a whole, where some parts are given in large classes and some parts in tutoring groups. Often, what sticks in the students' minds the longest is the work with their own projects where they apply what they have learned to real problems.

CONCLUDING REMARKS

In this chapter we have tried to inspire you to start thinking about working with *real* real world projects. We think the potential and the advantages of such approaches by far outweigh the effort and disadvantages. Working with *real* real world projects is exciting but also very challenging.

By giving the students a single sentence assignment (achieve *a sustainable change* in a real business firm) the students become responsible for a number of choices and are free to act, thereby enhancing their own learning experiences. Working with real changes, in real business firms, meeting real people, results in a different learning experience--a difference that is fundamental. Once you have started to use *real* real world projects you are stuck there! It is difficult to "step back" and use other forms of projects. Other types of projects tend to feel superficial in comparison.

At the core of this way of working is the design of the process seminars in the course that forces students to switch between different perspectives when discussing different projects, which enables them to avoid being blindsided to defects in their own work. The students are surprised how projects with different subjects still often face similar problems, how easily they get caught up in their own ideas, and how much they can learn from other projects.

We do not need universal geniuses to run this type of course. The knowledge needed is more focused on handling learning processes than on specific subject area expertise. The key is to find people interested in learning issues, and especially interested in supporting learning processes. Another key is to find people that truly can trust the process and are not too worried about not knowing in advance what the process is going to look like.

Why not give it a try at the institution where you are?

REFERENCES

Argyris, C., & Schön, D.A. (1974). *Theory in practice: Increasing professional effectiveness*. San Francisco: Jossey-Bass.

Bateson, G. (1979). *Mind and nature: A necessary unit*. New York: Bantam.

Bloom, B.S. (Ed.). (1956). *Taxonomy of educational objectives: The classification of educational goals: Handbook I, Cognitive domain*. New York: David McKay.

Christensen, C.R. (1991). Every student teaches and every teacher learns: The reciprocal gift of discussion teaching. In C.R. Christensen, D.A. Garvin, & A. Sweet (Eds.), *Education of judgment: The artistry of discussion leadership* (pp. 99-119). Boston: Harvard Business School Press.

Christensen, C.R., & Hansen, A.J. (1981). *Teaching and the case method: Text, cases, and reading*. Boston: Harvard Business School.

Kolb, D.A. (1984). *Experiential learning: Experience as the source of learning and development*. Englewood Cliffs, NJ: Prentice-Hall.

Korzybski, A. (1941). *Science and sanity*. New York: Science Press.

Lewin, K. (1947). Frontiers in group dynamics. In K. Lewin, *Resolving social conflicts & field theory in social science* (1997, pp. 301-336). Washington, DC: American Psychological Association.

Lundeberg, M. (1993). *Handling change processes: A systems approach*. Lund: Studentlitteratur.

Polanyi, M. (1966). *The tacit dimension*. Gloucester, MA: Peter Smith. [reprinted 1983]

Roethlisberger, F.J. (1977). *The elusive phenomena: An autobiographical account of my work in the field of organizational behavior at the Harvard Business School*. Cambridge, MA: Harvard University Press.

Schein, E.H. (1987). *The clinical perspective in fieldwork* (Qualitative Research Methods Series, 5). Newbury Park, CA: Sage.

Schein, E.H. (1991). Legitimating clinical research in the study of organizational culture. *MIT Working Paper Series*, No. 3288-91-BPS (May). Cambridge, MA: Sloan School of Management, Massachusetts Institute of Technology.

Schön, D.A. (1983). *The reflective practitioner: How professionals think in action*. New York: Basic Books, HarperCollins.

Schön, D.A. (1987). *Educating the reflective practitioner*. San Francisco: Jossey-Bass.

Watzlawick, P., Weakland, J.H., & Fisch, R. (1974). *Change: Principles of problem formation and problem resolution*. New York: Norton.

CHAPTER 4

MANAGING DIVERGENT AND CONVERGENT FOCUS OF LEARNING IN STUDENT FIELD PROJECTS

Susan M. Adams

The popularity of field-based student projects in business schools is growing. Even though the use of field projects is increasing, there are few guidelines for faculty supervising these experiences. This chapter advocates a stakeholder management approach to address the learning needs of the 3 main stakeholders for student projects: the students, project sponsor, faculty and the school. Using the example of the field-based student consulting project as typically conducted at Bentley College, an analysis of stakeholder interests guides practical suggestions for faculty to prepare, conduct and evaluate the experience and more importantly, harvest learning from the experience. Additional suggestions for administering other types of student projects are also discussed.

INTRODUCTION

A popular pedagogy for providing an opportunity to better prepare management students is the student project in work organizations (Tooley,

Educating Managers through Real World Projects, 65–90
Copyright © 2005 by Information Age Publishing
All rights of reproduction in any form reserved.

1997). These projects provide a way for students to apply concepts and to develop skills in unsanitized field situations. Student field projects are increasingly used in MBA programs (Baker & Schomburg, 2000; Adams & Zanzi, 2004). Baker and Schomburg found that approximately 40% of the MBA programs use a student field project in some form within the MBA program. Looking more specifically at management consulting courses, Adams and Zanzi, (2001, 2004) reviewed the use of field projects in management consulting courses and found a significant increase in the number of top tier schools incorporating field consulting from 18.3% to 30.9% during the 2001-2003 time period. Widening the view to all AACSB accredited MBA programs, the use of field consulting projects in management consulting courses was 15.3% in 2003 (a significant increase over 2002), indicating that the use of consulting field projects is beginning to attract a wider audience than just the elite schools.

Even though the popularity of student field project work is growing, there is little guidance for administering these experiences (Farinelli & Mann, 1994). How should instructors, attempting to start using student field projects, design the experience? How can instructors make their existing courses involving student field projects more effective? Using the example of a student consulting project, a framework is provided for effectively facilitating an effective student consulting experience to meet the needs of the various parties involved. This stakeholder management approach is based on a literature review, a stakeholder analysis of learning needs, and more than ten years of practice in conducting student consulting projects in a graduate school of business. The approach focuses on meeting the learning needs of all involved parties rather than benefitting a specific stakeholder. The ultimate goal is minimizing disappointments that can lead to derailment of projects and lost learning opportunities.

STAKEHOLDER ANALYSIS FOR STUDENT CONSULTING PROJECTS

Field projects can range from interviewing a manager to reporting on the use of particular course concepts in a field setting to full-blown consulting projects for client organizations. Such projects vary across a number of dimensions. See Figure 4.1 for a typology of the range of student field projects and associated characteristics.

The *field study* bears some similarity to a *consulting project* but the goals for each of the courses are generally different. A student *field study* project is usually undertaken to focus on specific content material such as operations, marketing, or strategy. It can entail activities such as an interview with a manager about organizational life or an observational study to cal-

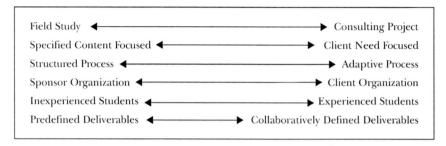

Figure 4.1.   Typology of student field projects in management education.

culate throughput time in a manufacturing organization. The learning objectives and student assignment deliverables are content centered focusing on what they saw and learned rather than the process of seeing and interpreting. Some field studies may have the added objective of behavioral competency building (e.g., producing a financial report) but the focus is still primarily on understanding how the sponsor organization handles a specific aspect of business (Young, 1996). The field study falls in the application stage of Bloom's hierarchy of learning. The project sponsor is not expecting much in return for the limited amount of time and effort put into accommodating students involved in field studies. At most, sponsors learn what is interesting to students.

At the other end of the continuum, a student *consulting project* focuses more on having the students learn the consulting process or organizational problem solving at a much higher level. An organization sponsoring the project is called a client with the expectation that the consulting team will provide a desired product or service. Since clients may even pay for services, students are expected to bring some expertise to the project to guide the client toward its desired goals. Therefore, most consulting project students are MBA students with some work experience (Adams & Zanzi, 2001). The students must work with the client to identify problems and potential solutions. Consulting project students may focus on specific content areas to assist the client but the course intent from the student perspective may also be for students to learn about the consulting and investigational processes to solve organizational problems. Students apply conceptual understanding of a process to build consulting competencies but, moreover, they learn ways to solve organizationally-specific problems. When used properly, the consulting model involves higher order learning that entails discovery, critical judgments, application, synthesis, and knowledge creation.

In a student consulting project the main players are the students, the academic institution, the client organization sponsoring the project, and the faculty supervisor (instructor). Typically, most schools use a student project model where a faculty supervisor is in charge of selecting client organizations, the initial project scope, assembling and supervising student teams, and evaluating final results. A popular variation of the procedure has students locate a client, often with assistance from the school. A consulting project usually involves tackling issues of strategic importance defined by the client organization. For example, a team might identify internal and external forces hindering expansion opportunities for the client organization. The client expects a final product that offers direction at a minimum and more often, implementable or implemented solutions. A team of 3-5 students works on-site gathering information and analyzing data to draw conclusions that are presented formally to client representatives, faculty, and sometimes, the whole class at the end of the course. Consulting projects require an academic understanding of the basic consulting process and investigational skills that can be provide throughout the project or as a prerequisite. Therefore, projects are usually part of a course in consulting or a sequel to prerequisite content-rich courses. Courses with consulting projects expect students to integrate ideas from multiple business functions and into different industries. Additionally, students must identify and obtain essential information that is not readily available. Since many MBA programs use the case method teaching approach with nicely packaged and organized information, the consulting project provides an opportunity to expand problem-solving skills. Projects allow for practice in a more realistic environment where a variety of methods (e.g., interviews and surveys) and sources (e.g., the client, other stakeholders, and archival data) must be used to identify and understand problems in the issue presented by the client.

Stakeholder Expectations

Understanding stakeholder expected benefits can suggest the type of learning that needs to take place. Since the nature of student field projects are varied, I am concentrating on the most complex and demanding type of projects, consulting projects, to identify stakeholder learning needs and then later discussing adaptations from this most complicated case. There are numerous reasons graduate business schools include student consulting projects in their graduate programs and more specifically, in management consulting courses. Likewise, there are a number of reasons client organizations engage students. These points are listed in Appendix A and discussed next as background for identifying stakeholder learning needs.

Expected Student Benefits

From a student's academic perspective, consulting projects provide an avenue for students to bridge their understanding of theory to practice. In the classroom, concepts are often presented as isolated issues. Consulting projects provide a forum for students to view concepts as they are integrated in real world complex situations. For instance, they are often thrown into organizational politics and must understand the complexity and limits of the client-consultant relationship. Many students may gain a deeper understanding of concepts from an experiential learning approach since classroom approaches rarely cater to all learning styles (Boyatzis & Kolb, 1991). Consulting projects provide opportunities for hands-on learning where students can view actions and results of those actions as they unfold. Actual teamwork with accountability to a client gives students the opportunity to hone their understanding of team dynamics under pressure.

There are also practical career development benefits of consulting projects that students find attractive. Networking is a critical factor for job search success. Consulting projects provide connections to individuals who may be in a position to aid in job searches. More directly, the client organization may actually be hiring graduates and/or interns giving student consultants an edge since they will be familiar with the organization (Coco, 2000). In our experience, exposure to the client goes beyond those actually involved in the project because the consulting class usually debriefs all team projects, providing connections to other organizations. Students considering career changes find consulting projects especially helpful to resume building and guidance for future career decision-making (Ornstein & Isabella, 1993). Consulting projects provide a new line on one's resume that expresses new accomplishments. Career changers find the opportunity to experience a different industry and a new company, or even a new country or culture especially helpful in determining the type of job to pursue upon graduation. For example, they may determine that consulting is not a career path they want to take but they would enjoy a management position in their client's industry.

Student learning goals to achieve these benefits include the development of knowledge and skills for effective consulting, gaining a more in-depth knowledge of organizational processes and practices, and a deeper understanding about personal career preferences.

Expected Client Benefits

Consulting clients may engage student teams as a community service, enhancing their social responsibility images. Yet, practical business reasons are cited more often as justification for the time and company access associated with engaging a student consulting team. Many of the reasons are the same ones for hiring a professional consulting firm: unbiased view; systematic investigation of anticipated or ongoing problems that cannot be attended to due to everyday duties; and expertise in content, techniques or tools not available inside the organization (cf. Block, 2000; Sekaran, 2002). The most cited reason in my experience is the unbiased or "fresh" views student teams can bring. Additionally, clients can preview potential hires and interns (Watson, 1995). All this is possible for a relatively low cost in most circumstances (Baker & Schomburg, 2000).

From examining what clients expect, learning goals need to include how to work effectively with student teams, acknowledgment of constraining practices, recognition of their own involvement in current problems and future solutions, and how to continue interaction with the institution.

Expected Faculty and School Benefits

Schools offering student teams enjoy benefits as well. They are seen as more connected to the corporate world and thus as providing more relevant programs for their current and potential students. Faculty members involved with consulting courses gain direct access to organizations to better understand their workings to enhance teaching and research. Organizational access may also be extended to faculty colleagues once the initial relationships are established. Field connections are also attractive to incoming faculty thereby facilitating the recruiting process. On a more practical note, career services and alumni relation offices receive an introduction to sites for jobs and alumni for donations. Institutions can offer their alumni consulting services that more closely connect them to the schools so they are more likely to think about the school when posting jobs or making donations.

Schools must continuously learn what is important to managers to offer what they need. In addition to learning more about current organizational concerns and practices, instructors need to learn how to continuously improve their management of student and client learning.

Approaches to administering student projects can provide less than optimal benefits when focusing on the separate players involved. A student-focused approach that seeks to maximize student benefits may do so to the detriment of their clients and the long-term benefits of their institutions. A typical example is when a consulting team has a specific type of project to perform regardless of the client's needs. Companies who want to maintain a friendly relationship with a school for recruiting needs or social responsibility reasons may agree to host teams whether or not they have compelling business needs for a consulting team. Students end up working on a project that has no real impact for the host organization. Client organizations spend a good amount of time and energy being nice with little or no return on investment. The school does not impress any-one and may, in fact, lose credibility as real-world connected.

A client-focused approach that tries to maximize client needs may be closely aligned to optimizing the interests of schools. A school that pro-vides teams for consulting projects in the community will likely have appreciative clients that are aware of the school thus creating bonds that can be tapped for payback. However, students lose if consulting teams provide whatever services the client needs without regard to students' learning goals or to students' career aspirations.

A STAKEHOLDER MANAGEMENT APPROACH EXAMPLE

A stakeholder management approach for conducting field projects maxi-mizes the benefits for all parties by paying attention to the needs of the various stakeholders and by avoiding potential problems at critical steps. I integrate a number of streams of research to provide helpful information about how to manage learning for the stakeholders involved in student field projects.

The most apparent connection to previous studies is the work regard-ing learning from student apprenticeships, internships, and field projects. These studies primarily focus on student learning with little regard to cli-ent or faculty learning but offer numerous lessons for maximizing student learning. Students engaging in apprenticeships and internships are gen-erally self-managed and paced so that relevant knowledge and skills are acquired as needed, ideally, for increasing complex tasks. Critics say that there is little evidence that learning is guaranteed with this approach to learning (Hamilton & Hamilton, 1997) since instructors are not on-site to harvest lessons (Raelin, 2000). Students may achieve daily objectives but not learn anything to transfer to real jobs in other places. Despite the crit-icism of transferability, most authors analyzing the student field projects as pedagogical tool are generally pleased with the approach in providing students insights into applying classroom knowledge to the more complex real world (e.g., Bloomfield & Paschke, 1997). These studies provide prac-tical advice to manage student learning by dealing with the challenges of team dynamics and project management (e.g., Congram & LaFarge, 1995) and with acknowledgment and extension of lessons learned from the student project experience (e.g., Bloomfield & Paschke, 1997).

Work-based learning research (e.g., Raelin, 2000, 1997) provides a broader view of how individuals can learn from work activities, in general. Raelin (2001) advocates public and critical reflection both in the moment and after activity to discover what is being learned and to share it for col-lective learning. He concedes that the organization must be prone to appreciating learning so that the environment will be conducive to honest dialogue (Raelin, 2001) since managers often see the facilitation of learning distinct from their role of manager (Ellinger & Bostrom, 2002).

Another current stream of research has focused on project-based learning (e.g., Arthur, DeFillipi, & Jones, 2001; Ayas & Zeniuk, 2001; Gunasekara, 2003; Keegan & Turner, 2001). These studies are primarily concerned with promoting organizational learning from the activities of project teams formed to address specific organizational problems. Issues such as team dynamics, individual learning capabilities, and organizational culture receive attention in these studies as input variables. These authors tend to focus on practices for creating new knowledge and transferring it to the organization. Garrick and colleagues (Garrick & Clegg 2001; Rhodes & Garrick, 2003) question the project-based learning as a viable learning approach for business students because students tend to focus too much on the project's product rather than learning. They argue for integrating critical distance for dialogue and critique with project-based learning as a remedy.

Tightly embedded in the project-based and work-based learning research is the recent flurry of work regarding knowledge management and learning. Knowledge management studies focus on the creation and sharing of knowledge at the individual and team level drawing on cognitive theory, social construction, psychodynamics, and complexity theory (e.g., Beech, MacIntosh, McLean, Shepherd, & Stokes, 2002; Nahapiet & Ghoshal, 1998; Nonaka & Takeuchi, 1995; Van der Sluis & Poell, 2002). They delve into learning processes, such as the use of boundary objects (Carlisle, 2002), to transform implicit knowledge to explicit knowledge.

Finally, academic studies about consulting and the plethora of consulting books provide insights from practical experience. For example, Block (2000) describes a collaborative process to lead clients toward learning how to solve their problems and Clegg et al. (2004) caution that consulting is disruptive rather than orderly if the consultant is willing to take the risk of challenging current organizational practices in exploring new options.

In summary, these research streams provide guidance in dealing with separate parties and aspects of facilitating student field projects. In the next section an example details how integrating earlier research findings and lessons from experience into a stakeholder management approach has been used for graduate consulting projects in a management consulting course at Bentley College. The three main categories project steps of before, during, and after the project is described, highlighting actions and considerations along the way to promote desired learning for all stakeholders.

Before the Project Begins

Initially, learning needs for students, the client, and the instructor are different. The instructor needs to learn what the client needs and about the students as learners. The client needs to learn about what to expect from a student team and how to interact with the team. Students need to learn about course and client expectations and how to work together. Before the project begins, the instructor has a number of tasks to complete to attend to the learning needs of each stakeholder. The job is preparing the stakeholders for what is to come.

Preparation

Consulting projects entail key preparation issues. Students need a realistic preview of the client's and the school's expectations regarding the time involved and the quality of work expected. Individual student advising by a program director or faculty advisor familiar with the project course is recommended. A superficial examination of a student consulting course often reveals high grades awarded for the course. This leads students to believe it is an easy course. Some mechanism needs to be in place to spread the word that the high grades are a function of the intense workload and quality checks by faculty, teammates, and the client to ensure topnotch work. I have used an application process with mixed results. What seems to work best is to lay out the course requirements with prospective students before the course begins and on the first day of class in a brutally honest fashion, mentioning that students that find they are not up to the task should withdraw. This point focuses on making sure students are prepared to benefit but also protects the client, school, and faculty.

Students need to be academically prepared to handle the project work. The use of prerequisites is advised. Students often think consulting is equivalent to sharing opinions. In advising sessions, they need to be told about client demands for evidence to back recommendations and that being able to supply valid and convincing evidence usually comes from content-rich coursework prior to undertaking a field consulting project. This point is another readiness issue for students to enhance student learning and ultimately, to benefit consulting firms that may hire the students. It also protects the quality of the product clients receive and the integrity and credibility of faculty and the school.

Students need to be socially prepared. This is especially important when projects involve students from a different national culture than the client. Business protocols around the world are different. Seemingly little things, such as how to communicate with a high level manager, is not trivial. For instance, an e-mail saying, "Hey Joe," to a Fortune 100 senior manager that the student has not met does not reflect well on the school. Business protocol lessons about communication, dress, and business routines are suggested. It is also imperative to stress the ethics of the situation in excruciating detail. I might have missed the case of a student manufacturing data to back a recommendation if a teammate had not alerted me to the situation. Now I provide specific examples of unethical behavior in consulting early in the experience and ask questions throughout to make sure no one is unintentionally headed for trouble.

Faculty need to be trained to oversee client management and student progress. Things happen. Faculty will need to deal with problems involving student team difficulties, client-student interface issues, difficult clients, and project management issues. Some advanced notice about how to handle and ward off typical problems helps. At a minimum, faculty need to know resources for seeking help and their parameters of control. For example, can a faculty team supervisor fire a team member, or at what stage can a client be dropped to pick up a more appropriate project? An entire paper could easily be dedicated to this topic alone so guidance from an experienced instructor can be a tremendous help. There are so many ways instructors can influence the success of a project from supplying additional resources to intervening at critical points to halting the project. I have found that dropping a client in mainstream is a great learning experience for all involved if done delicately in a way that quickly transitions students to another project and keeps the client happy. On one occasion I found another colleague to complete a project for a nominal fee since the project had become much more complicated than anticipated when students unearthed major company problems.

The school needs to commit resources to proper supervision of students. If a team approach is used, extra faculty may be needed to monitor team dynamics or serve as content experts. Students are learning and will make mistakes. It serves everyone to turn those mistakes and near misses into teachable moments. For example, a broadcast e-mail to the whole class about how to handle a difficult client that a team recently handled well is possible if there are enough faculty to capture and distribute the lesson. There is a misconception among some administrations that field project courses involve less faculty time. Since the student consulting project is primarily focused on the consulting process, faculty involvement is intense and time consuming to correct actions in progress. If additional faculty resources are out of the question, I suggest negotiating a reduced course load or at a minimum, a lower number of students admitted to the course or the use of new technologies such as groupware. If the faculty is unable to provide in-the-moment lessons for timely feedback, student learning is limited and clients may not receive an optimal result.

Client Identification

Identifying an appropriate client and project can be time-consuming but when done well, prevents problems later on. Be sure the client is accessible and will provide necessary resources to complete the project properly. I use a test to size up the situation and to measure the client's willingness to share necessary information and provide access to key people in the organization by asking to speak to specific people or to see certain documents associated with the project. Do not be reluctant to meet with the client on several occasions before the project begins. Also, ask to meet other key individuals in the organization so you can provide students a realistic preview of individuals they will be working with. Discuss project expectations, compensation issues, and necessary confidentiality constraints.

Be sure the client understands what the commitment entails and mention potential project issues that will not be possible to address. For example, it is not unusual to have clients ask for a team to go undercover to get competitor information. Being very clear up-front will avoid the potential for such expansion of a project as it progresses. The faculty member can provide an information document that outlines client involvement, a typical project timeline, and typical student deliverables. Meetings to size up a client also help the client assess the situation to determine if the faculty can deliver what is desired. This is where client learning begins. A hesitant client will likely have problems later so provide the time and information needed to establish a ready client. This step prepares the potential client to accept an offer to sponsor a project and prevents problems later that could derail the project.

Make sure there are back-up clients in case a project needs to be abandoned. As a project unfolds, information could reveal a situation that a student team is not prepared to handle or the client determines that the sponsoring organization is no longer interested in pursuing the project. Keep a list of former clients or sure bets that can be called on at a moment's notice in case a project falls apart. At a minimum, have a plan ready for redistributing students to other teams if a project does not go well. I have found that abandoning a project is better than sticking with what will be a bad experience for students or the client. While lessons can be drawn from failures, I have found that even the most positive experiences contain enough difficulties for painful lessons. Students tend to disengage from learning about consulting and concentrate on merely surviving the course when a project turns into a negative experience. Clients quickly trained not to use student consulting teams when they have a negative experience.

Client Contracting

Contracting with the client to engage a student team involves attention to key issues to maximize benefits. Make sure there are back-up client contacts in the client organization in case the primary contact leaves or is otherwise unavailable. I have had client contacts that were promoted, transferred, left the organization, were hospitalized, or took a leave of absence for a family tragedy. To keep a project from falling apart I suggest at least two client contacts for each project although one can and should serve as the lead contact.

At the contracting step, the client needs a customized but general preview regarding boundaries of the project noting probable exclusions, the general nature of promised deliverables, the expected pace of the project, compensation issues, confidentiality terms, and the amount and nature of expected client interaction with students. Only about 25% of the schools conducting field study projects ask for compensation with an average of about $4,500 for a fee (Baker & Schomburg, 2000). It is my opinion that clients will provide a more realistic consulting experience for students when a project entails a fee. However, students tend to focus intensely on deliverables to the exclusion of skill development and other course lessons. For example, a team may elect the best speaker to be the only person to present information to the client instead of allowing everyone the practice. Another consideration is that in some markets charging a fee is not plausible because local competitor schools do not charge fees. Written boundaries of confidentiality are also important. Knowing a client's desire for extreme confidentiality led me to reassign a student from a project when that student's employer bought a company that competed with the client's company. In that case I also had to make sure that class presentations about the project were thoroughly screened by the client. Client screening of information for classroom use was included in the work scope agreement (Step 8) in that case. Had I not spent time at this early stage understanding client needs, we may have missed ways to console the client later on. Dealing with client anxieties this early in the project provides the level of comfort needed later when the client will likely be asked to view their organization and issues associated with the project from a different perspective.

Team Assembly

Team composition has long been seen as an influential factor in team performance and satisfaction. How the student consulting team is formed and the mix of team members really matters (Parker, 1990; Watson, Kumar, & Michaelsen, 1993). Beyond consideration of individual expertise, assembling the student teams requires attention to personalities, work styles, communication abilities, and personal life constraints such as business travel for employed students and childcare issues. Career aspirations and personal interest in available projects should also be assessed to maximize student benefits. This can be done with a series of personal assessments, class discussions, individual student interviews, class exercises, and forms where students prioritize their interests in available projects. I recommend making sure each team is capable of filling the vital roles of (a) client liaison with a good oral and written communicator, (b) team coordinator with a good administrator who can run team meetings and manage the project flow, and (c) content expert with an individual who has more extensive experience and knowledge about the project's topic. If the team is large enough, other helpful roles are faculty liaison who continuously updates the instructor, knowledge manager who compiles and categorizes all collected data, a writer who edits all client communications and presentations, and a separate project manager who can create and maintain the project plan.

Team Building

Once a group is assigned to a team, the individuals need to learn to work together as a team. High performing teams must gel (Gammage, Carron, & Estabrooks, 2001; Seashore, 1954). I use two or three team-building exercises to help teams learn how to work together. Clients can be confused by mixed messages if a team does not act as a single unit from the beginning.

High performing teams focus on a common cause. I suggest the use of a team contract that clearly identifies performance standards for work quantity and quality as well as process issues such as promptness of answering e-mails and meeting attendance and tardiness. Each team can develop this contract as a team building exercise. It should state the issues to be evaluated for each individual and as a team plus how to measure performance for each issue. This promotes a common focus and language for performance standards. This makes what was previously implicit for individuals, explicit for the team.

During the Project

Once the project is underway, all the stakeholders concentrate their learning on how to address the project's objectives. The instructor tries to keep students working together and with the client to understand underlying issues affecting the problem that stimulated the project and options for helping the client deal with the problem. The suggestions outlined next are intended to focus learning on the client's problem and eliminate distractions that could derail such learning.

Preliminary Investigation

Before students meet the client, they have some homework to do. Students should understand the client's current organization and its history: its strategic goals, its competitive environment, the industry challenges, the organization's immediate challenges, and the culture of the organization.

Next, students should conduct secondary research focused on the problem to be addressed through their project work. A thorough literature search of the issues involved will help students develop fruitful questions for the initial meeting with the client and give them a jumpstart on creating the pieces of the work scope agreement. Since the students will become the client's teacher as they offer options for the client to deal with the problem, they need to know as much as possible about their student, the client and the client organization.

Initial Client-Student Meeting

The initial introduction meeting is key to setting the tone, establishing a productive relationship between the student team and client (Ulvila, 2000), and providing data to more clearly define the work scope and potential pitfalls. Students should come prepared to ask specific questions about the client's concerns, expectations, and resources available. A one to, at most, two hour meeting is typical. This is the first step in client management for the student team. They need to establish a relationship (i.e., learning environment) that will see them through the project and beyond.

Work Scope Agreement

There should be some type of agreement about the specific boundaries of the project and procedures expected from the client and student teams (Gibson, 1996). I highly recommend a formal, written agreement at this point that describes project boundaries and deliverables in more detail than the initial informal agreement. A clear understanding of what is and is NOT included in the project will prevent "scope creep" (project expansion) that often happens when clients get excited about the project's potential to really help the organization. It is best to have this follow two to three weeks after the initial client meeting so that the team has time to understand what is realistically possible following the initial client meeting and so that there is enough time to complete the project.

Monitoring and Crisis Management

As alluded to earlier, there is a misconception that faculty sit back as the projects kick into gear. Wrong, wrong, wrong. This is when faculty need to be on their toes to catch students doing things right to share with the class and to correct individual mistakes more privately to promote individual learning. Periodic meetings with student teams are recommended. This will help faculty spot any emerging problems not evident in the weekly written, e-mail, or class time updates from the team that I also suggest. When a problem does arise, it can be dealt with quickly or allowed to develop to the best time to share a lesson.

Midterm Student Evaluations

Whether or not student team contracts suggested above are used, a midterm student evaluation is recommended to reinforce that the course's intent is to learn about consulting. About midterm is when students tend to start focusing only on producing client deliverables, forgetting about process issues such as team dynamics and continuous management of client expectations. I have each team use the team contract it developed at the beginning of the course to evaluate the contributions of individual team members and the performance of the team as a whole. Then they meet with me as a team to discuss progress through course goals, not client goals.

Midterm Client Update

Once the project is underway, clients tend to think about expanded issues to include in the project because student teams often uncover new issues during the discovery stage that create excitement about solving aggravating problems. Even though a work scope agreement may have been signed, scope creep is common. A midterm update for the client gives students the opportunity to reinforce the boundaries of the project or if necessary, renegotiate deliverables. Clients are usually worried about benefits from the project at this point so it helps if students can summarize and actually show the client what has been accomplished to date. For example, a team can say, "From the interviews we have conducted thus far, we are beginning to see some trends emerge toward … we will be conducting a survey with … to test that hypothesis." Students should share findings, to date, to help the client start processing the view students are getting of the organization's problem they are addressing. I suggest a face-to-face meeting so students can better gauge client response. Faculty may also want to attend to spot potential client resistance that often arises if students see the situation differently than the client. The instructor can share signs of such resistance with the students in a teachable moment following the meeting and work with students to prepare a plan for helping the client and students delve into why they have different perspectives. Such conflicting perspectives often provide wonderful learning experiences for the client and students to see problems through a different lens and to work toward a common understanding of the problem and its underlying issues.

After the Project Is Completed

Stakeholder learning goals diverge as the project concludes. Students transition from learning what is important for finishing the project to learning what they have learned to enhance their careers. Clients are interested in how to use the team's recommendations, actionable knowledge about transitioning student perspectives to organizational action. The instructor is still learning how to facilitate learning for the client and students and is additionally interested in helping the client learn how to stay connected to the school for future projects.

Client Feedback Presentation

The culminating experience for clients and students is the client feedback presentation. This is when the client is given the deliverables and students unveil the whole picture they have discovered through their project work. This can be held at the client site where there is a higher chance to invite more organizational members or at the school where the school can be on display to more closely connect the client to the school. Either way, the presentation needs to be carefully orchestrated with appropriate scheduling, invitations, a token gift for the client, refreshments and breaks. If the typical Power Point presentation is used it should be engaging and supplemented with handouts to prevent boredom and to promote discussion following the presentation. A great sign of success is when members of the client organization have a heated debate about how many interns they can afford to hire to implement the team's recommendations quickly. A good feedback presentation is compelling enough to stage such a debate. The tone of the feedback session should be instructive but not demeaning; in short, it should provide hopeful help to the client. The client should leave the meeting know what steps to take to deal with the issue at hand. Students are thrilled when they hear clients excited about using their results. Faculty can help the teams shape their feedback presentations toward that end through preliminary practice sessions. I have students practice their presentations in class before presenting to the client. The whole class learns about how to present their recommendations from each other.

Student Debriefings—with Class and Individually

A final class to debrief client feedback sessions and the entire experience is recommended. Students can share their lessons learned with one another in public reflection and share the exhilaration of a job well done. The debriefing should include a broad array of topics since most consulting projects cover multidisciplinary issues as well as skill-building, such as teamwork. A set of questions can be provided to stimulate thinking and identify lessons that may be overlooked. Group pictures and food are a nice touch. Additionally, individual interviews or specifically focused comments on individual project debriefing papers personalize the experience and lessons for each student. Client bashing should not be allowed but rather faculty should force an understanding of the client perspective if a team dealt with a particularly difficult client, complex project, or troubled organization.

Post Mortem Evaluation of Project and Database Updates

Not all projects achieve the perfect balance advocated in this article. An evaluation using input from students, the client, and any additional faculty involved is recommended (Muir, 1996). Direct client feedback about meeting the project's goals is useful. The client is also a wonderful source of information about the student team's performance. The client may have a different view of student contributions and evaluate the project differently than the instructor. Such information can be used for grading student performance and more important, for constructive feedback to students about how to craft and present solutions to organizational problems. Review short- and long-term outcomes for all the stakeholders and how goals were, or were not, achieved. A final part of the post mortem evaluation should be a listing of lessons learned and, if necessary, a revision of guidelines for conducting student consulting projects. The guidelines I share here are mostly the result of post mortem lessons learned and continue to learn from experience. Capturing this information in a database can serve as a knowledge management system to spot underlying issues that may need addressing. The database can include the client organization, nature of the project, client contact information, deliverables, response from students and clients, problems and how they were handled, and lessons learned. This provides a history that can be shared with new faculty, data for developing client information sheets during the preparation phase, data for information sheets for prospective students, and success stories for the school's public relations.

Client Follow-up

Show appreciation for the client's efforts by having an appreciation event for all clients and other people involved in helping students such as guest speakers and internship sponsors. This helps clients connect with others struggling with similar issues. It also provides an opportunity for public relations to highlight companies that support the school and makes the clients look good in their organizations. If consulting firms that recruit on campus are invited, they can hear first-hand from clients about the wonderful training the school is providing.

Connecting the client to other interested parties in the school can help maximize the school's benefits. It can be a delicate task to protect the client from being overwhelmed so it helps to find ways to do this in the least time consuming and painless way possible for the client. If the client feedback session is hosted at the school, other interested campus personnel, such as those in career services or faculty interested in research with the client organization, can attend and meet the client then. School personnel can also be invited to the appreciation event to make it more convenient for the client and gauge client interest in pursuing further connections.

REALIZING BENEFITS OF
STAKEHOLDER MANAGEMENT APPROACH

The stakeholder management approach acknowledges and manages to needs of all parties throughout the consulting project. The first five points in the process relate to preparatory work suggested before a project begins. Shortcutting the preparation work can lead a project toward failure or, at minimum, unnecessary problems. In particular, choosing an inappropriate project or unruly client can spell disaster for the project. A second major roadblock to avoid is not building the necessary introductions and contacts between the student team and the client. A stranded team runs in circles and becomes frustrated.

The next six points outline suggestions for keeping the project on track. Once the project is underway, the main task of the faculty is to keep it moving according to plan and harvest lessons. Nothing can be worse than a stalled project due to the lack of checkpoints and crisis management. Monitoring to notice potential problems or roadblocks is essential to preventing a derailed project and lost learning opportunities.

The final five points are necessary for making learning explicit, and the post mortem analysis is crucial to the learning experience for students and faculty. Even the client can benefit from an honest analysis. When a client asks, "What can I do better next time?", you have an excellent sign of a productive experience and a strong potential for future engagements. A checklist for conducting student consulting projects is provided in Appendix B. It summarizes the points above for instructors embarking on this type of experience.

EXTENDING THE STAKEHOLDER MANAGEMENT APPROACH

Thus far, this chapter has focused on conducting effective student *consulting projects* but there are implications for student *field study* projects as well.

Faculty involved in field study projects can and should use a stakeholder management approach with minor adjustments. Most of the stakeholders and interests will be the same. The biggest difference between a field study and a consulting project will be the course objectives for student learning so some guidelines will need to be altered slightly to put more focus on application of course content and less emphasis on consulting skills such as client and project management.

Before the Project Begins

Since field studies have more narrow content-related objectives, the appropriate site needs to be checked for specific fit. There can be a tendency is to lean too far to please the client, losing focus on the course objectives or focusing too much on the course, providing nothing for the project sponsor and perhaps, burning the chance to go back to that organization for future projects. Managers and organizations sponsoring the project are less likely to gain much unless there is an arrangement for a report, debriefing, public recognition, or thank you letter for the sponsor. In preparing a field study, faculty should identify exactly what sponsor organizations will receive from the experience with an equitable exchange as the goal.

Another issue to consider before the project begins is the mechanism of structure that will be used to ensure attention to course objectives. Written guidelines, interim deliverables, and direct faculty supervision are possible ways to keep students focused on the topic and prevent the sponsor from imposing different objectives. It also protects the sponsor from being imposed upon more than necessary once the project begins. For example, many undergraduate operations management courses require plant tours for students to see different types of manufacturing processes in action. Structure can be provided by having a step-by-step assignment sheet complete with introduction, agreement, and thank you letter templates, and peer review forms for the teams. This keeps students focused on course objectives rather than client management and project planning.

Field studies often focus on common aspects of business, so students are usually equipped to find sponsors on their own. However, students from other cultures or those with little or no work experience may not know where to start. They may need some guidance or assistance. Since field studies are usually less involved than consulting projects an agreement letter for the sponsor to sign is probably more appropriate than a detailed work scope document to make sure that the sponsor understands the commitment.

During the Project

If there has been careful project sponsor selection and there is a defined process for conducting the study, the instructor's job becomes one of monitoring, crisis management, and capturing valuable lessons. Typical problems are sponsors who back out or become inaccessible or yes, student cheating. Since the use of field studies are so prevalent, there are field study papers available online and in fraternity files. Random phone calls to project sponsors to confirm activity can keep cheating in check and foster a stronger relationship between the faculty and project sponsor.

After the Project is Completed

A nice touch is for faculty to send thank you letters to the sponsors. This accomplishes two things. First, a letter gives the sponsor something to put in a performance evaluation and second, it establishes another way to build the connection between the school and sponsor, particularly if the project sponsor was found by the student.

CONCLUSION

Field study projects and field consulting projects can achieve learning goals for all stakeholders by intentionally focusing the separate needs of each stakeholder as the project evolves through different phases. In summary, the big picture is to create an experience that provides an environment conducive to learning and activities that promote learning for the stakeholders. Key components include relationship building, management of expectations for learning readiness, planned reflections, and opportunistic reflections.

All the stakeholders need to be aware of and appreciative of the interests of the other stakeholders. Some underlying objectives in the guidelines in this article, such as the use of a work scope agreement and the no client-bashing rule, are designed to create an awareness of and appreciation for the interests of other involved parties. Other suggestions, such as how a project is chosen, focus on creating mutual goals. In student field projects using the stakeholder management approach, each party is student and teacher at some point in the project. For example, as instructor, I learn from student naiveté about how what needs to be taught and from student functional expertise about better ways to approach organizational problems. I learn about emerging organizational concerns and much more from clients. Students learn about consulting from me and more about organizations and career preferences from clients. Clients learn new perspectives from students and ways Bentley can help them from me. In closing, I should caution that the suggestions provided in this chapter are simply a starting point for designing and managing student field projects because the instructor's continuous learning will obsolete the course template. I have found that the curious students that take this course and the open-minded clients that engage our teams are ingenious creatures in constant motion. Just when I think I have the perfect template for future replication another issue will arise. A number of years ago, the issue of confidentiality came to the forefront, and it still is but with additional constraints. The issue of student cheating is now more prevalent than in the past. Technological advances such as groupware for knowledge management and communication have changed the way I monitor students and capture teachable moments while the vast amount of information available online can be tempting for students who want to avoid the tough work of collecting primary data. Therefore, the changing nature of our world and the many variations of student projects from consulting to field studies makes each time the course is run unique. This chapter provides suggestions for building and managing the field projects that integrate findings from research and experience that instructors can use to meet stakeholders need and assure student learning.

APPENDIX A:
BENEFITS OF STUDENT CONSULTING PROJECTS

STUDENT BENEFITS:
 Academic opportunities
- Bridging theory to practice
- Deeper understanding of concepts
- Learning style accommodation
- Competency building

 Career development opportunities
- Networking
- Resume building
- Exposure to new work situations career decision making
- Opportunity to experience new cultures

CLIENT BENEFITS:
- Objective, unbiased viewpoint

- Access to new techniques and resources
- Inexpensive assistance
- Guided, systematic attention to necessary issues
- Preview of potential interns or hires
- Enhanced social responsibility image/community service

FACULTY AND SCHOOL BENEFITS:

- Closer connection to alumni
- Faculty development
- Faculty access to organizations for research
- Corporate connections for career services job postings
- Enhanced image in corporate world

APPENDIX B:
INSTRUCTOR CHECKLIST FOR WORKING WITH STAKEHOLDERS

Before Project Begins

School/Administration	*Student Team*	*Client(s)*
Consider prerequisites (e.g. content centered consulting course or progress in degree) or application process	Clarify workload expectations in advising	Identify potential client list
	Clarify expectations in first class	Check availability and problem scope
Obtain contacts and support from alumni, career services, and development office	Decide on number teams, size, composition and mix of expertise and background. Examine: resumes/vitas personal assessments interviews class discussion dynamics ice breakers	Meet with the client to determine willingness and readiness and to preview relevant facts / documents
Negotiate: extra resources class size reduced teaching load graduate assistant/other clerical support	Establish team members roles team supervisor faculty liaison knowledge manager project manager	Identify key contacts and back-ups for the team
	"Socially prepare" students for client culture	Generate a back up client list and team redistribution provision in case of severe problems
	Establish business protocols	
	Use recent examples to illustrate potential problems	Clarify with client: project scope duration & intensity budget compensation confidentiality issues
	Conduct ice breaking and team building exercises	
	Reach agreement on performance standards	
	Formulate a "team contract"	

(Appendix continues)

Appendix B (continued)

During Project

School/Administration	Student Team	Client(s)
Engage assistance as needed from campus resources	Supervise initial investigation of industry and client organization	Monitor project progress on a weekly basis with the client
	Encourage secondary search on focal problem(s)	Arrange for a mid project client update and possible renegotiation of deliverables
Keep other parts of school informed about projects in case they have contact with clients	Arrange for the initial client-team meeting	
	Establish a semi-formal work scope agreement	Seek informal feedback on team performance from client counterparts
	Follow up in 2-3 weeks to evaluate the discovery phase of the project	
	Monitor the team on a regular basis for crisis or emerging problems	
	Require weekly advancement reports from the team-faculty liaison	
	Arrange for a mid project student evaluation	
	Evaluate draft of findings before client presentation	
	Attend practice client presentation	

After Project

School/Administration	Student Team	Client(s)
Invite key administrator(s), other faculty and alumni to the final feedback presentation	Organize the logistics, review content of, and attend the final client feedback presentation	Conduct a private evaluation session with the client
Generate list of contacts for future reference	Debrief individual students and the whole team in class	Follow up on mid-range outcomes of project suggestions
Generate "success stories" for PR consumption and advertising	Compare experience and learning in a joint session with other teams	Maintain contacts for future engagements or follow-ups
Generate a data bank of project experiences, problems and learning	Conduct a post mortem of the project particularly in case of a negative experience	Contact the client for other school activities: guest speakers, seminars, ceremonies, appreciation events
	Generate revised guidelines for future engagements	

REFERENCES

Adams, S.M., & Zanzi, A. (2001). Are we producing information age consultants?: Reflections on U.S. business schools' course offerings. In A. Buono (Ed.), *Current trends in management consulting (Research in management consulting*, Vol. 1, pp. 189-206). Greenwich, CT: Information Age.

Adams, S.M., & Zanzi, A. (2004). Academic development for careers in management consulting. *Career Developmental International, 9*(6), 559-577.

Arthur, M.B., DeFillipi, R.J., & Jones, C. (2001). Project-based learning as the interplay of career and company non-financial capital. *Management Learning, 32*(1), 99-117.

Ayas, K., & Zeniuk, N. (2001). Project-based learning: Building communities of reflective practioners. *Management Learning, 32*(1), 61-76.

Baker, H.K., & Schomburg, A. (2000). *MBA Field Study Survey.* Washington, DC: American University.

Beech, N., MacIntosh, R., MacLean, D., Shepherd, J., & Stokes, J. (2002). Exploring constraints on developing knowledge. *Management Learning, 33*(4), 459-475.

Block, P. (2000). *Flawless consulting* (2nd ed.). San Francisco: Jossey-Bass/Pfeiffer.

Bloomfield, S.D., & Pashke, P.E. (1997). Quality assessment projects as teaching and learning tools. *Journal of Management Education, 21*(1), 73-86.

Boyatzis, R.E., & Kolb, D.A. (1991). Assessing individuality in learning: The learning skills profile. *Educational Psychology, 11*(3&4), 279-295.

Carlile, P.R. (2002). A pragmatic view of knowledge and boundaries: Boundary objects in new product development. *Organization Science, 13*(4), 442-455.

Clegg, S.R., Kornberger, M., & Rhodes, C. (2004). Noise, parasites, and translation: Theory and practice in management consulting. *Management Learning, 35*(1), 31-45.

Coco, M. (2000). Internships: A try before you buy arrangement. *SAM Advanced Management Journal, 65*(2), 41-44.

Congram, C., & LaFarge, V. (1995). Student advisory teams: A new approach to managing field projects. *Journal of Management Education, 19*(3), 347-353.

Ellinger, A.D., & Bostrom, R.P. (2002). An examination of managers' beliefs about their roles as facilitators of learning. *Management Learning, 33*(2), 147-180.

Farinelli, J.L., & Mann, P. (1994). How to get the most value for your internship program. *Public Relations Quarterly, 39*(3), 35-38.

Gammage, K.L., Carron, A.V., & Estabrooks, P.A. (2001). Team cohesion and individual productivity. *Small Group Research, 32*(1), 3-18.

Garrick, J., & Clegg, S. (2001). Stressed-out knowledge workers in performative times: A postmodern take on project-based learning. *Management Learning, 32*(1), 119-134.

Gibson, D.C. (1996). Criteria for establishing and evaluating public relations internship systems. *Public Relations Quarterly, 41*(1), 43-46.

Gunasekara, C. (2003, Winter). Project-based workplace learning: A case study. *SAM Advanced Management Journal,* 37-48

Hamilton, M.A., & Hamilton, S.F. (1997). When is work a learning experience. *Phi Dleta Kappan, 78*(9), 682-689.

Keegan, A., & Turner, J.R. (2001). Quantity versus quality in project-based learning practices. *Management Learning, 32*(1), 77-98.

Muir, C. (1996). Using consulting projects to teach critical-thinking skills in the business communication. *Business Communication Quarterly, 59*(4), 77-88.

Nahapiet, J., & Ghoshal, S. (1998). Social capital, intellectual capital, and the organizational advantage. *Academy of Management Review, 23*(2), 242-266.

Nonaka, I., & Takeuchi, H. (1995). *The Knowledge Creating Company.* New York: Oxford University Press.

Ornstein, S., & Isabella, L.A. (1993). Making sense of careers: A review 1989-1992. *Journal of Management Review, 19*(2), 243-268.

Parker, G. (1990). *Team players and teamwork.* San Francisco: Jossey-Bass.

Raelin, J.A. (2001). Public reflection as the basis of learning. *Management Learning, 32*(1), 11-30.

Raelin, J.A. (2000). *Work-based learning: The new frontier of management development.* Upper Saddle, NJ: Prentice-Hall.

Raelin, J.A. (1997). A model of work-based learning. *Organization Science, 8*(6), 563-578.

Rhodes, C., & Garrick, J. (2003). Project-based learning and the limits of corporate knowledge. *Journal of Management Education, 27*(4), 447-472.

Seashore, S.E. (1954). *Group cohesiveness in the industrial work group.* Ann Arbor: University of Michigan.

Sekaran, U. (2002). *Research methods for business* (4th ed.). New York: John Wiley & Sons.

Tooley, J.A. (1997). Working for credit: How to make the most of semester-long internship. *U.S. News & World Report, 123*(19), 76-79.

Ulvila, J.W. (2000). Building relationships between consultants and clients. *American Behavioral Scientist, 43*(10), 1667-1681.

Van der Sluis, L.E.C., & Poell, R.F. (2002). Learning opportunities and learning behavior: A study among MBAs in their early career stage. *Management Learning, 33*(3), 291-311.

Watson, B.S. (1995). The intern turnaround. *Management Review, 84*(6), 9-13.

Watson, W.E., Kumar, K., & Michaelsen, L.K. (1993). Cultural diversity's impact on interaction process and performance: Comparing homogeneous and diverse task groups. *Academy of Management Journal, 36*(3), 590-602.

Young, R.R. (1996). Brief field experiences: An instructional tool for undergraduate political science classes. *Political Science & Politics, 29*(4), 695-697.

PART II

SERVICE LEARNING PROJECTS

CHAPTER 5

EDUCATING MANAGERS THROUGH SERVICE LEARNING PROJECTS

Karen Ayas and Philip Mirvis

Project-based learning can be a powerful method for educating managers and developing leaders at all levels. This chapter looks at the design and delivery of several executive programs that involved service learning projects. It reports first-hand observations from the authors along with reflections from executives who participated in them. Using cases that differ in scope, sponsorship, and centrality to the business agenda, it demonstrates the effective use of service learning for developing self awareness, understanding others, dealing with diversity, and connecting business and society. The chapter concludes with a review of design elements that can enhance the impact of service learning on executive development.

INTRODUCTION

Smith and Dodds (1997) define "project-based learning" as the theory and practice of using real-world work assignments on time-limited projects to achieve performance objectives and to facilitate individual and collective learning. Project-based learning is based in the tradition of learn-by-doing exemplified in action research (e.g., Lewin, 1946), action

Educating Managers through Real World Projects, 93–113
Copyright © 2005 by Information Age Publishing
All rights of reproduction in any form reserved.

science (e.g., Argyris & Schon, 1978), and action learning (e.g., Revans, 1971). In the past decade there has been a growing body of literature pointing to the benefits of learning through projects.

Studies find that management training that rely on classroom experiences, even with case studies, small group exercises, and computer simulations, fall short of developing the wide range of skills and learning capabilities managers need to master real life situations (Hall & Mirvis, 1995). Project-based learning, while limited by the content, scope, and duration of a specific project, typically features more stimuli, ambiguities, and dilemmas than classroom training along with a steady stream of changing opportunities, problems, and stakeholders—like in real life. In addition, it provides managers with clear and consequential feedback—whether or not the goals were achieved and why the project was a success or failure.

Organizations also see benefits in project-based learning beyond the immediate results. For instance, even as projects stretch individual managers with challenging tasks, they often demand teamwork and collaboration across levels and organizational boundaries. This not only enhances individuals' social and relational skills, it often develops relationships between trainees and across a company that endure beyond the project time frame. Furthermore, in their choice of projects and in the mentoring and educational input that supports trainees, organizations can send signals about what is expected of future company leaders, important to the enterprise, and essential to progressing in one's own career.

Given these benefits, the past decade has seen widespread adoption of and a variety of innovations in project-based learning in organizations. Ever increasing numbers of business schools and corporations, for example, feature project-based learning in their management development programs (Vicere & Fulmer, 1996). Vanguard programs at ARAMARK, Johnson & Johnson, and IBM offer tiers of project-based programs aimed at entry, operational, and strategic levels of management. GE has trained a generation of leaders through its "workout" projects. Noel Tichy, who helped to set up the GE program, has carried this philosophy and methodology to several other companies under the banner of leaders developing leaders (Tichy, 2002). In these programs, senior leaders sponsor projects undertaken by younger managers and coach and evaluate them over the course of the program.

THE CASE FOR SERVICE LEARNING

Our interest here is with the role of service learning projects for educating managers. Jacoby (1996)—similar to Kendall (1990) and other service-learning advocates (Bringle & Hatcher, 1996)—defines service learning as "a form of experiential education in which students engage in activities that address human and community needs together with structured opportunities intentionally designed to promote student learning and development" (p. 5). For the purpose of this chapter, managers are the "students" of service-learning. The service learning projects described here vary from a half day limited engagement with a community to ongoing sustained business-community partnerships but key components of service learning—achieving the learning objectives through the service, mutual benefit for the managers and the community, and structured reflection—are enacted in all.

Cultivating habits of reflective practice in the project environment to benefit the individual, the organization and society is one of the key goals of project-based learning (Ayas & Zeniuk, 2001). In the special issue of *Management Learning* on project-based learning, Raelin (2001) argues that reflection is fundamental to learning and provides a basis for future action. Service learning provides its own rich mix of intellectual, emotional, and experiential stimuli that can aid in the development of managers (Carver, 1996). The milieu opens manager's eyes to social and economic conditions outside their traditional realms of operation and encourages them to reflect on being effective in a resource-poor environment and challenges them to act. This is especially true when learners have "structured opportunities" to reflect on their experiences (Eyler & Giles, 1999). McAleavey (1996) describes reflection as a crucial part of service programs and the key "to making community service yield real learning."

Brown (2000) illustrates how teaching project management to MBA students through service learning can enhance students' higher-level cognitive skills, and the retention of lessons learned. Service projects typically put trainees into an environment where they are dealing with people who may have very different outlooks, motivations, and goals (Godfrey, 2000). Most managers, lacking formal power in this context, have to learn to listen to different points of view, exercise "soft" influence skills, and empathize with others if they are to be effective and deliver on project goals. Carver (1996) offers her version of the essence of service learning: agency (learning to be a change agent); belonging (belonging to the community); and competence (the ability to apply what is learned).

To this point, much of the literature and commentary about service learning concerns school or university-based programs and the experience of student learners rather than executives (Bringle & Hatcher, 1999; Eyler, 2002; Jacoby, 2003). Studies of service learning in the corporation generally cover apprenticeship programs, volunteer initiatives, company-sponsored community service projects, or extended private-public partnering (Galen et al., 1994; Yerkes, 1998). As laudable as these efforts can be, they tend to be localized and/or primarily philanthropic. Furthermore, they seldom include senior executives nor are they aimed specifically at leadership development.

This chapter looks at the design of several executive development programs that involved service learning projects. It reports first-hand observations from the authors along with reflections from participants that are derived from individual journal entries and group reflection sessions that were taped and transcribed, and reflection on the experience once they returned to their workplace. In each case—Ford Motor Co., Unilever and Shell—service learning was integral to but by no means the only element of leadership development. The programs also involved to varying degrees team development, and business-related inputs and deliberations. The intent here is to parse the features of project-based service learning in these programs that are most relevant to executive development and describe their impact with regard to the following learning objectives:

- developing self awareness,
- understanding others,
- dealing with diversity, and
- connecting business and society.

As we discuss these learning objectives, we include a vignette that describes the service learning experience.[1] We conclude the chapter with a review of design elements that can enhance the impact of service learning projects on executive development.

CULTIVATING SELF-AWARENESS

Unilever Managers at the Village of Hope

The director of Village of Hope, home to 200 orphans and disabled children in Danang, had been a primary school teacher who had very few resources but a big dream and an abundance of hope. When asked what drove him, he answered, "Faith and love. I have a dream that keeps me going, where I see each child is happy." And he added: "When you are 50 years old, you feel there is not much time left to do something worthwhile; one needs to share all he has." When one of the young leaders questioned him, "What would happen to the children if something were to happen to you?" there was a moment of silence. Then his inscrutable face was overcome with emotion. He trembled and could not stop his tears. Seven or seventy years old, every person in the room cried with him.

This was a moment of truth characterized by participants of Unilever's Young Leaders' Forum (YLF) as "looking humanity in the face." This was also a moment of collective commitment of some thirty-five managers from Unilever Asia to the Village of Hope (VOH) project.

For the young Asian leaders who meet biennially for the purpose of leadership development, the life story of the director of the orphanage has been a source of inspiration. Howard Gardner's (1995) comments on identity stories apply: "It is the particular burden of the leader to help other individuals determine their personal, social, and moral identities." (p. 25). Many corporate programs cultivate leaders' self-awareness through, say, personality tests, 360-degree feedback, coaching, and myriad forms of experiential learning. Personal reflection on one's life course and the sharing of life stories with others also serves this purpose and helps to build a sense of common humanity among a group of leaders.

The VOH project in Vietnam has been an integral part of the leadership development program and has played a major role in sustaining the forum. Unilever's young managers have assisted in the physical upgrade of the facility, developed an IT infrastructure, and today continue to meet regularly with the headmaster and children to ensure their well being. The dialogue between the young leaders, staff and children—sustained for five years—has yielded rewarding emotional bonds and deepened the young leaders' self-picture. "With your help, not only I was able to get to know a great number of enlightened souls but I also discovered myself" reported one young leader.

Almost every leadership program emphasizes how important it is for a leader to "know thyself." This means, among other things, being in touch with one's emotional make-up and being able to recognize strengths and weaknesses and the impact a person has on others (Goleman, 1995). Service learning is a particularly apt experience for executive self-development. On this count, Edgar Schein (1990) reminds that involving people in unfamiliar situations that stretch their understandings and boundaries often triggers self-reflection. He finds business people particularly open to introspection and questioning when they are abandoning "career anchors" and transitioning into new roles. In a complementary light, Krieger (1990) contends that immersion in symbolic social situations can be a "formative experience" as people prepare to assume new responsibilities.

The young leaders of Unilever took on themselves to create a better home for all the children and successfully completed the renovation project at a total cost of US$120,000. The project included raising the necessary funds and collecting donations across Unilever. At the reopening of the village, the young leaders planned a huge celebration with the aim of creating a memorable experience for the children. After an official ceremony, they headed out with everyone from the village for a bus ride, stroll in the nearby town, and three-hour boat ride. The day ended at a restaurant where a small feast and festive party that brought out the child in everyone; there was dancing between tables, songs around a huge campfire, mirth and a food-fight with a giant creamy birthday cake for the 200 children.

With the renovation project complete, the young leaders extended their engagement with the orphanage. Their annual project is to design and facilitate a daylong "birthday" celebration with the children.

The reciprocity of benefits to community and business is clear. What was meant to be a memorable experience for the children of the VOH turned out to be more so for the young managers of Unilever. The lessons learned would not be forgotten. One said: "I've learned that when a young child from the Village of Hope holds your little finger in his fist, you're hooked for life." Said another "I never thought that an organization could teach you about humanity or love. Ten years from now, we will not just have become business leaders, but we will have had an impact on a lot of other people's lives."

Ford Executives at the Home for Black Children

Another example, albeit a briefer service learning engagement, comes from Ford. The Ford program with Homes for Black Children (HBC) also strongly emphasized self-discovery and aimed to prepare Ford executives to move into general management positions where they would be leading a large workforce and interacting with public. Prior to meeting their counterparts in the orphanage, each of the Ford leaders prepared an "emotional lifeline." This technique, developed by Herb Shepard (1984), has people chart their life's journey from childhood to present with careful consideration of emotional highs and lows.

After discussing their lifelines with fellow executives, the Ford leaders were then asked to abstract "life stories" and prepare to share them with their counterparts from HBC. The sharing began with the president of HBC telling her story of growing up in Detroit, guided by God-fearing parents, earning a college degree, and finding a calling in caring for underprivileged children and families. She then recounted a story of how her college roommate had married an employee of an auto company, who was subsequently laid off when his job was outsourced. The husband took employment at lesser wages, received no benefits, and was laid off again. He went into debt, and ultimately turned to drink, drugs, and adultery. In a very real and moving way, the director's story of her friend's sad fate was a story all-to-familiar to the Ford executives who had, after all, overseen outsourcing and layoffs and would be in a decision making role in the years ahead.

They, in turn, shared heartfelt stories of growing up, of in some cases adopting children, and of trying to do the right things as parents, community members, and corporate leaders. Members of the two groups paired off to talk more intimately of their lives, their leadership stories, and what might be done to strengthen families and safeguard children in the inner city. These kinds of conversations, integral to community service projects, necessarily open up questions about personal identity, values, and priorities. Furthermore, the emotional content can range from guilt, to sympathy, to mutual respect. Whatever the range, such feelings are a window into the soul.

Although Ford's formal engagement with HBC was limited in duration and participation, many of the participants established voluntary connections with the home and the children that continue to this day. After this encounter, many Ford executives were moved to continue their involvement with HBC by, for example, advising Board members on business issues, coaching HBC staff, talking with parents about adoption or mentoring children—depending on their personal interests and inclinations.

Interestingly, several based in the region brought their own teams (and, in one case, an entire factory) to HBC for community service and a few, in faraway lands, brought their teams to local orphanages or social service settings to replicate the experience and lessons. All of this community service was self-generated by the Ford executives acting on personal values that were reawakened or, at least, newly channeled by service learning.

UNDERSTANDING "OTHERS"

Unilever Best Foods Top Leaders in Xingping

Two hundred travelers invited by the president of Unilever Best Foods (UBF) Asia join the company's top leadership on a "Journey to Greatness." From seventeen Asian countries, stretching from Japan and South Korea to India and Pakistan to Australia, they head to the little eighteen-hundred-year-old village of Xingping, sixty kilometers south of Guilin, in the heart of China's wondrous Li River valley. The UBF Asia team leaders begin their transformational journey by "getting into the skin of another," working on different projects alongside the local villagers for a whole day.

It's well established that human relations develop and deepen as people see themselves in another person and see another in themselves (Friedman, 1983). Another way service learning projects enhance leadership development is the way it can stimulate a greater understanding of others. Empathizing is central to what Erich Fromm calls the "art of loving" (1956). It is integral to socialization and growth. Indeed, psychologists posit that just as seeing the world through another's perspective helps people to grow beyond egocentrism, so empathizing with another is the antidote to human selfishness. Alfie Kohn (1990), among others, suggests that empathy, more so than sympathy, is the basis for the "helping relationship."

Drawing on practices of whole systems intervention, community building, small group process, and individual development, the UBF Asia top leaders program was aimed to open eyes and minds, and stimulate heads and hearts. Working on different projects alongside villagers in rural China they would be pushed outside of their comfort zone in many different dimensions. Reflection points and quiet times were built into the program so as to create a "learning zone" wherein the UBF leaders could individually and collectively make sense of their experiences.

In their various service learning projects in China, the leaders spent some time listening to themselves (Schein, 2003). They reflected on questions such as: "What has this person's life been like? Why do they see things the way they do? How am I reacting to this situation or this person? What are my reactions telling me about my own assumptions about life and people?" This is a different sort of self-listening in which the self makes inferences about what makes others tick and how they relate to their world.

An Australian leader elaborated on the impact: "It's helping us develop empathy, to put yourself in the other person's shoes—that could be your customer, your colleague or one of your managers. Working alongside with villagers was a very good device for us to step outside of our own paradise and get a deep understanding that the way we do things is not the only way."

One group of leaders learned about giving and receiving from buffalos and the farmers who trusted them with all they had. Another group worked in a small noodle factory, making dough, cutting it into long strings, drying the noodles outside on bamboo poles. It was a primitive operation by any standard, but the ingenuity and ambition of its owner/operator were inspirational to the UBF leaders. He had once been a farmer but decided to become a noodle maker to earn more money to educate his children, though it was a craft he knew nothing about—and he knew even less about marketing his product. At first, his noodles had been poorly made and hard to sell, but he learned to send samples to potential buyers to ask for improvement and eventually to win their business.

Others helped to build a road. Seeing the enormous lumps of stone that needed to be carried, this group first thought that they were on a short straw. Yet they ended the day as a triumphant team with powerful lessons on greatness. "From the construction work I learned that doing a piece of work well requires dedication, rigor and discipline" said one, "humility and humbleness also came to the fore." Explaining how his team had laid a fence with stones, said an Indian leader, "One big learning is that as a team, we can move mountains." These were just some of the many lessons earned with sweat.

Still others worked at repairing bicycles, trimming hedges, making ropes. Said one of the plant managers, "The grand old man in the family—the way he taught us to make ropes, the way he kept his cool throughout despite our silly mistakes—made me think about my style of management when it comes to teaching the new managers who join my team at the factory." No matter what the task at hand was there seemed to be important lessons to be learned. "I thought my day with the 71-year-old Chinese 'sweeper' would not really yield anything," said another, "Now I know the sweeper as a human being with a family that has its own challenges and aspirations. I know the incredible ambition of his granddaughter aspiring to be a model one day. I guess this is what dreams are made of."

The UBF top leaders program triggered deep reflections on behavior, attitude and style. Many went home with the resolution to be more sharing, loving, giving and receiving. "I have started to practice it," noted one of the leaders in his post-meeting reflections, "and the response I have received from my team gives me the strength to carry on."

APPRECIATING AND DEALING WITH DIVERSITY

Connecting with others of a different background can also yield lessons on diversity. The top leaders of UBF Asia met villagers in rural China whose income was less then U.S.$125 per annum. "70% of our 140 million population is similar to the family of the man I met today" said a Pakistani leader "while only 5% has a lifestyle similar to mine. I need to respect them and to value them for whom they are and what they deliver to all of us." An Indonesian added, "I am Asian, 40 years old, living in a country that is 80% rural, but I have never planted a tree nor talked to rural people who buy our products every day. This is critical when we aim to improve their nutrition, their health, their happiness, life and future."

After "getting into the skin" of the villagers in Xingping, the top leaders of UBF Asia also came to realize that intellect, wisdom and virtues were not the heritage or property of any particular nation or a group of people. Every individual, irrespective of his or her country, religion, beliefs or culture did amply display, intellect and wisdom, although some were more articulate in expressing their viewpoint more philosophically and effectively.

Sustaining a dialogue among Unilever's Asian leaders, from seventeen countries—stretching from Japan to Indonesia, and from Pakistan to Australia—posed its own challenges. Here was a mix of men and women, and Christian, Hindu, Buddhist, and Moslem. And the difficulty was exacerbated because of uneven mastery of English, as well as, cultural differences in style of communication. Some, for instance, were culturally more reserved, others were more expressive. Some seemed to be interpersonally relational and others more transactional. "In an Asian culture, it's not easy to speak up" explained one of the leaders to the group. "It's very risky to stand up and say something. It must be the right thing."

Cultural awareness and developing the capability for effective communication in a multicultural environment is a must for the executives who take on increasingly global assignments but dealing with the emotional conflicts remains a challenge (Von Glinow et al., 2004). Early and Peterson (2004) stress the importance of developing cultural intelligence and suggest that global managers need skills in cultural sense making, empathizing, and understanding culturally-acceptable behavior.

The service learning experience in Xingping encouraged the leaders to reflect on their differences in their own cultures and ways of communicating. A Malaysian admitted: "This was difficult for me because it made me do things against my norms. However, I am grateful that I was forced to face it and reflect on myself, my future and my job." Said a Japanese, "I discovered many touching stories and started to appreciate the diversity and richness of the human being." An Indian added, "Whilst there were differences in our appearance, speech and food, we were bonded by a feeling of friendship and caring. Sharing inner most feelings and fears so openly bonded us emotionally." Said another, "We all have different backgrounds, so I have to look into that deeply and I have to open my mind up and be big enough to accept each one of you in my heart. So we can have some sort of same understanding and then become more united together."

CONNECTING BUSINESS AND SOCIETY

Learning from Communities in India

As a next leg on their "Journey to Greatness," UBF top leaders spend two to three days in ashrams, spiritual centers, micro-enterprises and charities in India to learn about community life. They tend to the needy, offer what help they can, and wonder how swa-

mis, selfless caregivers, community entrepreneurs, and energetic dabbawallas (who deliver thousands of lunches prepared at home to workers all over Mumbai) are able to accomplish so much with so few resources. In a desert campsite, for three days thereafter, they reflect on the meaning of their experiences, talk over its relevance for them, and rediscover what a true mission is—and what a great business should aspire to.

The service learning projects were spread across Mother Teresa's Missionaries of Charity, the Dalai Lama's monastery, the Sikh Golden Temple, the Brahma Kumaris in Mt. Abu, Bah'ai Lotus Temple, as well as cloth spinning communes, the self-employed women's association (SEWA), ashrams, and so forth. During the visits with the diverse communities the leaders engaged in service to others, recorded observations, feelings, and insights about community practices and needs, and talked these over in informal and structured group reflections over several days thereafter. The leaders were asked to assume the role of an anthropologist for the visit, that is, to use their five senses—sight, hearing, smell, taste, and touch—to make sense of what was going on in the communities and to rely on their sixth sense—intuition or gut feel—to connect to the universal rhythms of human and community life. In so doing, they are urged to pay attention to preconceived cultural or intellectual assumptions; to be sensitive to their feelings and judgments; and to open up to what they might experience during the visit. All were provided with workbooks to record thoughts on the physical environs, the social organization of the communities, the ties that seemed to bind people together, and their very purpose for being together.

Broadly, any such encounter with a "foreign" community has the potential to deepen understanding of how different groups of people live and work and invites consideration of how one also lives and works (Schindler-Rainman & Lippitt, 1980). The purpose of these projects was for the leaders to experience communal living in its many forms and deepen their understanding of communities that they served. The expectation was set that as the leaders informed themselves about the people and circumstances of the communities they visited, they would also ponder the meaning and implications for their own leadership body and business.

After their community visits, the two-hundred plus leaders reflected together over three days. In solo, in small groups, and as a top leadership community, they probed deeply into the existential questions of "who am I?", "who are we?" and "what are we here for? The case here could be just an exception, but the mind-opening and heart-rending experience of being connected to people who dedicate their lives to serving others sparked the desire of UBF leaders to build a business that serves a "higher purpose"—promoting the well-being of everyday Asians and reaching out to the poorest of the poor.

Ongoing dialogue brought them closer to the conclusion that organizations have to be driven by their missions rather than by numbers and processes. "We should be able to serve the larger community by being relevant for them—not by just being providers of products," said one, "How else can organizations like Brahma Kumaris, Missionaries of Charities, etc. be managed without systems, procedures and controls and yet handle millions of dollars effectively?" The leaders also talked about what kind of an organization they would need to fulfill this aspiration; one where, in effect, people would be willing to "volunteer" their time and talents. One asked, "What can I contribute to the society and have I fulfilled my duty to mankind?" and then answered her own query, "we could all work toward leaving a legacy that transcends the borders and barriers of culture, religion, or race." Said another, "The communities we visited reminded me of an 'itch' that has been bugging me for the longest time, that is, to give my time and effort to a cause which is beyond myself (and even beyond my family). I have been blessed so much in this life that the least I can do is to help my fellow men. I need to act now."

Unilever was stimulated by community service to reexamine the ways it does business in Asia. Through reflection on their experience the UBF Asia top leaders came to the conclusion that they should serve the larger community by being relevant for them—not by just being providers of products. Commitments were made to pursue a worthy mission that would emphasize the healthy, nourishing aspects of food even though this would mean dropping several current offerings in the market. And it would lead to the launch of a children's nutrition campaign to bring affordable foods to the "bottom of the pyramid."

Shell's Wake Up Call

Another example, from the Royal Dutch Shell Group, shows how service learning projects can help transform the company's relationship with society. This story begins in 1995 with a public outcry over the Group's plans to scuttle its Brent Spar oil rig in the North Sea. Even as Shell's leaders were digesting the implications, a crisis in Nigeria erupted, resulting in the arrest and later the execution of an Ogoni tribal leader, Ken Saro Wiwa, who was protesting Shell's shoddy operations in the Niger delta. Within the Shell Group, there was scant denial that the company had damaged the natural environment and mishandled relationships with local tribes and Nigeria's ruling regime. There was, in turn, considerable frustration that company leaders had not fully factored social and environmental criteria into their plans and operations or into the response to these twin crises.

Thereafter Shell took steps to revise its Business Guidelines, survey its stakeholders, and reassess its role in society. A team composed of young managers and professionals was formed to study and make recommendations about Shell's social performance and reputation. With help from Tichy and Michael Brimm, and advice from Charles Fombrun (1996), the team showed how social and environmental issues, such as the Spar and Nigerian crises, affected perceptions of Shell by customers, investors, employees, and recruits.

Leaders today are being tasked with becoming "global citizens" and developing a point of view about the role of business in society (Waddock, 2002). Service learning can certainly help promote civic responsibility (Zlotkowski, 1996). Executives that take this responsibility seriously have a chance to become better informed about corporate citizenship and gain some experience filling an ambassadorial role for their company. Knowledge of and exposure to human and environmental calamities can itself be a "wake up call" and stimulus to action. But consciousness-raising requires some degree of internalization of the problem-at-hand and the placing of oneself psychologically into the situation (Prochaska et al., 1994).

To spread the findings, and reassert its commitments to society, Shell hosted core-purpose workshops for all staff in nearly fifty countries. As a part of this endeavor, the Group launched service learning projects where leaders in all its businesses would work hand-in-hand with community groups and NGOs—in London, The Hague, and around the world—to build a playground, clean up the environment, or provide service to the sick and needy. In preparatory workshops, they would reflect on their values, write a personal obituary, and script a personalized story about Shell's role in society (Tichy, 2002). They would then share these stories with community groups, work alongside them, and reflect together with top management over Shell's core purpose. In this case, service learning certainly reinforced Shell's new responsiveness to society.

What is apparent in both cases is that service learning was a spark to changing the way these companies do business.

DESIGN CONSIDERATIONS

According to Kolenko et al. (1996) service learning programs in business schools are effective to the extent they:

- Build a coalition of corporate managers, faculty, and community agencies to support and execute the service learning agenda;

- Build networks and structures to support service learning for students; and
- Build lifelong commitments to community service.

As illustrated in each of the corporate cases, the same prescriptions apply to service learning in executive development. In the case of Ford, alumni from prior programs maintained connections to the leaders at Homes for Black Children and helped prep newcomers for the experience. In the case of Unilever's Young Leaders Forum the leadership development agenda was based upon meeting the needs of the children of VOH as well as the development needs of the young leaders. And, in all cases, it was conveyed that community service was an expected executive commitment in the company.

Increased self-awareness, an improved ability to understand and relate to others, and heightened sensitivity to how social, political, and economic forces interplay in the service setting are to some extent organic byproducts of service learning projects. Programs where these are the learning objectives for executive development would therefore highly benefit from service learning projects.

Paying attention to the design of service learning projects and facilitation of the learning experience is critical. The consequences of poor design or implementation affect not only the executives but the communities the projects intend to serve. Design of executive development programs that involve service learning are therefore more challenging. Consider these design elements.

Sense of purpose.   Perhaps the most crucial element in the design is a shared understanding of the intent of the project and clarity around learning objectives: "What are we individually and collectively striving for?" An inquiry into purpose might go beyond the specific project engagement to an agenda connected to a higher purpose—such as reaching out to those who are less fortunate as illustrated in the case of Unilever.

Leaders as role models.   Needless to say, not all executives warm to the idea of service learning projects, nor are comfortable with exercises in self-disclosure. However, when their superiors self-disclose and speak to the link between service and business, some of the resistance lessens. It is worth noting that, in the programs described, the very top leaders of Shell and Ford, and the president of UBF Asia, frequently joined in the service learning projects with their company teams.

Preparation for learning.   Techniques like the emotional lifeline, discussion of it with colleagues, and preparation of vignettes for storytelling can help prepare leaders operationally and emotionally to meet people with different life experiences and stories to tell. The connection of the experience to self-awareness, interpersonal understanding, and dealing with diversity are relatively transparent and easy to preview in preparatory conversation.

When there is a desire to look into the social, political, and economic factors shaping the service setting, some pre-reading, talks by subject matter experts, and open discussion help to ready the mind for thoughtful questions and the senses for what is to be seen and heard. A workbook to organize thoughts and record observations during the project can also be helpful.

Immersion in the experience.   Experiential learning is most profound when it stretches the imagination and takes people to the edge of their comfort zones. Stretching the "classroom" to rural villages and sublime nature with community leaders and indigenous people as teachers create the context for a whole new learning experience. Attention to atmospherics, staging, and the flow of energy through the experience— all part of experience management—need to be carefully considered in the design of these programs. The aim is to create a multi-sensory experience that can stimulate leaders' heads and hearts(cf. Mirvis et al., 2003, on performativity). The design of these service learning projects should include individual, small group, and whole system activity. Reams have been written on how to design meaningful learning experiences at each of these levels (cf. Senge et al., 1994).

Service learning programs involving, say, house construction, painting, trash pickup, and such are useful for stimulating informal interaction, building bonds, and illustrating vividly social and economic cleavages between business and society. They also demonstrate, substantively and symbolically, what can be accomplished when business and community people work together. Given the focus on personal development here, emphasis was given to connecting deeply to people in their service setting or community. In addition, the content of the service learning project was to some extent "themed" to relevant issues in the firm's leadership development programs (e.g., self-knowledge, storytelling, learning from others, diversity) and, where appropriate and feasible, to strategic considerations of the business (e.g., corporate citizenship, consumer understanding, core purpose).

Reflections—before, during, afterwards.   Many studies suggest that focus on effective reflection is a primary enforcer of the power of service learning. Where self-awareness and consciousness-raising are intentions of the service learning project, it is essential to make personal as well as group reflection an integral and ongoing part of the program. There are a variety of tools that can aid reflection including materials and practice in journaling, "time outs" for note taking, and episodic group reflection (Raelin, 2002). Eyler (2002), as an example, offers a "reflection map" as a tool for organizing types of reflection for service learning activities. In several of the cases described, the leaders were introduced to learning concepts such as the ladder of inference, differences between advocacy and inquiry, and other reflection-in-action methodologies (Argyris, 1982; Schon, 1983). In addition, they were exposed to and practiced group dialogue techniques, including sitting in a circle. In the Unilever cases, this included the use of "I" statements to claim personal knowledge, "emptying" oneself of preconceptions and judgments, and "dealing with difficult issues"—precepts for group communication advanced by M. Scott Peck (1987, 1993) and a part of community building tradition (Mirvis, 2002).

Collective reflection. Certainly individuals can gain from service learning and make significant contributions to the service setting as solo participants. Learning as a group through collective reflection as described in the cases here has several advantages. First, otherwise reluctant individuals can be pulled into engagement by the group-as-a-whole and in any case find safety-in-numbers. Second, peer learners can be a source of orientation, stimulation and social support, and aid in interpreting what's going on and considering any implications. Third, there is the cohort effect whereby a group begins to see itself and is seen by others as having a unifying identity. This is a prerequisite to taking common action. But time needs to be given to developing the collective's capacity to work together. Here an exercise in setting expectations and joint ground rules between the execs and service setting members can be useful. Third-party facilitation of collective dialogue and reflections is of benefit, too.

Communities of practice. An additional design consideration in service learning programs, as illustrated by the two Unilever cases, is to ensure formal continuity of the programs to enable building communities of practice. YLF whose members have been meeting biennially over the past five years operates as a learning community where personal inquiry, small group dialogue, and communal reflection continuously broaden the curricula and deepen shared experiences (Ayas & Mirvis, 2002). The top leaders of UBF have been meeting annually to continue their transformational journey for the past three years. Unlike the YLF, they have been engaged in a variety of service learning projects over the years. Yet in both cases, the continuity of the program has enabled meeting the learning objectives more effectively. More time together, practice with dialogue, experience in sharing personal stories and expressing vulnerability, and a degree of psychological safety established from past encounters are no doubt factors contributing to success. Furthermore, over time, some of the norms of building community in a circle—speaking personally, listening thoughtfully, raising difficult issues, and talking from the heart—while originally "foreign" to these Asian leaders proved agreeable. Said one, "Last year it was hard an dpainful to talk openly as we were so new to each other. This year, it was great to see that words just poured out from everyone." Through repeated encounters, the process certainly matures to the point of collective thinking. "When we talk about building this community, we are very serious about it" added another, "so it takes time for us to progress, to make it happen."

FURTHER CONSIDERATIONS

We have chosen to elaborate on service learning projects in this chapter as it is a much less developed arena of project-based learning. We would argue, however, that executive development programs should be project-based and involve both service learning and business cases. Service learning projects often deepen and inform self-reflection that is crucial to the leadership development agenda and mostly missing from corporate training programs. While lacking in the depth on understanding the other or dealing with diversity or raising consciousness, projects on strategy, growth, and competitiveness counterbalance this introspective bent. The combination can be extremely beneficial.

In all of the cases illustrated here, service learning has been an integral part of the program but by no means the only element. For instance, at meetings of the YLF, academic and business experts have presented concepts and case studies on leadership, best practices in product innovation and marketing, and trends in branding. Several case studies on growing a business have been covered. In addition, young leaders regularly report on their home country markets and present case studies from their own businesses.

At their meeting in India the young leaders participated in a 3-month project where they developed a proposal for launching ice tea in India. Separated into three teams they undertook field studies of consumer segments and distribution channels in three major cities with mentors from the organization. After an intense week of working together they presented a joint proposal to the host country chairman and the board. Later a team worked on incorporating the requests of the board and helped the marketing team to prepare a trial launch.

For a recent gathering the young leaders organized into teams for a project on children's nutrition in Asia, each one of them focusing on their own region. At the meeting where they presented the findings to one another they prepared the input for the regional team in charge of the project that would be launched in Asia. No question that the learnings from all these projects were essential to and very enriching for the young leaders development.

While the focus in this chapter has been on service learning projects for executive development, the many linkages to self-awareness, learning from others, and deepening understanding of social and environmental conditions in the world is only sketched and illustrated here. Thankfully, other contributors to this book have delineated them more fully and provided a thoroughgoing reference list (see also Kendall, 1990; Cohen, 1994; Furco, 1996; Kolenko et al., 1996).

Showing, objectively, the connection between service-learning and the future behaviors necessary for effective management will always remain a challenge. Note, however, that the reflection quotations were collected through recording of reflections during the projects—taped and transcribed—and individual written entries once participants resumed their regular work. Since in two of the cases the groups continue to meet, there is ongoing evidence that the service learning experience has impact on their behavior. A plausible conclusion would be that the participants, their managers and their organizations are satisfied with the results as they choose to continue to participate and commit to the service.

Certainly in considering the organizational impact of service learning, factors of purpose and fit to corporate strategy and culture must be considered. Unilever's young leaders have made a strong connection to the orphanage and use their time spent in Vietnam to also renew their own sense of community. The UBF top leaders have been "awakened" to a new corporate purpose by their connections to nature, villagers, and communities. But whether or not service learning experiences will remain a part of the corporate strategy as their mission matures or a new generation of leaders takes charge remains to be seen.

There are, in turn, other dimensions of service learning for executives that might animate further research. What, for example, are the discrete benefits of service to versus interpersonal communication with community members? What are the tradeoffs in deciding between the depth and duration of each? Can the experiences described here, particularly given costs and demands on time and travel, be approximated in a classroom environment? Certainly they can be scaled accordingly: Shell US, for instance, has nonprofit entrepreneurs visit its corporate training center, rather than the other way around. Our own sense is that what matters are hands-on engagements in real-world subject matter and imagination-stretching experiences connecting to people, no matter the logistics and locale.

Finally, it is important to look into the impact of service learning experiences on the host setting. It's easy enough to equate sending executives out into orphanages or rural villages with industrial tourism or outright exploitation. Certainly, that was not the motivation of the companies discussed here. Moreover, they all made financial and material contributions to the groups and communities that hosted them and most of the executives offered valuable advice and service. Still, a closer look at the perceived degree of reciprocity between corporation and community groups (cf. Jacoby, 2003), and between individual business leaders and community members would help in assessing the value of these connections and inform the design of future encounters.

NOTE

1. More detailed accounts of some of these experiences and development programs can be found in Ayas and Mirvis (2002, 2004); Mirvis (2000); and Mirvis and Ayas (2003).

REFERENCES

Argyris, C. (1982). *Reasoning, learning, and action*. San Francisco: Jossey-Bass.

Argyris, C., & Schon, D.A. (1978). *Organizational learning: A theory of action perspective*. Reading, MA: Addison-Wesley.

Ayas, K., & Mirvis, P.H. (2002). Young leaders' forum in Asia: Learning about leadership, abundance, and growth. *Reflections, 4*(1), 33-42.

Ayas, K., & Mirvis, P.H. (2004). Bringing "mission" to life: Corporate inspiration from Indian communities. *Reflections, 5*(10), 1-12.

Ayas, K., & Zeniuk N. (2001). Project-based Learning: Building communities of reflective Practitioners. *Management Learning, 32*(1), 61-76.

Bringle, R.G., & Hatcher, J. A. (1996). Implementing service learning in higher education. *Journal of Higher Education*, 67, 221-223.

Bringle, R.G., & Hatcher, J. A. (1999, Summer).Reflection in service-learning: Making meaning of experience, *Educational Horizons*, 179-185.

Brown, K.A. (2000). Developing project management skills: A service learning approach. *Project Management Journal, 31*(4), 53-58.

Carver, R. (1996). Theory for practice: A framework for thinking about experiential education. *The Journal of Experiential Education, 19*(1), 8-13.

Cohen, J. (1994). Matching university mission with service motivation: Do the accomplishments of community service match the claims? *Michigan Journal of Community Service Learning, 1*, 98-104.

Earley, P.C., & Peterson, R.S. (2004). The Elusive Cultural Chameleon: Cultural Intelligence as a new approach to Intercultural training for the global manager. *Academy of Management Learning & Education, 3*(1), 100-115.

Eyler, J., & Giles, J. (1999). *Where's the learning in service learning?* San Francisco: Jossey-Bass.

Eyler, J. (2002). Reflection: Linking service and learning-linking students and communities. *Journal of Social Issues, 58*(3), 517-534.

Fombrun, C.J. (1996). *Reputation: Realizing value from corporate image*. Boston, MA: Harvard Business School Press.

Friedman, M. (1983). *The confrontation of otherness: In family, community and society.* New York: Pilgrim Press.

Fromm, E. (1956). *The art of loving.* New York: Harper & Row.

Furco, A. (1996). Service-learning: A balanced approach to experiential education. In The Corporation for National Service's (Eds.), *Expanding boundaries: Serving and learning* (pp. 2-6). Columbia, MD: Cooperative Education Association.

Galen, M., Greising, D., & Forest, A. (1994, September 26). How business is linking hands in the inner city. *Business Week*, 81-82.

Gardner, H. (1995). *Leading minds.* New York: HarperCollins.

Godfrey, P.C. (2000). A moral argument for service-learning in management education. In P.C. Godfrey & B.T. Grasso (Eds.), *Working for the common good: Concepts and models for service-learning in management.* Washington, DC: American Association for Higher Education.

Goleman, D. (1995). *Emotional intelligence.* New York: Bantam.

Hall, D.T., & Mirvis, P.H. (1995). Careers as lifelong learning. In A. Howard (Ed.) *The changing nature of work* (pp. 323-361). San Francisco: Jossey-Bass.

Jacoby, B. (2003). *Building partnerships for service learning.* San Francisco: Jossey-Bass.

Jacoby, B. (1996). Service-Learning in today's higher education. In B. Jacoby (Ed.), *Service learning in higher education: Concepts and practices* (pp. 3-25). San Francisco: Jossey-Bass.

Kendall, J.C. (1990.) *Combining service and learning: A resource book for community and public service, Vol. 1.* Raleigh, NC: National Society for Experiential Education.

Kolenko, T.A., Porter, G., Wheatley, W., & Colby, M. (1996). A critique of service-learning projects in management education: Pedagogical foundations, barriers, and guidelines. *Journal of Business Ethics, 15*(1), 133-142.

Kohn, A. (1990). *The brighter side of human nature: Altruism and empathy in everyday life.* New York: Basic Books.

Krieger, M. H. (1990). Broadening professional education: On the margins and between the niches. *Liberal Education, 76,* 6-10.

Lewin, K. (1946). Action research and minority problems. *Journal of Social Issues, 2*(4), 34-46.

McAleavey, S.J. (1996). Service-learning: Theory and rationale. In D. Droge (Ed.), *Disciplinary pathways to service learning.* Mesa, AZ: Campus Compact National Center for Community Colleges.

Mirvis, P.H. (2000). Transformation at Shell: Commerce and citizenship. *Business and Society Review,* 105-1, 63-84.

Mirvis, P.H. (2002). Community building in business. *Reflections, 3*(3), 45-51.

Mirvis, P.H., & Ayas, K. (2003). Reflective dialogue, life stories, and leadership development. *Reflections, 4*(4), 39-48.

Mirvis, P.H., Ayas, K., & Roth, G. (2003). *To the desert and back: The story of one of the most dramatic business transformation on record.* San Francisco: Jossey-Bass.

Peck, M.S. (1987). *The different drum: Community making and peace.* New York: Simon and Schuster.

Peck, M.S. (1993). *A world waiting to be born: Civility rediscovered*. New York: Doubleday.

Prochaska, J.O., Norcross, J.C., & DiClemente, C.C. (1994). *Changing for good.* New York: William Morrow.

Raelin, J. (2002). I don't have time to think! versus the art of reflective practice. *Reflections, 4*(1), 66-75.

Raelin, J. (2001). Public reflection as the basis of learning. *Management Learning, 32*(1), 11-30.

Revans, R. (1971) *Developing effective managers: A new approach to business education.* New York: Praeger.

Schein, E.H. (2003). On dialogue, culture, and organization learning. *Reflections, 4*(4), 27-38.

Schein, E.H. (1990). *Discovering your real values*. San Diego, CA: Pfeiffer.

Schindler-Rainman, E., & Lippitt, R. (1980). *Building the collaborative community: Mobilizing citizens for action*. Los Angeles: University of California Extension.

Schon, D. (1983). *The reflective practitioner*. New York: Basic Books.

Senge, P., Roberts, C., Ross, R., Smith, B., & Kleiner, A. (1994). *The Fifth Discipline fieldbook*. New York: Doubleday.

Shepherd, H.A. (1984). On the realization of human potential: A path with a heart. In M.B. Arthur, L. Bailyn, D.J. Levinson, & H.A. Shepherd (Eds.), *Working with careers*. New York: Graduate School of Business, Columbia University.

Smith, B., & Dodds, R. (1997). *Developing managers through project-based learning.* Aldershot/Vermont:Gower

Tichy, N. with N. Cardwell. (2002). *The cycle of leadership*. New York: Harper Business.

Vicere, A.A., & Fulmer, R.M. (1996). *Leadership by design*. Boston: Harvard Business School Press.

VonGlinow, M., Shapiro, D.L., & Brett, J.M. (2004). Can we talk, and should we? Managing emotional conflict in multicultural teams. *Academy of Management Review, 29*(4), 578-592.

Waddock, S. (2002). *Leading corporate citizens: Visions, values, and value added*. New York, NY: McGraw Hill.

Yerkes, R. (1998). Service learning revisited. *The Journal of Experiential Education, 21*(3), 117-118.

Zlotkowski, E. (1996). Opportunity for all: Linking service-learning and business education. *Journal of Business Ethics, 15*(1), 5-19.

CHAPTER 6

REAL WORLD TRANSFER OF PROFESSIONAL KNOWLEDGE

A Modification to Internship Learning

Jan Brace-Govan and Irene Powell

The pedagogical innovation described here was the addition of business mentors to an out-of-classroom, real world marketing internship project for final year undergraduate students. Where tertiary education passes on formalized and articulated knowledge, and internships offer the opportunity for experiential learning, the addition of mentors significantly enhanced the tacit knowledge available to the student interns. The inclusion of an experienced professional facilitated a "consultant-to-client" approach for the student in real world projects in non-profit sector SMEs. By giving students different kinds of relationships to manage, the exchange of tacit knowledge was extended beyond the usual supervisory role encountered in industry placements. Furthermore, the inclusion of a business mentor enabled the coordinating academic staff member to seek out placements where the marketing specific professional expertise was more limited. Presented through 3 cases studies, the evaluation of this transfer of knowledge draws out the significance of communication and problem solving. It also points to the increased reach of the internship process, improved industry links for the university, and a valued role for alumni.

Educating Managers through Real World Projects, 115–147
Copyright © 2005 by Information Age Publishing
All rights of reproduction in any form reserved.

INTRODUCTION

Internships are widely used to provide students with relevant work experience. However, while the nonprofit context is often of great interest to some students, it can have limited access to appropriate business expertise. This is not to suggest that the nonprofit sector is not of economic significance. Indeed Andreasen and Kotler have pointed to the rising interest in this sector over the last 20 years and the substantial contribution that non-profits make to the American economy (2003, pp. 8-12). Moreover many nonprofit undertakings are businesses of significance (Andreasen & Kotler, 2003). In practice though, there are very many smaller nonprofit organizations that can benefit from the involvement of supervised student projects. This chapter is based on the findings from an evaluation of an educational innovation that brought real world transfer of professional knowledge for marketing students into the nonprofit environment. The key point of difference here was the addition of business mentors to an out-of-classroom marketing internship project for final year undergraduate students. This enhanced the transfer of tacit knowledge, enabled experiential problem solving, and supported the extension of communication skills. Where much tertiary education passes on formalized and articulated knowledge, internships offer the opportunity for experiential learning. The addition of mentors significantly enhanced the tacit knowledge available to the student interns. The inclusion of an experienced professional facilitated a "consultant-to-client" approach for the student in real world projects in the nonprofit sector. By giving students different kinds of relationships to manage, the exchange of tacit knowledge was extended beyond the more commonplace supervisory role encountered in industry placements. Furthermore, the inclusion of a business mentor enabled the co-ordinating academic staff member to seek out placements where the marketing specific professional expertise was more limited. Finally, each case study draws out different communication processes that utilize variations of electronic and face-to-face communication, demonstrating the high level of flexibility that this innovation introduces to the internship process.

EXPERIENTIAL LEARNING AND INTERNSHIPS

Increasing interest in reality-based or experiential learning has brought a focus on internships and service learning. Experiential learning theory forms the rationale behind the value of the internship and is derived initially from Dewey's (1938/1963) assertion that learning benefits from doing, which was later developed into Kolb's (1984, p. 42) well-known experiential cycle. Kolb suggested that learning progressed through, and

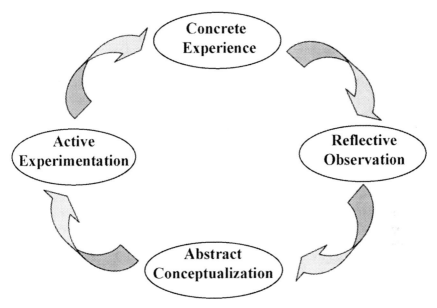

Figure 6.1.   Adapted from Kolb's experimental learning cycle (1984).

was encompassed by, four phases: concrete experience of the real world; reflective observation; abstract conceptualization; and active experimentation to discover cause and effect relationships, as shown in Figure 6.1. While a learner can start at any point on the cycle, Kolb asserted that all four processes needed to be incorporated for quality learning to occur. Kolb's model has underpinned the development of a range of experiential approaches to undergraduate teaching in business schools for example in marketing strategy (Razzouk, Seitz, & Rizkallah, 2003), services marketing (Gremler, Hoffman, Keaveney, & Wright, 2000), retailing (Seitz & Razzouk, 2002) and principles of marketing (Young, 2002). Others have utilized Kolb's framework for learning external to the classroom in field-based service learning (Petkus, 2000) and internships (Toncar & Cudmore, 2000).

Service learning does not have the exact same intention as an internship. Petkus (2000) describes a stronger element of community service, in this case in the nonprofit sector, that is not expected within an internship. Rama, Ravenscroft, Wolcott, and Zlotkowski's extensive literature review demonstrates the history and value of service learning. Often linked to civic responsibility and volunteering, service learning "is a form of active learning that involves service to one's community" (Rama et al., 2000, p. 658). This facet prompts Rama et al. (2000, p. 680) to specify in their guidelines for service learning that there needs to be a link to the curriculum. In contrast the internship is closely linked to the learning outcomes of the business course and generally refers to part-time field experience (Gault et al., 2000, p. 46) that "bridge(s) the gap between classroom learning and knowledge application in the real world" (Toncar & Cudmore, p. 55). Internships require a specified number of work hours, which may be paid or unpaid, where credit is awarded and supervision by an academic is provided (Gault et al., 2000; Toncar & Cudmore, 2000). The internship is widely recognized through a number of disciplines such as law, medicine and accounting, as well as the experience-based learning that is utilized in teaching, nursing, social work and psychology (Lewis & Williams, 1994, p. 7). Marketing too, has found the internship to be of value in training graduates for the workplace. Shuptrine and Willenborg (1998, p. 6) established a "statistically significant relationship" between students participating in a marketing internship and the satisfaction of their first employers and Floyd and Gordon (1998, p. 108) recommended internships as a key step in getting that first job. Gault et al. (2000, p. 52) offer empirical evidence that internships bridge the gap between university and the reality of the workplace reporting that students with internship experience earn higher salaries and have higher levels of job satisfaction. Toncar and Cudmore (2000, p. 55) assert that internships "combine a resume-building, career test drive with a hands-on, learning-by-doing work experience and afford students the opportunity to integrate theory and practice."

However, placing students in nonprofit organizations is not always straightforward. Many non-profits rely on volunteers or members who do not have formal marketing training or, do not fully understand the fundamentals of marketing (Klink & Athaide, 2004, p. 145; Petkus, 2000, p. 65). Marketing student interns can make a significant and desirable contribution in the spirit of service learning to the nonprofit organization's business approach and thinking (Petkus, 2000). Nonetheless, this poses a challenge to the organizing faculty member to ensure that students have a rewarding learning experience (Klink & Athaide, 2004). While nonprofit organizations are a valuable source of experiential learning and one that suits some students' interests, there is a potential lack of marketing expertise from the on-site professionals. These professionals have their own expertise of course. Moreover, working with differently qualified professionals is an excellent mirror to the real world where marketers are regularly required to work in team settings with a mixture of professional backgrounds. The situation does not arise for interns with large consumer-based organizations where a marketing professional is allocated to act as an on-the-job supervisor, in addition to the academic supervision of the faculty member. With rising student interest in the nonprofit sector, it was decided to proceed with a small scale trial of an educational innovation that would offer students an experiential learning opportunity with nonprofit organizations in a fully supported manner. The scale of the trial was principally determined by the number of students with the appropriate personal attributes and interests to tackle the situations available. This paper reports on the evaluation of this trial and makes recommendations for its continued implementation.

THE NUB OF THE PROBLEM: THEORY INTO PRACTICE

In many respects the nonprofit sector offers an excellent real world context for a marketing internship: interesting marketing issues, often challenging constraints that require ingenuity, and a welcoming, supportive culture for a novice professional. Furthermore it is a sector that is growing in size and influence (Andreasen & Kotler, 2003). There is one essential ingredient of the experiential learning model that is potentially incomplete in the nonprofit context and one for which universities receive a lot of criticism. The real world transfer of professional knowledge. As novices, the marketing students need a professional with expertise with whom they can consult for guidance. Although the academic supervisor is available to all internship students, a crucial element in commercial enterprises is the transfer of knowledge through working closely with a professional marketer. There are several different kinds of knowledge (Jarvis, 1992) and several different stages of expertise (Cornford, 1999; Daley, 1999). Experts have more context-specific knowledge, more experience, better organized knowledge structures, better thinking and problem solving strategies and special ways for handling information (Misko, 1995). Essentially experts know more about themselves as problem solvers and are better able to control their thinking than novices (Misko, 1995, p. 14). They tend to use more holistic knowledge (Cornford, 1999; Daley, 1999) where knowledge becomes tacit and internalized (Jarvis, 1992). Novice learners are different and they tend to have trouble sorting out what is important from what is not. They can be comparatively rule-governed and rely heavily on codified knowledge. They can become quite anxious about making mistakes and have a greater need for validation (Daley, 1999). While this has implications for selecting internship sites, it also draws our attention to the role of tacit knowledge, the situatedness of learning (Lave & Wenger, 1991) and, therefore, the value of problem-based learning (Wee, Kek, & Kelley, 2003). Recent discussions in the management literature around these issues has also renewed interest in mentoring (Cornford, 1999; Swap et al., 2001). A feature of internships is that there is a transfer of experience and knowledge through working along side an experienced professional. The authenticity of this real world experience is a key component of the internship (Toncar & Cudmore, 2000).

However, this also clearly implies that proximity to an experienced professional not only makes available the explicit knowledge of that professional practice, but can also draw on their tacit knowledge through being engaged in practical problems with them, thus replicating some elements of mentoring.

A POTENTIAL SOLUTION: "REFLECTIVE" COACH

The key contribution and innovation here were the inclusion of a business mentor into the internship process. Mentoring has a long history but is notoriously difficult to define (Friedman & Phillips, 2002; Bennetts, 2002) having moved into the vernacular to refer to a wide range of supportive relationships formed between a more expert adult and a novice (Cawyer, Simonds, & Davis, 2002). Kram's (1985) seminal and detailed work on the nature and influence of organizational mentoring identified several functions for the mentor: sponsorship; exposure-and-visibility; coaching; protection; and challenging assignments as well as psychosocial elements. In the context of a time-limited project not all of these functions would be either possible or desirable and a more narrowly focused definition is required. Sharing experience across the novice/expert divide (Gray & McNaught, 2001) was the essential support required for the nonprofit internship, and most closely resembled "coaching" (Kram, 1985, p. 28). Coaching in specific areas facilitates learning (Lankau & Scandura, 2002, p. 780) and would be a valuable student support in an organization where there was limited marketing knowledge. However, the role of the mentor was envisaged as much broader than solely coaching on marketing practices. Mentors are also helpful in influencing attitudinal responses to tasks (Lankau & Scandura, 2002, p. 782) and in developing reflectivity (Friedman & Phillips, 2002, p. 281).

Reflection on learning is a significant constituent of Kolb's experiential learning model and, furthermore, has been an important facet of management training. Schon's (1987) arguments in favor of the reflective practitioner are widely known and forge a link across experiential learning and mentoring. The conceptualization of the mentor as "reflective coach" is a valuable way in which to support novices and a mechanism to encourage reflective practice (Argyris & Schon, 1996; Nonaka & Takeuchi, 1995; Senge, 1990) within the specific framework of a nonprofit internship. The intended learning cycle of the internship that begins with concrete, real world tasks, requires abstract conceptualization, active experimentation and reflective observation, also relies on the presence of an "expert" with whom the student can engage to discover the role of the professional in a real life setting. This less tangible, more tacit knowledge of the professional is often conveyed through informal mentoring in the workplace (Cawyer et al., 2002) and in the more conventional internship is offered by the in-situ, supervisor professional. Tacit knowledge is the often unformulated and usually unarticulated knowledge that is an essential component of professional expertise which develops with experience and practice. Externalizing tacit knowledge is a complex process (Stenmark, 2000) often best achieved through personal interaction and "storytelling" (Swap et al., 2001). The transfer of this kind of knowledge from expert to novice is best achieved within a one-to-one relationship, through role modeling reactions and approaches to context specific tasks, such as writing and implementing a marketing plan. The mentoring process supports professional socialization and the internalization of knowledge (Swap et al., 2001, p. 98), both of which are integral to experiential learning theory. Acquiring the beginnings of such knowledge is the crucial element in the novice professional's experiential learning that has often been overlooked. Business mentors, or "reflective coaches," enabled students to enter the nonprofit sector where there was limited business support available and engage fruitfully with an internship.

INTERNSHIP AT MONASH UNIVERSITY

The internship at Monash University has been offered as a final year undergraduate option for ten years.[1] Initially around 60 students completed annually but more recently enrollment is twice that with the internship offered in each semester. Internships comprise fully assessed work experience in commercial workplaces with companies such as, Coca Cola, Nike, and Foote, Cone and Belding are usually undertaken within the marketing function. Interns work, unpaid, for either one day a week over a thirteen-week semester or, an equivalent block of time. This gives both students and organizations some flexibility in the arrangements. During the internship the student may be working on a specific project or, on day to day activities. Prior to the student intern going to the organization there are several processes in place. Firstly contact is made between the academic supervisor and the organization to discuss the guidelines for internship experiences and scrutinize the intended activities. The guidelines include a list of benefits of internships, examples of previous internship activities, an indicative list of activities that are considered appropriate, the responsibilities of the sponsoring company's supervisor (client supervisor) and details of the assessment the intern will undertake. To clarify which person will take responsibility for the intern, there is an agreement signed prior to commencement. The guidelines for the organizations are also reproduced in the outline provided to students in order that the process is transparent. This essential step establishes and manages expectations and ensures the scope of the project is appropriate to the individual student to be assigned. While reality-based learning should enlarge the student experience (Smith & Van Doren, 2004), nevertheless, the individuality of experience needs to be taken into account if the internship is to work at its best (Lee & Caffarella, 1994). In addition, when the academic supervisor establishes the extent of the project with the external organization and manages their expectations regarding the student capabilities, they are also able to ensure that the task and its assessment can be individually tailored, as well as valid and reliable. Once the groundwork has been done, the student is introduced to the organization and their intended work experience, usually through a meeting with the academic supervisor, the client supervisor and the intern all present. This is another opportunity for the academic supervisor to manage expectations, this time with both parties present. Although quite detailed in the initial stages, this process gives the intern the best opportunity for self-directed learning and fosters personal autonomy in the student (Lee & Caffarella, 1994, p. 45).

It is important that the objectives for internships are expressed broadly but clearly to the students in terms of what they should be able to do on completion of the internship. For example students will be able to provide a thorough analysis of a marketing task; critically and realistically appraise the applicability of theory in a marketing task area; demonstrate an understanding of the practicalities of working within an organization. The skills that will be developed and reinforced during the internship include observation, reflection, application, research, literature searches, in company research and report writing. This approach is consistent with the template proposed by Klink and Athaide (2004) to incorporate service learning in their marketing course.

Measuring the outcome of learning is expected of any university education. However in the case of internships, as in other applications of knowledge, there is no specific body of curriculum content that would benefit from being examined through a conventional examination paper. Instead alternative assessment strategies are required that more appropriately evaluate the stated objectives of internships. This "authentic assessment" may use a wide variety of techniques such as performance evaluations; criterion referenced appraisals; systematic observation by instructors, clients, peers and self; portfolios and journals (Wellington, Thomas, Powell, & Clarke, 2002). Authentic assessment is designed to evaluate learning outcomes that require students to demonstrate competencies and skills in real world settings using relevant problem solving techniques. In instances where students are required to be able to apply their knowledge rather than simply know facts, authentic assessment has provided better measures of student learning. For example Fall (1998) suggests that the area of authentic assessment research in higher education, especially in her specialty of public relations, is virtually untapped, but the resulting motivation and critical thinking skills are much improved for students if real world projects are used.

Thus assessment is an important part of the educational value of business internships (Clark, 2003) and in this instance there are three components. Reflection on the experience by the learner is encouraged and supported through a reflective journal (Birenbaum & Amdur, 1999). At the end of the internship students submit an academic report which is assessed by the academic supervisor on the basis of its relevance to their learning, its originality, its professionalism and business standards, and that it is a worthwhile topic for both the organization and the student's learning. In some instances this report can be a practical document for the organization, such as a marketing plan. Lastly the student is assessed by the organization on their progress and this offers the student an opportunity for constructive feedback on their performance from their client supervisor. The students' overall grade is made up of the reflective journal (10%), the academic report (60%) and the organization's assessment of the student (30%).

An opportunity arose to place some students as marketing interns in state run schools in Melbourne, the metropolitan center of Victoria, Australia. There were three students for whom this opportunity for experiential learning in the nonprofit environment was appropriate. Innovation was required to overcome the reduced access to professional marketing experience in comparison to other internship placements. The Alumni organization was contacted to find suitable business mentors who had studied marketing to either bachelor or master level and had successfully practiced marketing for at least five years. Academic supervision of course remained in place. Several Alumni volunteered to mentor, and three were selected based on the suitability of their professional experience to the proposed nonprofit-based marketing projects. The academic supervisor prepared guidelines for the mentors and the client supervisors, established the general scope of the projects and arranged meetings to introduce the interns to their assigned supervisors and mentors. A careful balance between mentored activity and independent student work for both the nonprofit client and academic assessment needed to be established by the academic supervisor. As well the project was discussed with the nonprofit client in some detail to ensure, firstly, that there was a project of reasonable size for the student and, that it relied sufficiently on the principles of marketing to be appropriate. However, it needs to be made clear that the nonprofit supervisor was a professional in their own right, with valuable expertise and tacit knowledge to share, not only with

Academic staff member
responsible for Internship
co-ordination and communicates
with all participants

Experienced Professional
(Business Mentor
Reflective Coach)
brings
Explicit and tacit professional
knowledge to the project

Novice Professional
(Student)
brings
Idealised, or codified, knowledge
that is predominantly theoretical
to the project

**Differently Experienced
Professional**
(Client Supervisor Principal)
brings
Context specific explicit and
tacit professional knowledge
to the project

Figure 6.2.   Lines of interaction and knowledge sharing in a mentored internship learning experience.

the student, but also with the mentor. During the course of the projects it emerged that there were three different kinds of communication and exchange taking place as shown in Figure 6.2.

- between the novice professional (the intern) and the experienced professional (the mentor);
- between the novice professional (the intern) and the differently experienced professional (the nonprofit client supervisor);
- between the experienced professional (the mentor) and the differently experienced professional (the nonprofit client supervisor).

The experiences of students, nonprofit supervisors and mentors were evaluated using the student learning outcomes as criteria. The learning outcomes for students suggest that this is a valuable, well-supported way in which to introduce nonprofit internships to fully assessed fieldwork options and are described below.

METHOD FOR EVALUATION

Although Kolb's learning cycle is the basis of experiential learning, it is also the case that marketing as a business discipline has criteria which its graduates need to meet. In other words what components are required of real life experiences that will encourage a student to reflect, conceptualize and experiment in an appropriate way for marketing? Floyd and Gordon (1998) established that four skills were of particular importance and were teachable (or able to be developed) through university education: communication skills; problem-solving skills; work experience and interpersonal skills. Employers paid particular attention to problem solving skills (Floyd & Gordon, 1998, pp. 104-105). The aim of the evaluation would be to ascertain the presence of these four important learning areas for the student.

A qualitative case study methodology was the most appropriate to assess the potential for this innovation in field-based experiential learning for marketing in the nonprofit context. Yin (1994) suggests that case studies have a "distinctive place in evaluation research" (p. 15). A point on which Stake (2000) would concur. This evaluative project is an "intrinsic case study" (Stake, 2000, p. 437) where the investigator seeks clarity and understanding about a particular case in order to make decisions or extract implications. Evaluative research can be more pragmatically based than other kinds of research (Pitman & Maxwell, 1992, p. 736) with a focus on describing and interpreting (Patton, 1990). In education this approach to evaluation is commonplace where research is "predominantly practical work that provides concrete and specific guidance" (Pitman & Maxwell, 1992, p.736). Qualitative methods are especially relevant when the experience of the students and others are of paramount interest (LeCompte, 1994, p. 32) and where there are multiple sources of data from an uncontrolled naturalistic environment (Yin, 1994). At the same time the case study is "tailor made for exploring new processes with the intention of illuminating those processes and allows the contextualization of meanings and actions" (Hartley, 1994, p. 212).

There were three nonprofit sites and therefore three triads of an intern, mentor and client, making nine participants in all. The students, two female and one male, were in their last semester of an undergraduate business degree and aged around 21 years. The clients were all principals of state government schools: two were principals of primary schools of around 350 pupils (one male and one female) and one (male) was the principal of a secondary school of around 1200 pupils. The principals were in their late forties or early fifties. One primary school was located in an economically disadvantaged suburb and the other two schools were in suburbs of moderate economic status. The mentors, two women in their thirties and one man in his late forties, were alumni of Monash University with a range of business experience in terms of years and type of expertise. The triads were arranged by the faculty member who co-ordinates the internship unit.

There were a number of sources of data available to the investigator. The investigator was present at some meetings held through the projects. This gave information about the actual projects and their progress, which was noted in the investigator's field diary. The meetings also gave the investigator a sense of the rapport amongst the various teams. All participants were aware of the investigator's role and had given their permission to have notes taken and documents examined. The assessment documents were made available to the investigator at the end of the internships which included the reflective journals, academic reports and the assessments by the client organization. Lastly the investigator conducted a semi-structured in-depth interview, lasting approximately an hour with each participant. The interviews described what the projects entailed and the tasks students had pursued, and explored the support offered by the mentor and the nonprofit client supervisor. They were asked about their communication with each other and about the advantages and disadvantages of taking part in such a process. The interviews were transcribed and then read closely for significant information around the themes identified earlier as important to marketing graduates: *communication; problem solving; transferring theory into practice; and interpersonal skills.* All the materials were analyzed and integrated to form a case study narrative using a modified version of the constant comparative technique (Strauss & Corbin, 1998).

The evaluation set out to ascertain whether the nonprofit environment offered the students an appropriate internship experience. Sweitzer and King (1999) identify five stages of experience for the student intern. Stage one, *Anticipation*, is when the student first starts their internship and experiences a combination of excitement, trepidation, eagerness and anxiety. Questions for the student that are to the fore include who will help and at this stage they need to work on building relationships. Stage two, *Disillusionment*, occurs when the difference between the anticipated experience and the reality that is possible becomes clear. Sweitzer and King advise students to work through these differences as they can be a great opportunity to learn and to learn about oneself. The third stage they call *Confrontation*, and it is during this phase that the student needs to acknowledge issues and problems and take another look at their expectations, goals and skill set. They may need to take steps to bolster their support system but most importantly they need to keep on working because confidence comes from grappling with the issues and finding a resolution. Stage four, *Competence*, brings feelings of excitement, accomplishment and invest-

Table 6.1.   Five Stages of Internship

Anticipation
Introduction to the project
Initial communication

Disillusion
Problem identification
Task requirements

Confrontation
Problem solving
Seek help/support/information

Competence
Knowledge sharing
Transfer of expertise
Mentor input

Culmination
Outcomes
Evaluation

Source: Adapted from Sweitzer and King (1999).

ment in work. There is a sense of emerging professionalism with a realization that excellence is not synonymous with perfection. The final and fifth stage is *Culmination* where there is pride in the work and some sadness about leaving the context. There can be guilt about not doing enough and leaving tasks that seem to be midstream.

The links to Kolb's experiential learning model are clear with experience, reflection, experimentation and abstraction contained in the chronology of stages through the internship reflecting the development of the learner from excited novice to emerging professional. Themes of communication, problem solving, transferring theory into practice and interpersonal skills were used in conjunction with the chronological framework provided by the five stages of the internship to structure a coherent, comparable narrative for each case as shown in Table 6.1. The evaluation's focus was on the educational experience of the students and so the learners' experiences were the base across which the triads were compared, with other materials and the interviews with the client supervisor and the mentor contributing either supporting or contradictory evidence. Thus, the presentation of each triad case continues with the learner-centered orientation of the experiential model. This is justified on the basis that it is the learning outcomes that are paramount here, although, as will be shown later, there are positive outcomes for all parties.

Although the academic supervisor established that there was a suitable project, there was flexibility in the arrangement too. Therefore, the first task for each student was to meet the academic supervisor, the mentor and client to take an initial briefing. It was then the student's responsibility to define the tasks for the project and carry it through with as much or as little support as they negotiated.

CASE STUDIES

The following case studies each illustrate different issues that arose through the evaluation of the mentored internship process in the nonprofit environment. In the first case study the business mentor supported the student in selecting a project in an unfamiliar area. The student went on to perform well in the task but this case draws attention to the need for flexibility in timing. Often marketing education's focus on the for profit sector assumes significant budget allocation. The challenge in the second case study was to apply learning within the constraints of a limited budget. With the support of her mentor this challenge was successfully met but this case raised some issues around communication. The last case illustrates the value of best practice to deliver better than expected outcomes to the client. All three cases show the supportive knowledge sharing role of the mentor and the broader, enhanced learning experience for the student.

CASE STUDY STORY 1: THE PROPOSAL

Anticipation

Introduction to the Project

The student in the secondary school internship was introduced to the client, school and mentor at a meeting in which he was offered a choice of three well defined projects. The client gave an outline of each project and the meeting was a free flowing exchange of information. Then the group was taken on a tour of the school.

Initial Communication

At first the student, John,[2] leaned toward taking a project that slotted in well with his previous study interests, developing a direct mailing campaign for the performing arts facility. However, when he telephoned his business mentor to discuss his choice, the student was persuaded that he had the requisite skills to tackle the larger, and more daunting project of writing the brief for a $4.3 million community access information technology center. The mentor's specific expertise lay in this area and the student was reassured that he would get the support that he needed to overcome his qualms. This initial communication went well and John had taken a protected step toward extending his written communication skills.

He also made an appointment to go and discuss the detail of the project with the client supervisor.

Disillusion—Daunted

Problem Identification

The project was quite well defined before John took up the internship [Principal 1, p. 7: Mentor 1, p. 3]. For example, there was access to a range of supporting material such as: targeted audience research and financial information. In addition, the client supervisor "knew exactly what output he wanted" [Mentor 1, p. 7]. However, John's initial excitement was turning to trepidation as he began to realize the nature of the work before him. The requirement of the task was that the student sift through the information that was available and decide how best to approach the writing task, but as noted earlier, identifying priorities is difficult for novice professionals. As John notes in his journal, "I am not sure how to begin to put together a government proposal" [Journal 1, p. 2].

Task Requirements

The outcome of the project was to be an application for government funding for a large entrepreneurial information technology venture, partly attached to the school itself and partly situated in a local center of commercial activity. John would need to identify relevant information, prioritize and then present appropriately for the audience for which it was intended. And at this stage he expressed his conflicting responses. On the one hand it was "my first real exposure to a practical experience … seeing how business and government are related" but he also thought it would be "a massive exercise where you'd have marketing consultants and it would take you know a good year to get the funds" [Student 1, p. 2].

Confrontation

Problem Solving

The project also required that the student obtain financial and strategic support from local businesses, an understanding of the processes of lobbying government, and the needs of writing a business proposal. There are significant learning opportunities provided for the student in this nonprofit internship. However, the scale of the exercise was a problem that needed to be addressed by this student.

Seek Help/Support/Information

Most of the information for this project and its intended direction came from meetings and discussions with the client supervisor. After gathering information from the client, John began by writing a first draft and sending this to his mentor for comment. All communication with the mentor, after the initial meeting, was through email with drafts and comments being sent between the two.

Competence

Knowledge Sharing

The knowledge that the mentor was able to pass on to the student occurred primarily through their email exchanges. John learned that business communication is succinct, to the point and follows an expected order. The mentor also pointed out that John "didn't have any financials in the first draft and he ended up being pushed into going to (the principal/client) and sitting down and working through all the financials" [Mentor 1, p. 13].

Transfer of Expertise

However, there was more to these exchanges with the client supervisor than simply gathering information. As the mentor suggested that John "hadn't really understood the information up to that stage and so there was a bit of discussion backwards and forwards about the financials and how it would work . . . what was infrastructure capital and what was working capital and what was recurrent expenditure" [Mentor 1, p. 13]. Therefore, in addition, to accessing the mentor's expertise in business documentation, John also had access to the client supervisor's expertise in financial planning.

Mentor Input

The student described the mentor's input as "pretty extensive," "really helpful" and "really specific" [Student 1, p. 5]. Indeed, the mentor was instrumental in driving the student toward a higher standard of performance. Toward the end of the project the mentor and the student engaged in an email discussion around the point at which to conclude the project. While the student expressed being content with a document that would gain him a pass mark with the University, the mentor argued, successfully that "next year you are going to be out there working professionally as a marketeer, . . . and you need to be able to produce professional standard documentation and you haven't quite got there yet. So let's keep going" [Mentor 1: p. 15].

Culmination

Outcomes

In practical terms, the outcome for John was the opportunity to "make decisions and show initiative" [Principal 1, p. 7] in a project that was more entrepreneurial than the usual day-to-day running of a school [Principal 1, pp. 4-5]. This was invaluable experience and John appreciated the usefulness of this and felt better equipped and "more confident out in the workforce" [Student 1, p. 7]. Furthermore the student's practical experience included the encouragement to be meet professional standards. "This internship . . . has made me realize that what I have learnt in the last 4 years can be applied to 'real' working environments" [Journal 1, p. 6]. The outcome for the school was not only a proposal for funds, but also the creation of new relationships for the school [Principal 1, p. 6]. The principal reported these relationships were the result of the school having access to "someone who has a level of expertise that is not normally available to the school" [Principal 1, p. 10], ergo the mentor.

Evaluation

Overall then this triad reported an exchange of knowledge and skills between the student and mentor. This was confirmed by both participants and culminated in concrete benefit for the client/principal. In addition, the student engaged in problem solving through his interactions with the client supervisor as well. All three were able to identify beneficial advantages from their participation: additional expertise for the school and a proposal written; valuable practical experience and increased work confidence for the student; and for the mentor the project was an interesting way to refresh some knowledge as well as a source of altruistic pleasure.

The disadvantage that all three participants identified was the narrow and somewhat forced time frame for the project. The issue here was that the semester did not fit exactly with the timelines driven by the project itself. For example, at the mentor's suggestion, the student had arranged a high level meeting with a significant politician to further the lobbying process. The Principal had invited the student to join them but the student was caught up in examinations and could not attend, much to his disappointment. In addition, although the student produced a report for the end of semester, in fact the project still had some further iterations to work through, including feedback from the politician. This somewhat false ending to attend to the University's needs for assessment had not disadvantaged the student in any way, but it would have removed him from the process before the project's real completion. All three wanted there to be a more flexible approach to allow students to work through to completion and allow for timing delays and unforeseen developments in projects. In this instance, the student continued his involvement in the project in any case on a casual basis.

CASE STUDY STORY 2: ONLY $2,000

Anticipation

Introduction to the Project

Initially this student, Trish, toured the school and met briefly with the principal. The student was formally introduced to the primary school project through a meeting that included the client/principal, the academic supervisor, and the business mentor. During this meeting there was discussion around the school's background, current circumstances and needs. The suggestion from the client was that the school needed a "promotion plan." In stark contrast to the first case study, the budget for this was a challenging $2,000.

Initial Communication

The first meeting was informative and useful and the student left with the impression from the client that she was to write a promotion plan. She duly pursued the marketing communications tack and found an outline of a promotion plan from a reputable textbook and proceeded to organize her work schedule to deal with the problem before her. There was a meeting with the school's marketing and promotions committee and a further exchange of information with a focus on a marketing communications plan.

Disillusion

Problem Identification

However, the first meeting with her business mentor revealed that the client had not used the appropriate marketing vocabulary and that what was actually required was a marketing plan. Trish "got over the initial anguish of having to start again" [Student 2, p. 1], and recognized the extensive support and direction that she was receiving from her mentor.

Task Requirements

The mentor explained to Trish what was required of her through examples of marketing plans and outlines of the tasks that matched with those plans. Effectively this was a complete restart on the project.

Confrontation

Problem Solving

With a clearer picture of what was required of her from the practical support of her mentor, Trish returned to the school and conducted a second meeting with the marketing and promotions subcommittee. This time she ran a SWOT analysis with the group and "brain stormed strategies" [Student 2, p. 3]. There were also further meetings with the client supervisor to clarify directions and maintain a good flow of information in addition to the research that the student was doing on the local area and its primary schools.

Seek Help/Support/Information

The combination of meetings with the school's subcommittee and the client supervisor, as well as her research, were building a detailed perspective on potential marketing strategies. There were also regular meetings with the mentor to discuss issues and to review drafts of the developing marketing plan. This student preferred face-to-face meetings and made only cursory use of email and telephone.

Competence

Knowledge Sharing

Sharing knowledge was a dynamic element of this particular case. Firstly there was the direct business input from the mentor which was invaluable to the student, not only in terms of practical advice in constructing and writing the marketing plan but also important in being able to decipher the needs of a client. This was particularly evident when the client/principal, who was experienced in the education sector, but had limited marketing experience and therefore did not use exact vocabulary when describing the needs of the school. Secondly, there was the shared knowledge that the student brought to the school. This was a source of great delight to Trish and a significant boost to her confidence in terms of presenting herself in the business world. She had not realized the extent of her own knowledge until she had needed to explain business concepts such as a SWOT analysis and the 7Ps to the sub committee [Student 2, pp. 5-6]. Moreover, during meetings with the principal, when the student used marketing terminology the principal jotted these down with meanings attached in a "glossary type thing" [Student 2, p. 5].

Transfer of Expertise

In this instance the transfer of expertise had not been solely one way. Certainly the student had learned a great deal both from her business mentor in making the shift from theory to practice, and from the client/ principal in developing a clear idea of the concerns of a non profit organization, which is an area of interest for future paid work for this student [Student 2, p. 8]. In addition Trish had passed on some business concepts to the school and the principal. There was one last connection that was made where the business mentor supported the principal in sourcing a piece of promotional material quickly and at an affordable price.

Mentor Input

The business mentor was especially supportive over the shift from theory to practice. There were differences in the way that marketing plans were set out and the kind of information that was required, particularly in the strategy section. In this section the student was following a format from a class exercise but the mentor showed her that what was required were the advantages, disadvantages and costs so that the client could make informed decisions for themselves. The mentor was also helpful when it came to identifying appropriate strategies for the school's business environment. It was not appropriate to be directly aggressive with a closely located competitor [Mentor 2, p. 1]. However, the mentor had some experience in the corporate sector with a covert less direct approach [Mentor 2, p. 3].

Culmination

Outcomes

The client/ principal was extremely pleased with the input from the student and described the marketing plan as a "comprehensive document" [Principal 2, p. 5] and they will "implement a lot of the ideas" [Principal 2, p.11]. The principal also noted the business concepts that the student had introduced saying "she was very good at explaining that (SWOT and 7Ps) and we took that on board" [Principal 2, p. 4]. Trish said her "experience in the real world just seems to be invaluable" [Student 2, p. 4] most particularly because she has an interest in working the in the nonprofit context. With special mentions of realizing her own depth of knowledge, this student clearly received a boost to her confidence as well as developing the practical aspects of her skills.

Evaluation

In general then this triad was very successful with knowledge transfers along several lines in the relationship: client to student and student to client; mentor to student; and mentor to client. The student's confidence and practical skills improved and she also confirmed the area of marketing that interested her. The school received a "thorough," "practical," "affordable" marketing plan" [Principal 2, p. 5] and were able to communicate the special needs that the school faced in its specific business context. All three participants were able to find advantages to their experience: a comprehensive document for the school and an opportunity to do some self-evaluation and "pull their socks up" [Principal 2, p. 2]; an understanding of marketing in a real context for the student; and for the mentor it was good "professional development" [Mentor 2, p. 38].

Although all three were positive about their experience, they were also able to offer some constructive criticism. The student was very positive about the support that she received from the mentor and from the academic in charge of the internship. However, she suggested that a syndicate group of other internees would have been a good source of peer support. The mentor was enthusiastic about the extent of her involvement but she found the need for face-to-face meetings onerous and would have preferred a more time efficient method of communicating with the student, such as email.

CASE STUDY STORY 3: SURVEY-BASED STRATEGY

Anticipation

Introduction to the Project

The third student's initial contact with the client was in the company of the academic in charge of the internship. This was a pleasant, informative meeting in which the client/ principal described the school environment and business context. The mentor was not able to be present.

Initial Communication

This principal had some business training and was familiar with business language. Even so the student, Stella, had trouble at first discerning whether the project was to design a brochure or to write a marketing plan. However, she took on additional discussions with the academic supervisor who had been present at the meeting, and initiated contact with her mentor.

Disillusion

Problem Identification

This early confusion put Stella a bit off balance [Student 3, p. 6], but through these early discussions, and additional contact with the principal/client via email, it was established that the aim of the project was to increase enrolments at the school. Stella was guided toward writing a marketing plan to address this issue with a particular focus on enrolments for the first year of school, called "Prep" in Australia.

Task Requirements

With the overall direction of the project agreed on as a marketing plan to increase Prep enrolments, Stella identified which tasks to pursue. Her mentor was especially helpful in coaching her on how to approach a brain storming session with the school committee and also in the structuring of the marketing plan. "Mentor provided some really useful advice in relation to the report structure and things to include and what not to include. Her advice took me away from my academic mind set on the structure of the report to make it suitable for the reader. I now have a clear idea of what I need to do and how" [Journal 3, p. 2].

Confrontation

Problem Solving

In order to give the marketing plan some direction, the student believed that it was important to have a clear concept of the target audience. Stella resolved to conduct a survey of the preschool and child care centers in the area that would have children preparing to go to school for the first time the next year. Although neither the principal nor the mentor were particularly supportive of this task, Stella decided that knowing the audience well had been a key concept from the theories taught during her course and proceeded to hand-deliver the surveys–a strategy which netted her almost a 20% response rate in a week.

Seek Help/Support/Information

At first the student returned to the academic in charge of the internship to clarify the role of the mentor. Once that was clear in her mind, throughout the project this student relied on the ongoing support from her mentor. They met only three times face to face. The rest of their communication was through email where the student used her mentor as an effective sounding board "just to confirm" what she was doing [Student 3, p. 7] and "run things past her" [Student 3, p. 11]. The process of the survey was itself a useful one for Stella because she found that she got a better understanding of the context in which the school was located through "talking to the kinder teachers and just sort of seeing the parents" [Student 3, p. 4]. Although the principal had initially been informative about the school's situation, by this stage in the project he was unavailable due to illness and then away through the school holiday period, so Stella had difficulty contacting him. However the mentor is easily accessible via email and the relationship developed well through the process of designing the survey.

Competence

Knowledge Sharing

The mentor was especially helpful in how to approach the report and putting the marketing plan into a format and structure that was informative for the school, for example fleshing out the recommendations with a calendar. Another example of students sharing knowledge with members of the nonprofit organization occurred in this internship. Stella was pleased to discover that her ideas and strategies were well received by the school committee, and said this "boosted my confidence" [Student 3, p. 13].

Transfer of Expertise

The transfer of expertise from the mentor to Stella was clear with ideas for the marketing plan's final report and how to approach a survey. The mentor also made suggestions on how to conduct a brainstorming session and met with the student to run her through some meeting strategies. She used many of the tips that she would normally use in supporting her staff [Mentor 3, p. 7] and found the student to be "independent and self-sufficient" [Mentor 3, p. 4].

Mentor Input

The mentor's advice was welcomed by Stella and sought on a regular basis through email and included suggestions on how to incorporate the findings from the survey, and how to develop recommendations.

Culmination

Outcomes

Overall the experience of the student and the mentor was very positive. The student had initially expected to take her internship with a large corporation and initially was disappointed with her final option. However, after the experience she was enthusiastic and had changed her mind completely because it was a "lot more involving" [Student 3, p. 12]. Furthermore she was bowled over by the positive reception she had at the school committee [Student 3, p.13]. The mentor enjoyed the altruism of supporting programs such as this and found that it dovetailed nicely with work that she does with her junior colleagues. The principal/client expressed concerns about the time frame for the project finding it difficult to fit it into that stage in the school year. However, the marketing plan that the student presented to the school became "part of the Assistant Principal's performance management plan" [Principal 3, p.10], which seemed to be a strong indication of the success of the student's strategy advice.

Evaluation

In general then the triad had a successful outcome: a marketing plan for the school that will be implemented; a mentoring experience with a willing student; and a more diverse and rounded internship experience for the student. There was knowledge transfer from the mentor to student and also for the student the practical experience of the project.

There were also some issues that each of the participants raised. In the light of her failed application to a large corporation, the student suggested a list of questions in the format of an interview schedule for the students to use when trying to arrange internships with bigger companies. The mentor demonstrated keen involvement and would have liked some kind of formalized reporting procedure, along the same lines as the client supervisor's assessment of the intern. The principal suggested that the timing of the project could have been improved by the intern working half time across two semesters. In spite of the inherent difficulty arising out of the differences in term dates between universities and schools, there are advantages for the student in a more focused time frame.

CONCLUDING REMARKS

The case studies detailed above clearly show the value of problem-based learning in a service oriented experiential learning environment (Petkus, 2000; Wee et al., 2003). A number of elements need to be present such as good quality support from the academic supervisor including clear guidelines for all stakeholders, a willing supervisor on-site and a suitable project. The addition of a business mentor offered a dynamic, consultant type role for the student and enhanced their learning experience. These case studies also drew out some particular themes from the grounded analysis: communication; interpersonal skills; problem solving' and the-

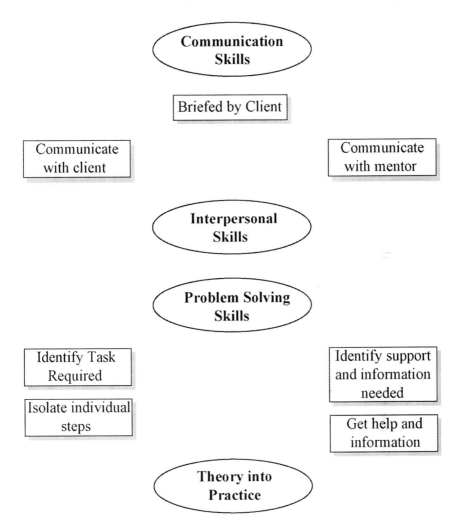

Figure 6.3.   Events that encourage skill development and knowledge exchange.

ory into practice. Furthermore, these skills were especially apparent through certain exchanges and loosely linked to each other as shown in Figure 6.3.

Communication

Communication was a key skill (Floyd & Gordon, 1998) and came through these internships strongly as a central pivot on which other learning depended. For example, all the processes that were part of Stella's internship involved communication of some kind. There was verbal communication with a broad range of people: the client to establish parameters around the identified task; contacts who knew the target audience (kinder teachers and school council members); her mentor for access to valuable expertise; and there was written communication in the survey and the report. Apart from giving Stella real world experience in communication across a diversity of people this also mirrored the skills required of a "team worker." This valuable experience was closer to the real world than the more usual group project at university. In addition, for various reasons most of the communication in this triad was conducted through email, thus arriving even closer to the real world of today. Moreover, the mentor and the principal never met or spoke to each other; therefore, Stella was the "driver" behind all the communication. This gave Stella experience in a consultant-type role that held far more reality than role-playing at university.

In the second case, Trish preferred face to face communication. However, this mentor found the process to be quite demanding and remarked that it was harder to manage one's time when there are face-to-face obligations. On the other hand, the principal in this case found face-to-face meetings preferable, as did the parents of the school. Once again the intern found the reality of the process and her pivotal communication role invaluable in her personal development. Communication in John's case was a balance between a client/principal that allowed time for meetings and a mentor that preferred the flexibility of email. Again the experience extended the student.

The crucial question in the evaluation was how did the student interns find their experiences? At first Stella had been disappointed because she had wanted to go to a large well-known multinational. So how did the primary school match up? Stella had conferred with her friends who had got into the large multinational and where they had been "assistants," whereas she had done everything "from the consulting to the research to the end result to the implementing" [Stella, p. 12]. In comparison to her friends, she believed she had experienced a broader range of tasks and acted more independent. John too had conferred with friends and thought theirs had been a very different experience. Perhaps his had not been so "cut throat as corporate life" [John, p. 8] but it had still been very much about business and was a "valuable experience" [John, p. 11] as well as a pleasant social one. Trish was especially pleased with her work experience because it was real, and people might actually do some of the things she had suggested. This intern was also delighted because her interest lies with the nonprofit sector and she had become a bit jaded with the focus that marketing has on the larger corporations. The culmination of the communication experiences and the setting meant that overall this was closely linked to improvements in interpersonal skills.

Interpersonal Skills

Developing lines of communication with older adults who have the expertise of senior professionals to offer was also practical, real world experience in developing interpersonal skills. Moreover, the mix of more than one professional background gave a taste of reality that was extended through their interactions with lay clients. Marketers frequently have to convey the intentions and meaning of their professional practice to those less informed about marketing and this experience was not only valuable but very difficult to replicate in the classroom. In all instances the mentors went to some lengths to support the students in this through being available, responding to emails and role modeling appropriate communication skills for leading meetings. Also, in all cases, there were opportunities to interact with members of the public in the role of advising professional for the nonprofit organization. This type of interpersonal skill building was particularly re-enforcing and positive for the interns and showed a generosity on the part of the client principals in providing these opportunities.

Problem Solving

A broad range of problems were presented to these interns who responded to the challenges well, in spite of having moments of doubt. The comments offered around the value of the nonprofit internship and the elation the students express conveys the value of the skills developed here. During his interview the principal of the secondary school specifically mentioned the need to remember that these are student projects and that students need the opportunity to choose. He certainly went to some trouble to offer John three options and in so doing also presented John with the need to choose and thus make a commitment. It is a strategy that is worth considering, although not having the options available in the smaller organizations did not seem to be a hindrance to the experiential learning process. There was evidence of the transfer of expertise, both tacit (demonstrating how to conduct a brainstorming session with non-marketers) and explicit in examples of marketing plans, surveys and business report writing. These outcomes were accomplished through the students' identifying the tasks required, identifying the support that they needed, isolating individual steps, and sourcing help and information. Through these mechanisms the projects were progressed, utilizing the aforementioned communication and interpersonal skills and in the experience the theoretical knowledge conveyed by universities was converted into practice.

Theory into Practice

The transfer of theory into practice encapsulated the invigorating moments that the interns experienced. Leading a brainstorming session, explaining SWOT analysis and the 7Ps to discover that they are part of a professional marketer's toolkit, and composing a report that was presented to a politician were all significant moments. In this process, the role the mentors played was crucial and the transfer of experience from expert to novice through a practical, real world context was demonstrated in every case. The structure of a marketing plan, the expression used in business documents, and the dress rehearsal for leading a meeting were all conveyed effectively.

Finally there is the reflection that the interns provide in their journals which conveys in vibrant tones the excitement that they feel from their first experience of practical, real world marketing. Sweitzer and King (1999) note the importance of the journal for the student experiential learner is recording the feelings and events that bring out the key moments in the internship. It was also important for the students to find individually tailored, concrete learning experiences that allowed them to grow and develop as novice professionals. Furthermore the support they receive to achieve this needs to be flexibly offered and delivered. The key skills of communication, interpersonal relations, problem solving and thus theory into practice are important ingredients in this process (see Figure 6.4), as they will be throughout the professional's working life. The role of the business mentors as "reflective coaches" allowed significant flexibility for the students and the type of projects that could be included. Furthermore, the relationship between the business mentor and the auspicing university contributes positively to the links between academic theoretical learning and professional practice and experience both in terms of supporting student learning experiences and also in terms of building relationships between the business sector and the university.

As a trial of this innovation of a business mentor in an internship that combined service learning and experiential learning, this evaluation has been generally positive with some small alterations noted. However, there are always limitations to a study that is devised as a pilot and as such it was a trial of only three triads. It would be useful to increase the numbers and consolidate the findings. For example it could be extended into other types of nonprofit business activity. As well it is a process of work experience that could be viable in the SME environment. There is also further research needed on the role of email as a flexible way to deliver mentoring support. For example, research could explore the transfer of tacit knowledge in more depth and also patterns of effective coaching. Overall though the students found this to be a very valuable experience that they would recommend to others. Almost paradoxically these projects offered them a very broad experience with a good deal of responsibility. As more and more employers understand the value of sound experience in addition to the theoretical foundation (Floyd & Gordon, 1998), so students are selecting these electives in their courses. Furthermore there are valuable relationships to be built for marketing departments, their alumni and industry.

RECOMMENDATIONS

Nonprofit internships are a source of invaluable experience to business students. There is diversity in the projects that challenge the learner, while also being offered in a welcoming environment. However, a key recommendation is the inclusion of the business mentor to enrich the process and bridge any shortfall in marketing, or other relevant business experience.

Organizationally the supervising academic must pay close attention to the scope of the project. Moreover, the combination of written guidelines and meetings encourage open and transparent communication amongst the parties involved, as well as managing expectations. Although quite some effort is required by the academic supervisor to establish the experiential learning projects, the combination of client supervisor and mentor offers comparatively comprehensive support to the student for the duration of the project.

Generally the participants in this trial were very positive about their role whether as student, client supervisor or mentor. The value to the students' has been detailed above. The value to the clients included access to new business relationships, access to business advice, planning and writing that was individually negotiated and otherwise out of reach, as well as the altruistic benefits of offering a novice professional an opportunity to experience the real world. The mentors valued the experience of passing on their expertise to a novice professional too. They also appreciated the opportunity to maintain contact with the University and to achieve recognition from their peers as a mentor. The University derives benefit from extending its industry network both through the nonprofit organizations and also through links to its alumni, but mostly the benefit is through providing a memorable, quality educational experience.

Overall then the combination of nonprofit project with "reflective coach" provides learners with a real world experience that facilitates a range of valuable outcomes:

- the provision of experiential learning with a service element;
- the nonprofit sector offered a welcoming environment to the novice professional;
- the extended access to business sites, which increases the reach of the internship process;

- the enhanced transfer of tacit knowledge;
- The supported "consultant style" relationship for the student;
- the extension of the student's communication skills;
- the extended reach of the industry links to the university; and
- the valued role for alumni from diverse professional positions.

NOTES

1.   See Polonsky et al. (1999) for an overview of marketing education in Aus-
     tralia, where 90% of 36 universities offer a three-year undergraduate mar-
     keting degree comprising 4 units per semester in a two-semester year.
2.   Participants were given pseudonyms. Journal quotations are referenced by
     number [i.e., Journal 1] and page and, interview transcripts are indicated
     by participant type and number [Mentor 1] with a page reference.

REFERENCES

Andreasen, A.R., & Kotler, P. (2003). *Strategic marketing for nonprofit organizations*
   (6th ed.). Upper Saddle River, NJ: Prentice-Hall.
Argyris, C., & Schon, D. (1996). *Organizational learning II: Theory method and practice.* Reading, MA: Addison-Wesley.
Bennetts, C. (2002). Traditional mentor relationships, intimacy and emotional
   intelligence. *Qualitative Studies in Education, 15*(2), 155-170.
Birenbaum, M., & Amdur, L. (1999). Reflective active learning in a graduate
   course on assessment. *Higher Education Research & Development, 18*(2), 201-
   218.
Cawyer, C.S., Simonds, C., & Davis, S. (2002) Mentoring to facilitate socialization:
   The case of the new faculty member. *International Journal of Qualitative Studies
   in Education, 15*(2), 225-242.
Clark, S.C. (2003). Enhancing the educational value of business internships. *Jour-
   nal of Management Education, 27*(4), 472-484.
Cornford, I.R. (1999). Skill learning and the development of expertise. In J.A.
   Athanasou (Ed.), *Adult educational psychology* (pp. 263-289). Katoomba, NSW:
   Social Science Press.
Daley, B.J. (1999). Novice to expert: An exploration of how professional learn.
   Adult Education Quarterly, 49(4), 133-144.
Dewey, J. (1963). Experience and education. New York: Collier Books. (Original
   work published 1938)
Fall, L.T. (1998). Using management by objectives to measure results of classroom
   projects through authentic assessment. *Journal of Education for Business, 73*(3),
   172-176.
Floyd, C.J., & Gordon, M.E. (1998). What skills are most important? A comparison of employer, student and staff perceptions. *Journal of Marketing Education,
   20*(2), 103-109.

Friedman, A., & Phillips, M. (2002). The role of mentoring in the CPD programmes of professional associations. *International Journal of Lifelong Education, 21*(3), 269-284.

Gault, J., Redington J., & Schlager, T., (2000). Undergraduate business internships and career success: Are they related? *Journal of Marketing Education, 22*(1), 45-53.

Gray, K., & McNaught, C. (2001, December 9-12). Evaluation of achievements from collaboration in a learning technology mentoring program. 18th annual conference of the *Australasian Society for Computer in Learning in Tertiary Education,* 217-224, Melbourne.

Gremler, D., Hoffman, K.D., Keaveney, S., & Wright, L. (2000). Experiential learning exercises in services marketing courses. *Journal of Marketing Education, 22*(1), 35-44.

Hartley, J.F. (1994). Case studies in organizational research. In G. Cassell & G. Symon (Eds.), *Qualitative methods in organizational research* (pp. 208-229). Thousand Oaks, CA: Sage.

Jarvis, P. (1992). Learning practical knowledge. *New Directions for Adult and Continuing Education, 55,* 89-94.

Klink, R.R., & Athaide, G.A. (2004). Implementing service learning in the principles of marketing course. *Journal of Marketing Education, 26*(2), 145-153.

Kolb, D.A. (1984). *Experiential learning: Experience as the source of learning and development.* Englewood Cliffs, NJ: Prentice-Hall.

Kram, K.E. (1985). *Mentoring at work: Developmental relationships in organizational life.* Glenview, IL: Scott, Foresman and Co.

Lankau, M.J., & Scandura, T. (2002). An investigation of personal learning in mentoring relationships: Content, antecedents, and consequences. *Academy of Management Journal, 45*(4), 779-790.

Lave, J., & Wenger, E. (1991). *Situated learning: Legitimate peripheral participation.* Cambridge: Cambridge University Press.

LeCompte, M.D. (1994). Sensible matchmaking: Qualitative research design and the Program Evaluation Standard. *Journal of Experimental Education, 63*(1), 29-43.

Lee, P., & Caffarella, R.S. (1994). Methods and techniques for engaging learners in experiential learning activities. In L. Jackson & R.S. Caffarella (Eds.), *Experiential learning: A new approach* (Vol. 62, pp. 43-54, *New Directions for Adult and Continuing Education*). San Francisco: Jossey-Bass.

Lewis, L.H., & Williams, C.J. (1994). Experiential learning: Past and present. In L. Jackson & R.S. Caffarella (Eds.), *Experiential learning: A new approach* (pp. 5-16). San Francisco: Jossey-Bass.

Misko, J. (1995). *Transfer: Using learning in new contexts.* Leabrook, South Australia: National Centre for Vocational Education Research.

Nonaka, I., & Takeucki, H. (1995). *The Knowledge Creating Company: How Japanese companies create the dynamics of innovation.* New York: Oxford University Press.

Patton, M. (1990). *Qualitative evaluation and research methods.* Newbury Park, CA: Sage.

Petkus, E., Jr. (2000). A theoretical and practical framework for service-learning in marketing: Kolb's experiential learning cycles. *Journal of Marketing Education, 22*(1), 64-70.

Pitman, M.A., & Maxwell, J.A. (1992). Qualitative approaches to evaluation: Models and methods. In M.D. LeCompte, W.L. Millroy, & J. Preissle (Eds.), *The handbook of qualitative research in education* (pp. 729-771). San Diego, CA: Academic Press.

Polonsky, M.J., Fry, M-L., Mankelow, G., Morgan, P., & Rugimbana, R. (1999). A structural overview of undergraduate marketing education in Australia: Implications for defining core competencies. *Marketing Education Review, 9*(2), 33-42.

Rama, D.V., Ravenscroft, S., Wolcott, S.K., & Zlotkowski, E. (2000). Service-learning outcomes: Guidelines for educators and researchers. *Issues in Accounting Education, 15*(4), 657-692.

Razzouk, N.Y., Seitz, V., & Rizkallah, E. (2003). Learning by doing: Using experiential projects in undergraduate marketing strategy course. *Marketing Education Review, 13*(2), 35-41.

Schon, D. (1987). *Preparing professionals for the demands of practice: Educating the reflective practitioner.* San Francisco/London: Jossey-Bass.

Seitz, V.A., & Razzouk, N. (2002). Teaching retailing and merchandising: An experiential approach. *Marketing Education Review, 12*(1), 53-60.

Senge, P. (1990). *The Fifth Discipline: The art and practice of the learning organization.* New York: Double Day.

Shuptrine, K.F., & Willenborg, J.F. (1998). Job experiences of marketing graduates—implications for marketing education. *Marketing Education Review, 8*(1), 1-11.

Smith, L.W., & van Doren, D.C. (2004). The reality-based learning method: A simple method for keeping teaching activities relevant and effective. *Journal of Marketing Education, 26*(1), 66-74.

Stake, R.E. (2000). Case studies. In N.K. Denzin & Y.S. Lincoln (Eds.), *The handbook of qualitative research* (2nd ed., pp. 435-454). Thousand Oaks, CA: Sage.

Stenmark, D. (2000). Leveraging tacit organizational knowledge. *Journal of Management Information Systems, 17*(3), 9-24.

Strauss, A., & Corbin, J., (1998). *Basics of qualitative research: Techniques and procedures for developing grounded theory.* Thousand Oaks, CA: Sage.

Swap, W., Leonard, D., Shields, M., & Abrams, L. (2001). Using mentoring and storytelling to transfer knowledge in the workplace. *Journal of Management Information Systems, 18*(1), 95-114.

Sweitzer, H.F., & King, M.A. (1999). *The successful internship: Transformation and empowerment.* Pacific Grove, CA: Brooks/Cole Publishing Co.

Toncar, M.F., & Cudmore, B.V. (2000). The overseas internship experience. *Journal of Marketing Education, 22*(1), 54-63.

Wee, L.K., Kek, M.A., & Kelley, C.A. (2003). Transforming the marketing curriculum using problem-based learning: A case study. *Journal of Marketing Education, 25*(2), 150-162.

Wellington, P., Thomas, I., Powell, I., & Clarke, B. (2002). Authentic assessment applied to engineering and business graduate consulting teams. *International Journal of Engineering Education, 18*(2), 168-179

Yin, R.K. (1994). *Case study research: Design and methods* (2nd ed.). Thousand Oaks, CA: Sage.

Young, M.R. (2002). Experiential learning = hands-on + minds-on. *Marketing Education Review, 12*(1), 43-51.

CHAPTER 7

CREATING ACTIONABLE KNOWLEDGE

Practicing Service Learning in a Dutch Business School Context

Judith M. van der Voort, Lucas C.P.M. Meijs, and Gail Whiteman

This chapter examines the benefits and challenges of introducing service learning at a leading European business school (RSM Erasmus University), given the different cultural context of service learning and the relationship between the private and nonprofit sectors in The Netherlands. Based on 3 initiatives, with different levels of service involvement, Dutch business students' perceptions of service learning were evaluated. Students agreed that the experiential nature was by far the biggest added value of service learning, although we found mixed responses to the added value of the "community context" of service learning. Overall, our study strongly suggests that this type of innovation in management education offers appealing benefits to Dutch business students. However, we also found interesting cultural influences on the acceptance of service learning, particularly at the institutional level.

Educating Managers through Real World Projects, 149–180
Copyright © 2005 by Information Age Publishing
All rights of reproduction in any form reserved.

INTRODUCTION

European business schools have not yet discovered the added value of service learning (Van der Voort, 2003a). Although U.S.-based research has explored the definitions, benefits, success factors, and challenges of service learning, there is no current research on Dutch perceptions with respect to service learning. This chapter delves into the possibilities of introducing service learning at the Rotterdam School of Management (RSM Erasmus University in the Netherlands), confronting the "U.S.-based" teaching method of service learning with a different set of profit-nonprofit/nonprofit-government relationships and a different institutional attitude to change.

During the academic year 2003-2004 we were able to develop both a course assignment as an informal stepping stone toward service learning and a real service learning course. We were also able to interview students who did a 4-6 month internship at a nonprofit organization. Our research objective was to evaluate how Dutch business students perceive the concept of service learning. The first informal stepping stone (writing a letter to the editor) focused on getting the idea of business—nonprofit (public policy) involvement into the "heads and hearts" of the Business Administration student. This initiative lacked a real service learning component, but functioned as an informal and "no real involvement" introduction to the service learning concept in which students are required to act as if they are active members of society. It also functioned as an informal situation to experiment with service learning without going full flag within the institution. The second initiative (giving management advice to a nonprofit organization) focused on training management skills and creating mutual acceptance between nonprofits and Business Administration students in a "medium-involvement" service learning context. The internships, our third initiative, are perceived as "high-involvement" service learning experiences.

The structure of the chapter is as follows. First, we provide a short introduction to service learning. We also outline some of the U.S. research on student perceptions and on the impact of service learning on management education. Second, we describe the Dutch cultural context including the nonprofit regime and community relations between businesses, nonprofits, universities and the government. This section is also concerned with Dutch perceptions with respect to organizational change. Third, we outline our research design and research results. The chapter will end with an in-depth discussion on the feasibility of service learning in a corporatist nonprofit regime such as that which exists in the Netherlands, and provides an outline for future research.

AN INTRODUCTION TO SERVICE LEARNING

Service learning aims at enhancing student learning by reflecting in-class on real world practice within a community service context and is based upon the notion that "experience enhances understanding: understanding leads to more effective action" (Eyler & Giles, 1999, p. 8). One of the most frequently cited definitions of service learning and the one we will use in this chapter is that of Bringle and Hatcher (1996, p. 222): "Service learning is a credit-bearing, educational experience in which students participate in an organized service activity that meets identified community needs and (students) reflect on the service activity in such a way as to gain further understanding of course content, a broader appreciation of the discipline, and an enhanced sense of civic responsibility." In service learning, students are first and foremost awarded for their learning experience and not the service (McCarthy, Tucker, & Lund Dean, 2002). Nevertheless, "the thing that separates service-learning from other field-based and experiential forms of learning is the service, the giving to others, and students seem aware of this particular value" (Eyler & Giles, 1999, p. 37).

Eyler and Giles (1999, p. 7) emphasize the experiential nature of service learning by stating that "Learning occurs through a cycle of action and reflection, not simply by being able to recount what has been learned through reading and lecture." Service learning builds upon the four-stage experiential learning cycle of Kolb (1976). In Kolb's learning cycle, concrete experiences are connected to more effective action (active experimentation) through reflective observations and abstract conceptualizations. People learn by applying theory in practice, reflect on that experience, and propose new actions on the basis of observations. This may lead to new concrete actions/ experiences and through these actions the process of learning continues. Kolb states that the learning is most effective when a student goes through all the stages of the learning cycle. Linking service learning to a four-stage cycle implies that successful service learning initiatives needs elements of theory, experience, reflection, and experimentation based on abstract conceptualizations (see Rama, Ravenscroft, & Wolcott, 2000).

Petkus (2000) also underlines the experiential element in service learning, but emphasizes its mutually beneficial nature by arguing that the "organized community service" in service learning differs from the more traditional forms of community service or volunteering in that service learning must be course-relevant (see Markus, Howard, & King, 1993; Kraft, 1996; Eyler & Giles, 1999), must be part of the curriculum (see Astin, Vogelgesang, Ikeda, & Yee, 2000), must be reflection-oriented (see Eyler, 2002; Kohls, 1996) and directed toward the mutual benefit of all parties involved (see Zlotkowski, 1996). Mutual benefits include, students gaining career relevant experience while "doing good," community organizations being able to improve their effectiveness and efficiency, and the university benefitting from positive public relations as faculty and students are more involved in outreach activities within the community.

Not all academics agree on the goals of service learning. Rhoads (1998) describes the dualism found in service learning literature in which one school of thought perceives service learning predominantly as a pedagogical model aimed at cognitive learning and one school that views service learning first and foremost as a form of citizenship education. McCarthy et al. (2002, p. 68) categorize these different approaches as those which emphasize intentional learning versus those which emphasize intentional transformation. From an analysis of the theoretical basis of service learning, they summarize three themes related to service learning: the learning of theory through application; skill development; and the development of civic responsibility. They argue that service learning projects differ in their emphasis on intentional learning of theory and skills on the one hand, and intentional transformation of students and society on the other hand. From their perspective, service learning is an example of learning theory and skills through real world projects with the added value of teaching civic engagement through experience in a unique service context. To be called service learning, real world projects should emphasize either student learning, or underline both student learning and citizenship education (see also Kezar & Rhoads, 2001; Eyler & Giles, 1999; Kolenko, Porter, Wheatly, & Kolby, 1996).

PREVIOUS (U.S.) RESEARCH ON STUDENT PERCEPTIONS

In our study we are interested in Dutch business student perceptions of service learning. However, there is little, if any, previous research on this topic in the Netherlands. Previous research on service learning tends to be from within a U.S. context. This is not surprising since service learning has not traditionally occurred within the Netherlands. In contrast, a number of high ranking U.S. business schools have for some time offered their students a variety of service learning opportunities.

For example, the Wharton Business School (University of Pennsylvania) emphasizes the added value of innovative teaching using experiential learning. Service learning is a key part of this approach. In addition to a wide range of opportunities for students to experience community service outside the formal curriculum, the University of Pennsylvania also provides more than 120 different service learning courses, and in 1991 Wharton introduced its first service learning course: Management 100, a course on leadership and communication. This course attempts to provide students with an experiential context to develop as leaders, to practice communication skills, to learn about the nature of group work, and to build a sense of community.

Similarly, the Kellogg School of Management offers a course on management of nonprofit organizations in which students work with local nonprofit organizations to address management concerns. At both the Harvard Business School and the Columbia Business School, students are able to participate in a social enterprise program which combines elements of teaching social responsibility, and nonprofit and public management, with team experiences in community problem solving. At UC Berkeley, the use of service learning as a teaching tool has been institutionalized through the initiation of the UC Berkeley Service-Learning Research and Development Center.

Although these programs are not always specifically referred to as service learning or community-based learning, they do fit its definition of combining community service and classroom learning through experience and reflection. Most appear to be based on the explicit assumption that management students can learn relevant management skills and knowledge through community service experiences, and the concept of service learning appears to complement a university/ business school culture in which both (extracurricular) student community service and experiential learning have high priority.

The research on (U.S.) student perceptions with respect to service learning can be divided into perceptions as regards service learning benefits and effectiveness on the one hand and service learning acceptance in a (BA) curriculum on the other hand. For a thorough analysis of student outcomes from participation in service learning courses with regard to theory application, skill application, and civic responsibility, we refer to McCarthy et al. (2002). We focus on those studies emphasizing student perceptions of service learning and service learning effectiveness in a business school context.

In his experience of integrating service learning in a business ethics course, Kohls (1996) concludes that students perceive their experiences as the most fulfilling and rewarding when those experiences include direct encounters with the clients of the nonprofit organizations.[1] According to Hogner (1996) one of the most important outcomes of a service learning management course was the realization of many of his students that service learning is first and foremost about student learning; "they do 'get it', i.e., that the service activity has its greatest impact on students and not on the community." The team experience of service learning assignments is also perceived as an important impetus for student learning (see Tucker et al., 1998; Kenworthy-U'Ren, 2000).

Eyler and Giles (1999) conclude from their comprehensive research on student perceptions (which also included business students) that students value the team experience in terms of communication and interpersonal skills. According to their research, students perceive service learning as different from learning through books and lectures and they claim to have learnt more than they are used to in traditional classroom-bound courses. Kenworthy-U'Ren refers to this as "real-world" learning. Easter-ling and Rudell (1997) describe student perceptions of a marketing consultancy service learning project. Their students found the project challenging because of group dynamics and also because they were not sure that they could offer added value to the nonprofits.

There has also been some previous U.S. research which examines initial student reactions toward integrating service learning in their curriculum. This may be particularly relevant to our study given the introductory state of service learning within the Netherlands. McCarthy and Tucker (1999) hypothesized in their research on student perceptions that students would feel anxious to get the job done, that the perceived importance of the service task coupled with an emotional connection with the service client would influence the student's felt need to help, and that students would see service learning as beneficial, but time-consuming. They argue that an initial negative student perception is one of the most important barriers to integrating service learning in the business curriculum. Kolenko et al. (1996) also refer to initial student resistance as a barrier to introducing service learning in management education, especially because of its questioned relevance to management education, and the perceived "requirement to volunteer." McCarthy and Tucker (1999, p. 557) conclude that "students have a positive perception about community service but are less positive about having college courses incorporate a service-learning component into the curriculum." They conclude that although U.S. business students may value the importance of community service, they seem to be less uniform and slightly less positive in their perceptions concerning service learning due to high expected time commitments and low perceived benefits. Even students with prior service experience did not necessarily have a more positive view on service learning, although it was expected that these students would be better able to estimate real time commitments and their abilities to do the service. "It is clear that even limited experience may help reshape the way students think about obligations and opportunities for service and about people who need social services" (Markus et al., 1993, p. 337).

Sax and Astin (1997) argue that not all students will voluntarily choose service learning courses. They state that especially female students with prior high school volunteer or tutoring experience, and/ or involvement in religious activities and who are not predominantly motivated by materialistic values, are more inclined to self-selection. Eyler and Giles (1999, p. 46) suggest that a mandatory low-intensity service learning project "with limited opportunities for reflection and integration with the study" may be a useful way to encourage students to engage in service learning. Kolenko et al. (1996) refer to this as obligatory, low involvement "exposure experiences" to undergraduates, vis-à-vis elective "high involvement experiences" in which skills are applied in a more in-depth way to address real issues in nonprofit organizations.

While useful, previous research has largely been conducted in the United States. The outstanding question is whether these conclusions hold across cultures and more specifically for the Dutch context. In our review of the literature, we did not find any references to possible cross-cultural differences with regard to student perceptions of service learning in a European Business Administration context. Nor is there any existing discussion on potential cultural differences within the institutional structure of European business schools which may (or may not) affect implementation of service learning curriculum. Yet Bringle and Hatcher (1996, p. 232) implicitly refer to the importance of the cultural dimension in planning and implementing service learning initiatives at least at the micro-level, by emphasizing that is it important "to know the nature of the student climate and culture, including student attitudes toward voluntary service activities (individual or through student groups) and student attitudes toward service learning course development."

Our study attempts to address the "cross-cultural" research gap in the service learning literature by conducting research on service learning as it is introduced for the first time within the Business Administration curriculum at RSM Erasmus University in the Netherlands. Before we describe the details of our study, the next section provides a brief overview of relevant aspects of the Dutch cultural context.

THE DUTCH CONTEXT OF SERVICE LEARNING

The phrase "service-learning" is virtually unknown in the Netherlands. Nevertheless, just as in the United States, volunteering is a rather common act in the Netherlands. For example, Salamon and Sokolowski (2001) conducted a cross-national comparative study in 24 countries, and found that volunteering on average constitutes 2.5% of non-agricultural employment. The top five in this sample were Sweden (8.0%), the Netherlands (7.5%), France (5.2%), the United Kingdom (4.9%) and the United States (4.6%). In the Netherlands, about 30% of the adult population volunteers in any given year,[2] with organized sports as by far the largest area of volunteering (Roques, 2004).

There are also many examples of Dutch students who are active in volunteering (Njiokiktjien, Talavera, & Lugtenberg, 2004). Volunteer work in the form of board or committee membership within student associations is especially popular. Building up an impressive résumé seems to be of particular importance to Business Administration students in the Netherlands, just as it may be with students in the United States. Student associations (especially the larger ones) are also slowly becoming active as socially involved members of society.

According to Burger and Dekker (1998), the Dutch nonprofit sector is of considerable size and importance. However, business schools (and in fact Dutch universities in general) do not typically have institutional linkages with the nonprofit sector. In contrast, top ranked U.S. business schools do have some well established institutional linkages with the nonprofit sector. U.S. examples include the Leader to Leader Institute (the former Peter Drucker Foundation for nonprofit management) which has links with the Initiative on Social Enterprise at the Harvard Business School, and also Wharton's Center for Community Partnerships.

The lack of institutional interaction between business schools and the nonprofit sector may stem from different cultural patterns of relations between the government and the nonprofit sector. Based upon an international project run in some forty plus countries, Salamon, Sokolowski, and Anheier (2000) describe four different nonprofit regimes, or patterns of relations between the government and the nonprofit sector using social origins theory (see Table 7.1).

These models are differentiated by two key dimensions: role of the state (the extent of government social welfare spending), and scale of the nonprofit sector. In the so-called liberal model, low government social welfare spending is combined with a relatively large nonprofit sector. The nonprofit sector is privately funded. At the opposite extreme is the social democratic model. In this model, state-organizations dominate the field. In between these two models, there are two models characterized by strong states. In the corporatist[3] model the state has made an arrangement or "common cause" with (different) nonprofit institutions. In practice this often implies that there are no pure governmental agencies performing services. Nonprofit organizations, also those based upon reli-

Table 7.1.   Nonprofit Regimes

	Small Nonprofit Sector	*Large Nonprofit Sector*
Low government social welfare spending	Statist	Liberal
High government social welfare spending	Social democratic	Corporatist

Source: Based on Salamon, Sokolowski, and Anheier (2000)

gion, are to a large extent funded with public money, which reduces the need to fundraise within their own constituencies. The fourth model is the statist model. In this nonprofit regime, the state also runs the social institutions on behalf of business and economic elites.

According to Salamon et al. (2000), the United States operates according to the liberal model. Private actors, such as private donors, foundations or companies, traditionally finance the nonprofit sector. We believe that in a liberal model Business Community Involvement (BCI) or profit sector involvement in addressing societal issues is part of the history, tradition and policy of both companies and nonprofit organizations to some degree.

In contrast, the Netherlands has a corporatist model in which government spending and growth of the nonprofit sector operate hand in hand. The corporatist model is characterized by indirect relationships, in which the government serves as a link among actors in the business and nonprofit sectors. In this model businesses pay taxes and do not invest directly in business community development.[4] We argue that in countries with a corporatist nonprofit regime, like the Netherlands, BCI is only a recently introduced strategic instrument for businesses. Nonprofit organizations in the Netherlands still perceive BCI in many cases as a second-best solution to governmental funding. Nevertheless, Dutch companies and nonprofit organizations are beginning to see the advantages of (strategic) BCI. This may also explain why BCI has only very recently been recognized by Dutch business schools as a relevant topic, and further helps to explain why service learning initiatives have been unknown in the Netherlands until our study.

While experiential learning has been integrated to some degree into Dutch business schools (for example through case-based learning and internships), service learning has yet to be identified as a possible innovation in management education. While societal internships have been introduced at a very small number of secondary schools over the last five years, they have not yet appeared at Dutch business schools. These internships also do not include structured reflection nor do they typically emphasize service learning goals. Nevertheless, this development does suggest that a new link between universities (educational institutions) and the nonprofit sector is possible.

This slow pace of innovation within Dutch business schools may be due, in part, to the rather conservative nature of the management culture within the Netherlands. In general, Hofstede (2003) classifies the Dutch as a somewhat risk-averse culture, where innovation in organizational change is not as common as in the United States. Dutch institutions do not typically emphasize innovation in program design. For example, Fagenson-Eland, Ensher, and Burke (2004) compared organization development and change interventions in seven nations, including the Netherlands and the United States, based upon the cultural concepts of Hofstede. They found that OD instruments based upon rewards and performance appraisals are used less in the Netherlands than expected. They suggest that these methods are "less necessary in a society where there is high demographic homogeneity and where roles and expectations of individuals in distinct social classes and work positions are very well defined. Instead, managers may be more likely to rely on informal systems of feedback and well-defined social sanctions and norms" (Fageson-Eland et al., 2004, p. 458). Within Dutch organizations, change and innovation per se is not embraced and supported immediately but only after the "innovation" has been tested in many informal situations, often relying upon smaller preliminary "stepping-stone" styled interventions.

Service learning does not appear to be a concept that is easily embraced by university administrators as having potential educational value. Perceived problems are, for example, the different conceptualization of volunteering in the Netherlands (Meijs et al., 2003), the general societal idea that the government should organize "this" and the institutional belief that there is a reluctance amongst students against volunteering. The question that we are interested in is whether or not Dutch business students are open to service learning initiatives, and what perceptions they have after participating in different forms of service learning.

OUR RESEARCH

Although some of the high-ranked business schools like Wharton and Berkeley have a variety of service learning programs, European business schools do not have this tradition (Van der Voort, 2003a). But this is starting to change. At the Rotterdam School of Management (RSM Erasmus University), the department of Business-Society Management devotes itself to the teaching and research of globalization issues, internationalization strategies, stakeholder management, ethics, nonprofit management and Business Community Involvement (BCI). As members of this department, we were able to introduce the first service learning initiatives to business students within the Netherlands. RSM Erasmus University is the top-ranked Dutch business school in the *Financial Times* ranking (*Financial Times*, 2005).

The aim of our research is to explore Dutch student perceptions of service learning in a management education context at the RSM Erasmus University. We have chosen to study three different initiatives with a varying degree of service intensity to find out whether student perceptions with regard to service learning change when their involvement increases.

In the Appendix, we have enclosed a more detailed description of these initiatives. For the purpose of this chapter we call the operational activities carried out by students to get in touch with the nonprofits' clients direct service, as opposed to indirect service like the consulting advice through which students support the nonprofit organization indirectly in achieving its mission.

The first initiative (December 2003) was aimed at creating awareness of a social issue while learning argumentation skills. It was also meant as an informal situation or stepping stone for service learning at the Rotterdam School of Management. The initiative was aimed at "planting the seed" that managerial decision making takes place within a societal context. It was not, however, a "real" service learning exercise according to Bringle and Hatcher's definition. It did not include any real form of service to a nonprofit organization; it was a one-time only assignment of at a maximum a day work: it only slightly touched upon a community issue; and "citizenship" learning objectives were limited toward "planting a seed." Students were not expected to reflect upon this experience in a formal way although they would receive feedback from their mentors.

All Business Administration students at RSM Erasmus University have to follow the course Business Administration skills as part of their Bachelor 1 curriculum. We chose to study student perceptions of this activity since the BA Skills course is a general management course, yet it does contain some introductory business-society content. This course is given in small groups headed by (advanced student) mentors. They coach the students in the acquisition of, among others, writing, argumentation and presentation skills. One of the obligatory assignments was to write a letter to the editor. The students were allowed to choose to write about either the recent accountancy scandals or high CEO salaries. The students needed to read background material on their issue, to form an opinion, to support their opinion with relevant arguments and to transform these into a well-written, well informed and convincing letter to the editor. A total of 500 letters (out of 550 students) were handed in. The mentors were responsible for providing the students with feedback on their letter's argumentation. The citizenship element of this assignment was reflected upon during a Bachelor 1 public debate on corporate social responsibility. The students did not receive a separate grade for this assignment. The assignment was part of a set of obligatory assignments for the course. Students were not aware that this was part of a study on service learning.

For our second initiative (December 2003-February 2004), we integrated a service learning component in the Master elective in Nonprofit Management. This Master elective prepares students for managing and governing of nonprofit organizations. It takes a functional and diverse approach to nonprofit management, teaching students among other things about profit-nonprofit (dis)similarities, fundraising, nonprofit effectiveness, public accountability and volunteer management. Representatives of nonprofits are involved in this course through guest lectures as well as the service learning "consultancy" initiative.

Unlike the students of the first initiative, the students of the second initiative (37 in total) were well informed about their participation in a service-learning initiative. In this second initiative, the students did not just write a report on a hypothetical problem in a hypothetical nonprofit organization, but attacked real issues in teams as consultants to six preselected nonprofit organizations. They had to conduct interviews, do background research, write a policy and managerial advice, and present that advice at both the university and the nonprofit organization. The nonprofit organizations were selected on the basis of prior contacts/involvement in the course, the presence of a willing contact person who would be available at least three days in a seven-week period, and the content/ feasibility of the management issue they identified. In dialogue with us, our nonprofit partners wrote down one-page assignment descriptions themselves, which we presented during the first class of the master elective. We also discussed with our nonprofit partners the minimal time and information investment expected from the organizations in order for the students to successfully attack the formulated nonprofit issues. The nonprofit organizations knew beforehand that the students had to follow classes and to complete other assignments besides this consulting project, and that two days a week were booked for research, meetings, and report writing. The issues ranged from business partnership strategies to the program versus membership management of volunteers and the financing of a welfare website. Students were allowed to choose their own team members and to select, as a team, one of the six nonprofit organizations. Each student team had to visit their organization in the first week of the nonprofit management course, in order to get to know the organization, its management issue, and to discuss the course of action for the coming seven weeks. The objectives of this initiative were for students to gain relevant experience in a nonprofit context while applying theory to practice, to learn to work in teams and to train presentation, writing and communication skills.

We characterized this service learning case in advance as a medium-involvement service learning activity. Students dealt with real strategic issues in real nonprofit organizations; learned a diverse set of skills from team-building to presentation skills; and experienced first-hand nonprofit management issues. The students time commitment, however, was limited to a seven-week period, and the students were not involved in the "active experimentation" phase of Kolb's learning cycle in which their contribution would go further than simply writing a consultancy report (i.e., students were not involved in the implementation of their consultancy advice). All students were required to participate in a classroom collective discussion on the relevance of the service learning activity in terms of course content. Furthermore, the student teams were required to write a research report in which they explicitly had to refer to the theories that were discussed in the classroom. All student teams also received feedback from their classmates and their "client" nonprofit organization through presentations. The consulting experience was graded on the basis of informal nonprofit organization reactions, the written report, and the classroom presentation. This grade constituted 50% of the final course grade.

For our third case we examined the impact of nonprofit internships (Academic year 2003-2004) on student perceptions of service learning.[5] Some students choose to do their internship at a nonprofit organization. Six of these students were asked to participate in our research in order to gather their experiences and perceptions concerning service learning. We characterized these internships in advance as high-involvement service learning activities as the time commitment is large (at least a three-month period), and the students are involved in both the proposal and implementation of management policies. We considered these internships at nonprofit organizations as a service learning experience, since students did not receive any payment from their nonprofit organizations other than compensations for costs incurred, and because students were required to write down their experiences, and to reflect on the relevancy of these experiences from a business administration perspective.

EMPIRICAL RESEARCH METHODOLOGY

To evaluate student perceptions we conducted individual interviews and two sets of three focus groups (see Krueger & Casey, 2000). Steyaert and Bouwen (1994) suggest that focus groups are especially relevant to get a first impression of the field and to provide the context in which different perspectives on a certain topic can be shared and discussed. The benefit of focus groups is that the interview protocol allows for structured but dynamic discussions between focus groups participants that can produce a wealth of information. We acknowledge the fact that the focus group methodology does not lend itself for easy generalization, but the use of a pre-structured interview protocol and the organization of six focus groups in total does provide a basis for finding patterns in student perceptions. In total, two sets of three focus groups were held to evaluate student perceptions of the first two initiatives. To evaluate students' perceptions of nonprofit internships, we did not organize focus groups, but instead we conducted a total of six individual in-depth interviews. For the second initiative, we also interviewed the contact persons of the participating nonprofit organizations.

To stimulate focus group participation with regard to the first service learning initiative, each participating student was awarded a 15 euro (18 dollar) reward. These students were recruited via the university email and blackboard system, to make sure that the researchers had no opportunities to influence the final focus group composition. With regard to the second initiative, each team was obliged to delegate three of their team members to participate in one of the three focus groups. All focus groups have been held at university premises and have been moderated by the same professional moderator. They have been taped and fully transcribed with our respondents' consent. The respondents have remained anonymous in our research.

While our participants were all Dutch, interviews and focus groups were held in English, to prevent misinterpretations and alterations to our respondents' original statements when translated to English for the purpose of writing this chapter. All participants thus spoke English fluently or to an adequate degree.

FINDINGS

Our findings are presented first separately for each of the three initiatives, followed by a broad comparison across the initiatives in order to understand the main differences and similarities between the student perceptions of the stepping stone initiative (the letter to the editor exercise), along with the medium and high involvement service learning activities (the consultancy report to nonprofits and the nonprofit internship respectively).

The Letter to the Editor

The overall impression based on the focus groups is that students were strongly interested in experiential learning yet felt that the first assignment was too limited, and provided no real opportunities to link theory to practice. Students felt that the letter to the editor did not allow for any real involvement with society on their part, and it provided only a limited degree of freedom with respect to the issue topics. Furthermore, all reported that they liked the concept of service learning (which we explained in the focus groups), first and foremost, because it gave them the opportunity to learn theory by practice, even in the first year. "You can read about how to ride a bike, but if they say here is your bike, go ahead, you will fall. Business Administration is just like that, you just have to do it." Another student added: "I learn most by doing things. I learn faster that way." Thus experiential learning was perceived to be the key success factor of a service learning assignment and students felt that a "stepping-stone, no-real involvement"—initiative did not satisfactorily meet their desire for more in-depth experiential learning.

Yet at least half of the respondents in this set of focus groups did not see any added value of service learning beyond the experience. Some of them claimed to be indifferent with respect to the context of learning practice in terms of profit or nonprofit. Others seemed to have trouble understanding the added value of a nonprofit context to a Business Administration student. For instance, one student said, "I think it is a good thing, it is like an internship. But I do not think it has to be in a nonprofit. Our study is all about profit." Most of these students had difficulties understanding the added value of this assignment beyond learning argumentation and writing skills. The other half of the students did see some added value in gaining experience in a nonprofit context, especially as a learning laboratory for some management skills. Only in the first focus group the respondents discussed the extra added value of service learning in terms of personal transformation (see McCarthy et al., 2002); "I think they wanted to teach us something else. During this period it is all about the most efficient way of production. With this topic they want you to think a little bit more socially responsible. That it is not all about making profits." Another student referred to this as "planting the seed of social responsibility."

Strikingly, almost all respondents had a distorted view of nonprofits, viewing them as excellent learning laboratories for the inexperienced Business Administration student. According to these students, nonprofits do not have to make a profit, and therefore have more space to make mistakes and can avoid the managerial stress inherent in profit making: "I think in a nonprofit organization you have very little stress, because you do not have to be concerned about profit." Taken together, these findings suggest that a significant portion of students were interested in high-involvement experiential learning yet at least half were not particularly sold on the value of service learning per se or had troubles perceiving the added value of experience in a nonprofit context.

The focus group discussants seemed to reach consensus with respect to the success factors for future service-learning assignments. They should be study-related, backed up by rigorous feedback, and graded, in order to be really motivating for students. Especially in the first focus group, the need for reflection was central to the discussion, particularly the students perceived lack of it in their assignment. "I do not get a grade for it; I do not get any good commentary on it personally, so why should I pay so much attention to this assignment?" Another student continued by stating that "my article was evaluated by my teacher and I got some very good feedback on it. On my argumentation techniques, the structure of my argumentation, and the use of references. It is only useful when you get feedback." Several students emphasized the added value of repetition in reflection and student learning: "Perhaps it is better to let the students write some sort of these assignments every trimester. So that you can correct yourself and really learn something." In two of the three focus groups, some students even mentioned service learning as an opportunity for reflecting on student learning after every trimester: "first you get some theory, then you have the practice, and then you have to review yourself. You have to say these were my goals, this is what I have done, and this is what I have learnt."

The question as to whether a service learning assignment should be mandatory received no straightforward answer. Some saw the added value of making service learning obligatory, which would act as a little push to get students involved in volunteering: "If your heart is not in the right place, let other people put it in the right place. Everybody needs a little push." Others seemed to foresee that an elective would only attract those students already active in the community. Still, others referred to the link between student enthusiasm and offering service learning as a voluntary elective: "If you do it in an elective, the student will be much more enthusiastic. I think it is a two-way street." Another student added, "in an elective you can make it more specialized, because then you are in a smaller group."

In each of the three focus groups, the respondents concluded that it would be best to integrate service learning into the whole BA curriculum; starting with an essay assignment along with some classes on social responsibility to get a preliminary grasp of the unique context of service learning and then quickly move from class-based learning to experiential learning in the form of a mandatory course including some hours of direct service (the students could not arrive at a consensus with respect to the minimum or maximum amount of hours to spend on direct service) and concluded by an elective with a more rigorous service learning assignment that is experientially based. "Integrate it into the four years; you can pull a line with the courses you get in every trimester." Despite the fact that a number of students were unclear about the added value of a nonprofit context, only two focus group discussants actively questioned the need and possibility to integrate service learning in the BA curriculum: "I think people who really want to do it, something like this, they will find their way anyway." The second student added: "I think it starts with the individual. You have to do it in your own time. With social work you can integrate it into the program, but with BA you cannot." Thus, the general

BA students that participated in our focus groups were generally in support of the concept of service learning particularly if it gave them the opportunity for some interesting experiential learning. One of the final remarks summarizes the groups sentiments' with respect to the potential value of service learning within the BA curriculum: "The biggest turn off would be putting students in a classroom and let them listen to some boring people."

Medium-involvement Service Learning: The Master Elective Nonprofit Management

All respondents participating in this second set of focus groups said that they chose this Masters' elective either to expand their horizons and learn about something other than profit, or as preparation for a future job in a nonprofit context. This is in contrast to the first group, who were general BA students. These Masters' students also already had significant volunteer experiences, with most of them volunteering for a local sports association or student association. About a quarter reported that they were actively involved in the church.

Without exceptions, all respondents were enthusiastic about their mandatory service learning assignment of preparing a consultancy report for a real nonprofit. Some liked the needed creativity, others the ability to work in a self-selected team, and still others the fact that they worked with real problems in real nonprofit organizations. "You really get the opportunity to see how it works in an organization. Now you can see that when you have a theory it does not work in reality, you have to adapt it first." All students agreed that their service learning experience had been a valuable team experience.

In addition to the development of communication, research, presentation, writing, and team-building skills, they also referred to the added value of service learning with respect to awareness building and nonprofit understanding: "I can only say that it creates awareness. Ok, we can't make a profit, but we still need to raise funds to continue our activities." Another student emphasized the added value of learning in a nonprofit context: "It is another way of learning and it stimulated me more, because you have the idea that you are doing something useful and not only something you just do to get a grade." In class, attention was also paid to the relevancy of structured reflection in terms of group discussions, research reports, and class presentations. Although the students did like the idea of learning from other teams' ideas and experiences, they questioned its added value due to a perceived presentation overload. "The last range of presentations was really boring. We could have learnt something from the ideas of the other groups, but after one and a half presentation you don't listen anymore." All focus group discussants seemed to value the idea of reflecting upon experiences with their nonprofit organizations, in order to ensure that these organizations would actually implement the students' advice in their organizations. These students also perceived service learning as an instrument to reflect learning experiences across a set of courses.

Some linked their satisfaction with the assignment to the nonprofits' motivation: "Those people are more motivated from the start, because they really want to do something with your policy advice. For-profits think they know it all themselves." According to all respondents (with the exception of three representatives from one student team) this organizational motivation was apparent in the well-preparedness of the nonprofit organizations and their willingness to share contacts and information.

Although they were enthusiastic, these master students also shared the feeling that the service learning assignment could be improved by extending the time frame of the assignment: "A problem was the time lapse. It would be nice if we could conduct research to see if some of our brainstorming ideas could be implemented." Interestingly, most of the respondents had the feeling that nonprofits and the community would gain more if students undertook some form of direct service: "It was not like that what we were doing, that the community could really prosper by helping this organization. I could not imagine that what we did would be the service that you were talking about." Another student continued by stating that "we wrote a policy advice which may help the nonprofit and that is indirect, because it is the nonprofit which ultimately address the community need. You are just facilitating that organization in doing that." Another student also addressed the perceived difference in indirect and direct service: "Isn't service learning, learning by doing something for the community? I didn't really get that from the assignment. Ok, you do something for an organization which does something for the community, but that is too indirect to really get the nonprofit idea."

Furthermore, all respondents, with no exceptions, had trouble defining their added value to the nonprofit organizations apart from being an eye-opener to some people in the organization. "I think it is indeed important that you get the feeling that you really helped them and if you do not have that feeling, it is not a nice assignment. You have to know that they are really going to use your recommendations."

Strikingly, both the nonprofit organizations and the respondents in this second set of focus groups (without exceptions) indicated that they perceived the "win-win" of service learning to students and nonprofits to be out of balance, but in the opposite way. Students perceived that their own advantages exceeded those given to the nonprofit organizations respectively. "I think I learnt more than I gave them service." In contrast, the nonprofit organizations felt that their benefits may have outweighed the value for students, since the organization time investment was lower than expected while the students appeared to be able to produce a relevant report in a relatively short time period. The organizational members all seemed to be satisfied with the consulting advice that they received from their student team; "My expectation is that we can easily find issues in our organization that lend themselves to service learning projects." They were positively surprised about the open communication with the teams, their work ethic and autonomy, their focus on delivering a useful end product, and their recognition of the strategic importance of the issues at hand. "The students have delivered a top job. They have written a very practical and applicable piece of work." The contact persons from all six participating nonprofit organizations assured us that they would be very much interested in participating in next year's service learning assignment. Even more striking is the fact that both students and nonprofit organizations proposed the same strategy to rebalance their "partnership," namely by extending the service commitment to include direct service. "In our view, our time investment was not a problem at all, certainly not in relation to the benefits we earned from this assignment. The learning experience for the students could be further expanded by working in the organization for a certain period of time."

Although all students were enthusiastic about the assignment, they did not have that same shared euphoric feeling as regards service learning in general. One respondent claimed that "I think we are all positive, not because of the fact that it is about service learning, but because finally we get to do something in practice and that could also be a totally different concept." Interestingly, these Masters' students also saw themselves as different from the general BA student. All participating students in the second set of focus groups stated that they question whether "the general BA student" would be interested in service learning. Some students even declared that the nonprofit part would be the biggest turn off for service learning for general BA students. Yet at least one student was aware of the potentially misleading stereotypes of such beliefs. "The question is how well do I know the general BA student? To be honest, I have no idea, because we are making all these generalizations about all these people that they only care for their résumé and that they are not interested in nonprofit management or service learning, and is that really true?"

Finally, these participants also indicated that service learning should be integrated throughout the whole Business Administration curriculum, starting with an assignment that could be characterized as introductory and possibly non-experiential, and followed by more intensive courses in which theory is learnt through practice. There were even a couple of students who declared that they appreciated the added value of service learning so much that they suggested organizing new courses or changing an existing one to include service learning: "The educational program is in every trimester based around one specific topic. Maybe it is possible to do three courses and one extra course that expand and links the other three courses and that would be the service learning assignment." One other student added: "I would change the courses, so that you give in every course, whenever possible, a nonprofit aspect."

High-involvement Service Learning: Nonprofit Internships

The service learning internships covered a variety of tasks, ranging from writing a business plan for a nonprofit, or training employees of a nonprofit in the area of web management, to exploring opportunities for sustainable development in the area of Puerto Williams and Cape Horn, and organizing a public debate about higher educated refugees. All but one of the interviewees were exceptionally enthusiastic about their internship at a nonprofit organization. They were by far the most enthusiastic about their service learning experiences compared to the other students that participated in this research. The one student that was not particularly enthusiastic about her experience said the following: "It was a good experience to work with two small organizations like X and Y, even though I would never want to work with organizations like these again. It was quite disappointing to find out that in the case of X the employees were mostly interested in their own research projects without any interest in the goals and main projects of their NGO." The same student perceived service learning as a "win-win" opportunity especially in a high-involvement context, although she thought that her particular assignment did not meet the requirements of service learning: "I would not qualify my internship as service learning, since it did not require management skills on my behalf." Another student expressed his very positive experience by stating that "it makes students aware of another world besides business, business, and business. For me, it assured me in the fact that I want to work in a nonprofit organization. Nonprofit organizations are also important stakeholders to business and BA students should therefore know them, as they could be negotiating partners in the future."

Students liked the idea of working in nonprofit organizations because of their smaller size, providing students with more freedom and responsibilities. One student said, "I didn't expect the level of responsibility I had toward the nonprofit and the stakeholders involved." These students were particularly positive about the learning potential of such long-term internships: "I have learned how to function like a true manager. I have also learned how to make relationships between different disciplines of management like Strategic Management, Information Management, Marketing Management, Logistics Management and Financial Management. But most importantly I have learnt how to communicate effectively to people from diverse backgrounds." Another student said: "We were able to experience how the triangle of NGO's, businesses, and government works. Besides that, I have learnt to work with people from very different backgrounds and interests." All six students that were interviewed in the course of our research stated that their nonprofit internship gave them a broader appreciation of management: "That it isn't always about money." Internships also allowed students to recognize the importance of stakeholders in general management and more specifically, about the nonprofit as an important stakeholder to businesses.

With respect to service learning, they all emphasized in their first reaction the relevance of such practices to the BA program, for instance as an internship or an elective. As with the other students, experiential learning was a critical dimension of this. "I think service learning will be a good possibility for students to develop their management skills in practice. I personally like to do as many practical projects as possible, because I think this is the best way to learn." Another student added "If I got it right and service learning is more practical than theoretical, than I think it should definitely be included in the BA curriculum. I have learnt more about organizations and management during my two internships than from all the cases I have written during my study." Five out of six students emphasized the added value of student learning in a nonprofit context. "The basic management skills can be put in practice, and at the same time your experience provides a basis for learning about local needs, involvement, development issues, and empowerment." One student explicitly emphasized the added value structured reflection next to gaining experience: "It sounds to me that service learning can be a real added value. If indeed it meets community needs while at the same time puts theory into practice and allows for a reflective learning process, it seems beneficial for all parties involved." To one student, it was not so much the opportunity of structured reflection that will enhance student learning, but the student attitude: "It was up to me as an individual to gain as much as possible from this experience. It depends totally on the individual interest and willingness to learn, how much he or she is able to glean from new experiences. The study of BA only taught me the why's and what's but not the how's. I have learnt the art of communication and managing people by experience and not through pedagogy."

When asked how service learning could be integrated into the Business Administration curriculum, they all referred to offering nonprofit internships and electives. Only one student mentioned the possibility of integrating service learning in the already existing Business-Society Management course, as an extra team project. One student emphasized the role of the university in stimulating service learning: "The University could begin by actively offering possible projects at nonprofit organizations to the students." This student continued by stating that "Yes, I think it is desirable to integrate service learning into the BA curriculum, because students will have the practical experience, will learn more about nonprofits and their objectives, and they will contribute to the community environment." Two students emphasized the reputational added value of providing service learning to the Rotterdam School of Management: "I think that ethical business and corporate responsibility will increase in importance in the future and therefore it wouldn't do any harm to the Rotterdam school of Management to take a proactive position in service learning and be an example for others."

FINDINGS: COMPARISON ACROSS CASES

Across all three initiatives, students agreed that the experiential nature of each of the initiatives is by far the biggest added value of service learning. They all seemed to be of the same opinion that every opportunity to apply theory to practice should be welcomed since experiential learning experiences provide the basis for long term learning as opposed to the more traditional and short term "classroom and exam" approach to student teaching. Low intensity or "no real involvement" service learning did not appear to be appealing, even to those students (e.g., the general BA student) who were not necessarily predisposed to working in the nonprofit environment. Even with the medium-involvement service learning initiative (i.e., the consultancy report within the Masters elective on Nonprofit) seemed to be dissatisfied with the "service" intensity of their assignment. Experience is key; the more, the better.

The students were less unanimous about the added value of the nonprofit or "community context" of service learning. Perceptions regarding this aspect of service learning can be divided into four sub-aspects. First, some students really perceived the added value of the nonprofit context in terms of bringing the rational study of management education and emotions together. They valued their ability to make a difference to the community while they learn at the same time. A second group also saw the added value of practicing in a nonprofit context, but then in the shape of an "experimental learning laboratory"—that is, as a place where they could make mistakes and learn at the same time. A third group did not see any added value or at least no difference between acquiring practice in a nonprofit or profit context. To the fourth and final group belong those students who held the opinion that Business Administration students would only want to focus on profit and therefore strictly work with companies. The nonprofit context would not provide any real opportunities to learn management skills except through the experience of working in a team and improving communication skills. Strikingly, most students participating in the research did not hold that view themselves, but thought that the "general BA student" would react like that.

Some of the debate in the six focus groups was directed toward the apparent contradiction between direct and indirect forms of "organized community service" and the related discussion with respect to the intensity of that service. In the first set of focus groups (letter to the editor assignment) the students could not come to a consensus for the minimum or maximum amount of hours to be spent on service. In the second set (Masters' students consulting advise nonprofit), the students perceived direct service, the hands-on work, as the biggest added value to non-profits, as opposed to the indirect service of consultancy advice of which they thought they themselves benefitted the most. The first year students from the first initiative seemed to have trouble perceiving the added value of service learning above and beyond organizing community service projects for students to create awareness, although they do saw the added value of a nonprofit context as a learning laboratory. They focused their discussion on the amount of hours to be spent on direct, voluntary service and some questioned the role of the university in organizing these service opportunities. The participants in the second initiative (nonprofit consultancy report), conversely, linked the idea of indirect service as an instrument to train management skills in a controlled environment (e.g., consulting projects) to the idea of getting to know the nonprofit organization and its clients by doing some direct service work. It seemed to them that community service should include a direct service element to optimize the learning experience. At the same time they had the idea that nonprofits would benefit most from students' direct service. It seemed that these students perceive service learning especially as a learning tool for students and have difficulties perceiving the mutually beneficial nature of service learning.

The length and intensity of the service seemed to determine the quality of the learning experience across each of the initiatives. Students from the first two ("no involvement" and "medium involvement") initiatives seemed to agree that their learning would improve if their involvement increased in terms of depth and length. Students in the third initiative, the internship, felt that the length and intensity of service learning were strongly related to their already high level of satisfaction and enthusiasm. Since internships provided the greatest amount of experiential learning, it is not surprising that the third group was the most supportive of the value of service learning.

With respect to the future design of service learning programs, students from the first two initiatives supported a "service learning package" that included guest lectures in the first year to "plant the seed of social responsibility" moving into a small mandatory service learning experience and culminating in an in-depth, elective-based "consultancy experience" for those students that were really interested in service learning. Students from both these groups perceived service learning as the (potential) glue that could bind the functional areas of the BA program together. This finding is surprising given that some of the focus group discussants also declared that they had difficulties visualizing service learning benefits beyond the advantage of the mere practice. The students that had an internship experience at a nonprofit also liked the idea of integrating service learning in the curriculum mainly because of its experiential nature, emphasizing that service learning could be integrated in the form of internships and electives. Taken together with the previous findings, it may be that students were so enthusiastic about the experiential nature of service learning that it smoothed over concerns from students who did not find nonprofits as particularly appealing organizations.

Across all three initiatives, students could not give a clear answer to the question as to whether service learning initiatives should be mandatory or elective. On the one hand, making it mandatory would ensure that all students are confronted with service learning, and not only those who are already interested in the subjects of nonprofits and volunteering, emphasizing the citizenship education element of service learning. On the other hand, some students believed that offering service learning as an elective, thus in smaller groups, would increase student enthusiasm, as well as the opportunities to organize high-involvement service learning initiatives.

Our research indicates that across all three initiatives, students did not believe that their peers, the general BA student, would be interested. But the results from the first set of focus groups (which was conducted among general BA students) implies the opposite: the general BA student that participated in our research quite liked the idea of service learning, at least from an experiential learning standpoint. It seemed that hands-on participation and experiential learning were appealing for general BA students regardless of whether they were interested in the service dimension of service learning. In this way, service learning may be generally appealing, and may actually lead to greater commitment to service-related content through concrete experience.

DISCUSSION

While service learning is largely unknown in Dutch business schools, our study strongly suggests that this type of innovation in management education offers appealing benefits to Dutch business students. Despite the lack of institutional innovation, Dutch students showed openness and enthusiasm among both the general BA population and among more specialized Master students who already had a predisposition to work in nonprofit environments.

While the students in our sample come from a Dutch cultural background, our results show clear similarities with the previous literature which is largely developed from a U.S. data set and theoretical perspective. For instance, our findings show strong support for Eyler and Giles (1999, p. 8) idea that "experience enhances understanding." Our qualitative research shows that students strongly believed that the more intense the service learning experience, the better they were able to state what they have learnt from their experience. Intensity in this case related to more experiences. This conclusion underlines Kolb's experiential learning model which suggests that learning will be enhanced when a person is involved in all stages of concrete experience, theoretical reflection, abstract conceptualization, and active experimentation.

The students in our study also agree with Petkus' (2000) argument that service learning initiatives should be course relevant, integrated into the curriculum, directed toward mutuality of benefits, and reflection oriented. With respect to learning, the Dutch students identified skills like team work, creativity and communication skills. These skills are also linked to service learning experience by Tucker et al. (1998), Kenworthy-U'Ren (2000), and Giles and Eyler (1999). Especially the students participating in the nonprofit management consulting assignment perceived the working in teams as both a learning experience and a coordination challenge (see also Easterling & Rudell, 1997).

The results of our research suggest that there may be some cultural influences on the acceptance of service learning, particularly at the institutional level. For instance, none of the Dutch students perceived service learning as an expression of their university's community involvement (e.g., Zlotkowski, 1996), since in general, they did not perceive the university as having an institutional role in community involvement. Although two out of the six students who did a nonprofit internship declared that they perceived service learning as a beneficial opportunity for RSM Erasmus University to invest in its reputation. Students did not expect an institutional linkage between business schools and the nonprofit sector, which fits with the Dutch social origin of a "corporatist" nonprofit regime, where the key institutional linkages lie between the government and the nonprofit sector.

We expected that the Dutch tradition of a nonprofit corporatist regime (with no previous history of university-community involvement) would result in a lower service learning acceptance, or at least a lower understanding of the added value of experience in a nonprofit context to future business leaders in comparison to U.S. students' service learning acceptance as described by McCarthy and Tucker (1999) and Kolenko et al. (1996). But, our research shows that this is not the case, at least not for the students. Service learning was perceived rather positively, especially from an experiential learning standpoint, even by those students from the first service learning initiative who would come closest to the notion of the "general BA student." Gaining experience and learning theory through practice are by far the most important aspects of service learning for the majority of students, which would be in line with McCarthy et al.'s (2002) reasoning that service learning is first and foremost aimed at intentional student learning of theory and management skills. None of the Dutch students were in support of isolated low or no-involvement exercises. Our findings suggest that for Dutch students, deeper involvement (with greater possibilities for experiential learning) may be a more effective means of overcoming initial student resistance. Expressing the experiential value of service learning may be therefore sufficient to overcome initial cultural resistance to business-community involvement (and/or business school-community involvement), if it does exist at all. We also think that in this corporatist regime, service learning may be an important method to raise the awareness among future business managers of their role in the community as well as help to train them in the skills needed in this new function. Service learning could thus contribute to changing Dutch managerial attitudes (over the long run) toward the role of businesses, and universities, in their communities.

Markus et al. (1993) suggests that even a minimal service learning experience (low-involvement) would be effective in building awareness for social issues and to reconnect U.S. students to the notion of community service (see also Eyler & Giles, 1999). We found this was not the case for Dutch business students. They did discuss the added value of some hours of direct service to get acquainted with the nonprofit context, but they were not able to reach a consensus on the number of hours to be spent in a "low involvement" service learning experience. Furthermore, they only saw the added value of these low involvement activities as part of a "service learning package" in which the emphasis is on an intense experiential learning-based service learning experience. This maybe links to the Dutch perception and practice of volunteering which is based upon long time commitment of volunteers and a membership approach to managing volunteers of organizations.

Mutuality of benefits was extremely important to the Dutch students (e.g., Zlotkowski, 1996), particularly in the second service learning initiative, and students linked mutuality of benefit to direct service levels. Our results indicate that while students saw the value of managerial service (an example of indirect community service) they were also interested in doing more direct forms of service such as non-managerial work. Their motivation was not necessarily to engage directly with the end-clients of the nonprofit organization (which would be in line with McCarthy & Tucker, 1999 and Kohls, 1996) but above all because they felt that direct service may increase the added value for the participating nonprofit organizations. This was especially the case for students from the Master elective Nonprofit management who thought that some hours of direct service would be of most interest to their nonprofit organizations, as opposed to providing a "medium involvement" indirect service which they perceived to be mainly beneficial to the students themselves in terms of student learning (see Hogner, 1996). The question is where this form of direct service connects to the intentional learning versus intentional transformation distinction of McCarthy et al. (2002). Or to put more broadly, where this result would fit the dualism found in the service learning literature (Rhoads, 1998; Kezar & Rhoads, 2001; Eyler & Giles, 1999; Kolenko et al., 1996).

While the Dutch students were clearly interested in intentional learning (and the development of managerial skills), they also felt a strong need to make a direct concrete contribution to the nonprofit through hands-on work (or through the implementation of their managerial recommendations). These findings fit more with the suggestion by Dumas (2002) that service learning is first about addressing real needs and applying theory in real life. Although the students of the second service learning initiative like the idea of addressing real needs in real organizations in real life, they did not believe that a medium-involvement experience like theirs would be sufficient to really address those issues. This bothered them. These students seemed to evaluate the success of their service learning initiative implicitly on Kolb's (1976) experiential learning cycle, emphasizing that the initiative could be improved by extending the length of the assignment to include "active experimentation" in the shape of student involvement in implementing consulting recommendations.

With regard to the issue of integration, our research suggests that Dutch students are extremely receptive about the possibilities of integrating service learning into their curriculum, as opposed to the students in McCarthy and Tucker's (1999) research who declared that they were more positive about the idea of community service in general than about integrating community service in their curriculum, due to the expected time commitment. Although McCarthy and Tucker's work may not be generalizable to the broad U.S. context, we have reasons to believe that this difference could be explained from a cultural perspective. There might be two explanations for this difference. First, emphasizing the added value of learning by experience (the experience) instead of the added value of community service (citizenship), provides students with the needed motivation to invest heavily (time) in a service learning initiative because this might be one of the rare occasions to actually learn by experience. Second, there is a difference between a short term approach (community service and volunteering as unpaid labor for a program) and a long term approach (volunteering as active membership with a nonprofit organization). The latter approach is more connected to the Dutch culture and explains why some Dutch students seem to have less opposition against the idea of investing more time in service learning initiatives, as that would mean a larger commitment to a nonprofit organization. The proposal to make a "service learning package" with both mandatory and optional courses seems to fit with Kolenko et al.'s (1996) idea of "exposure experiences" and "high involvement experiences" combining the goals of creating awareness and increasing students' involvement in the service learning initiatives.

In summary, our findings suggest that Dutch students are extremely open to service-learning opportunities, particularly if these initiatives offer interesting forms of experiential learning. While different groups of students had different levels of support for the added value of service learning, they were all in support of experiential learning via such initiatives. While the Netherlands may exist within a different nonprofit regime (in this case, a corporatist regime), this did not seem to result in student perceptions that were markedly different from their U.S. counterparts. Thus, the lack of previous innovation and non-adoption of U.S. approaches toward service learning among Dutch business schools cannot easily be traced to strong cultural differences in student perceptions. While there may be some cultural differences in terms of intensity of service desired among Dutch students (which fits with Dutch preferences for a membership-approach to volunteering), our findings lend support for the cross-cultural viability of service-learning.

Our findings also lend support to the notion that it may be the institutional framework within the Netherlands that has unduly resisted such innovations in management education. Based upon the second author's extensive experience in conducting research on Dutch volunteerism and nonprofit management (combined with many informal discussions with business faculty and administrative staff at universities and vocational schools in the Netherlands), we have found that service learning is not easily organized in the Netherlands at the institutional level. While many

Dutch administrators have informally told us that Dutch students are not open to such approaches, our research strongly suggests the opposite. Instead, it may be that Dutch administrators are not open to such approaches and such preferences may indeed be culturally based.

FUTURE RESEARCH

While our findings among Dutch students demonstrate that their perceptions on service learning have many similarities with US studies, this field of cross-cultural research deserves greater attention. More research is needed to explore the relationship between national cultural contexts and the possibilities of using service learning. Research on the effectiveness of service learning as it relates to levels of managerial innovation would also be valuable, particularly from a cross-cultural perspective.

We also believe that the Dutch institutional resistance (or inertia) may stem in part from the Dutch corporatist nonprofit regime which does not typically emphasize the link between business (and business schools) and the nonprofit sector. However, this requires further research. Thus future cross-cultural research may need to be carried out by selecting based upon the four different nonprofit regimes of Salamon et al. (2000). A related topic would be comparative research into the cross-cultural perceptions of service learning by students, university faculty and administrators, non-profit organizations and their clients in order to identify both institutional and individual cultural preferences for (or resistance to) service-learning initiatives.

APPENDIX: SERVICE LEARNING EXPERIMENTAL DESIGN

	No Real Involvement Letter to the Editor	*Medium Involvement Nonprofit Consulting*	*High Involvement Nonprofit Internships*
Student level	Bachelor 1	Master students	Master students
Status curriculum	Curricular	Curricular	(Extra)curricular
Status course	Obligatory	Elective (obligatory within master elective)	Elective
Student learning	Awareness building, argumentation skills	Diverse skills and 'nonprofit management'	Diverse skills, and "nonprofit" management
Nature service*	Indirect	Indirect	Indirect/ direct
Nature experience	Individual	Team	Individual

*Direct: direct involvement in nonprofit services/direct contact with service clients.
Indirect: management level support/ no direct contact with service clients.

ACKNOWLEDGMENTS

We would like to acknowledge the support of our colleagues Cynthia Piqué and Linda Bridges Karr in data collection. We would also like to thank the two anonymous reviewers for their helpful comments. In addition, we want to thank our Research Institute ERIM for their financial support.

NOTES

1. These direct encounters are similar to the direct service (activities helping clients) in volunteer administration, as opposed to the indirect service (activities for management, boards and policy making).
2. Caution must be used with these numbers. Dekker and De Hart (2002) found in surveys on volunteering in the Netherlands that somewhere between 15 and 50% of the Dutch adults volunteer. According to these authors, the variation depends on factors such as the context of the survey, the expected intensity, and definition of volunteering.
3. The word "corporatist" relates to a way of organizing society and does not relate to the role of companies.
4. The funding of nonprofit organizations provides the most visible evidence of this regime, but it is manifested in a number of other areas as well. Van der Voort (2003b) for example finds an indirect "partnership model," in which the government finances local intermediary organizations to stimulate social involvement among businesses. Dutch local governmental bodies support nonprofit organizations in recruiting volunteers in contrast to the American approach in which local governmental agencies recruit volunteers directly for tasks as cleaning parks or working in libraries (Brudney, 1990).
5. Since the academic year of 2003-2004, student internships are no longer officially required by the Business Administration program at Rotterdam School of Management. However, our department still strongly encourages students to do an internship on a voluntary basis.

REFERENCES

Astin, A.W., Vogelgesang, L.J., Ikeda, E.K., & Yee, J.A. (2000). *How service learning affects students: Executive summary* (Executive summary). Los Angeles: Higher Education Research Institute, University of California.

Bringle, R.G., & Hatcher, J.A. (1996). Implementing service learning in higher education. *The Journal of Higher Education, 67*(2), 221-239.

Brudney, J.L. (1990). *Fostering volunteer programs in the public sector: Planning, initiating, and managing voluntary activities*. San Francisco: Jossey Bass.

Burger, A., & Dekker, P. (1998). De grootste nonprofitsector ter wereld [The biggest nonprofit sector in the world]. *ESB, 83*(4181), 944-946.

Dekker, P., & Hart, J.J.M. de (2002). Ontwikkelingen in de deelname aan vrijwilligerswerk in Nederland [Developments in Volunteering in the Netherlands]. In L.C.P.M. Meijs, & Voort, J.M. van der (Eds.). *Vrijwilligerswerk in Nederland en*

Vlaanderen 2002 [Volunteering in the Netherlands and Flanders 2002], Proceedings research meeting 2002, pp.11-27. Rotterdam: Erasmus University.

Dumas, C. (2002). Community-based service-learning: Does it have a role in management education? *International Journal of Value-Based Management, 15*(3), 294-264.

Easterling, D., & Rudell, F. (1997). Rationale, benefits, and methods of service-learning in marketing education. *Journal of Education for Business, 73*(1), 58-61.

Eyler, J. (2002). Reflection: Linking service and learning-linking students and communities. *The Journal of Social Issues, 58*(3), 517-534.

Eyler, J., & Giles, D. (1999). *Where is the learning in service learning?* San Francisco: Jossey-Bass.

Fagenson-Eland, E., Ensher, E.A., & Burke, W.W. (2004). Organizational development and change interventions. *The Journal of Applied Behavioral Science, 40*(4), 432-464.

Financial Times (FT.com). (2005). *Global MBA rankings 2005.* Retrieved February 16, 2005, from http://rankings.ft.com/rankings/mba/rankings.html.

Giles, Jr., D.E., & Eyler, J. (1994). The impact of a college community service laboratory on students' personal, social, and cognitive outcomes. *Journal of Adolescence, 17*(4), 327-339.

Hofstede, G. (2003). *Culture's consequences: Comparing values, behaviors, institutions, and organizations across nations* (2nd ed.). Newbury Park, CA: Sage.

Hogner, R.H. (1996). Speaking in poetry: Community service-based business education. *Journal of Business Ethics, 15*(1), 33-44.

Kenworthy-U'Ren, A.L. (2000). Management students as consultants: A strategy for service-learning in management education. In P.C. Godfrey & E.T. Grasso (Ed.), *Working for the common good: Concepts and models for service-learning in management* (pp. 55-68, *AAHE's Series on Service-Learning in the Disciplines*). Washington, DC: American Association for Higher Education.

Kezar, A., & Rhoads, R.A. (2001). The dynamic tensions of service learning in higher education: A philosophical perspective. *The Journal of Higher Education, 72*(2), 148-171.

Kohls, J. (1996). Student experiences with service learning in a business ethics course. *Journal of Business Ethics, 15*(1), 45-57.

Kolb, D.A. (1976). Management and the learning process. *California Management Review, 18*(3), 21-31.

Kolenko, T.A., Porter, G., Wheatley, W., & Colby, M. (1996). A critique of service learning projects in management education: Pedagogical foundations, barriers, and guidelines. *Journal of Business Ethics, 15*(1), 133-142.

Kraft, R.J. (1996). Service learning: An introduction to its theory, practice, and effects. *Education & Urban Society, 28*(2), 131-159.

Krueger, R.A., & Casey, M.A. (2000). *Focus groups: a practical guide for Applied Research.* Thousand Oaks, CA: Sage.

Markus, G.B., Howard, J.P.F., & King, D.C. (1993). Integrating community service and classroom instruction enhances learning: Results from an experiment. *Educational Evaluation and Policy Analysis, 15*(4), 410-419.

McCarthy, A.M., Tucker, M.L., & Lund Dean, K.L. (2002). Service learning: Creating community. In C. Wankel & R. DeFillippi (Ed.), *Rethinking management education for the 21st century* (pp. 63-86). Greenwich, CT: Information Age Publishing.

McCarthy, A.M., & Tucker, M.L. (1999). Student attitudes towards service-learning: Implications for implementation. *Journal of Management Education, 23*(5), 554-573.

Meijs, L.C.P.M., Handy, F., Cnaan, R.A., Brudney, J.L., Ascoli, U., Ranade, S., Hustinx, L., Weber, S., & Weiss, I. (2003). All in the eyes of the beholder? Perceptions of volunteering across eight countries. In P. Dekker & I. Halman (Eds.), *Value of volunteering: Cross-cultural perspectives* (pp. 19-34). New York: Kluwer/ Plenum.

Njiokiktjien, M., Talavera, C.D., & Lugtenberg, G. (2004). *Supporters van Rotterdam; Studentenorganisaties actief in de stad* [Supporters of Rotterdam: student associations active in the city]. Rotterdam: Erasmus University Rotterdam.

Petkus Jr., E. (2000). A theoretical and practical framework for service-learning in marketing: Kolb's experiential learning cycle. *Journal of Marketing Education, 15*(1), 21-32.

Rama, D., Ravenscroft, S.P., & Wolcott, S.K. (2000). Service-learning outcomes: Guidelines for educators and researchers. *Issues in Accounting Education, 15*(4), 657-692.

Rhoads, R.A. (1998). In the service of citizenship: A study of student involvement in community service. *The Journal of Higher Education, 69*(3), 277-297.

Roques, C. (2004). Tweemeting vrijwilligers in de sport, een samenvatting [Double measurement volunteers in sports, a summary]. *Vrijwillige Inzet Onderzocht* [Voluntary effort studied], *1*(1), 4-9.

Salamon, L.M., & Sokolowski, S.W. (2001). *Volunteering in cross-national perspective: Evidence from 24 countries.* Baltimore, MD: The Johns Hopkins University Press.

Salamon, L.M., Sokolowski, S.W., & Anheier, H.K. (2000). *Social origins of civil societies: An overview.* Baltimore, MD: The Johns Hopkins University Press.

Sax, L.J.,& Astin, A.W. (1997). The benefits of service: Evidence from undergraduates. *Educational Record, 78*(3-4), 25-32.

Steyaert, C., & Bouwen, R. (1994). Group methods of organizational analysis. In C. Cassell & G. Symon (Eds.), *Qualitative methods in organizational research: A practical guide.* London: Sage.

Tucker, M.L., McCarthy, A.M., Hoxmeier, J.A., & Lenk, M.M. (1998). Community service learning increases communication skills across the business curriculum. *Business Communication Quarterly, 61*(2), 88-99.

Voort, J.M. van der (2003a). *Integrating service learning into the business curriculum.* Rotterdam: Rotterdam School of Management.

Voort, J.M. van der (2003b). *Partnerschappen in perspectief. Over duurzame relaties tussen bedrijven en vrijwilligersorganisaties* [Partnerships in perspective: about sustainable partnerships between companies and voluntary organizations]. Rotterdam: Erasmus University Rotterdam.

Zlotkowski, E. (1996). Service-learning and the academy. *Change, 28*(1), 20-27.

PART III

ACTION LEARNING

ACTION LEARNING AS A VEHICLE FOR MANAGEMENT DEVELOPMENT AND ORGANIZATIONAL LEARNING

Empirical Patterns from Practice and Theoretical Implications

Lyle Yorks

As action learning (AL) programs have proliferated, so have their design characteristics. This chapter uses an integrated model of action learning program dynamics as a framework for an analysis of three case studies of distinct variations in AL program designs. The integrated framework is organized around an empirically based typology of action learning programs, and incorporates constructs from the literatures on adult learning theory, communities-of-practice, and transfer of learning. The discussion includes the impact of program design on learning dynamics, learning transfer, and important decision points for implementing AL within various organizational settings.

Educating Managers through Real World Projects, 183–211
Copyright © 2005 by Information Age Publishing

INTRODUCTION

Although action learning has a long history (Casey & Pearce, 1977; Foy, 1977; Revans, 1965, 1971, 1978, 1982) it has more recently become fashionable, especially in the context of executive development (Boshyk, 2000; Dotlich & Noel, 1998; Marquardt, 1999; Noel & Charan, 1988; Vicere, 1996). Along with this increasingly wide use of action learning methodology has come a number of compromises that human resource development managers in organizations have had to make in bringing what is advocated as a best practice into their organizations. Action learning is an intensive and demanding approach to development, and participants can struggle with the requirements of working on projects while also being accountable for their work responsibilities in downsized workplaces characterized by "24/7" work loads. Many action learning programs are being designed in contexts that require significant compromises in terms of budget, timing, and visible senior executive support as learning and development professionals strive to demonstrate the use of action learning as a "best practice." As these programs proliferate there is a need for bringing relevant conceptual lenses to bear for critical analysis with the intention of better understanding the learning dynamics of these programs. Such understanding is fundamental to the further development of theoretical frameworks useful for guiding both research and practice.

Four general questions of concern to both researchers and practitioners that are fundamental to any actionable theory of action learning have guided the inquiry reported in this chapter:

- How does program design influence the learning dynamics in action learning?
- What is the pattern of learning transfer taking place from different program designs?
- What factors in the larger transfer system appear to inhibit or facilitate learning transfer, and consequently?
- What are some important decision point considerations for implementing action learning within various organizational contexts?

These questions are systemically interconnected with one another. Learning dynamics influence the pattern of transfer, and contextual factors in the larger transfer system shape program design as well.

Over the past decade the author and his colleagues have studied seven different action learning programs in depth.[1] This chapter draws on data from three field case studies, supplemented by insights from the other four. These three cases represent different program types (described below), and the organizational settings vary considerably in terms of the strategic issues facing the companies, market size and dynamics, and organizational culture and legacies. We will provide more information on the programs and development of the cases below. First, however, it will be helpful to define how the terms "action learning" and "learning" are used in this project.

ACTION LEARNING DEFINED

Although there is no one definition of action learning (cf. Marquardt, 2004, pp. 2-4; McGill & Beaty, 1992, p, 17; McNulty, 1979, p. 12; Pedler, 1991, pp. xxii-xxiii; Revans, 1982, pp. 626-627) certain principles distinguish action learning from other forms of experience-based learning. Common to virtually all definitions of AL is working in small groups in order to take action on meaningful problems while seeking to learn from having taken this action (Yorks, O'Neil, & Marsick, 1999). This process of learning from taking action is often conceptualized as involving cycles of action and reflection. Some authors advocate the use of learning coaches who facilitate the process of learners questioning their actions, reflecting on their assumptions, and committing to new actions. Within these general parameters there are several variations of how action learning programs are structured, including designs in which individuals share their own particular work-based challenges versus group designs where a team collectively works on a problem typically sponsored by a senior executive. Group designs can vary according to whether the problem is a familiar one in a familiar setting, an unfamiliar problem in an unfamiliar setting, or one of the other two possible combinations. Further design variations include the number and the spacing of meetings, the composition of the group, and whether the objectives of the program are centered on individual learning and development or also include some form of organizational learning.

Incorporating the above principles, the definition of action learning that has guided this inquiry is: *An approach to working with and developing people that use work on an actual project or problem as the way to learn. Participants work in small groups to take action to solve their problem and learn how to learn from that action. Often a learning coach works with the group in order to help the members learn how to balance their work with the learning from that work* (Yorks et al., 1999, p. 3). As an approach to management and executive development, action learning takes an actual "real-life" dilemma or quandary confronting a manager, or his or organization, as a vehicle for learning and development. The terms "dilemma" or "quandary" denote a complex challenge that is highly unstructured, and reasonable people are likely to disagree over proposed solutions. These kinds of challenges have been differentiated in the seminal action learning literature (Revans, 1978) from "puzzles" that may be very challenging and the answer unknown, but the relevant variables and methodologies for solving the puzzle are known. Resolving quandaries requires the development of what Revans (1982) calls questioning insight (although "just-in-time" input from experts may be utilized as part of the learning process), the latter the application of expert knowledge.

Action learning can be differentiated from other active learning strategies such as simulations, experiential learning exercises that provide vicarious experiences, and adventure Outward Bound type rope courses in that action learning is directly linked to the learner's work setting. However, all of these pedagogical methods may be used in combination with action learning in extensive management development programs, along with presentations by outside consultants and case studies.

WHAT DO WE MEAN BY LEARNING?

The defining characteristic of learning is that it involves personal change (Bateson, 1972; Hilgard & Bower, 1966; Knowles, 1990), and in the context of executive development this change may take place in any of number of domains: specifically content knowledge, skills and competencies, cognitive frames of reference, personal awareness, and the emotional capacity for change. Revans' concept of questioning insight implies what Cell (1984) calls situation learning—a change in how one interprets a situation. This requires what Mezirow (2000) refers to as changing one's meaning perspective: the structure of assumptions and expectations through which we filter experience and sense impressions by elaborating existing frames of reference, learning new frames of reference, or transforming frames of reference through critical reflection on underlying premises and reformulating reified mental models. These frames of reference may relate to instrumental learning (learning to manipulate the environment or other people in the service of task accomplishment) or communicative learning (sensemaking).

Mezirow's ideas parallel those of Bateson (1972) who describes level I learning as learning within existing meaning schemes, level II learning as changing the set of alternatives from which one selects alternatives, and Level III learning as changes in the premises on which our main frame of reference is based. When learning results in changed underlying premises, it can be described as transformative (Mezirow, 1991).

Additionally, many action learning programs are intended to make participants more cognizant of their learning processes per se, or learning how to learn. This is what Cell refers to as transsituation learning— learning how to change our interpretations of a situation—and Bateson as deuterolearning. This kind of learning requires that learners reflect on the processes that characterize their learning—using reflexive inquiry practices for critical self-reflection on *how* they have engaged in testing their assumptions and attributions.

Effective executive development involves integrating content and self-knowledge into practical *knowing how* (Quinn, 1992; Vaill, 1996) that can be applied in diverse, and often changing and uncertain, contexts. This kind of learning transfer is referred to in the literature as far transfer, being able to generalize learning across contexts that are very different from the ones encountered in the original learning setting (Butterfield & Nelson, 1989; Holton & Baldwin, 2003; Laker, 1990; Royer, 1979). This is in contrast to near transfer, the application of learning in contexts that are the same or only slightly modified from those encountered in the learning environment. Under the conditions of rapid change confronted by most of today's organizations, the notion of far transfer can be extended to include the more developmentally advanced forms of transsituation and deuterolearning posited by theorists such as Cell and Bateson. What needs to be transferred are not only competencies and knowledge of general principles, but the capability for engaging in learning in which even past experience may not be a guide: in other words, a capacity for continuing to pursue questioning insight.

A RESEARCH-BASED TYPOLOGY OF ACTION LEARNING PROGRAMS

Action learning programs can be designed in a variety of ways, and for a range of purposes. The organizing framework for this inquiry is a typology of action research programs originally developed by O'Neil (1999). Based on an analysis of interviews with a wide range of prominent action learning practitioners, O'Neil identifies four "schools" of action learning practice, the tacit or incidental school, the scientific school, the experiential school, and the critical reflection school. Each of these 'schools' represents a cluster of action learning practices, forming a typology that captures some central characteristics of the different ways in which action learning initiatives are organized and implemented. Although the four schools share in common an emphasis on working on actual work-based challenges, each of these "schools" is also distinguished by different assumptions regarding learning. Consequently, each approach designs the learning experience in a different way. Not surprisingly, these different designs lead to different learning outcomes, and by extension, what is potentially transferred to the workplace beyond the learning program itself.

The four schools are described in detail elsewhere (O'Neil, 1999; Yorks et al., 1999; Yorks, 2003). In summary form, the tacit school approach assumes that learning will take place so long as carefully chosen participants are put together, some team building is done, and experts provide background and contextual information relevant to the projects to be worked upon. While the program is planned, the learning process *per se* is not structured. The learning that takes place from the project work is largely what Marsick and Watkins (1990) have categorized as incidental. Consequently, the project teams do not use learning coaches (see, e.g., Downham, Noel, & Pedergast, 1992; Noel & Charan, 1988). The scientific school is rooted in the work of Reg Revans and reflects his original professional training as a physicist. The overall framework of this approach reflects the scientific method, and places importance on problem setting and resetting. In practice it has many of the characteristics of co-inquiry oriented action research. The emphasis is on asking questions (questioning insight) and solving the problem rather than the development of interpersonal and leadership competences. The role of the learning coach (called a "supernumerary" in Revans' work) is minimized. Casey and Pearce (1977) and Foy (1997) provide case discussions of AL initiatives that are examples of this type.

The experiential school places emphasis on the experiential learning cycle (i.e., Kolb, 1984; Mumford, 1995) of having an experience, reflecting on that experience, conceptualizing the experience, and experimenting with new ideas. Practitioners of this tradition emphasize the role of intentional, explicit reflection throughout the process and a learning coach works with the learners, actively designing practices toward this end. Personal learning goals are set and there is considerable emphasis placed on personal development. Mumford (1993) provides a good introduction to this approach and Vicere's (1996) discussion of ARAMARK provides a nice example. Practitioners in the critical reflection school are also influenced by the experiential learning cycle as a theoretical framework, but take reflection to a deeper level by focusing on the underlying premises in the thinking of managers. This critical reflection is focused on taken-for-granted organizational norms and examines the deep culture of the organization (Marsick, 1990). The goal is personal and organizational transformation (see Dennis, Cederholm, & Yorks, 1996, for an example). It should be noted that these four types represent analytical categories that capture the general elements of distinct approaches found in practice. Any particular program will vary somewhat from type.

An Action Learning Pyramid

Based on experience and case studies, Yorks, O'Neil, and Marsick (1999) subsequently structured the typology into a pyramid model to help practitioners make choices among different programs based on desired outcomes (Yorks et al., 1999). Preliminary evidence suggests that these different approaches become increasingly inclusive in terms of the learning outcomes they produce. Essentially, as one goes from the base of the pyramid (tacit school) to the top (critical reflection), each successive level incorporates the primary learning outcomes of the previous one with the depth of the questioning insight and developmental and transformative potential of the learning experience increasing. However, the level of "organizational noise" also increases as one goes up the pyramid. As program designs progress up the pyramid from tacit to critically reflective, there is an increasing sense of learners feeling out of their comfort zone. This is particularly true of participants who are used to very structured learning environments. Consequently, more initial "noise" is produced in terms of feedback into the organization. By "noise" is meant comments made by participants challenging the program as they are asked to reflect

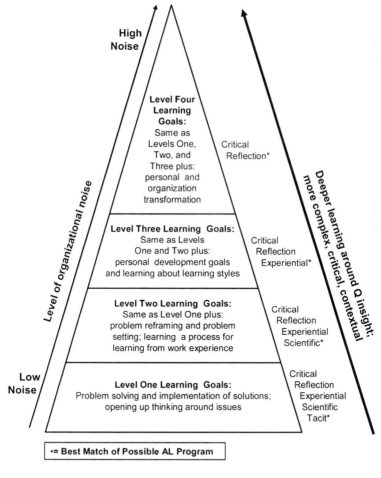

Adapted from Yorks L, O'Neil J, Marsick VJ (1999, p. 14)

Figure 8.1.   Work-based learning pyramid.

on long-held assumptions, mental models, and issues that have been pre-viously treated as givens, not open to discussion, and other "undiscuss-ables" (Arygris & Schon, 1978). Figure 8.1 illustrates this pyramid model.

Using the Typology as a Basis for Further Inquiry

This pyramid is a product of the broader stream of inquiry on which this chapter is based and has been used as part of the analysis reported here. The three cases described here were selected as prototype examples of critical reflective, experiential, and tacit designs. For purposes of com-parison, all three involve group designs with teams working on projects sponsored by more senior executives, and multiple meetings of the teams. To date, we have not had access to a program that closely fits the group project model using the scientific approach.

The three cases have been selected through a combination of conve-nience and theoretical sampling. Opportunities for researching two of the programs presented themselves when those administering them approached the author about providing an independent assessment of the program. In the case of the third program an internal assessment pro-cess was overseen by one of the author's colleagues. This assessment was subsequently made available to the author. The author was not involved as a consultant in the delivery of any of the programs.

The cases were studied at different points in time, and the methodol-ogy had to be adapted to meet the circumstances that presented them-selves. In the critical reflection case, the data were gathered through extensive participant observation. The researcher traveled with the pro-gram and conducted interviews with participants, program faculty, and peers and subordinates of the participants. Additionally, pre and post-program developmental 360 feedback data used during the program were available. In the tacit case, there were partial field observation and audio-taped interviews with both participants and leaders of the program. In the experiential case, the data sources were audio-taped critical inci-dent interviews with participants and program leaders, and archival data, supplemented by first-hand knowledge of the program's design. The emergent patterns are verifiable through multiple sources, lend them-selves to the development of theory that can inform action, and suggest implications for future testing and revision. Table 8.1 provides a brief summary of each program.

All three programs were viewed as successful by both the internal learn-ing staff and senior management. Participants subsequently evaluated their program as a significant learning experience that exceeded their ini-tial expectations and was substantially different from prior management development programs (essentially level 1 evaluation in Kirkpatrick's 4

Table 8.1.   Summary of the Three Case Studies

The Critical Reflection Program

Goals and Format: Facilitate the transition to a global organization with a one company profit & loss statement mentality by:

- Developing appropriate global leadership competencies
- Developing the parameters and core framework for the organizational infrastructure & systems for a global company
- 3 programs of 4 six day meetings. Each program held across a period of 3 months, with program meetings held in different global locations. All three programs held during a period of two years.
- 20 participants in each program, divided into 4 project teams, each team sponsored by a member of the executive committee including the CEO. Participants are senior and upper management in the operating companies.
- Each team has a learning coach who is on the program staff

The Experiential Program

Goals and Format: Build capacity for performance in the deregulating business environment by:

- Enhancing interpersonal communication skills, especially problem solving and coaching skills
- Creating an environment where conflict can be productively surfaced and resolved
- Build the use of quality tools and practices
- 9 programs/25 to 30 participants in each program/ participants are divided into project teams of 5 to 6 members/ each team has a project sponsored by senior functional management. Participants are operational level supervision
- ½ day orientation, a 2day kick off meeting, 2 day interim meeting, and 2 day final meeting of the entire program/ 6 days of project team meetings spread over 6 weeks/ each team has a learning coach

The Tacit Program

Goals and Format: Developing executive capacity and 'bench strength' among the 'top 100' executives below the executive committee by:

- Developing strategic thinking through working on projects in E business product distribution that would reposition the business within the value chain
- 1 week meeting with training delivered by outside experts and project team development around learning styles/some project work, a 21/2 day interim meeting focusing on projects, and final week preparing project presentation with additional training in leadership and presentation skills. No learning coaches but a expert on strategic thinking (B-school executive professor of practice) works with the program.

---

level evaluation typology). Additionally, our research into the programs provides evidence of individual learning aligned with program goals (level 2), and some evidence of application (level 3). While there were insights from all three programs as to how each might be improved in future offerings, all three were assessed by management as meeting their objectives. The cases were selected for more intensive study to allow for the emergence of important differences among effective representatives of each type.

AN INTEGRATED MODEL OF
ACTION LEARNING PROGRAM DYNAMICS

The patterns observed in our three cases can be framed in the context of a diverse set of existing literature. The literatures of communities-of-practice, team and organizational learning, adult learning, and learning transfer are all relevant for understanding the dynamics of action learning programs. Indeed, systemic analysis of AL programs provides insight into important connections among these theoretical frameworks from a research perspective. The integrated model presented here (Figure 8.2) has evolved over time from the streams of literature sources summarized below. The various components of the model provided the basis for the coding scheme for developing this paper. Iterations of the field research have produced insights into the relevance of these various theoretical foundations for understanding the dynamics to a broader understanding of AL.

Communities-of-Practice

While there are important differences between action learning programs and communities-of-practice, Marsick (2002) has argued that critical dimensions of learning communities are useful for the analysis of action learning programs. Like communities-of-practice, action learning programs incorporate principles of social learning theory, striving to create a social space in which a group can thrive in working together on a problem or challenge (Marquardt & Waddill, 2004, p. 191). Both can be conceptualized as organizational learning mechanisms (OLM's) (Popper & Lipshitz, 1998); organizational structural and procedural arrangements facilitating both learning-in-organization (when members learn on behalf of the organization) and learning-by-organization (when this individual learning has organizational level output in the form of changes that are captured and widely used by the organization). Action learning teams can be conceptualized as potential organizational learning mechanisms with participants learning-in-organization. If the results of their projects and/ or new competencies learned by participants in the program become embedded in the practices and norms of the organization, learning-by-organization can be said to have occurred. Drawing on the work of Brown and Duguid (1991), and Huang, Newell, and Galliers (2002) four mechanisms for creating and disseminating knowledge have been identified: structural, social, intellectual, and technological. These mechanisms can all be used to both generate and communicate knowledge about different learning domains (Marsick, 2002). Our discussion will focus on the design

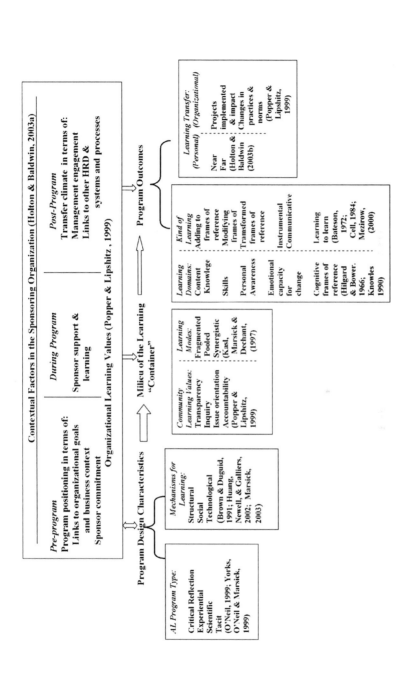

Figure 8.2. An integrated model of action learning dynamics (and literature).

of structural and social dimensions for action learning programs. We note in passing that there are interesting questions to be explored regarding how to most effectively use technology to allow globally diverse project teams to pursue their projects in a virtual space.

AL programs strive to create a collaborative social space (Yorks, Neuman, Kowalski, and Kowalski, forthcoming) that is a "container" for engaging in open inquiry that is critical for the kind of learning that occurs in an AL program. Fisher and Torbert (1995) describe this kind of collaborative social space as a "liberating structure," "turn(ing) tensions, dilemmas, and gaps ... into occasions for learning and improved competence ... that is productive and ... educates its members toward self-correcting awareness." Fisher and Torbert argue that organizations place significant barriers in the way of generative learning processes. Overcoming these barriers requires conscious intervention, since many, perhaps even most, are undiscussable defensive routines that have become embedded in the cultural fabric of organizations, leading them to continually reproduce obstacles even when they seek to overcome them. The extent to which these barriers are surfaced and recognized within programs' is a function of the structural and social dimensions of the learning community that are established through the length, timing, and location of the meetings (structural) and the activities and the focus and depth of the reflection and reflexive learning practices that are embedded in the program (social). These two dimensions contextualize and shape the intellectual (learning) content of the program.

In effect, structure creates opportunities for learning and the social dimension enacts it, both through the patterns of personal interaction that are created and the learning values that are established. These patterns of interaction and the norms and values that are established by them facilitate or constrain the kind of learning that is produced in the program. Popper and Lipshitz have argued that for organizational learning mechanisms like AL programs to promote collective learning, they must be embedded in shared values that promote productive learning. These values are transparency, inquiry, integrity, issue orientation, and accountability. Establishing these values within the AL program is partly a function of the design of the program, and partly a function of the extent to which the broader organizational context of the program is supportive of them. This support can be facilitated through interaction and learning on the part of sponsors.

By design, the project teams are the principle vehicles for learning in action learning programs. Three modes of team learning (Kasl, Marsick, & Dechant, 1997) can be potentially observed in the teams: *fragmented learning* (individual learning that is not shared by the group, nor necessarily shared with or by others), *pooled learning* (individuals share information and perspectives, and small groups of people learn together, but the group as whole doesn't learn), and *synergistic learning* (the group as whole creates knowledge mutually, integrating divergent perspectives in new ways and integrating team knowledge into individual meaning schemes). Design of the structural and social dimensions of the program, along with the values that are established facilitate the modes of learning that occur within the project teams and also the kind of learning that occurs.

Organizational context matters both in terms of how program participants approach their learning in the program and their work on the projects. These connections include both the strategic goals of the organization and their fit with the rationale for the program, the nature of senior management's engagement with the program (particularly the projects), and how projects relate to other organizational initiatives. Apart from influencing the learning that takes place within the program, these contextual characteristics are variations of what Holton and Baldwin (2003) have characterized as the learning transfer system. Depth of learning in terms of the five knowledge domains, augmented by the organization's contextual setting seems to be determinate factors in transfer patterns. Learning transfer can be personal, where participants change their behavior and actions in their regular jobs, and organizational, in terms of the impact of the projects on the organization, and changes in patterns of organizational practices and norms. Both personal and organizational transfer requires supporting contextual conditions.

PATTERNS ACROSS THE THREE PROGRAMS

Having shared the overall conceptual framework that has been emerging from our work, below we describe the impact of program design and context on the three cases.

The Impact of Program Designs

Patterns of design and learning in the critical reflection program. The most readily observable difference among the three programs directly relates to their respective designs. The critical reflection program provided evidence of the majority of participants becoming increasingly aware of the connections among the formal content of the program, their process of learning, and their projects. As the program progressed, participants also became conscious of how their behavior in their project teams and in the program initially replicated how people behaved in the organization. This led to discussions regarding the strengths and limitations of this organizational culture as the company was working toward becoming a global network. Cross-cultural assumptions began to surface. The resulting reframing of behavior also led to critiques of how their various business units functioned internally as well.

Perhaps the most graphic example of how behavior in the program reflected broader issues in the organization took place during the third meeting of one of the programs. From the start of the week, the learning coaches were aware of a sub-text of discussion among participants. During the Saturday evening reflection and dialogue session that started the week, one of the participants said, "There is something wrong with this group, I don't want to say what it is." Others seemed aware of the meaning behind his comment. While nothing was said directly, there was a different "feel" to the program. As this feeling got stronger, the coaches decided to call an unscheduled reflection and dialogue session following Wednesday's breakfast. As was customary for these "R&D" sessions, the entire community of 20 participants, four coaches, and the researcher were seated in a large circle for the dialogue. The lead coach started by stating that the coaches sensed something was an issue in the community, and simply said if the group was ready he would like for the entire community to discuss whatever the issue was.

After a long silence, one of the participants said that there was a rumor within the group that, even though this program had been established as a development opportunity and what happened in the program was confidential, the coaches were assessing people and feeding back information to management and others were compromising confidentiality. As the dialogue continued, the focus gradually shifted from the program to the company, and that the issue wasn't the program but how people are used to functioning in the organization. The coaches were not central to the dialogue as people spoke about the climate in the company and with an increasing awareness of what they as a global network of relationships could do about it. The R&D session ended an hour later; the air had been cleared and several "undiscussables" had been surfaced and discussed.

Another example of becoming aware of how behavior in the organization at large was being transferred into the learning community comes from within one of the project teams early in the first week. As the project evolved, one of the two more senior members of the group stood up to write on the easel and began leading the group. The other senior member, who had the same job title in a different geographic region, stood at the other end of the room, participating in the discussion. The other three members, all division level executives, but with less senior titles, remained seated. During the stop/reflect called by the learning coach, one of the other three, referring to the person who had been standing at the back of the room, and motioning toward the other said, "I think he's doing what you want to do." This triggered an open discussion with another member saying "with the pens we are being directed, we are being edited." Another stated, "I felt a certain competitiveness." The group discussed the need for asking questions, rather than asserting positions. Over time, as the team developed, one could observe the group becoming increasingly focused on building composite ideas. By the end of the third program meeting, one member commented, "as a group we made tremendous progress, we worked to a good result very fast, we had openness with one another." Another said, "our later performance over weighted the early. Everybody made changes. I never had the impression of one guy being in charge."

Similar patterns occurred in the other three groups. One of the members of another project team commented after the third meeting, "In regard to storming, norming, etc. depending on whether we are on a macro or micro issue, we are doing all three things at different times. We are aware of our process, stopping ourselves. We have raised awareness of ourselves. We have a different level of comfort about learning about that [process] then before."

This evolving awareness is a function of the evolution of the program as a learning community. Each six-day meeting of the community was a mix of community wide focused learning, experiential learning activities linked to the cultural setting where a particular meeting was being held, project work, and presentations by outside consultants and academics that provided content relevant to the stage of their project work. A typical week would include one day devoted to a cultural experience, with culturally diverse groups of participants engaging in varied activities that would then be shared with the entire community of twenty. For example, while in Singapore, groups of participants visited a Buddhist temple, a Hindu temple, a Moslem mosque, and a Christian retreat center, respectively. The groups' particular assignments involved not only touring these spiritual sites, but also engaging in inquiry with the religious leaders about how their religious traditions functioned in the larger Singaporean culture.

Another day in the program would have an external expert presenting on management issues relevant to the project work. For example, a presentation during the first week of the program was done by an internationally recognized expert on globalization, focusing on the key differences between operating as a multinational and as a global organization. A presentation during a later meeting focused on scenario planning as a way of testing ideas.

At least two days of each week focused on project work, with the learning coaches working with the teams to help them harvest their learning and surface issues for discussion. The learning coach would not try to facilitate the group's process, but would observe what was happening and periodically help the group to critically reflect on their team's process and the content of their work. The coaches would also suggest practices and methods that might help to move work on the project forward. Several times a week the entire community of twenty would participate in a 45 minute period of reflection and dialogue. Because the program traveled to different global locations, several of the participants would be outside of their comfort zone during each meeting. Learning was not limited to either formal content or the projects but was part of the experience as a whole, building capacity for dealing with uncertainty and change.

The resulting learning was very holistic and systemic, a function of the attention given to building a "learning community." Most participants came to develop a tacit knowledge about working in tense situations across cultures on issues that were very challenging. This was the only program in which the data provide evidence of deuterolearning, or being explicit about learning to learn. Many of the learning practices that were introduced became second nature to the participants by the conclusion of the program. Early in each run of the program, participants would be very method or technique oriented, looking for specific practices that they could take back to their home organizations. As the program progressed, participants began to realize that resolving process issues was less a matter of specific techniques, and more a function of how they related to other people. This awareness typically progressed through stages of differentiation and integration. Initially, participants struggled with establishing their own identity within the group, how to build on the ideas of others while maintaining their own individuality. Later, this same dynamic could be seen between the various project teams, as teams tended to make comments among themselves that reflected almost a competitive orientation with the other teams. Finally, the teams came to see themselves as part of a larger system, drawing on insights and ideas across team boundaries.

In the critical reflection program, the learning tended to get applied back in the workplace when there was an emerging cadre of former participants. About 80% of the people interviewed in two areas of the organization in which a significant number of managers had participated in the program could see some change in how these participants approached their jobs. These changes reflect personal transfer of learning apart from the content of the project. When asked about the percentage of former participants who demonstrated change, estimates ranged from half to 75%. The range of change varied from "significant change" to "some change" with the latter the most frequently mentioned. Most frequently mentioned changes were behaviors around sharing information (which was seldom done before) and an openness to the opinions of others. Also, there was a higher level of reflection and encouraging dialogue, reflecting the deuterolearning that took place during the program. Typical interview comments were:

> Well, there has been an impact in the way people are behaving, the way they are doing things.... When I look at my boss, for example, he was more willing, more open, to talk about ... things that he wanted to change.

Another person commented:

> The behavior of people has changed. Out of three (participants in the program), one didn't change at all. The other two became more open ... tried to delegate more ... it is a process that has to build.

In another interview a person stated:

> If you have a meeting (with people from the program), there is a difference. They become better listeners. They also take some time to have some reflection.... They take a step back. They evaluate what was said, this has a positive impact, making better decisions. There is a better understanding in a number of people.

These interviews were supported by a subsequent 360 feedback survey and further field observations in the program. Overall, the pattern of practices a year later suggested far transfer, although there was also some slippage back into old practices, especially without the support of others. It is also important to note that these patterns were not universal. In each run of the program there were one or two people who were clearly resisting many of the learning practices and the more intensive reflexive activities. These individuals participated with their project teams, but, for example, didn't speak up in program-wide reflection and dialogue sessions.

Patterns of design and learning in the experiential program.   In the experiential program, the primary focus was on the project work and the development of interpersonal communication skills, particularly in the area of surfacing and resolving conflict. Because the teams largely met separately, and on different schedules, there was not the same program-wide learning dynamic. During the two-day meetings of the program as a larger community, the teams shared their work with one another. There was no training content from outside experts. However, the learning coaches provided instruction in learning styles, the Johari Window, dialogue practices, giving feedback, and conflict resolution. In project meetings, the coaches then facilitated group learning using these various

Table 8.2.   Overall Percentages of
Responses from the Experiential Program

1. Have you found other people in the department who are able to say thing more openly with you and with others since the start of the program?

Yes without qualification	31	40.30%
Yes with qualification	19	24.70%
No with qualification	15	19.50%
No without qualification	12	15.50%
Total Interviews	77	100.00%

2. Do you feel people are acting any differently when there is a disagreement now than before the program?

Yes without qualification	37	48.00%
Yes with qualification	17	22.10%
No with qualification	16	20.80%
No without qualification	7	9.10%
Total Interviews	77	100.00%

3. Do you see the quality tools being used more now than before the program?

Yes without qualification	46	59.70%
Yes with qualification	15	19.50%
No with qualification	11	14.30%
No without qualification	5	6.50%
Total Interviews	77	100.00%

methods as the teams worked on their projects. Special attention was paid to using learning oriented approaches, such as balancing advocacy with inquiry, as ways of surfacing and resolving conflicts as well as application of quality management tools such as Pareto diagrams and process control charts in targeting and testing opportunities for new work practices. Each participant brought a learning goal to the program that was discussed with the coaches and shared with the team. The project team was used as a context for working on the personal learning goal, as well as trying certain changes and activities back in the workplace and reporting this back to the group.

The data from critical incident interviews following the program point toward individuals learning and a mix of near and far learning transfer. Table 8.2 provides a summary of seventy-seven interviews conducted a few months following the program. The questions reported in the table relate to the program's core objectives. Depending on the program objective being discussed, 65%-79% of the interviewees responded that they had seen positive changes reflective of the program objectives in their day-to-day interactions. The specific negative responses (that they had not seen the changes desired by the program) ranged from a low of 6.5% to a high of 15.5%. There is considerable evidence of participants being more aware of process and engaging in basic reflective learning. For example, "Yes, I think we have more consciousness ... let's say when we go to a meeting if we did not accomplish anything in the past we would have walked away. Now, whether on a conscious or unconscious level, we are asking ourselves what went wrong. We are asking more of the right questions if a meeting was not prepared to standards." A non-participant comment: "I think the program has allowed them to focus their attention in a manner that they are not afraid to speak up whether they say it in the right way or not."

Patterns of design and learning in the tacit program.   In the tacit case, the program focused primarily on the projects, but also had a heavy component of executive education content. Participants spent considerable time during each day of the first week being exposed to presenters from outside the company on topics related to "strategic drivers" of business success. While these presentations were not as closely linked to the specific development issues of the project work as in the critical reflection program, they were targeted toward expanding participants knowledge of strategic drivers of the business and stimulating their thinking around the projects. Topics included globalization and competitiveness, E-business, scenario planning, and brand management. These presentations were highly rigorous. Of the three cases, this program most closely corresponded to an advanced EMBA program with project work. During the first day of the program, participants were experientially exposed to learning style theory and spent time reflecting on the relative strengths and limitations of the mix of styles in the teams and the implications of this mix. The project work was largely scheduled for the evening and toward the end of the week-long session. Project teams got organized for working virtually during the time between the first and second meeting of the program. The second meeting allowed more time to be devoted to refining the projects.

Participants didn't receive any feedback on their project work from a senior executive committee member until early in the final week of the program. This feedback resulted in some tense rework of the project proposals that, nevertheless, demonstrated the group's ability to pull together and resolve some core issues. The learning from the program was very cognitive, with participants demonstrating new ways of thinking about the business, particularly the nature of strategic thinking and the implications of E-business for the company. A representative interview comment was, "we all learned about outside forces and then we all took that into a strategy for the company. We did it together. We had a group leadership experience as if we were the policy team. I am proud of how we did, how we included each other."

There was considerable discussion about how ready the organization was for embracing the kinds of changes that would be required for future competitiveness, but there was no systematic critical reflection on either the organizational culture or their own experience in the program. In many ways, the approach was what has been called "bounded critical reflection" (Yorks & Marsick, 2000, p. 274) where there was guided critical reflection on the instrumental issues of task performance at the organizational level and rethinking assumptions about the larger business environment, but discussions about the organization's culture was largely off limits. There was minimal structured dialogue in the total program regarding what the participants had learned. Whatever insights others were gaining from the program remained largely private or shared informally among friends, but not collectively harvested.

However, there was evidence of pooled learning around competencies as participants shared feedback informally with one another. In the words of one participant, "it was one of the best learning experiences of my life because I was in a peer team that will give you feedback. I am in a branch where my employees can't give me that feedback, so it was very useful even when it wasn't the most flattering feedback." Comments like this expressed the value of what they had learned, but didn't reflect the same learning about how to solicit feedback and structure more open conversations back on the job with employees and others. Learning transfer tended to take the form of participants importing learning content into their work. Often, this took the form of sharing ideas from the presenters with staff in their home settings. "I am a very practical person so I am sitting there experiencing all of these (presentations) knowing that I have an application for one of them coming up in the next month and thinking about that. I look at everything in terms of what am I going to get out of this?... There was more substance than I had initially expected.... I used (a strategy professor's) presentation to some management groups." When working within their project teams, team members initially functioned as individuals working within a team. With time, they improved their capacity for working together, resolving difficulties and learning to use each other's strengths. Essentially they were able to work effectively together as individuals and get the job done, and share considerable learning about the business. There was less evidence of achieving team synergy and learning how to bring out the potential for group learning that would tap less obvious individual talents and bring them into the team.

Organizational Context

A fundamental premise of AL is that the project is the vehicle for learning. Our data suggest that for the projects to provide a significant learning experience to participants, the project teams have to perceive their work as more than either a routine taskforce or simply a learning exercise that uses the organization as the case study. An important precondition for the depth of learning that takes place around the project itself is the perception of participants that the project is linked to significant business issues for which there is no preexisting organizational answer, and that their work is going to be relevant to eventual organizational actions. Additionally, participants are being "challenged" in that the issues involved in the projects stretch them beyond their previous levels of experience.

In all three of the cases, participants initially bought into the projects because they were linked to believable challenges that were confronting the organization. In the critical reflection case, the AL program had been preceded by a corporate search conference involving a broad cross section of managers that supported the need for the company becoming more globally integrated, supplemented by a corporate survey that also demonstrated wide spread support throughout the company for the globalization strategy. The survey also revealed that many employees had questions about the capability of managers in the organization for functioning in a global environment. The AL program was an extension of these initiatives. The projects laid the foundation for the subsequent organizational changes while accelerating the development of operational level management through significant cross-cultural exposure and cultivated an informal network of relationships that would later become formalized.

In both the experiential and tacit cases, changes in the external business environment provided a clear rationale for the projects. The experiential case involved a large public utility at a time when it was becoming clear that deregulation would have a significant impact on the industry's structure. It was clear that the traditional hierarchical and centralized structure was an impediment to effective adaptation to this new business environment. New approaches needed to be adopted. The participants in this program were lower in the organization than in either of the other two cases, but, although more operationally focused, the projects were linked to the need for coming up with new ways of organizing work that were consistent with evolving organizational strategy. In the tacit case, the advent of the web and its impact on the marketing value chain had also made clear the need for change in how the company distributed its products.

In all three cases, the participants in the program were challenged to surface assumptions they were holding about how things were done in the organization; they gathered data informing them about a range of issues relevant to the project, and made innovative proposals that reflected new thinking around the instrumental issues. The motivation driving the learning was intrinsic and extrinsic: intrinsic in terms of their interest in the project and extrinsic because of the opportunity of making an impression on senior executives.

These cases are in stark contrast to some AL programs we have also observed where the challenges appear to be manufactured for the program, or the sponsors seem disassociated from them. Often the sponsor will delegate contact with the team to a subordinate who is only marginally interested in the challenge, and many times view the assignment simply as another task that has been "put on his or her plate." These "de facto" sponsors can often be a de-motivator, or serve to limit the creative potential of the groups, channeling the teams into traditional courses of action. An aspect of the sponsor's role that is largely undiscussed in the literature is the notion of being a co-learner. Our data suggests that the willingness of the sponsor to have his or her assumptions about the project challenged, and to facilitate learning through questioning the team and engaging in dialogue without specifically directing them, is an important determinant of a team's willingness to embrace new learning. This kind of mentoring is often a new experience for senior executives.

In all three of our cases, the first time senior managers were confronted with the thinking of the teams, they acted in ways that ran counter to the way the participants had been functioning in the program. This discrepancy became visible in the critical reflection program where program participants had been not only working on projects but also developing competencies for working cross culturally, and fostering open dialogue and debate. During the presentation of the project recommendations, the members of the executive committee began arguing with one another, interrupting the presentations, and inserting their own opinions without listening—essentially bringing their own collective way of working into the room. A similar pattern occurred in the tacit program, with the senior executive group.

In the critical reflection program, the program participants interjected themselves into this dynamic, commenting "this isn't the way with talk with one another in here." In part, this intervention into the behavior of the executive committee was a function of both the cohesiveness of the total learning community and the connections that had been facilitated between the program teams and their sponsors during the program. In the tacit program, the strategy professor who had been working with the project teams and with the senior executive team called for a break and counseled the executives. One positive outcome was that the C.O.O. came to understand the value of the process and became a valuable ally in the structuring of future programs. A less dramatic occurrence took place in the initial presentations of the experiential program. The senior operations executive was initially very judgmental, but came to learn to inquire about the underlying logic of the proposed changes. By the ninth "run" of the program he and other senior managers were participating in dialogue sessions with the participants, something that helped to reinforce the climate for transfer.

In the critical reflection program, the work done on the projects was integrated into the transition plans for the global organization. As discussed above, the AL program was part of a larger process of organizational change. Hence, follow-up task forces used the ideas from the projects to develop and implement a global financial reporting system, a global logistics system, new human resource development practices, and the new organizational structure in which the senior executive team transitioned from regional authority and oversight to global functional responsibilities. In addition to incorporating the thinking of the AL program, and providing support and credibility to the changes, the informal personal networks established through the programs helped to facilitate the transition.

In contrast, at the conclusion of the tacit program, it was not clear to the participants how their work was going to be used, nor were there obvious ways for the relationships established during the program to continue to be leveraged by the organization. However, there was strong evidence of most of the participants coming away with a more strategic focus and knowledge about the business. The overall pattern was learning-in-organization rather than learning-by-organization.

The learning in the experiential program was also largely individual, although several of the projects got implemented because the participants were in a position to do so once they gained approval from management. These were projects relating to tasks over which they had supervisory responsibility. Examples are a reorganization of how service trucks got out into the community in the morning and the structuring of service groups. Additionally, there was strong evidence of changes in how supervisors and labor worked together. Overall, there was both individual learning in organization, and some learning by organization, although it was not transformational in nature.

SUMMARY OF THE THREE CASES

One of the most obvious differences among the three prototype cases was the depth of self-correcting awareness that occurred, which in turn was a function of the focus and depth of the reflection and reflexive practices that were introduced and facilitated by program staff. In all three programs the instrumental learning around the project issues took place. Only in the critical reflection program was there widespread evidence of transformative change in terms of both instrumental and communicative learning. The program was extensively structured as a holistic learning community that provided opportunity for intensive interaction. In the other two programs the structure and social dimensions were adequate for the purposes of the programs, but more moderate in design. In the tacit program, the participants functioned more as individuals who were committed to producing a collective product. The learning was a mix of what Kasl et al. (1999) have identified as fragmented and pooled learning. The experiential program more clearly produced pooled learning, but only the critical reflection had consistent evidence of synergistic learning.

While initially generating "noise" and discomfort among some participants, the resulting learning for most participants in the critical reflection program was in all five domains: knowledge content, instrumental skills, cognitive frames of reference, personal awareness, and emotional capacity for change. In the experiential program, there were changes in instrumental skills, cognitive frames of reference and personal awareness. In the tacit program, the dominant learning was in content knowledge and cognitive frames of reference, with some change in personal awareness.

In addition to driving the learning across the domains, the degree of reflexivity on the learning processes in both the overall program and within the project teams that was encouraged by coaches seems to impact on the team learning modes (fragmented, pooled, or synergistic) that occurs. It must be acknowledged that patterns described here are based on prototypical cases, are tentative, and intended to stimulate future inquiry about AL practices. Table 8.3 summarizes these relationships in the framework of the integrated model of action learning dynamics.

One should also avoid assessing one design as 'better' than the other. For example, the depth and comprehensiveness of the learning, along with the transfer patterns described above for the critical reflection program are very impressive. However our experience inquiring into other programs suggests that these outcomes were a function of its fit with the overall strategic context of the program. In other situations, the critical reflection design proved to be less effective.

For example, in one of the other seven programs studied, the program facilitators designed the program with practices consistent with the critical reflection type. In fact, a couple of the same learning coaches who were part of case presented above were also involved in the design and facilitation of this program. This program took place within the context of a financial institution, and while the projects were important, there was not the same compelling case for changing the patterns of interaction

Table 8.3. Summary of the Three Prototype Cases in Terms of the Integrated Action Learning Program Dynamics Model

Design Characteristics		Contextual Factors			Program Millieu		Program Outcomes		Transfer	
Program Type	Learning Mechanisms	Pre Program	During Program	Post Program	Learning Values	Learning Modes	Learning Domains	Learning Kinds	Personal	Org.
Critical Reflection	*Structural* Extensive 4 six-day meetings over 3 months. Different global locations. *Social* intensive Emphasis on learning community	Global Organization Strategy	Sponsors met with teams	Yes	All	Synergistic	All	All	Far	Yes
Experiential	*Structural* Moderate *Social* Moderate emphasis on basic reflection	Deregulated business environment	Limited sponsor contact	Yes	All	Pooled	Cognitive Skills Awareness	Adding to and modified frames of reference	Near	Yes
Tacit	*Structural* Moderate *Social* Focused on project	Changing business context	No	No	Inquiry issue account. (focused on project)	Fragmented and pooled	Content Awareness Cognitive	Adding to and modified frames of reference	Near	No

within the bank. The corporate culture was very individualistic and competitive. Consequently, the program actually unfolded much more closely like a tacit program. The project teams often tried to work without the coaches present, and clearly resisted any reflective practices outside of formally negotiated times. The mode of learning in the project teams was largely fragmented, although the project work was productive and subsequently utilized by the company.

Overall, it appears as though the tacit mode is very effective for developing competencies that are consistent with a strong corporate culture that management wants reinforced, while exposing high potential managers to broader ways of thinking. The experiential type is effective when the company is supportive of development, but the overall context is not ready for critical reflection on the taken-for-granted culture of the organization. An initial experiential approach can create an expanded context for a more critically reflective program if these programs are part of a broader change process.

What is important is making explicit design choices that take into account the purpose of the program, the type of support necessary for achieving the learning goals, and the readiness of the organizational culture to support the learning. There is need for program developers being cognizant of the many possible variations and connections among the components of the integrated model. With additional field research and experience, we can better explicate the individual and organizational dynamics of AL.

NOTE

1.   This research has evolved over the course of the past decade and besides the author has involved Judy O'Neil, Victoria Marsick, Robert Kolodny, Sharon Lamm, and Glenn Nilson. Some papers have been published by this group under the name ARL Inquiry.

REFERENCES

Arygris, C., & Schon, D. (1978). *Organizational learning*. Reading, MA: Addison-Wesley.

Bateson, G. (1972). *Ecology of the mind*. New York: Balentine.

Boshyk, Y. (Ed.). (2000). *Action learning worldwide: Experiences of leadership and organizational development*. Hampshire, U.K: Palgrave Publishers.

Brown, J.S., & Duguid, P. (1991). Organizational learning communities-of-practice: Toward a unified view of working, learning, and innovation. *Organization Science, 2*, 40-57.

Butterfield, E.C., & Nelson, G.D. (1989). Theory and practice of teaching for transfer. *Educational Research and Development, 37*(4), 5-38.

Casey, D., & Pearce, D. (1977). *More than management development: Action learning at GEC.* Hampshire, England: Gower.

Cell, E. (1984). *Learning to learn from experience.* Albany: State University of New York Press.

Dennis, C., Cederholm, L., & Yorks, L. (1996). Learning your way to a global organization. In K.E. Watkins & V.J. Marsick, (Eds.), *In action: Creating the learning organiztion* (pp. 165-153). Alexandria, VA: American Society for Training and Development.

Dotlich, D.L., & Noel, J.L. (1998). *Action learning.* San Francisco: Jossey-Bass.

Downham, T.A., Noel, J.L., & Pendergast, A.E. (1992). Executive development. *Human Resource Management, 31*(1&2), 95-107.

Fisher, D. & Torbert, W. R. (1995). *Personal and organizational transformation: The true challenge of generating continual quality improvement.* London and New York: McGraw-Hill.

Foy, N. (1977). Action learning comes to industry. *Harvard Business Review, 77*(5), 158-168.

Hilgard, E.R., & Bower, G.H. (1966). *Theories of learning.* New York: Appleton-Century-Crofts.

Holton, III., E.F., & Baldwin, T.T. (2003). Making transfer happen: An action perspective on learning transfer systems. In E.F. Holton, III & T.T. Baldwin (Eds.), *Improving learning transfer systems in organizations* (pp. 3-15). San Francisco: Jossey-Bass and the Society for Industrial and Organizational Psychology.

Huang, J.C., Newell, S., & Galliers, R.D. (2002, April 5-6). *Inter-organizational communities of practice.* Paper presented at The Third European Conference on Organizational Knowledge, Learning, and Capabilities, Athens, Greece.

Kasl, E., Marsick, V.J., & Dechant, K. (1997). Teams as learners: A research based model of team learning. *Journal of Applied Behavioral Science, 33,* 227-246.

Knowles, M. (1990). *The adult learner: A neglected species* (4th ed.). Houston, TX.

Kolb, D.A. (1984). *Experiential learning: Experience as the source of learning and development.* Englewood Cliffs, NJ: Prentice-Hall.

Laker, D.R. (1990). Dual dimensionality of training transfer. *Human Resource Development Quarterly, 1,* 209-223.

Marquardt, M. J. (1999). *Action learning in action. Transforming problems and people for world-class organizational learning.* Palo Alto, CA: Davies-Black.

Marquardt, M. J. (2004). *Optimizing the power of action learning: Solving problems and building leaders in real time.* Palo Alto, CA: Davies-Black.

Marquardt, M. J. & Waddill, D. (2004). The power of learning in action learning: A conceptual analysis of how the five schools of adult learning theories are incorporated within the practice of action learning. *Action Learning: Research and Practice. 1*(2), 185-202.

Marsick, V.J. (1900). Action learning and reflection in the workplace. In J. Mezirow and Associates. *Fostering critical reflection in adulthood* (pp. 23-46). San Francisco: Jossey-Bass.

Marsick, V.J. (2002, August 9-14). Building and sustaining networks through action learning. Symposium: Building and sustaining networks using action learning. *The Academy of Management Meeting*, Denver, CO.

Marsick, V.J., & Watkins, K. (1990). *Informal and incidental learning in the workplace.* London and New York: Routledge.

McGill, I., & Beaty, L. (1992). *Action learning: A practitioner's guide.* London: Kogan Page.

McNulty, N. G. (1979). Management development by action learning. *Training and Development, 32*(3), 12-18.

Mezirow, J. (1991). *Tranformative dimensions of adult learning.* San Francisco: Jossey-Bass.

Mezirow, J. (2000). Learning to think like an adult. In J. Mezirow and Associates. *Learning as transformation: Critical perspectives on a theory in progress* (pp. 3-33). San Francisco: Jossey-Bass.

Mumford, A. (1993). *How managers can develop managers.* Brookfield, VT: Gower.

Mumford, A. (1995). *Learning at the top.* London/New York: McGraw-Hill.

Noel, J.L., & Charan, R. (1988). Leadership development at GE's Crotonville. *Human Resource Management, 27*, 433-447.

O'Neil, J. (1999). *The role of the learning adviser in action learning.* Unpublished doctoral dissertation, Teachers College, Columbia University, New York.

Pedler, M. (1991). *Action learning in practice* (2nd ed). Brookfield, VT: Gower.

Popper, M., & Lipshitz, R. (1998). Organizational learning mechanism: A structural and cultural approach to organizational learning. *The Journal of Applied Behavioral Science, 34*, 161-179.

Quinn, J.B. (1992). *The intelligent enterprise.* New York: Free Press.

Revans, R.W. (1965). *Science and the manager.* London: Macdonald.

Revans, R.W. (1971). *Developing effective managers.* New York: Praeger.

Revans, R.W. (1978). The a,b,c, of action learning: A review of 25 years of experience. Salford: University of Salford.

Revans, R. W. (1982). *The origins and growth of action learning.* London: Chartwell-Bratt.

Royer, J.M. (1979). Theories of the transfer of learning. *Educational Psychologist, 14*, 53-69.

Vaill, P. B. *Learning as a way of being: Strategies for survival in a world of permanent white water.* San Francisco: Jossey-Bass.

Vicere, A. A. (1996). Executive education: The leading edge. *Organizational Dynamics*, 67-81.

Yorks, L. (2003). Beyond the classroom: Transfer from work-based learning initiatives. In E. Holton, III & T.T. Baldwin (Eds.), *Improving learning transfer in organizations* (pp. 138-160). San Francisco: Jossey-Bass.

Yorks, L., & Marsick, V.J. (2000). Organizational learning and transformation. In J. Mezirow and Associates, *Learning as transformation: Critical perspectives on a theory in progress* (pp. 253-281). San Francisco: CA: Jossey-Bass.

Yorks, L., Neuman, J., Kowalski, D., & Kowalski, R. (forthcoming). *Developing and sustaining social space for the creation of actionable knowledge* (Working paper). Adult Learning and Leadership Program, Department of Organization and Leadership, Teachers College, Columbia, University, New York.

Yorks, L., O'Neil, J., & Marsick, V.J. (Eds.). (1999). Lessons for implementing action learning. In *Action learning: Successful strategies for individual, team, and organizational development. Advances in developing human resources* (pp. 96-113). San Francisco: The Academy of Human Resource Development and Berrett-Koehler.

Yorks, L., O'Neil, & Marsick, V.J. (Eds.). (1999). Action learning: Theoretical bases and varieties of practice. In *Action learning: Successful strategies for individual, team, and organizational development. Advances in developing human resources* (pp. 1-18). San Francisco: The Academy of Human Resource Development and Berrett-Koehler.

CHAPTER 9

ACTION LEARNING FOR MANAGEMENT DEVELOPMENT

Lessons from a
Leadership Development Program

Richard T. Harrison and Claire M. Leitch

There has been a significant reawakening of interest in action learning as a paradigm for management development, particularly as a pedagogical device in both classroom and executive development contexts. The implications are twofold: first, the range of teaching techniques must be extended to include process-oriented approaches; second, and more fundamentally, there is a need for an expanded definition of the learning arena itself, and of the role of management schools within that. This chapter reviews a number of key developments in contemporary management education and development, and presents a summary of a program built as an action-and-implementation oriented approach to entrepreneurial senior executive development. This program aims to support the development of leadership in both large and smaller, growth-oriented companies, in a partnership which breaches the conventional separation both between the encapsulated learning arenas of the university and the organization and between management and entrepreneurship education and development. This partnership emphasises the impact of intra-group and interorganizational learning on both the participants and on the context of their organizations.

Educating Managers through Real World Projects, 213–239
Copyright © 2005 by Information Age Publishing
All rights of reproduction in any form reserved.

INTRODUCTION

Although not extensively represented in the literature, the subject of entrepreneurship education has been subject to increasing scrutiny in recent years and research in the area is growing (Block & Stumpf, 1992; Gorman et al., 1997; Young, 1997; Kourilsky & Carlson, 1997; Greene et al., 2004). Despite a growth in the number of entrepreneurship programs offered there is little uniformity with respect to the nature, relevance, content and appropriateness of such courses (Henry et al., 2003). It is thus, difficult to classify entrepreneurship education activities due to the level of differentiation and disaggregation of concepts and objectives (Gibb, 1993; Vento, 1998). However, in an attempt, to trace the evolution of entrepreneurship education and development Harrison and Leitch (1994) have proposed a three-stage model. In the first, and earliest, stage, entrepreneurship education was characterized as simply a subset of general management education; the second approach reacted to this as entrepreneurship grew in importance as a focus for academic debate, and was based on the argument that entrepreneurship education (and education and development for smaller businesses in particular) must be qualitatively different from conventional large company-based management education which dealt with essentially different problems, organizations and contexts (Vesper et al., 1988; Filion, 1991). The third stage in the evolution of approaches to entrepreneurship education is an emerging reconceptualization of the field, based in part on a renewed interest in the nature and role of leadership in changing organizational structures, which provides the basis for the reintegration of management education and entrepreneurship education.

In parallel with this, there has also been a growing interest in the processes by which individuals and, increasingly, organizations learn (Argyis & Schon, 1974, 1978; Pedler et al., 1991; Senge, 1990; Dixon, 1994; Edmondson & Moingeon, 1996; Easterby-Smith, 1997; Easterby-Smith & Lyles, 2003; Dierkes et al., 2001). This interest has begun to influence the entrepreneurship literature (e.g., Gibb, 1997). For example, Block and Stumpf (1992) draw on the earlier work of Cooper (1982) and House (1982) in discussing the learning needs of entrepreneurs; Slevin and Colvin (1992) parallel, without directly referring to, the emphasis in Senge (1990) on team learning and team development as a key entrepreneurial process; and Guth et al. (1991) address specifically the relevance of models of experiential learning, and of the learning from failure in particular (Brehmer, 1980; Janoff-Bulman & Brickman, 1982; Levitt & March, 1988; Sterman, 1989), to entrepreneurial cognition and enactment. One of the critical areas where learning has been identified as a strategic imperative is the growth transition between the founder-owner led business and the professionally managed business (Flamholtz, 1990; Mazzarol, 2003). As Day (1992, p. 137) argues, "all organizations must be able to learn if they are to move into new businesses. In fact, virtually every aspect of organizational learning has relevance either directly or indirectly for entrepreneurial management"—a point reiterated in the growing literature on organizational competencies and learning in strategic management and entrepreneurship (McGrath et al., 1993; Dubini & Paulato, 1993; Leitch & Harrison, 1993; Leitch & Harrison, forthcoming).

As in other areas of management research and practice, research into entrepreneurship education has followed a number of distinct avenues (Block & Stumpf, 1992; Vesper et al., 1988; Gorman et al., 1997). Within this range of interests and approaches, however, "the most difficult and costly research on entrepreneurship education will involve the examination of different program content pedagogical methods used to accomplish educational objectives" (Block & Stumpf, 1992, pp. 38-39). This is a wider problem, and is still an area of major concern:

> Even though executive education is an increasingly large proportion of teaching at some schools ... we know of no published studies, or even informal but systematic data, that would enable us to assess the effects of executive education on either the individuals who receive it or their organizations. In fact the absence of much assessment of any kind is one of the defining characteristics of contemporary business education and one reason that problems are likely to persist. (Pfeffer & Fong 2002, p. 80)

In this chapter we begin to respond to this challenge by discussing the design and outcomes of an executive development program (which has a particular focus on leadership development[1] as a bridge between conventional management and entrepreneurship education and development—Harrison & Leitch 1994). The paper is structured as follows: following a brief summary, for contextual purposes, of recent developments in management education, the paper briefly reviews the basic principles of action learning which underlie recent discussions of the learning company concept (Lessem, 1993; Pedler et al., 1991) and which have informed the design of the program under discussion. Following a presentation of the key features of and background to this entrepreneurial executive development program, the paper presents an initial evaluation of the impact of this program on the development of personal leadership, operational organizational development and strategic business development.

CHANGES IN MANAGEMENT EDUCATION

As Grey and French (1996) indicate, management education is an activity of growing significance and influence, which has recently attracted extensive attention and criticism, partly because of the rapidly changing context in which it is located, and partly as a result of wider concerns about the changing role of the business school (Pfeffer & Fong, 2002; Friga et al., 2003; Mintzberg, 2004). The established understandings of managerial practice and education are currently being reassessed, and increasingly doubt is being cast upon "the relevance and efficacy of established nostrums about the work of managers and about how they should be educated to do it" (Willmott, 1994, p. 105; see also Mintzberg 2004). In essence, as Spender (1994, p. 387) notes, "management education ostensibly designed to equip managers to deal with the world seems to have changed little in recent years." This concurs with Hamel and Prahalad's (1996, p. 257) belief that, "as we career from the machine age into the information age the more questionable become the traditional practices and precepts of management." Given that orthodox management education appears to have failed, by producing managers who cannot manage adequately in the modern world, this has led to a questioning of the intellectual inadequacy of the content of management education itself. Indeed Grey (1996, p. 8) posed the question: "how should management education proceed in the late twentieth century?"

Alternative approaches to management education, including action learning, are more committed to bridging the gap between "the formal knowledge derived through theory and the informal knowledge experienced in practice" (Raelin & Schmererhorn Jr., 1994, pp. 196-197). Argyris and Schon (1974) and Raelin (1993), inter alia, note that separating theory and practice is not a modern US invention. Instead "it is the central thrust of the German Wissenschaft tradition of old science wherein the professor-scientist perceives his activities to be quite different from those of the manager-doer" (Raelin, 1993, p. 85). In association with these new approaches there has also been a shift in emphasis on the pedagogical method considered appropriate. In the professional model a didactic approach to teaching and learning is still apparent, in that "the teacher and the text are the repository of what needs to be known about a discipline" (Beck, 1994, p. 238). Although applied in a management development context within companies Pedler's (1988) comment (quoted in Willmott, 1994, p. 122) can equally be applied to management education within universities where "management education is largely done to managers rather than done by them, socializing them into existing norms, practices and values and treating them as 'patients' rather than 'agents'." Indeed, as Chia (1996) suggests, changing the pedagogic process itself demands a suspension in the belief that the often passive and alienated approaches to teaching and learning are the most effective. A great challenge therefore faces management academics to develop alternative curricula and modes of delivery, which not only stimulate but facilitate a process of active and continuous learning (Salaman & Butler, 1990). The pedagogical methods inherent within the concept of action learning as developed by Revans (1982) are akin to Friere's (1972, p. 53) description of critical pedagogy, "through dialogue, the teacher-of-the-students and the students-of-the-teacher cease to exist and a new term emerges: teacher-student with student-teachers. The teacher is no longer merely the-one-who-teaches, but who is himself [sic] taught in dialogue with the students, who in their turn while being taught also teach." Employing a practice such as action learning obviously alters the traditional teacher-student role to one where the teacher fulfils not only a facilitating role but also a learning one. In fact the balance of power has shifted from one of "leader-follower" to one which is much more equal in nature. More generally, this shift in management education from a classroom-based teaching and learning model reflects a wider shift away from a transmissionist model of teaching and learning (which privileges the lecturer's choice of relevant material to be transmitted to a passive student) to a constructivist model of teaching and learning (which recognizes that the student actively constructs their own learning by choosing what is relevant to them and making sense of it in the light of their past and imagined future experiences) (Boud et al., 1993; Boud & Garrick, 1999). In such a framework, the role of the lecturer-facilitator is to design a learning event or process which facilitates active and deep learning through the design of experiences (including action learning sets and processes) which enable the student to connect new information to past knowledge in meaningful and relevant ways (Ramsden, 1992; Laurillard, 1993; Zuber-Skerritt, 1993; Harrison et al., 1996).

Action Learning

Action learning, although subject to multifarious interpretations (Marsick & O'Neil, 1999; Marquardt, 1999; Weinstein, 1999; McGill & Beaty, 1995), is an approach to management learning in which a manager learns by reflecting on actions being taken in solving a real organizational problem with managers of similar position also experiencing challenging situations (McLaughlin & Thorpe, 1993; Eden & Huxman, 1996; Zuber-Skerritt, 1995). Revans (1971), who proposed this approach, based it on the scientific method and thus conceptualized action learning as a model of problem solving in three stages. He believed that learners (in this case, managers and other workers) learnt most effectively with and from others in comparable circumstances while attempting to find solutions to actual, real-life problems. In the process of doing so they not only discuss the practical implications of their solutions but also the applications or misapplications of theories and concepts to proposed actions and solutions. To achieve this they engage in a learning cycle that involves a number of stages, including action and reflection, until the issue under consideration has been resolved. Such a process represents a valuable learning experience for through talking and reflecting people can learn to recognize their taken-for-granted values, appreciate the connections between their own practices and the organizational contexts in which they are embedded and potentially engage in a learning process "that may transform their world by their very participation in it" (Raelin, 2000, p. 185).

Revans' (1971) learning cycle has many similarities with that of Kolb's (1984) experiential learning cycle and indeed Lessem (1993) asserts that Kolb's model is an adaptation, consciously or otherwise, of Revans'. While learning is deliberately built into each stage of these two cycles, McLaughlin and Thorpe (1993) have observed that for proponents of Kolb's approach the starting point for learning is action. Along with other colleagues group members reflect on experience with the support of others. Indeed, action learning is based on "the straightforward pedagogical notion that people learn most effectively when working on real-time problems occurring in their own work setting" (Raelin, 1999, p. 117), which should encourage more effective problem solving (Marsick & O'Neil, 1999). In addition as Blackler and Kennedy (2004, p.182) observe "an action learning approach that includes significant opportunities for reflection, can help participants develop a resilient approach to the conflicts and tensions in their organizations and re-engage with their objectives."

In addition to the learning cycle, Revans distinguished between two types of learning, P and Q. P represents programmed knowledge and includes facts, theories or problems with known solutions and is the predominant learning mode in the traditional paradigm. On the other hand Q is more aligned with the ideology and assumptions underlying an alternative approach in which the ability to ask penetrating questions about problems, for which there are no known solutions, is a necessity. The concept of action learning by implication is in opposition to the status quo, not least because it challenges the passive approach to learning characterized in the traditional approaches. Indeed, the concept has been described as more than just a pedagogical approach, and "at its most profound it is a form of personal therapy, a means of social and economic transformation, and even a way of life" (Lessem, 1993, p. 12).

Those who are modernist supporters of the professional education approach have been critical of an action learning approach to management education. This is because they claim that such an approach is antithetical to theory and thus can be considered "anti-intellectual" (Raelin, 1994, p. 302). However, their fears may be allayed by the fact that both P and Q types of learning are encouraged in action learning—it is not just simply a case of throwing the baby out with the bath water. Raelin (1994, p. 305) believes that in the model of "action learning, theory is not separated, either temporally or epistemologically from practice." Indeed the model of action learning provides a good example of the paradigm of synthesis articulated by Forray and Mir (1994). They explain that it is also an important critique of the paradigm of balance "insofar as it attempts to falsify the dichotomies between subject-object, stability-change and theory-practice, and attempts to replace them with a synthesis which helps us appreciate the relationship between knowledge and experience" (Forray & Mir, 1994, p. 211).

Action learning emphasizes learning by doing and, as Raelin (1994) indicates with reference to adult education programs, the doing is often preceded by a theoretical modular unit so that the whole exercise in fact requires both P and Q learning. Action learning, which encourages both P and Q learning, contradicts the view that management can be learnt in an isolated lecture excluding experience. This is because principles only become meaningful to the extent that they are deliberately introduced into practice (Raelin, 1994). Indeed, McLaughlin and Thorpe (1993) proposed action learning as a new paradigm in management education, and identified a number of caveats. While they found that the model appeared to work in principle they discovered a number of anomalies. First, self-development assumes that a learner is able to accurately define his/her own learning needs. Frequently though, guidance is needed in defining this, and therefore McLaughlin and Thorpe (1993, p. 25) suggest that an action learning framework needs to provide structure so that students are able "to reflect in action, illuminate practice and criticize both." Second, they claim that there is no a priori reason why a manager could not use the model to develop his/her manipulative techniques. However, they state that proponents of self-development techniques would argue that these tendencies are likely to be decreased rather than increased. Third, action learning encourages "a desire to move on the higher plains" (McLaughlin & Thorpe, 1993, p. 25). Students who are thus challenged to take a broader view of the world may seek further enlightenment and ignore practical action. Pedler (1988, p.11) states that in fact "some beings in their wisdom often choose to refrain from action in favor of contemplation." Fourth, McLaughlin and Thorpe (1993) acknowledge the fear that cognitive knowledge may be dismissed completely, thus impoverishing the action learning experience. As Sutton (1990, p. 9) states, "action learning's emphasis on Q type learning has obscured the need for continual growth in P material, both as knowledge in its own right and also the base from which future Q learning can take place." Having identified these anomalies they recommend that a contingency approach which "lacks the philosophical underpinning of the other two and is much more pragmatic" (McLaughlin & Thorpe, 1993, p. 26) is adopted as a potential way forward. This approach is based on the premise that the most appropriate type of management education depends on the type of manager required.

Thus, a more traditional approach will be suitable to a manager who seeks knowledge based on theory, while an action learning perspective will be more appropriate for a manager requiring a focus on action.

Based on this characterization of action learning McLaughlin and Thorpe (1993) have identified a number of ways in which it represents a radical change in view compared with traditional management education. These characteristics of the action learning paradigm (McLaughlin & Thorpe, 1993) dovetail neatly with the shift of emphasis identified in management and entrepreneurial education and development (Porter & McKibben, 1988; Limerick & Moore, 1991; Harrison & Leitch, 1994), and are reflected in the aims and objectives of an internationally focused leadership program developed by the authors.

EXECUTIVE LEADERSHIP PROGRAM[2]

This program was developed to meet three interrelated needs. First, it was designed so that the international competitiveness of the regional economy[3] might be improved. Second, as the basis for achieving this, the program focused on increasing the efficiency and proficiency of key companies within the regional economy. Third, the course aimed to develop flexible and adaptable leadership in senior executives within these companies to provide a basis for, and stimulus to effective organizational transformation and development. In addition the focus of this program has been on developing the leadership capabilities of managers so as to enable them to cope with what Vaill (1989) has termed the "Grand paradox of management," to take responsibility for controlling what is less and less controllable.

The overall structure of the program, in terms of the link between needs, objectives and benefits, is shown in Figure 9.1. The achievement of this was designed around a structured action learning process which allowed both group and individual learning to be supported as well as encouraging critical reflection and practical discussion (Blackler & Kennedy, 2004). The program was structured as follows: First, the program was organized around eight residential workshop sessions over a 12-month period focused on personal leadership, strategic organizational and operational development. Second, within each workshop session, the program design required close integration of workshop content and personal and organizational context as the basis for content development and delivery. Third, each workshop finished with an agenda-setting exercise in which participants were required to identify (a) how and when they would act on and apply the lessons learned from the workshop and (b) how and when they would disseminate workshop learning more widely within the organization, either to other members of the top management team or more widely. Fourth, participants were encouraged to commit to action on the agendas they set for themselves, both through the mechanism of reporting on and evaluating these actions as part of the accreditation process for the qualification associated with this program, and through a commitment to report back to their peers on actions and progress at a subsequent workshop session. Fifth, between sessions, and in the final six months of the 18-month program on a monthly basis, participants met in action learning sets of 4-6 participants, facilitated by members of the program faculty. Finally, although not all participants registered for it, the accumulated learnings from the program (both in terms of process and content) provided the basis for the completion of a final dissertation, assessed for the award of the degree of MSc in Executive Leadership. This degree-level qualification was an attraction for a number of the participants on the program, and was based entirely on the reporting and evaluation of the action learning activities undertaken throughout the program.

The overall objective of this course was, to assist senior executives in both large and entrepreneurial small companies to develop the knowledge, skills and awareness which will enable them to transform their companies by providing team-based leadership through the creation and communication of vision and values. The emphasis on leadership, establishing and articulating both a vision and values, developing strategic awareness and building a team are among those issues which were identified as absent from the professional model of management education. In addition to addressing the criticisms advanced by Cheit (1985) and Porter and McKibben (1988) the approach developed in this program has recognized the need to define an enlarged learning arena in management education. As discussed above, traditional approaches have considered that two separate learning arenas within the field have existed, the university and the organization.

Alternative perspectives, in which a more integrative strategy toward management education is emphasized, focus on the acquisition of action skills in the field, and the collapsing of borders "between schools … between the business functions … between and among 'students' and 'instructors' … between the process of educating and the process of managing. All get in the way" (Mintzberg & Gosling, 2002, p. 64). This necessitates a high level of reciprocal integration and requires a fusion of the two learning arenas. Action learning (Revans, 1971) provides one of the mechanisms by which participants on this particular executive education program may transfer between the two learning areas which have been identified. As the context for this type of learning is a participant's organization, integration is encouraged not only between theory and practice

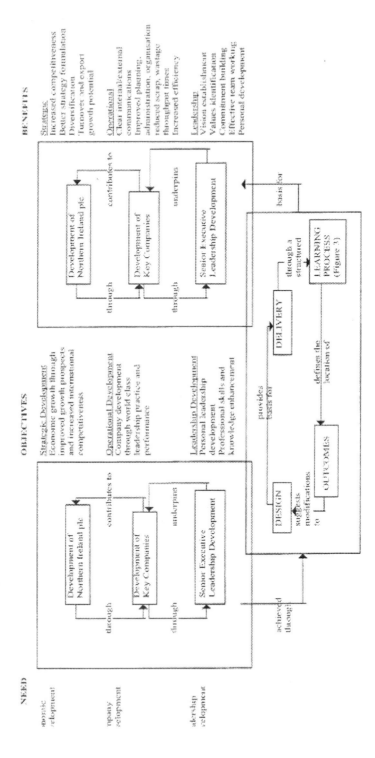

Figure 9.1. International directors program in executive leadership.

but also between academic institutions and industry. The approach adopted within the design of this program parallels the proposed alternative to the professional model of action learning discussed above.

Participants

Over the first six years of the program 64 senior executives and business owners participated in this personal and organizational development process. Reflecting the male/female ratio in the wider senior executive population, and the wider difficulty in encouraging female executives and business owners to participate in executive development programs dominated by their male counterparts, only five (8%) participants have been female, although this has increased significantly in recent years (Table 9.1). In terms of role and sector, there have been some significant shifts in the nature of the program since its inception (Tables 9.3 and 9.4). Overall, 59% of participants have been at managing director/CEO level and 41% have held senior executive-level positions (Table 9.2). However, there has been a major shift away from primarily owner managers in the program: in the first three years three-quarters of participants were MD/CEOs; in the following three years this had fallen to only 43%.

In sectoral terms there has been a shift away from participants from organizations in the manufacturing sector, down from 79% to 63%, and a

Table 9.1.   Gender Analysis of Participants

	Cohorts 1-3		Cohorts 4-6		Total—All Years	
	No	%	No	%	No	%
Male	34	100	25	83	59	92
Female	0	0	5	17	5	8
Total	34	100	30	100	64	100

Table 9.2.   Managerial Level of Participants

	Cohorts 1-3		Cohorts 4-6		Total—All Years	
	No	%	No	%	No	%
MD/CEO	25	74	13	53	38	59
Senior executive	9	26	17	57	26	41
Total	34	100	30	100	64	100

Table 9.3.   Industrial Sector of Participants' Organizations

	Cohorts 1-3		Cohorts 4-6		Total—All Years	
	No	%	No	%	No	%
Manufacturing	27	79	19	63	46	72
Non-manufacturing	6	18	7	23	13	20
Public sector	1	3	4	14	5	8
Total	34	100	30	100	64	100

Table 9.4.   Stated Objectives for Participating In Program

	Yes (%)	Cannot Say (%)
Prepare business to export	94	6
Assess and develop personal leadership	97	3
Identify and pursue leadership opportunities	91	7
Develop strategic abilities	85	15
Identify opportunity for competitive development	82	18
Key factors for world-class leadership/performance	85	15

rise in participation from the private services sector (up from 18% to 23%) and the public sector (up from 3% to 14%) (Table 9.3). This sectoral shift in part underlies the shift away from MD/CEO level participants as the program participation has become more "managerial" in nature. It also reflects a relaxation in an artificial constraint on recruitment to the program in the early years imposed by the core development funding provided by the region's Training and Employment Agency, which had a statutory obligation to support the development of the manufacturing and tradable services sectors. Given that the program was designed originally to meet the needs of both the growing entrepreneurial business and the senior executive in larger organizations faced with the challenge of responding creatively to increasing change, the growing interest of non-owners in the program is not unexpected. What is of interest is the growing interest in the program in the public sector, particularly in education and healthcare management, which reflects the increasing introduction of "private sector" management practices in recent years.

One unexpected development reflected in these figures is the impact of program recruitment being primarily through word-of-mouth recommendation (more than 50% of participants found out about the program this way, compared to only 21% who responded to direct university-originated materials and contacts): for the large company executives on the program the opportunity to interact with and learn from entrepreneurial business owners was consistently identified as a major benefit, and this formed the basis of the recommendation of the program to others. However, as the proportion of non-business owners have grown, there is a possibility that the program is perceived to meet the specific needs of the entrepreneur less well: success in meeting the original aims of an integrated and diverse participant group may well have had the unintended effect of reducing the program's perceived relevance to this key group. At the point of the first formal assessment and evaluation of the program (reported here), which collected responses from participants in the first six cohorts, a minimum of two years after completion of the formal 12-month workshop program, 22 participants had completed the requirements for the degree of MSc in Executive Leadership, of which six were awarded the degree with distinction, and no participant who has registered for the degree (which is not compulsory) has failed. Overall, only around 15% of those participating in the program have not opted to register for the Masters program, despite the MSc being an important factor in deciding to do the program for only 5% of them.

Outcomes and Benefits

Assessment of the outcomes and benefits of the program has been undertaken in a number of stages as part of a rolling program of formative evaluation. In this paper we report briefly on three phases of this evaluation, which is ongoing: first, both participants and, where appropriate, their companies were asked to indicate the benefits and outcomes attributable to the program, and 34 responses were obtained (with a further 15 company responses); second, a slightly smaller set of responses ($n = 25$) were obtained to a more detailed probing of the impact of the program on leadership development, operational business development and strategic business development; third, in order to set these results in context, a small number of detailed behavioral event interviews with selected participants were held ($n = 3$).

STAGE I EVALUATION: PARTICIPANTS AND COMPANIES

Participants in the first five cohorts were asked to indicate their perceptions of the extent to which the program met course, personal and business objectives. The vast majority of participants considered that the program had met its stated objectives (Table 9.4), with "internal"-oriented objectives such as leadership development and strategic ability being rather more highly ranked than "external"-oriented objectives such as competitive development and world-class leadership development. This is reflected in the achievement of personal objectives in the area of improved leadership development, self-confidence and improved professional skills and knowledge, a direct consequence of the emphasis of this part of the program on the assessment and development of leadership skills and behaviors. In terms of business objectives, the majority of participants reported benefits in terms of the development of strategic planning and increased export market development (see below) and in implementing changes within the organization (Table 9.5), although almost a quarter of respondents were unable to indicate benefits because it was still too early to identify the impact of the program. Overall, participants expressed high levels of satisfaction with the content of the program (Table 9.6): in this, the caliber of the other participants and, interestingly, the overseas visits (which involved both international management seminars and industrial visits) score particularly highly, emphasizing the need in executive education to give full attention to the opportunities for peer learning and development to occur in a high quality and highly motivated peer group.

Table 9.5.   Stated Business Objectives

	Yes	No	Too Early to Say
Improved operational efficiency	78	3	19
Improved motivation in workforce	66	9	25
Exposure to/implement world-class leadership practice	63	9	28
Introduction of new systems/procedures	47	25	28

Table 9.6.   Evaluation of Course Content and Structure

	Very Relevant	Quite Relevant	Not Very Relevant	Not at All Relevant
Coursework	52	48	0	0
Assignment work (action learning)	57	40	0	3
Caliber of participants	68	32	0	0
Overseas visits	66	17	11	6

These reactions were broadly confirmed in the company responses (by their nature, these responses relate to senior executive participants on the program and not to owner-managers/MDs, and the line manager responses have yet to be complemented with the views of those managed by the participants). In all cases where the participating executives had staff reporting to them, it was reported that their skills as a manager had improved, there were positive changes in performance and/or behavior and an underlying broadening of managerial capability reflected in longer-term thinking, improved communication skills, improved decision-making, a more methodical approach to management and a wider marketing focus. For 80% of the companies surveyed, the program was felt to have enhanced the competitive advantage of the company (a stronger response than from the individual participants themselves) in terms of efficiency, organization, responsiveness to change and improved communication among staff. For both participants and companies, a key but intangible and unquantifiable benefit of the program has been the development of contacts and peer networks which have continued as an informal learning (and in some cases business development) mechanism beyond the life and confines of the program itself.

STAGE II EVALUATION: PARTICIPANTS

A more detailed assessment of the benefits and outcomes of the program for both the individual executives and their companies has been undertaken at three levels, namely: leadership development; operational business development; and strategic development.

These correspond with the three levels of need and objectives identified. A total of 32 personal and company development dimensions have been measured for the 25 senior executives who completed the program in 1992 and 1993. Each participant was asked to assess the impact of their participation in the program on each dimension using a five-point scale (1 = major effect, 2 = considerable effect, 3 = some effect, 4 = minor effect, 5 = no effect). Participant comments are included under each heading (leadership development, operational business development and strategic development) to indicate the precise nature of some of these effects.

Leadership Development

Program impact has been greatest on leadership development. All ten leadership dimensions were reported as experiencing "some effect" at least by participants, and for six dimensions the average scores were under 2.5, indicating a considerable program impact. Overall, the program has been responsible for participants establishing a clear vision, identifying core shared values for the company, building more effective working teams, building commitment to the vision and values by the management team, and developing the personal leadership skills of influencing, networking, facilitating, empowering, learning and deciding. In other words, the program has achieved its primary goal of enabling senior executives to create a future for their company (vision) by providing a purpose (values) and establishing a process (effective working teams) to generate an outcome (commitment) through personal capability (leadership skills).

> I joined IDP to assist me in determination of the strategy necessary to take my company forward to a point where I would step back from all the day-to-day issues and concentrate on the strategic issues of future development. This was essential to allow my management team to develop and especially to allow development of my two sons to give them the opportunity to take over running the company. These ambitions are now well on the road toward achievement.

> A clearer vision of the future, improved confidence in achieving vision/goals and a clearer definition of company culture.

> My total outlook on everything has changed or is changing.

> I now understand the difference between leading and managing. Before IDP I wasn't 70% managing and 30% leading, now it is 80% leading and 20%.

> I now have a clear idea of my objectives and how best to help my people set and achieve their own objectives. I now understand better the need for "soft" skills when leading people and the importance of a vision, values and personal commitment.

> A superb course, most of which would benefit "higher flyers" at least in our company. I wish I (and my management) had this course 15-20 years ago.

> I have developed a clearer focus on the future direction and development of the company. I am putting greater emphasis on multi-functional teams.

Operational Development

The development of executive leadership provides the basis for operational business development—in only three of ten dimensions identified does the impact measurement fall below "3.0—some impact." The primary operational development impact of the program occurs through efficiency gains—improved internal and external communications provide the basis for better planning, administration and organization. Together with reduced scrap and wastage rates, and reduced throughput and cycle time, these support overall efficiency improvements as the basis for improved competitiveness (see below).

Improved product quality is also reported as a result of these operational improvements:

> In a high tech manufacturing plant, cycle time has been reduced from 42 to 14 days, resulting in the elimination of 12 days work in progress and representing an annual saving of £125,000.

> The course has initiated a complete general review of distribution policy with regard to frequency, computer hardware and software replacement and personnel requirements.

> The planning and operational review has produced a new dimension, the customer. By a questionnaire and customer forum we have asked how it should be done instead of continuing our normal policy which we have been operating for 20 years.... Customer and supplier involvement has and will result in us being well ahead of the competition.

> Profits have increased by 232% since completing the course.

> A division returning a period loss of £30k has been turned round to return profits of £50k.

Strategic Development

Leadership development at the most senior levels of the participating companies, and organizational and technical efficiency improvements, are reflected in strategic developments in the companies, and hence in their contribution to the development of Northern Ireland PLC. For participants the program provides the basis, to date, for increased competitiveness through improved business strategy formulation and diversification, resulting in increased turnover and market development opportunities.

> Participation in IDP has focused my attention more on strategy issues ... this has helped in the development of staff.

> The course helped provide improved focus on expansion opportunities and on complementary business opportunities (which are) not possible/applicable to quantify.

> A contingency analysis is underway with regard to training needs at all levels within the group to take effect over the next three years.

All the IDP modules have a slightly different slant but are on an absolutely consistent theme.

The whole theme throughout has been personal leadership thus preparing Northern Ireland business for the next century and ensuring these businesses become high performers.

Within five years the business will grow from £4m p.a. total sales to >£10m, from 100 to over 200 employees, expand from one to at least two production sites and investment will rise from £400k p.a. to £1m p.a.

Business Performance

In order to overcome some of the limitations of the self-report perception data discussed so far, respondents were asked to provide tangible evidence of changes in business performance attributable to the program. Over the three years post-program assessment there has been a significant improvement in key aspects of business performance as a direct result of program participation, based on responses from these 25 senior executives in 21 different companies (see Table 9.7).

Total employment in participating companies increased by an average of 15 percent in the two-year period/preprogram year/first year post-program, total turnover increased by an average of 25% and exports as a percentage of turnover rose by an average of eight percentage points. These results provide the basis for concluding that the program is achieving: final linkage established at the outset, that between company development and the development of the Northern Ireland economy in the con-

Table 9.7. Post-program Business Performance

	Increase Significantly[a]	Increase[b]	No Change	Decrease[c]	Decrease Significantly[d]
Employment	25	50	15	8[e]	7[e]
Total sales	55	40	5	—	—
Export sales	25	50	25	—	—

[a]more than 10% pa for employment and sales; more than 10 percentage points for export sales.
[b]between 5 and 10% pa for employment and sales; between 5 and 10 percentage points for export sales.
[c]between 0 and –5% pa.
[d]in excess of –5% pa.
[e]these responses indicate the outcomes of major company division restructurings to achieve productivity and efficiency gains and realize significantly increased sales and export growth at lower employment levels.

text of the fundamental need to become more internationally competitive. It is, therefore, even in the short term, beginning to have an impact on the fundamental need—regional economic development—which was the original stimulus for the development of the program.

STAGE III EVALUATION: CASE STUDY

It is not always possible or appropriate to capture all aspects of the impact of a wide-ranging program such as this on the personal and organizational development of the participants in "normal" quantitative and qualitative research contexts, not least because the program is primarily designed to stimulate and support long-term rather than short-term changes in attitude and behavior. To compensate for this, we have begun to undertake a series of more detailed case interviews to provide additional insight into the program and its impact. One of these cases is summarized below.

Participant A is, in many ways, a classic example of the stereotypical self-made entrepreneur: he has had 50 years experience in business, and for 30 years has been operating his own businesses rather than working for others, having left school with nothing other than the basic qualifications. Based on his experience in the construction industry, participant A established a small joinery works initially, later expanding this to a full service construction business, which together employ 64 people today. Diversification into the manufacture of PVC window systems followed in 1980 and, although competition in this sector has increased greatly, this business continues to employ 35 people. The third main company in the group, in which participant A now acts as chairman (a change in role developed during the period of participation in the program), was established in 1989 to manufacture toughened safety glass. Currently the group employs 200 (100 in toughened glass manufacture) and has a turnover of £13m.

The development of the toughened glass facility became the main focus of the application of the learning developed through the program for participant A. As he tells it:

> as a result of my travels looking for a double glazing line in Milan, I met a man who persuaded me that tough (or safety) glass was a much better bet. I invested some £2.5 million [against a then turnover of c. £6m] and the result was the forming in 1989 of company X which today employs over 100 people ... [and] ... exports to Great Britain and the Republic of Ireland. Since its formation company X has exported between 2.5 and 3 million panes of glass to GB and always delivers within five days on a two day per week scheduled run. The company has adopted the Confucian maxim

"When a young bird learns to fly, some old birds get knocked off their perch."

This represented a major shift in emphasis for the group, involving radical changes in the level of technological sophistication of the business and the development for the first time of a market outside the region. To date the development and success of the company has been based on a deep commitment to the development of quality in relation to the product, an overriding commitment to meeting and exceeding clients' expectations and winning commitment from the employees to these values. By late 1994 the company was investing in additional glass-toughening facilities to double production capacity and support the further development and penetration of the UK market, and it was at this time that participant A joined the program:

> Throughout my working life and, particularly when I worked for someone else, I kept abreast of skills by doing all the short courses I could get my hands on. But I always regretted that I hadn't been to university. During the 1980s, I undertook short courses at the University of Ulster and in the 1990s I undertook a course leading to an MSc in Leadership Studies [sic].
>   That not only gave me confidence, but it taught me to develop a vision and to delegate within that vision—an important lesson to learn at the stage that the group was and is, and at my age entrepreneurs want to do everything themselves and there is a time to step back from that.

In particular, participant A's role progressed from the hands-on direct management role of the entrepreneur to one of leadership through the empowerment of others, through the appointment of an "outsider" as managing director of the business, through a range of initiatives to recognize the potential and achievements of the workforce (based on observation from successful organizations visited on the overseas study tour). As a result of the program, participant A has devoted more time to "walking the talk," demonstrating the consistency between management style and management expectations, and has seen improvements in his listening skills, in how to communicate his ideas, in his ability to manage and work with people, in thinking strategically and in allowing others to develop their talents. Since participating in the program, participant A has embarked on a further expansion of the glass business, investing £9 million in facilities to produce curved tough glass, primarily for the European market. This will see employment in the company increase from 100 to c. 170 employees within two years.

Perhaps most significantly, however, and symbolic of the impact of the program on encouraging participant A to "think out of the box" as he expressed it, is the fact that this expansion program is based on the injection of outside venture capital into the business for the first time—given the traditional equity aversion of the typical entrepreneur, this injection of outside equity after 30 years of purely family ownership of the business is quite radical and indicates the potential of the program to stimulate and support major changes in personal leadership and business development.

CONCLUSIONS

The approach adopted in the development of this program, taking a cue from Limerick and Moore (1991) and Porter and McKibben (1988), recognizes the need to define an enlarged learning arena in management education and development. Traditional approaches have conceived of two separate encapsulated learning arenas: the university and the organization. The university has provided cognitive, intellectual frameworks and the organization has taught, often informally, skills in applying theory to practice. Too often those individuals participating in management education and development programs have been seen as moving from one arena to another in sequential fashion. Yet as Yavitz (1982) has pointed out, to cover a continuum of learning "requires a better articulation and integration of universities, management schools and corporate education, as well as an orchestration of professors, line managers and professional trainers." Such an interactive strategy toward management education and development focusing on the acquisition of action skills in the field necessitates a high level of reciprocal integration and requires a fusion of the two arenas.

Action learning provides one of the mechanisms by which the participants of this particular executive education program may transfer between the two learning arenas identified, most especially if the "action learning as a toolbox of techniques" perspective is taken. This is not necessarily to imply that the program does not address the issues of action learning as therapy or as philosophy. However, these perspectives raise issues which go beyond the narrowly defined purposes of the present chapter. In this approach, the assumption is made that this type of learning operates only within certain preconditions: a manager has a problem which needs to be solved and this problem is important to the organization. To enable him/her to solve this problem the individual joins an action learning set of managers in a similar situation, which is facilitated by a set advisor who acts as a tutor. In both overall design and in the context of several individual modules within the program in particular, the approach being adopted to the detailed evaluation of the impact of the program and of specific modules and process interventions is to seek experiential answers to five questions:

1. Who learns?
2. What do they learn?
3. How do they learn?
4. Where do they learn?
5. When do they learn?

In seeking answers to these questions, the nature of the learning alliance between faculty and participants is continually called into question. Furthermore, the answers to these questions themselves call into question the nature of and basis for the learning alliance which underlies the design, development and delivery of the program itself. This is important as, despite the great expansion in the volume of research on entrepreneurial education, there is still scope for "research on formal, structured education programs (which) should include niches for growth-oriented entrepreneurs and technology entrepreneurs, (are) areas which seem to have been neglected ... and greater emphasis on the development and evaluation of specific pedagogical methods and techniques, suitable for use for practicing entrepreneurs should be encouraged" (Young, 1997, pp. 233-234). This paper, and the program it describes, specifically occupies this niche and, in reviewing contemporary trends in management education, reinforces previous attempts to broaden the intellectual base for thinking about SME and entrepreneurial development (Harrison & Leitch, 1994; Gibb, 1997).

The experience of participants in the entrepreneurial executive development program described in this paper has demonstrated the applicability and efficacy of an action learning-based approach. As interest in the whole area of management, organizational and entrepreneurial learning continues to grow, the range of research issues to be addressed in assessing issues of program design, content, audience and delivery also expands. In a very real sense, therefore, our collective current state of knowledge represents no more than the establishment of an awareness of the boundaries of our ignorance. As Block and Stumpf (1992, p. 40) conclude in their review of the current state of entrepreneurship education:

> rigorous research is clearly needed to understand the target audiences for entrepreneurship education, their unique educational objectives and learning styles, and the types of content to be covered for each audience, and which specific pedagogical methods will most effectively meet their educational goals. Such research must look at both the proximal criteria of stu-

dent interest and immediate feedback as well as the more distal criteria of actual behavior over ten or more years.

This is an immense agenda—our perspective is, however, to suggest that the key to progress is, as Filion (1991) and Harrison and Leitch (1994) have argued, to recognize that entrepreneurial learning is not necessarily to be construed as unique but is capable of construal within a broader framework which allows for a comprehensive reconceptualization of the field of management education as a whole.

NOTES

1. As a number of recent writers have emphasized (Carter, Ulrich, & Goldsmith, 2004; Conger & Benjamin, 1999; Yukl, 2001; Storey, 2003) leadership development has been a significant and growing area of interest in recent years.

2. The account of this program refers to the program as developed and run by the authors at a university in the UK throughout the 1990s; both authors have subsequently changed their institutional affiliation and, in common with the majority of the teaching faculty originally involved in the program, are no longer associated with the program.

3. A key factor in the origin of the program was the perceived need to improve the level of knowledge, skills and competence of senior executives in companies based in one particular region of the UK, and through that to improve the international competitiveness of the regional economy. To that end, a significant proportion of the cost of developing the program was provided by the relevant government agency.

REFERENCES

Argyris, C., & Schon, D. (1974). *Theory in practice: Increasing professional effectiveness*. San Francisco: Jossey-Bass.

Argyris, C., & Schon, D. (1978). *Organisational Learning: A theory in action perspective*. New York: Addison-Wesley.

Beck, E. (1994). The new paradigm of management education: Revolution and counter-revolution. *Management Learning, 25*(2), 231-47.

Blackler, F., & Kennedy, A. (2004). The design and evaluation of a leadership program for experienced chief executives from the public sector. *Management Learning, 35*(2), 181-204.

Block, Z., & Stumpf, S.A. (1992). Entrepreneurship education research: Experience and challenge. In D.L. Sexton & J.D. Kasarda (Eds.), *The state of the art of entrepreneurship* (pp. 17-42). Boston: PWS-Kent.

Boud, D., Cohen, R., & Walker, D. (Eds.). (1993). *Using experience for learning*. Buckingham: Society for Research into Higher Education & Open University Press.

Boud, D., & Garrick, J. (Eds.). (1999). *Understanding learning at work*. London: Routledge.

Brehmer, B. (1980). In one word: Not from experience. *Acta Psychologica, 45*, 223-241.

Carter, L., Ulrich, D., & Goldsmith, M. (Eds.). (2004). *Best practices in leadership development and organization change: How the best companies ensure meaningful change and sustainable leadership*. San Francisco: Pfeiffer.

Cheit, E.F. (1985). Business schools and their critics. *California Management Review, 27*(3), 43-62.

Chia, R. (1996). Teaching paradigm shifting in management education: University business schools and the entrepreneurial imagination. *Journal of Management Studies, 33*(4), 411-428.

Conger, J. A., & Benjamin, E. (1999). *Building leaders: How successful companies develop the next generation*. San Francisco: Jossey-Basse.

Cooper, C.L. (1982). A theory of management learning: Its implications for management education. In R.D. Freedman, C.L. Cooper, & S.A. Stumpf (Eds.), *Management education: Issues in theory, research and practice* (pp. 45-55). New York: Wiley.

Day, D.L. (1992). Research linkages between entrepreneurship and strategic management or general management. In D.L. Sexton & J.D. Kasarda (Eds.), *The state of the art of entrepreneurship* (pp. 117-164). Boston: PWS-Kent.

Dierkes, M., Berthoinanthal, A., Child, J., & Nonaka, I. (2001). *Handbook of organizational learning and knowledge*. Oxford: Oxford University Press.

Dixon, N. (1994). *The organisational learning cycle: How can we learn collectively?* Maidenhead: McGraw-Hill.

Dubini, P., & Paulato, G. (1993). *Diversification and value creation: The case of Benetton*. Lyon: Third Global Entrepreneurship Research Conference, Groupe ESC.

Easterby-Smith, M. (1997). Disciplines of organisational learning: Contributions and critiques. *Human Relations, 50*, 1085-1116.

Easterby-Smith, M., & Lyles, M. (Eds.). (2003). *The Blackwell handbook of organizational learning and knowledge management*. Oxford: Blackwell.

Eden, C., & Huxman, C. (1996). Action research for management research. *British Journal of Management, 7*, 75-86.

Edmondson, A., & Moingeon, B. (1996). Introduction: Organisational learning as a source of competitive advantage. In B. Moingeon & A. Edmondson (Eds.), *Organisational learning and competitive advantage* (pp. 7-15). London: Sage.

Filion, L.J. (1991). Vision and relations: Elements for an entrepreneurial meta-model. *International Small Business Journal, 9*, 26-40.

Flamholtz, E. (1990). *Growing pains: How to make the transition from an entrepreneurship to a professionally managed firm*. San Francisco: Jossey-Bass.

Forray, J.M., & Mir, A.H. (1994). Envisioning a new paradigm: Synthesis in management education. *Management Learning, 25*(3), 201-14.

Friga, P.N., Bettis, R.A., & Sullivan, R.S. (2003). Changes in graduate management education and new business school strategies for the 21st century. *Academy of Management Learning and Education, 2*, 233-249.

Freire, P. (1972). *Pedagogy of the oppressed*. Harmondsworth: Penguin.

Gibb, A.A. (1993). Do we really teach small business in the way we should? *Proceedings of the Internationalising Entrepreneurship Education and Training Conference*, Vienna.

Gibb, A.A. (1997). Small firms' training and competitiveness: building upon the small business as a learning organisation. *International Small Business Journal*, *15*(3), 13-29.

Gorman, G., Hanlon, D., & King, W. (1997). Some research perspectives on entrepreneurship education, enterprise education and education for small business management: A ten-year literature review. *International Small Business Journal*, *15*(3), 56-77.

Greene, P.G., Katz, J.A., & Johannisson, B. (Eds.). (2004). Special issue: Entrepreneurship education. *Academy of Management Learning and Education*, *3*, 238-342

Grey, C. (1996). Introduction: Special section on critique and renewal in management education. *Management Learning*, *27*(1), 7-20.

Grey, C., & French, R. (1996). Rethinking management education: An introduction. In R. French & C. Grey (Eds.), *Rethinking management education* (pp. 1-16). London: Sage.

Guth, W.D., Kumaraswamy, A., & McErlean, M. (1991). Cognition, enactment and learning in the entrepreneurial process. In N.C. Churchill et al. (Eds.), *Frontiers of entrepreneurship research* (pp. 242-253). Wellesley, MA: Babson College.

Hamel, G., & Prahalad, C.K. (1996). Research notes and communications—competing in the new economy: Managing out of bounds. *Strategic Management Journal*, *17*, 237-342.

Harrison, R.T., & Leitch, C.M. (1994). Entrepreneurship and leadership: The implications for education and development. *Entrepreneurship and Regional Development*, *6*, 111-215.

Harrison, R.T., Leitch, C.M., & Burgoyne, J. (1996). Understanding the learning company: A constructivist approach. *Learning Company and Executive Development* (Working Paper). Belfast: Ulster Business School, University of Ulster.

Henry, C., Hill, F., & Leitch, C.M. (2003). *Entrepreneurship education and training*. Aldershot: Ashgate Publishing Ltd.

House, R.J. (1982). Experiential learning: A social learning theory analysis. In R.D. Freedman, C.L. Cooper, & S.A. Stumpf (Eds.), *Management education: Issues in theory, research and practice* (pp. 23-44). New York: Wiley.

Janoff-Bulman, R., & Brickman, P. (1982). Expectations and what people learn from failure. In N.T. Feather (Ed.), *Expectations and actions: Expectancy-value models in psychology* (pp. 207-237). Hillsdale, NJ: Lawrence Erlbaum Associates Inc.

Kolb, D.A. (1984). *Experiential learning*. Englewood Cliffs, NJ: Prentice Hall.

Kourilsky, M.L., & Carlson, S.R. (1997). Entrepreneurship education for youth: A curricular perspective. In D.L. Sexton & R.W. Sanlow (Eds.), *Entrepreneurship 2000* (pp. 193-213). Chicago: Upstart Publishing.

Laurillard, D. (1993). *Rethinking university teaching: A framework for the effective use of educational technology*. London: Routledge.

Leesem, R. (1993). *Business as a learning community*. New York: McGraw-Hill.

Leitch, C.M., & Harrison, R.T. (1993). *Learning, culture and the diversifying corpora-tion*. Paper to the Third Global Entrepreneurship Research Conference, Groupe ESC, Lyon.

Leitch, C., & Harrison, R. (2005). Entrepreneurial learning: Researching the interface between learning and the entrepreneurial context. *Entrepreneurship Theory and Practice, 29* (forthcoming).

Levitt, B., & March, J.G. (1988). Organisational learning. *Annual Review of Sociol-ogy, 14*, 319-40.

Limerick, D., & Moore, L.F. (1991). A winning relationship: Managing the stu-dent-company learning interface. *Journal of Management Education, 15*, 397-411.

Marquardt, M. J. (1999). *Action learning in action: Transforming problems and people for world-class organizational learning*. Palo Alto, CA: Davies-Black.

Marsick, V.J., & O'Neil, J. (1999). The many faces of action learning. *Management Learning, 30*(2), 159-176.

Mazzarol, T. (2003). A model of small business HR growth management. *Interna-tional Journal of Entrepreneurial Behaviour and Research, 9*, 27-49.

McGill, I., & Beaty, L. (1995). *Action Learning: A Guide for Professional, Management and educational Development*. London: Kogan Page.

McGrath, R., Venkataraman, S., & MacMillan, I. (1993). *Understanding organiza-tional competence: An alternative approach*. Paper to the Third Global Entrepre-neurship Research Conference, Groupe ESC, Lyon.

McLaughlin, H., & Thorpe, R. (1993). Action learning: A paradigm in emer-gence: The problems facing a challenge to traditional management educa-tion and development. *British Journal of Management, 4*(1), 19-27.

Mintzberg, H. (2004). *Managers not MBAs*. London: FT Prentice-Hall.

Mintzberg, H., & Gosling, J. (2002). Educating managers beyond borders. *Acad-emy of Management Learning and Education 1*, 64-76.

Pedler, M. (1988). Self-development and work organizations. In M. Pedler & T. Boydell (Ed.), *Applying self-development in organizations*. Englewood Cliffs, NJ: Prentice-Hall.

Pedler, M., Burgoyne, J., & Boydell, T. (1991). *The Learning Company: A strategy for substantive development* (2nd ed.). London: McGraw-Hill.

Pfeffer, J., & Fong, C.T. (2002). The end of business schools? Less successful than meets the eye. *Academy of Management Learning and Education, 1*, 78-95.

Porter, L.W., & McKibben, L.E. (1988). *Management education and development: Drift or thrust into the 21st century?* New York: McGraw-Hill.

Raelin, J.A. (1994). Whither management education? Professional education, action learning and beyond. *Management Learning, 25*(2), 301-317.

Raelin, J. (1999). Preface—special issue: The action dimension in management: Diverse approaches to research, teaching and development. *Management Learning, 30*(2), 115-126.

Raelin, J. (2000). *Work-based learning: The new frontier of management development*. Englewood Cliffs, NJ: Prentice-Hall.

Raelin, J.A., & Schermerhorn, J., Jr. (1994). A new paradigm for advanced man-agement education—how knowledge merges with experience, editorial. *Man-agement Learning, 25*(2), 195-200.

Ramsden, P. (1992). *Learning to teach in higher education*. London: Routledge.

Revans, R. (1971). *Developing effective managers*. Harlow: Longman.

Revans, R. (1982). *Origins and growth of action learning*. London: Chartwell-Bratt.

Salaman, G., & Butler, J. (1990). Why managers won't learn. *Management Education and Development, 21*(3), 183-91.

Senge, P. (1990). *The Fifth Discipline: The art and practice of the learning organisation*. London: Century Business.

Slevin, D.P., & Colvin, J.G. (1992). Creating and maintaining high performance teams. In D.L. Sexton & J.D. Kasarda (Eds), *The state of the art of entrepreneurship* (pp. 358-386). Boston: PWS-Kent.

Spender, J.C. (1994). Knowing management and learning: A dynamic managerial epistemology. *Management Learning, 25*(3), 387-412.

Sterman, J.D. (1989). Modelling managerial behaviour: Misperceptions of feedback in a dynamic decision making experiment. *Management Science, 35*, 321-39.

Storey, J. (2004). *Leadership in organizations: Current issues and key trends*. London: Routledge

Sutton, D. (1990). Action learning in search of p. *Industrial and Commercial Training, 22*(1), 9-12.

Vaill, P. (1989). *Managing as a performing art: New ideas for a world of chaotic change*. San Francisco: Jossey-Bass.

Vento, I. (1998). Promoting enterprise culture through education. *Proceedings of the Enterprise and Learning Conference*, Aberdeen.

Vesper, K.H., McMillan, W.E., & Ray, D.M. (1988). Designing and entrepreneurship program: What can we learn from other fields? *Revista Economica de Calalunya, 9*, 77-82.

Weinstein, K. (1999). *Action learning: A practical guide*. Aldershot: Gower.

Willmott, H. (1994). Management education: Provocations to a debate. *Management Learning, 25*(1), 105-36.

Yavtiz, B. (1982). *Institutional responses: Programs for action, managers for the xxi century: Their education and development*. Boston: Kluwer Nijhoff.

Young, J.E. (1997). Entrepreneurship education and learning for university students and practicing entrepreneurs. In D.L. Sexton, & R.W. Smith (Eds.), *Entrepreneurship 2000* (pp. 215-238). Chicago: Upstart Publishing.

Yukl, G. A. (2001). *Leadership in organizations* (5th ed.). New York: Prentice Hall.

Zuber-Skerritt, O. (1993). Improving learning and teaching through action learning and action research. *Higher Education Research and Development, 12*(1), 45-57.

Zuber-Skerritt, O. (1995). Developing a learning organization through management education by action learning. *The Learning Organization, 2*(2), 36-46.

CHAPTER 10

THE MANCHESTER METHOD

A Critical Review of a Learning Experiment

Tudor Rickards, Paula Hyde, and K. Nadia Papamichail

Recent critiques of management education have concluded that MBA programs are not equipping graduates adequately for organizational life. We contribute to this debate through a critical review of a learning experiment. Namely, the Manchester Method, a pedagogic approach to learning within business education, which involves students in a series of group projects set in real organizations for which they take increasing responsibility. While we argue that this approach to learning has acted as a platform for creating actionable knowledge, developing actionable skills, and supporting learning strategies we go on to challenge the provenance, claims for novelty and efficacy of the Manchester Method in the light of current changes to the wider business school environment.

INTRODUCTION

Recent critiques of management education conclude that the content and methods of management education require radical changes in the face of turbulently changing environments and that MBA programs are not equipping graduates for organizational life (Minzberg, 2004). To contribute to this debate we examine an educational experiment: The Manchester

Educating Managers through Real World Projects, 241–254
Copyright © 2005 by Information Age Publishing
All rights of reproduction in any form reserved.

Method, a pedagogic approach to business learning. It is innovative at the contextual level, retained within a community of practice of educators from behavioral and economic/technological paradigms, within an established MBA program. It supports a flexible culture, enabling agile changes in content and methods, as well as in supporting structures. The Method places students in a series of group projects set in real organizations for which they take increasing responsibility, over the course of the MBA program.

We draw from our experiences in applying the approach to illustrate how the Manchester Method has acted as a platform for creating actionable knowledge, developing actionable skills, supporting learning strategies and nurturing communities of practice. We demonstrate how collaboration across academic disciplines within the business school has been an important component in the development of the approach and specifically we indicate the inter-penetration of ideas from both social and technical traditions, which have provided sociotechnical grounding to the approach. Themes emerging from the application of the method are noted, and the provenance, claims for novelty, and efficacy of the method are examined critically in the light of current changes to the wider business school environment.

FROM EXPERIMENT TO METHOD

The Manchester Experiment was launched in conjunction with the opening of Manchester Business School in 1965 and involved a radically different approach to management education whereby only loose divisions between subject areas were maintained and most project work undertaken by students crossed disciplinary boundaries. The experiment was described as:

> a highly practical, learning by doing approach to management education, undertaken in a democratic, non-departmental organization which was only loosely co-ordinated from the top [which] symbolizes the continuous process of innovation which has typified the approach to course design at Manchester Business School. (Wilson, 1992, p. xi)

It was argued that this approach would confront what were seen as rigidities of business courses, identified in existing faculties around the world (Simon, 1969). The design decision was to cluster teaching and learning around multi-disciplinary experiences. To assist this process, the School avoided establishing departments organized around business specialisms such as finance or marketing. One of the essential features of the Experiment involved students in a process of learning whereby they played an increasing part in negotiating their learning experiences as they progressed through the course. Furthermore, as the course progressed, projects became less bounded and offered greater scope for individual and project-team negotiation. This formed the origins of the Manchester Method.

The nature of the Manchester Method remains highly contested, even within the Business School itself, however, it focuses on experiential learning and the pursuit of knowledge and skills acquisition through consultancy-based projects that involve students in group projects tackling current problems in real organizations. Although the present program continues to focus on the experiential nature of group-based project work the emphasis on cross-disciplinary working has all but disappeared.

DISTINGUISHING FEATURES OF THE MANCHESTER METHOD

The Manchester Method's claims for novelty arise from several distinguishing features. In order to identify differentiating factors, Table 10.1 contrasts the incorporation of the Method into the Manchester MBA program with other styles of MBA—lecture-centered and project-added. "Lecture-centered" relates to taught MBA programs with no supplementary project work. "Project-added" MBAs are those programs that offer opportunities for group work around set project areas. The delivery style of the Manchester Method was found to be distinguishable across a number of dimensions.

Table 10.1.   Differentiating Factors within the Practice of the Manchester Method

Dimension	Lecture-centered MBAs	Project-added MBAs	Manchester Method
Delivery style	Controlled and bounded delivery of established knowledge categories (marketing, finance, operations management etc)	Controlled and bounded projects designed to supplement established course lecture categories, while permitting some personal and experiential learning	Level of external control and boundedness of projects moderated and increased over the course of the MBA. Subject area boundaries loosely defined in relation to project work
Mode of assessment	Well established assessment procedures permitting external quality control and examination	Laboratory-based contributions to group development possible with well-codified pedagogic interventions	Facilitators have to approach the novelties within each project as presenting challenges and opportunities to students and facilitators

(Table continues on next page)

Table 10.1.   Continued

Dimension	Lecture-centered MBAs	Project-added MBAs	Manchester Method
Reflexivity	Personal and reflective learning has less emphasis	Personal and reflective learning possible under controlled conditions	Personal and reflective learning possible, with greater scope for personal experiences, challenges and setbacks
Experiential features	Psychologically safe learning zone within expectations of students and faculty	Experiential learning boundaries can be managed to permit some uncertainties, but avoid over-threatening challenges (Moderate scope for developmental 'stretching')	Challenges and setbacks require facilitated negotiation, so that they lead to qualitatively different experiential learning. The learning model permits reflective critique of group processes and anxieties
Degree of knowledge uncertainty	Lectures provide a coherent and convincing knowledge base	Projects provide realistic experiences equipping MBAs for industrial work as a unitary culture (shared goals etc), and less frequently as a negotiable pluralism	Projects reveal the 'messiness' of pluralistic and fragmented group cultures, which sometimes are susceptible to negotiable outcomes
Organization of learning opportunities	Personal and unintended learning opportunities few	Personal and unintended learning opportunities possible	Personal and unintended learning opportunities frequent
Scope for creativity	Presentational approach of teacher	Presentational approach of teams; some scope for exceptional insights in content	As for other project-based approaches, plus additional opportunities for resilient and creative responses to unanticipated challenges
Knowledge management	Knowledge management structures mostly codified	Knowledge management structures partly codified (with scope for some integration of learning)	Knowledge management structures integral to the method ensuring recurrent developmental features

Differentiating factors include the following: The program incorporates subject-based lectures with group projects in live settings; students take increasing responsibility throughout the MBA program for project acquisition, management and delivery; the mode of assessment necessarily incorporates project ambiguity in order to reflect group success in the award scheme and opportunities for reflexivity are high in the MBA program allowing for personal and reflective learning from the early stages. Furthermore, experiential features of the program are introduced from the beginning of the program; students are encouraged to acknowledge high levels of knowledge uncertainty as live project work ensures frequent opportunities for unintended and personal learning; and this approach generates high levels of creativity with the added opportunity to develop and incorporate innovations to the program (see section entitled Innovative Practices Generated From the Manchester Method).

THEORETICAL AND PRACTICAL DEVELOPMENT OF THE MANCHESTER METHOD

The Tavistock approach to organizational development was used as a model for development of the Method (Astrachan, 1975). This approach has, according to some authorities, two distinguishable tendencies (De Board, 1978; Smith et al., 1982). The first derives from the psychoanalytic work of Bion (1961); the second from the sociotechnical approach (Trist & Bamforth, 1951).

Firstly, Bion's work with groups explored both task and fantasy as features of group life (Bion, 1961). Subsequent psychoanalytical approaches to groups (Miller, 1998, 1997) had particular relevance to the initial development of the Manchester Method because of the group-based design for much of the project work. According to Bion (1961) only a minority of groups engage in what he called work group mode. These were psychodynamically "healthy" groups, dealing with their work issues in a realistic manner. For many groups there was a tendency to be driven by unrecognized emotionally powerful impulses which Bion referred to as Basic Assumptions. Bion considered that while groups could exhibit a strong grounding in reality they might alternatively demonstrate "basic assumption" behaviors where they were more influenced by unconscious and emotionally charged forces. He described the former as task activity and the latter as basic assumption activity (Bion, 1961). Indeed, his ideas were particularly useful as they refer to functional rather than dysfunctional groups (Rioch, 1970). Specifically he identified three forms of basic assumption: dependency; fight-flight; and pairing. Each assumption relates to a fantasy state, which affects group function perhaps through the formation of unhelpful coalitions, member-member, or leader-group dynamics and perpetuating the ungrounded assumption that some future resolution will overcome the unpleasantnesses of the present. Each basic assumption offers the group a world understanding which they act out without question. Notwithstanding the Manchester Method's bias toward experiential methods the importance of understanding group processes came to the fore particularly where student teams examined real or realistic organizational projects.

The influence of the second strand of the Tavistock approach, sociotechnical systems thinking, must also be noted. This approach was introduced particularly through the efforts of Enid Mumford (1981, 2000) and co-workers (Gunz, 1989; Morris, 1980; Thomas, 1997; Whitley, 1984). The Manchester Method evolved still further in its pedagogic grounding through the efforts of Stafford Beer. Beer argued for a cybernetically-informed educational structure ("the viable system") that would be self-adjusting (Beer, 1994). Beer, Mumford and the other earlier contributors to The Manchester Experiment were aware of the impact of people and innovations in information technology on modern organizations. The Manchester Method was to become inevitably reshaped by these influences (Rickards, 1987).

INNOVATIVE PRACTICE GENERATED FROM THE MANCHESTER METHOD

Each experience of the Manchester Method approach has offered scope for experience-based improvements to wider program content and management and the repeated challenge of dealing with new projects has helped to instil a flexible orientation to innovation among the faculty. A brief account of three recent innovations to the MBA program are given as illustrations of innovative practice arising out of the Manchester Method.

Recent innovations are illustrated through: project outputs, such as, "the incubator"; a developmental series of projects such as the UNESCO project; and the development of e-learning networks to support project work. Each of these innovations is outlined below.

Project Outputs: The Incubator

The development of the Business School Incubator in 2002 was a direct outcome of an internally generated Manchester Method project. A group of MBA students opted to find their own project and conduct it as a summer elective. They took responsibility for finding a sponsor (the head of school) whom they convinced of the benefits that would accrue from such an incubator. They also negotiated terms of reference for the project with their sponsor, conducted an investigation through direct interviews with leaders of existing incubators nationally and internationally, and reported their findings, which included evidence for the financial viability as well as the academic rationale for the incubator. As a direct result, an externally funded incubator was established, with the particular objective of providing learning experiences within future MBA programs. Moreover, members of the original project team act as operational executives. Financial support comes from several international financial and professional sponsors. New businesses are being created and supported, particularly through (yet more) Manchester Method type project teams. Several incubator electives are now offered within the MBA, giving a focus for those interested in entrepreneurial careers. New businesses supported by the incubator are being developed, offering a promising revenue stream to the University, as a major shareholder of the incubator holding company.

Project Development

Projects are initiated by dedicated project officers, through approaches made to the School from organizations, and by MBA participants, some of whom are studying part-time. Each project group has responsibility for meeting the (negotiated) business needs of the sponsor, and of meeting academic course requirements for examination purposes. The response from the sponsors is generally positive, as evidenced by subsequent requests for involvement with the School (see below). Some sponsors—from consulting, pharmaceutical, and IT sectors, for example—regularly use projects as means of identifying MBA participants for employment.

An illustration of the regenerating effect of these types of projects is provided by projects conducted for UNESCO (UK region). UNESCO operated world wide to find ways of transferring knowledge from first world regions for economic development purposes. Regional centers face enormous challenges of local knowledge capture and for global transfer. A pilot exercise in three regions was conducted by three MBA teams in a business and environment project in 2003. In 2004, the project was extended to a global challenge, involving twenty teams of MBA participants.

The Development of E-learning Networks

The Manchester Method engages participants in knowledge-intensive activities across organizational boundaries in the form of live projects, i.e., consultancy-based projects undertaken during the MBA program. These projects require students to work in groups and undertake consultancy work on a real-life project for a company, under the guidance of tutors. Over the years, a number of information and communication technologies ranging from e-mail to Lotus Team Workplace have been used to support the communication and information management needs of the Manchester Method participants.

An e-learning environment for live projects was recently designed, which allowed participants access to a number of workspaces including a common area that provided information about the project, a dedicated area that allowed the members of a group to share experiences, and an individual area that were used to record events and emotions. This followed an initial attempt to design an online collaborative template (Drinkwater et al., 2004). Tutors monitored online discussions, provided feedback and encouraged reflection on the learning process. All participants were able to be contacted via online services and were, therefore, more easily accessible. The online environment facilitated the transfer of knowledge and increased awareness of learning opportunities. Participants sought the advice of other members when they could not answer a question or solve a problem. The collaborative tool supported the social network comprising students, tutors, organizers and other support staff so as participants could benefit from other people's skills and experiences.

One of the advantages of using information and communication technologies to support group-based work, such as the project described above, was the creation of a record of learning, which captured behavioral patterns and extended the "Manchester Method memory." Online environments codify and store such forms of individual and collective knowledge which can be analyzed later in attempts to capture learning processes, articulate lessons learnt over time and identify best practice.

A critical element of this electronic-learning component of the Manchester Method was feedback. As teaching and learning projects unfolded, feedback loops were created that played a key role in fostering new innovations. Insights gained from past and current experiences therefore shaped the way that projects evolved. Tools such as e-mail and QuickPlace (www.quickplace.com) were used when electronic support was required to sustain the social network. The tools allowed for the codification of lessons learnt and for the dissemination of knowledge about decisions and actions taken. Thus, at the core of the Manchester Method lies a sociotechnical network that combines social actors (e.g., project participants) and technical structures (e.g., online infrastructure, codified knowledge) and acts as a platform for creating actionable knowledge through supporting learning strategies.

Instructional methods supported by information technology have been shown to enable the construction of sociocultural models of learning (Leidner & Jarvenpaa, 1995) and facilitate the implementation of instructional strategies (Alavi & Leidner, 2001). The literature on e-learning and instruction indicates that group support and collaborative systems improve group-based work (Alavi, 1994), enhance classroom interaction (Leidner & Fuller, 1997) and encourage a higher level of thinking (Lim et al., 1997). This example illustrates how collaborative computing tools have recently been introduced to enhance the learning experience before, during and after conducting the live projects in the MBA program. Such technologies have allowed participants:

1. To communicate information, action plans, decisions and research findings.
2. To collaborate by sharing documents and exchanging ideas.
3. To coordinate activities by assigning tasks and allocating resources.
4. To create a number of workspaces that enable access, anytime, anywhere, to collective knowledge.

EVOLUTION OF THE MANCHESTER METHOD

The Method, as it evolved, was to prove controversial, both to those who came into contact with it, from the wider University, and those from outside the University. Faculty joining the School, some years after its foundation, and familiar with more traditional departmental structures, sometimes proved difficult to convince of the virtues of such an unusual structure. Additionally, the concept of a loose, non-departmental structure presented difficulties for administrators seeking standardization of procedures and practices to permit quality assessment across departments, and across Universities. In contrast, the potential weaknesses of the experiment were easier to understand and articulate and, as we acknowledge, the experiment was indeed to become attenuated resulting in the emergence of more formal departmental groupings.

It should not be surprising though that the educational benefits of MBA programs, where traditional lectures and cases were complemented with project work, were easier to grasp: Firstly, the notion was less novel and secondly, team-working of itself was a familiar pedagogic approach in certain other university departments, and business schools. The differences lay more in the centrality of the concept to the pedagogy of Manchester Business School (MBS); the rationale developed for co-determination of teaching goals and context. In short, the Manchester Method could be seen as less radical than the original Manchester Experiment, while nevertheless remaining a potentially powerful differentiator of the Business School from its rivals, both conceptually and for the sake of marketing efforts.

TENSIONS AND DILEMMAS WITHIN THE METHOD

The conduct of any extended educational experiment reveals recurring themes, which challenge those involved. Participants involved in the Manchester Method have continued to encounter issues around personal and team development, leadership, reflectivity, and the management of ambiguity. The content uniqueness of projects as "living cases" have provided a context for these themes to be surfaced, explored and addressed. This is not to suggest that recurrent tensions are removed, rather they resurface with familiar and timely regularity for re-inspection and serve to emphasize the emotional effort required to sustain such a dynamic approach to student learning.

Student and Faculty Tensions

Experienced faculty have become familiar with recurring tensions related to the use of the Manchester Method. Perhaps it should not be a surprise that, such issues arise for students and faculty alike. Initially, on encountering the Method people grapple to understand its precise nature—it has a name but no clear form. At one level, the confusion is that of sense-making around a theoretical concept which is partially defined in practice and is presented as a new experience (Weick, 1995). The ambiguity around the Method is a necessary component of the pedagogic approach.

The case has been made for working with ambiguities around organizational knowledge and related constructs (Sparrow, 1998; Spender, 1996). Both staff and students at Manchester Business School have sought to either find ever more convincing characterizations of the nature of the Manchester Method or have dismissed it as an abstract concept.

For faculty and students alike, there is a recurrent and painful necessity to deal with uncertainty and anxiety. Such concerns are often expressed as a lack of understanding regarding the essential nature of the Manchester Method. The concerns are often crystallized around the absence of an unequivocal definition, and the issue is raised both informally and at formal committee meetings. Students and staff are often challenged by the ill-defined and fluid nature of their various tasks that involve working with businesses to focus on current (live) problems and develop plans for dealing with them. The lack of a clear answer, similar to one that may be attained from a case study approach, leaves the students with some level of uncertainty around what is expected of them. Additionally, they may be uncertain about what help they can expect from faculty and their host business. The resultant anxieties occasionally spill over into group meetings with the tutors. Recently there have been fewer Tavistock-trained staff available, and student anxieties have not always been contained or surfaced. Instead some members of faculty have absorbed the anxiety and colluded with the group in the search for the "right" answer. This has sometimes led to frustrations with the approach itself and to a push for more "concrete" student assignments. There is rarely a call to move away from the "live" element of projects, i.e., working with businesses on current problems, rather, the call is for tighter definitions, specifications or more written documentation about what is expected from whom. Notwithstanding these tensions, students who have completed the MBA program often record the Manchester Method as one of the most memorable and influential aspects of the program.

During engagement at the educational "coalface," however, diverse voices risk confusion. Specifically, the Business School comprises views including some agnostic toward the Manchester Method, and some prepared to express downright opposition. These voices typically, but not exclusively, come from the traditionally "hard" treatments of the core curriculum. According to the Tavistock principles informing The Manchester Method, the processes of encounter over time may help the voices converge through discourse and mutual development, although unresolved tensions and ambiguities remain a condition of "a democratic organization." In reality, boundaries between subject area groups in the Business School are more clearly delineated than hitherto resulting in perhaps a more conservative looking department at some distance from its radical roots.

Tensions between Sponsor/Client Roles

Business Schools have traditionally existed symbiotically with management consultancy firms with a proportion of MBA participants undertaking the course as a direct route into consulting. Consultant business models pass in an interactive fashion from top schools to consulting firms, to more general business and government consumers. Indeed, evidence has been presented of the benefits of approaching business projects in order to develop consulting skills (Clifford & Hillar Farran, 2004). There are, however, tensions between projects regarded primarily as consultant—type experiences and those more concerned with broader aspects of personal development.

The consultant-client relationship is often transactional and is generally exercised around preestablished and negotiated parameters. We distinguish this from developmental projects wherein the relationship is between project team and project sponsor rather than a client. Here learning is openly accepted as a central part of the rationale: the sponsor learns through fresh insights into key issues; the project teams acquire a range of knowledge, skills, and behavioral elements both directly and indirectly. We recognize that the distinction is far from clear-cut and that some projects are closer to the traditional consulting arrangements:

Indeed, some staff are themselves more disposed to encouraging the development of consulting skills. The key relationships appear to be between the sponsor, the team and the tutors. The calculus is not solely around a financial contract, but includes the additional recognition of a learning contract. Sponsors contribute financially in recognition of obligations and costs incurred by participants whilst achieving the mutually agreed objectives of the project. Furthermore, the choice of vocabulary is influenced by the preferences of the faculty team, and through them, the manner in which a specific project develops over time. These issues reflect the tensions inherent within the Manchester method approach, and the manner in which diverse views jostle for a negotiated acceptance.

Critical Evaluation of the Method

This critical evaluation of the Manchester Method has required examination of the novelty and practical outcomes achieved through this type of learning experiment, not least because this is one of the claims to originality of the approach. Collaboration continues across disciplines in spite of (or perhaps because of) disciplinary boundaries becoming more clearly delineated. Whilst we recognize that the Method no longer eschews disciplinary boundaries it continues to allow students to recognize group processes during live projects, to carry learning forward, and, subsequently, to put learning into practice in further group projects.

By engaging students in real organization-based projects, they are able to consider project group processes (taking account of both task and fantasy). The centrality of such concepts to MBS pedagogy has enabled rapid program innovation alongside a flexible, faculty orientation to such changes. The three illustrative examples of innovation presented above, demonstrated the recursive nature of project outputs both within the program and reaching outside of the University.

One further critical issue is that the type of learning system described represents a moving target, ever striving to address possibilities for self-initiated change and development. We argue that the approach can provide a coherent, well-grounded approach in the education of managers and leaders, facilitating the development of a community of practice and open to a variety of design elements supportive of developmental learning. At the same time we recognize the inherent difficulties of sustaining a dynamic approach to management education. Such approaches to learning generate tensions between faculty and staff and can conflate sponsor/client relationships. Furthermore, they require continuous emotional engagement of participants to manage uncertainties and anxieties arising from the negotiated nature of live projects. Such tensions concern personal and team development, leadership, reflectivity and the management of ambiguity. Live projects allow for the surfacing, exploration and resolution of conflicts. Rather than being removed they recur, upon the advent of each new live project, reemphasizing the emotional engagement required to sustain the approach.

The introduction of similar approaches to other settings would inevitably require an acceptance of its coherent broad sociotechnical pedagogy, and the introduction of modifications created to meet specific situational factors and antecedents. This analysis suggests that the evaluation of the merits of experiential programs will not be a methodologically or epistemologically straightforward challenge. As we have suggested, considerable emotional energy and investment are required of both students and staff in order to stay true to the philosophy of this approach. A critical mass of suitably trained or experienced staff is also necessary in order to support the process. These staff need to be embedded in the system as these approaches can be rapidly dissembled through the loss of staff central to delivery.

Notwithstanding these challenges, the Manchester Method offers an approach that forms a crucible for innovation in spite of, or perhaps because of, the emotional challenges it poses to the community of students, teachers, support staff and sponsors. Furthermore, the Method has provided a platform from which actionable knowledge may be generated through recursive interactions alongside skill development and supported learning.

REFERENCES

Alavi, M. (1994). Computer-mediated collaborative learning: An empirical-evaluation. *MIS Quarterly, 18*(2), 159-174.

Alavi, M., & Leidner, D. E. (2001). Research commentary: Technology-mediated learning: A call for greater depth and breadth of research. *Information Systems Research, 12*(1), 1-10.

Astrachan, B.M., (1975) The Tavistock model of laboratory training. In K.D. Benne, L.P. Bradford, J.R. Gibb, & R.O. Lippitt, (Eds.), *The laboratory method of changing and learning: Theory and application* (pp. 326-340). Palo Alto, CA: Science and Behavior Books.

Beer, S. (1994). *Beyond dispute: The invention of team syntegrity.* Chichester: Wiley.

Bion, W.R. (1961). *Experience in groups, and other papers.* New York: Basic

Clifford, P., & Hillar Farran, J. (2004). Wharton's global consulting practicum. In *Academy of Management Conference Proceedings.* New Orleans: AOM.

De Board, R. (1978). *The psychoanalysis of organisations.* London: Tavistock.

Drinkwater, P.M., Adeline, C.M., French, S., Papamichail, K.N., & Rickards, T. (2004). Adopting a web-based collaborative tool to support the Manchester method approach to learning. *Electronic Journal of e-Learning, 2*(1), 61-68.

Gunz, H.P, (1989). *Careers and corporate culture: Managerial mobility in large organizations.* Oxford: Blackwell.

Leidner, D.E., & Fuller, M. (1997). Improving student learning of conceptual information: GSS supported collaborative learning vs. individual constructive learning. *Decision Support Systems, 20*(2), 149-163.

Leidner, D.E., & Jarvenpaa, S.L. (1995). The use of information technology to enhance management school education—A theoretical view. *MIS Quarterly, 19*(3), 265-291.

Lim, K.H., Ward, L.M., & Benbasat, I. (1997). An empirical study of computer system learning: Comparison of co-discovery and self-discovery methods. *Information Systems Research, 8*(3), 254-272.

Miller, E. (1998). A note on the proto-mental system and "groupishness": Bion's basic assumptions revisited. *Human Relations, 51*(12), 1495-1508.

Miller, E. (1997). Editorial: On reaching the age of fifty. *Human Relations, 50,* 1-9.

Mintzberg, H. (2004). *Managers not MBAs: A hard look at the soft practice of managing and management practice.* San Francisco: Berrett-Koehler.

Morris, J. (1980). Joint development activities from practice to theory. In J. Beck & C. Cox (Eds.), *Advances in management education.* London: Wiley.

Mumford, E. (1981). *Values, technology and work.* The Hague: Martinus Nijhoff.

Mumford, E. (2000). Socio-technical design: An unfulfilled promise or a future opportunity. In R. Baskerville, J. Stage, & J.I. de Gross (Eds.), *Organizational and social perspectives on information technology,* IFIP Conference Proceedings (pp. 33-46). Kluver.

Rickards, T. (1987). Can computers help stimulate creativity? Training implications from a postgraduate MBA experience. *Management Education & Development Journal, 18*(2), 29-139.

Rioch, M.J. (1970). The work of Wilfed Bion on groups. *Psychiatry, 33*(1), 56-66.

Simon, H. (1969). *The sciences of the artificial.* Cambridge MA : MIT Press

Smith, M., Beck, J., Cooper, C.L. Cox, C., Ottaway, R., & Talbot, R. (1982). *Introducing organizational behaviour.* London: Macmillan.

Sparrow, J. (1998). *Knowledge in organizations: Access to thinking at work.* London: Sage.

Spender, J-C. (1996). Organizational knowledge, learning and memory: Three concepts in search of a theory. *Journal of Organizational Change Management, 9*(1), 63-78.

Thomas, A.B. (1997). The coming crisis of western management education. *Systems Practice, 10*(6), 681-701.

Trist, E.L., & Bamforth, K.W. (1951, February). Some social and psychological consequences of the Long Wall method of coal getting: An examination of the psychological situation and defenses of the work group in relation to the social structure and technical content of the work system. *Human Relations, 4,* 3-38.

Weick, K.E. (1995). *Sense making in organizations.* Thousand Oaks, CA: Sage.

Whitley, R. (1984). The fragmented state of management studies: Reasons and consequences. *Journal of Management Studies, 21*(3), 331-348.

Wilson, J.F. (1992). *The Manchester Experiment: A history of Manchester Business School, 1965-1990.* London: Paul Chapman.

CHAPTER 11

A MANAGEMENT EDUCATION MODEL FOR BRIDGING THE ACADEMIC AND REAL WORLD

Eugene Baten, David Fearon, and Cheryl Harrison

This chapter uses an education model that falls into that genre of management education models that use real world projects to provide real world education. Its authors recommend making the workplace (not just the physical building) the classroom; making the work the curriculum; approaching the curriculum by letting the organization's strategic plan reveal its content; and lastly, evaluating progress on what managers can do (not on what they know). This approach appreciates the concern that the traditional preparation of managers does not result in them being able to perform the tasks and envision the strategies that define their organization. The authors hold that educators can help managers unbundle their projects, determine what competencies are required to carry them out and design the appropriate competency-based education programs for each manager.

Teach with real world projects in that real world. First, we recommend making the workplace (not just the physical building) the classroom and second, we recommend making the work the curriculum. Third, we approach the curriculum by letting the organization's strategic plan reveal its content, and lastly, we evaluate progress, not on what managers know, but on what they can do.

Educating Managers through Real World Projects, 255–274
Copyright © 2005 by Information Age Publishing
All rights of reproduction in any form reserved.

INTRODUCTION

The purpose of this chapter is to present a model of work-based education that can be used for educating practicing managers as they work.

Many managers who move into management from functional areas or those that manage within functional areas often have a management blind spot. They have not had a management education; thus, their management style and knowledge are acquired through trial and error. They have no organized managerial frame of reference and thus lack some basic management knowledge. Management faculty at the authors' university are periodically requested to assist an organization in the education of their most promising operations managers, skilled in their discipline, but lacking certain management skills.

Our team of four, using released time from the School of Business to conduct research, worked with a local organization to develop an approach for educating their operations managers. The resulting model was different from the usual education programs in which we had previously participated. After our research was cut short by the University's decision to lower costs by eliminating released time, we continued to develop the model on our own. We have presented it at several conferences and it has aroused enough interest that we have been encouraged to continue to share it.

BACKGROUND

Collegiate management educators tend to use established approaches to the education of working managers and pre-managers alike. When we are in our classrooms, we present management theory, providing the opportunity to apply the theory through the use of case analysis, research presentations and simulations. We may even invite other managers (or other experts in some field) into the classroom to describe their world and experiences. Educators control the method of evaluation, which is usually focused on what knowledge has been retained.

Another approach for educating practicing managers is to provide on-site education. This moves management theory to the managers' work location. This is done to better represent the organization through the customization of the language, examples, anecdotes and cases used to support the theory. This approach is convenient and more relatable than teaching in the University classroom and when servicing one organization; however the approach is still based on the manager acquiring traditional management theory delivered by an instructor and being required to respond to a situation (such as a case) or questions about the subject matter.

Collegiate management educators may also act as a resource for a select group of managers, usually those of higher rank than the operations manager. The educators present a "hot" topic on some management phenomena or management technique, e.g., actionable knowledge, gender and leadership, cross-generational management or spirituality in the workplace. This approach goes beyond the classroom or onsite models but is usually limited to a very exclusive portion of management.

THE TWO WORLDS LEARNING MODEL: OVERVIEW

Our model focuses on bringing the best of the above educational models together with the addition of educational support for operations managers as they use the education to do their jobs. We have named it the Two Worlds Learning Bridge (TWLB) model because we see it as connecting the two worlds where management can be learned—the academic world and the world of management practice. The TWLB model is composed of six elements, a description of which follows:

- **Team of management educators**—a core team of educators is formed from management professors who are well versed in all aspects of their discipline, have strong analytic skills and extensive organizational experience. Professors from other business disciplines are asked to participate on an as-needed basis.

- **Establishing the partnership**—the team, with support from the Office of the Dean, searches for corporate partners that are interested in participating in a program that focuses on educating operational managers. Since the model focuses on using strategic projects as the learning vehicle, the organizations engaged in strategic planning and management would be the team's first choice. However, organizations that use projects to accomplish important non-strategic outcomes would also be of interest. A partnership is formed between the University and the organization when an organization is found that meets the model's criteria and the organization is interested in using our approach.

- **Identifying managers**—The organization identifies their promising operations managers, especially those in charge of strategic projects, and gives them an opportunity to participate.

- **Competencies are the curriculum**—the team assists each selected manager in "unbundling" his or her project(s) into tasks and the tasks into managerial competencies needed to perform the task. The education team then helps each manager determine what competencies he or she possesses and what competencies still need to be acquired. The educators construct a curriculum for each manager based on the competencies that each manager needs but does not possess. As the project activity is scheduled out, the commensurate educating is scheduled to be completed just before it is needed.

- **Execution**—the management educators (working as a team or as individuals), other supporting faculty, and/or resources within the organization, are available to help the manager apply newly acquired competencies as the project is executed. The faculty monitors the learning and its application.

- **Evaluation**—a manager's accomplishment is measured by the successful completion of the project, feedback from the manager, senior management's assessment of the project's execution and the assessment of the education team.

DETAILS OF THE MODEL

Each of the six elements is further explained in this section.

Team of Management Educators

The professors that participate on the team must be carefully selected. The model is designed around a core of management professors that are familiar with the workplace and comfortable working with managers. The team members must have an understanding of how adults learn. They must be analytic and good communicators. While they should be supportive, they cannot become part of the manager's decision-making and must remain separated from the management of the project. Each team member must realize his or her limitations and be willing to involve other team members, supporting faculty and internal resources, when appropriate, in educating the manager. Faculty must understand competency-based learning and how to develop a curriculum based on what a manager needs to know, respecting what he or she already knows.

Why would a faculty member be interested in participating? The opportunities for faculty are many. If the approach is successful, it becomes known and the number of organizations seeking to partner, grows. Thus participating faculty members will have access to a variety of organizations. Faculty will also have an opportunity to apply the management theory that they teach. This different approach to management education will drive the need for and result in more research opportunities. Relationships will be formed that will allow access for the development of new case studies. The partnership organizations will be a source for classroom speakers, worksite visits, work-study placements and internships.

Establishing Partnerships

The University

This is a University outreach program, located in the School of Business. The Dean of the Business School will fill a variety of roles, especially in qualifying faculty for the program and ensuring release time for those that participate. The Dean should be familiar with the model since (s)he has a key role in marketing it when in contact with the School's business community.

To support the model, the Dean must direct the needed resources to the program and encourage other faculty to participate. He or she can show support by leading the negotiations with selected organizations and participating in orientations and progress meetings.

The Corporation

If the university is ready to enact this approach, what sort of organization might also be ready to try something new to develop its operational managers? What is the nature of the organization that will take on the complexity of this approach? What type of organization would allow outsiders this much access to their managers, especially managers in charge of strategic projects? It should be:

- an organization that is authentically developing, implementing and evaluating its strategy.
- an organization that implements the strategy through projects.
- an organization that is never satisfied with what it has accomplished—one that is always looking to increase the competitive margin over its rivals.

Centrally, the company should be seeking more effective ways of developing its managers and future leaders.

The success of using work to develop managers in their own workplace rests upon selecting and being selected by the right kind of company. The right kind of company is one that is sustaining its competitive advantage through accomplishing its long-term strategic plan through shorter-term projects. An organization that has a history of accomplishing strategic initiatives through projects would be even better because the importance of good project management would be part of the culture. This organization may not be that easy to find. Fred David writes in his text on Strategic Management that less than 10% of the strategic plans that are formulated are ever implemented (David, 2004). An active search is necessary to establish the initial research sites.

When a potential partner is found, it is critical for the senior management of the organization to believe in and be committed to the Two Worlds Learning model. We were able to originate the Two Worlds model at our research site because of senior management's support. The organization's president saw the value of having operations managers increase their knowledge of management tasks and their application. Senior management also saw the logic of using the managers' projects as the vehicle for expanding their education; the managers would become more knowledgeable and projects would have a higher probability of being successfully completed. It is critical that senior management recognizes the links between managerial performance on the floor and fulfillment of the strategic objectives. The organization must be directed, by these leaders, to give access to the management education team, to devote the time and energy necessary to understand the program, to link the performance systems and the strategic planning systems with the program, to suggest the people to be educated, to trust its employees to the team, to help represent the program to others—at conferences, association meetings, etc., and to personally participate in the program, especially in the evaluation.

Identifying Managers

The focus of our program is the operations manager whose responsibilities include managing projects that are critical to the organization's success. We expect some of these projects to be strategic projects. By strategic projects, we mean projects that are the result of a strategic objective being translated into operational objectives and those objectives distributed to managers for accomplishment.

The model works best when managers are identified and selected as follows:

- The team establishes the ideal profile for managers. The managers would be generally described as performing well in their position, considered important to the organization's future, educable, and capable of moving beyond their current position.
- The organization identifies operational managers that fit the profile and in whom they are willing to invest. The organization shares the profiles of the identified managers with the team and describes the nature of their projects. Both parties agree on which managers should participate in the program.
- Managers that are selected to participate attend an orientation, at which time the model is explained, as are the program expectations.

- The operations managers, the managers to whom they report, and senior management meet to establish their own organizational objectives and expectations.
- The participating managers meet with the education team to start the program.

The education team and the organization's sponsors must make it clear to the participants, what is expected of them and what will and will not result from participation in the program. In our piloting of the TWL model, we experienced a few managers that thought participation meant promotion. A few managers were hesitant to decline the offer. The participating managers must believe, and it must be true, that if their participation results in no gain for them, they will not be worse off than they were.

The ideal arrangement would be the combination of well-defined projects and the most educable and experienced managers to head them.

We do have requirements for the TWL project, however. As stated before, we would prefer the projects to be part of the implementation of a strategic plan, but would include other projects that met the following characteristics:

- They have the greatest impact on plan attainment and are headed by managers who are described above.
- They have clear metrics and an activated design for measurement.
- They are directed at a clear and measurable strategic annual objective that is connected to the strategic plan or to an important operational goal.
- They have strong support from the organization's leadership—in other words, there is no doubt that these projects are important.
- They have a feasible completion plan. We understand that some strategic projects may take some time to complete since the strategic plan does not have a short-term focus. However, there are projects that have a shorter time of completion. It is important to find the project at the level of the annual objective. It is ideal to help managers understand and complete projects that last no longer than a year because an organization needs feedback and finality to measure the value of what we do and more than a year may not be tolerated.
- They have adequate resources to support them.
- They are supported by the availability of the right people needed to accomplish the tasks and provide the learning (serve as resources to the learner).

Competencies Are the Curriculum

In our design, the first activity is to determine the competencies required by the manager to successfully complete the project. This is done in conjunction with the education team. The manager is asked what he or she must know and be able to do in order to complete the project successfully. A member or members of the education team throughout the project will periodically pose this question. In our experience, projects are usually analyzed by what must be done and with little consideration given to the preparation of the individual to do what must be done.

The "teaching" comes in decisions on how to support the competency development on a "just in time/just needed to know" basis. The aim is to discover what they don't know and therefore can't get done and learn as fast as possible what they need to know to get the task done.

As stated above, the emphasis is on what is needed to know to do. The education team won't and can't teach/support the entire body of knowledge of any subject matter—we can only support those things seen necessary to get to the "know to do" stage.

Execution

First, the project is designed along the lines of any good project management system. This is principally the responsibility of the manager that heads the project. A less complicated approach of arriving at this point is to break the project down by tasks. We refer to this as "unbundling" the project. By determining what tasks are required, it is easier for the manager and the teams to determine what competencies are required.

The education team understands, in general, those non-skill areas that lead to project success and the manager will add to his/her management knowledge. In our research, we found that managers were positioned all along the continuum of required project knowledge. This can be understood if one thinks of the nature of a strategy that spawns the manager's project. Many times the strategy is requiring a change, a change with which the manager may have only passing knowledge but no actual experience in managing it. These are the teaching moments.

The education team's responsibility is to help the manager understand what knowledge and skills he or she already possesses and what knowledge and skills he or she needs to acquire in order to successfully complete the project. We are not suggesting that the manager spend time learning any subject matter totally, but only that portion of it that applies to the project. They may choose to learn more, at another time, in other educational venues. We believe that is what managers would do without our help but with the result of only "knowing what they know," that is, trying to force-fit skills that they already have to apply to the project. If this step is skipped, there is no way for the manager to gauge if he or she has all of the tools necessary to produce a superior outcome. As the saying goes, to he who has a hammer, all the worlds a nail. Too often it is a post mortem on a failed project that reveals the problem.

We acknowledge that managers are completing projects without complete knowledge all the time. We also know that projects, and therefore strategies, may be completed and implemented even though there are subtle and even glowing omissions or errors that result in unintended consequences. We know that often, the manager's skills *shape* the project. In the culture of an organization that does not recognize not knowing, it is often easier to manage a project without possessing all of the required competencies than to admit that competencies are missing. With no one to ask the difficult questions in a nonthreatening environment, the managers are on their own.

Another shortcoming of a manager's knowledge and opportunity is not knowing what resources are available, where resources can be found, and how to access them without giving the impression to others, that seeking them represents some shortcoming on the part of the manager. We believe that managers, supported by an arrangement endorsed by the top management of the organization, will find others that have the knowledge and experience are willing to support them. In this way, the culture of not sharing knowledge because it is seen as sharing power, can be changed or at least positively affected. Operating managers work closest to grassroots employees who, seeing their immediate leaders gaining fresh knowledge in collaborative learning, will be encouraged to create their working knowledge in the same vein.

Finally, managers who have experienced this approach, unbundling projects into tasks and determining what additional preparation and knowledge are required before spending resources on projects, will find the payoff is noticeably more valuable than plunging headlong in project management without understanding what is required of them to be successful. If this is so, learning managers will eventually adopt this approach without the presence of the education team. And if they are teaching managers and have a good experience with this approach, they will use it to develop their staff.

In summary, the management educator's job is to help the manager assess which of the *work tasks* form the basis of supportive *learning tasks*. We recognize that some tasks will need support and some won't because they are already part of the manager's skill set. For sake of speculation, we see tasks being divided into three groups. First, those that the managers feel competent to handle, second, those that the managers say they need to be supported, and third, those that the managers thought were in the first group but now want to move to the second group.

Grounding the Two Worlds Model

How is our project-embedded educational approach different from and a promising departure from other ways to conduct work-based management learning? Raelins research published in *Work-based Learning: The New Frontier of Management Development* provided us with this landmark to locate and advance our research on this "new frontier." He asks, "How can we introduce learning as an organizational property that extends to all mangers? (2000, p. 1) His answer is making the learning arise from the work itself.

We ground our model in our own variation on this theme. Organizational properties (e.g., structures, policies, processes, and sanctioned practices) *are* the work of managers. Thus, critical managerial learning arises from the work of managers at all levels, as they collaborate to build an organization capable of achieving its mission and strategic goals.

It is our view that managers build organizations by cultivating the natural process of organizational learning. We subscribe to the *capability* perspective of DiBella and Nevis (1998, p. 12) that organizations do not become learning organizations, because they already are so. Managers do not *become* learners in our program. They already are. Learning is an ongoing process. So we, as outside educators, need not view ourselves as bringing learning into a work-site, when we can "draft" onto the force of the learning that is already going on.

We realize that recommending entering the flow of ongoing organizational and managerial learning, rather than causing it, runs counter to deeply ingrained assumptions about whom we are as management educators and how we certify the differences we make in elevating individual and organizational knowledge. The convention is that learning must take place through intentional, teacher-designed and teacher-directed programs. Presenting this notion in *The Knowledge-enabled Organization*, Tobin (1998) frames the alternative vision for our model. "When a company learns to utilize and foster the growth of the knowledge and skills of all employees across all functions and levels, integrate learning activities into every employee's work, encourage and reinforce all models of learning, and align all of this learning with the company's strategic business directions, it becomes a knowledge-enabled organization" (p. 39). Our goal is to develop a model of pragmatic management learning integrated into their specialized work that is well-aligned with their company's strategies. We say *pragmatic* in recognition that management occurs as a practice by individuals. It is an experience of that individual—the manager—

and concomitantly experienced by members of the manager's organization. This is where and when managing counts. Thus, the closer we are able to efficiently and effectively educate managers in practice, the more like we are to bring theory into the flow of what is experienced by the organization as the product of managing. Garvin says that the best teachers are varied assignments, hardships and difficulties, missed opportunities and serving bosses with varying strengths and styles. He quotes McCall who observed: "The potential lessons in each kind of experience are determined by the overlap between what the experience demands and what a person does not yet know how to do.... Development results from doing something *different* from one's current strengths (Garvin, 2000, p. 93). While it may be logistically impossible for external or even internal management educators to manifest a helping presence in most moments when experience is doing its hard-knocks teaching, we have targeted a zone in which doing something different is the fundamental and predictable expectation of the manager. *The project.*

Cavaleri and Fearon (2000, pp. 251-258) posit that, while managers cannot directly make organizational learning happen in ways that favor performance goals, they do manage the context of organizational learning done collectively by all its members. They propose *project management* as powerful method for doing this. A project is distinctly different from managing regular operations. Its purpose is to do something for the organization that has not been done before, something unique. In order for the organization to be doing something unique and different, something must be done to the properties of the organization itself. Thus, the primary tasks addressed by manager(s) among those with technical specialties teaming to execute a project are about changes in organizational behavior. These *organization-transforming tasks* challenge the manager's present knowledge of the indicated aspect of the task such as resource allocation mechanisms, roles, distribution of authority. It is at these critical points of pending action that managers in projects will experience a heightened need to know. It is at these moments, when teaching that bridges the inquiring manager to clarifying concepts produce significant benefits to the learner and to the organization that is the object of that learning.

How shall management educators manifest a presence at these most teachable moments? We found an answer in this commendation by Cavaleri and Fearon. "Project management systems, because of their fundamental exploratory nature, provide a near-perfect vehicle and context for integrating organizational learning into existing business processes." Most organizations of any size and complexity have a viable project management system producing needed improvements and innovations. Our model emerges from our realization that this system can play a dual role. It can be a natural educational vehicle and context for practicing managers to learn their craft. It is their role in any project, strategic, operational, tactical, to see to the establishing or refurbishing of organizational properties. Raelin (2000, p. 67) writes, "Practitioners ... need the opportunity to merge theoretical principles with an understanding of the social construction of the organization in which they work." Again, we transform this conception into a rationale for bringing academic content to the worksite right into the projects run by managers. These practitioners need the opportunity to merge management and organizational behavior principles into their work of socially constructing the capacity of their organization to accomplish unique aims.

Where and how is this merging done and by whom? It is done on the ground floor of any projects selected for an additional educational purpose. This project management system is modified to heighten manager awareness of the organization transforming tasks that lay ahead, from the first to plan the project to the last to evaluate its results. Again, projects are only used for doing something that has not been done before. Consequently, not all of these tasks will be equally familiar to the manager-learner. Those tasks less known invoke teaching. To the extent that they may be anticipated, a teaching plan may be installed in the educational stream of the project management system. The rest of the teaching can be invoked when surprising knowledge gaps are encountered. The management educator facilitates teaching. It is the manager/learner who must do the merging of outside and inside knowledge.

Cavaleri and Fearon would call this *intelligent project management* (2000, p. 256). This accomplished by integrating cycles of project management (planning, implementation, documenting lessons learned) and action learning (concrete experience, reflective observation, abstract conceptualization, and active experimentation). "Projects aimed at increasing the value-yields of business performance serve concurrent purposes as projects of management learning."

Action learning is a natural process enacted by groups in the cause of solving real problems. Educators have formed it into a program by enjoining problem-solvers to also focus on what they are learning and how their learning may benefit the organization (Marquardt, 1999). We offer that intelligent projects may also be projects of management *education*. That is, they may be installed as powerful activities in comprehensive programs of on-site and off-site instruction.

Our focus is upon how this may be done by collegiate management educators for practicing managers, as they do their work to promote organizational learning. Doing this creates a living system of higher managerial learning that conjoins what Christensen and Raynor (2003) call the "street's" School of Experience with the "academy's" School of Management. Garvin says that these two schools have occupied center stage for well over a century. He would call them the Rationalists and the Empiricists. The Rationalist school is anchored in beliefs that knowledge is based on innate ideas and principles known independently of experience, while empiricists argue that knowledge come from only perceptions and sensory data. Among the latter, American pragmatist John Dewey, Garvin explains, established the counterintuitive theme that baffles and bothers institutional educators to this day. It is that all genuine education comes about through experience, espousing a curriculum that drew on a steady stream of hands-on projects rather than usual lectures and tests (Garvin, 2000, p. 91).

We would rather not choose one school or the other to house our teaching practice. However, because the practice about which we teach mainly only be simulated or treated as the object of instruction in the rationalist world of the University, we are attracted to the empirical world and the opportunity to learn from and with practicing managers. We think of the business unit in the real-world setting as also a school. The company's strategy frames the curriculum. Problems disclosed along the way of completing the strategic plan yield prime opportunities for experiential teaching and learning, concentrated in hands-on projects. We call our system the Two Worlds Learning Bridge (TWLB), envisioning a partnership bridging the two world "schools" of theoretical and practical management learning.

Our model lays out a process by which management educators to cross over to the worksite and go directly to extant and future projects to establish a reason to be there. The best bridge builders will be management generalists with both academic and real world experience. Teaching within the scope of the company's projects, they will serve as catalysts and guides over to the academic world that never interferes with the decision making of the manager, lest they unduly influence the outcome of a project. And, they seldom work alone. They locate needed expertise inside the organization and the University for creating and enhancing organizational properties such as budgeting, logistics, or personnel policies and practices and broker their use for project attainment.

BENEFITS OF THE TWO WORLDS MODEL

How does our approach add something new in the emerging field of work-based management learning? In a recent article in the Academy of Management Executive, *"Learning Versus Performance Goals: When Should Each Be Used?"* (Seijits & Latham, 2005), the authors state that organizations frequently assign major tasks or goals to managers without providing direction or guidance on any means to complete or attain them. This is not only a common practice, but the results are frequently disastrous.

Our model seeks to correct this practice and introduce an approach that is a win-win.

Seijits and Latham define the terms as a learning goal is focused on the discovery of effective strategies and not the end result (goal/task completion) versus a performance outcome goal that emphasizes an end result and distracts one from the discovery of effective strategies. The article makes the argument that assigning specific challenging performance goals creates such anxiety that the person, focused on being a high performer, scrambles "to discover the task-relevant strategies" in a non-systematic way The authors further state that "Once an employee has the knowledge and skills necessary to effectively perform the task, a specific challenging performance goal should be set . . . " We recognize the criticality of both types of objectives. We believe that our specific management education model focuses the employee on both objectives simultaneously. Our model addresses this by blending both learning and performance outcome objectives, making it an efficient and effective process with beneficial results for all parties.

Benefits for the Manager

The manager will benefit from this project approach because he or she has an opportunity to develop new skills and/or hone existing ones. The manager will develop more competencies in the learning-accelerated context of having to master new tasks. And, because the model emphasizes learning as well as goal completion, stretch goals that are frequently used as a development tool for high potential employees or succession potentials, becomes a much fairer test of one's ability and promise. We anticipate less dependency on the management education team and as increase in the manager's ability to use identified resources to complete task-by-task learning cycles.

Benefit for the Organization

This particular project-embedded educational approach both requires and emphasizes the importance of utilizing internal expertise. Appropriate utilization of an organization's human resources encourages knowledge sharing and skill building. The result is a *true* learning organization. As project goals are met, the accomplishment of each task has tested what both the manager and the organization know. As the manager learns and closes gaps in managerial knowledge, organizational knowledge is created and carried forward.

Corporate partners will see value added in the quality of the managers' projects. Those who manage the operations managers should see gains in their managers' capabilities, especially in their "ability to get things done." Are the costs of having a real time management learning program on site justified by the benefits? Our corporate partners must agree on what benefits are expected and how those benefits can and should be measured.

Companies will benefit from our program for additional reasons.

- First, the performance on the floor will more closely reflect the strategic objectives that were expected. This is a way of using the tasks of the organization to develop managers and to know in what areas they have gained skills.

- Compared to all other education and development tools, our approach is like to have a much higher lesson to practice transference ratio.

- After the initial research period has passed, the company may want to continue this approach. They can use either the research results or contract with the University for facilitation from a faculty team. The cost will be acceptable to companies that see it as an investment instead of an expense. It is an investment because there is an increased return on education. A two-year study of 575 U.S.-based companies revealed that companies investing $680 more in per person training than the average company improved their total shareholder return by 6 points. (Wagner, 2001).

- Finally, the corporate partner should see a steady growth in the number of effective project leaders.{\BL}

Benefit for the University

For the partnering academic institution, this type of initiative provides faculty members with a veritable research laboratory. Additionally, the participating faculty has an opportunity to connect with the "real world" and bring their newly acquired knowledge back to the classroom. Because their focus is on enabling task-by-task managerial learning, professors are witnessing the genesis of management skills at a granular level rarely afforded those conducting conventional on-site research. In turn, these insights into what works when theory is blended in action with practice. If there was ever a question in an educator's mind about whether his or her students were "getting it," it should be answered by using this approach. Thus, this experience may be converted into invaluable lessons for "traditional" students. Is it possible to assign our students to projects in the partnership companies, to work, in teams, on short, easily defined projects as part of their class work? The professor could play the role of the education team to give them guidance. They will be educated in a way that will better prepare them for the realities of managing to create a viable workplace.

Establishing partnerships will be an opportunity for the university to offer meaningful public service. The relationship or partnership will have value to the university because it will have value to the organization.

This program will broaden the understanding of those faculty members that are chosen to participate. Their understanding of strategies will be expanded beyond textbooks, case studies and articles. They will be exposed to the strategies of organizations that have something to lose. This working relationship will also expose faculty to some of the more subtle factors in successful strategic planning and implementation, such as personalities, group dynamics and power, available knowledge, and both internal and external competition.

All universities are concerned about the currency of the faculty. Requiring faculty to produce scholarly output usually addresses this. We think that research will be enhanced and complemented by having the opportunity of actually being on a work-site and dealing with real world problems. We see approach as a key for becoming and remaining current in management thinking and practice. Interestingly enough, it is still possible to, within limited agreement, to find opportunities to for scholarship. The Association for the Advancement of Colleges and Schools of Business (AACSB) calls for assessments that reveal if and how a person has learned (meaning will the individual be better able to perform as a business professional). This approach delivers both "if" and "how" information.

Universities are concerned, more and more, with increasing the usefulness of their curriculum and becoming more market driven. Universities know that a significant portion of their reputation is dependent on how well prepared students are and how students are seen by hiring organization as adding value. So universities need to do a good job in preparing students to make a contribution to the business that has taken a chance in hiring them. But a university's opportunity does not stop there. There are organizations that are managed by people who are not well trained in making a difference, in adding value. These employees have risen to the operating manager level because of their non-management skills—how well they sold the product, how much they know about the accounting system, etc. We believe that the manager's job requires more than his or her functional skills. Managers should also know how and be able to "make the company run better"; that they should possess business acumen. If universities could assist organizations increase the value of their managers' output, it would be doing a service that would be invaluable.

If the University made a difference, a new relationship would be established between the organizations that the university hopes to hire its graduates, serve on its advisory board, provide research sites for its faculty and support them in a variety of ways. This is an opportunity for a university to strengthen their relationships with companies.

Because a significant amount of the education will be one on one, the number of managers that participate at any one time, will be limited. If the experience is successful, the team will have an opportunity to strengthen the model and their ability to deliver education this way with another group of managers. Additional teams could be formed so that they might have an opportunity to experience this approach to management education. It may be possible for the model to become a program offered by the University as it attempts to reach out to its community.

SUMMARY

We think that there is no better vehicle for profound learning than the work itself. Our contention is based in adult learning theory. Malcolm Knowles (1980), the father of adult learning theory (andragogy), states that an adult learns best via hands-on problem solving. Further, the adult learner wants to be able to apply the new skills and knowledge immediately. Zemke and Zemke (1995) also support this approach to andragogy, in their principles. They state that person must be able to apply concepts gained through the learning experience to relevant problems.

In terms of motivation, importance to the learner, relevance, and access to necessary resources, the work of the workplace is far superior to classroom learning, classrooms transferred to the workplace, case studies, simulations, and all of the other vehicles presently in use that are supposed to give the manager practice in managing.

If the reader believes, as we do, that it is possible to know and still not be able to do, one can see how doing should be the goal of knowing. When we consider what makes a difference in a company's top line as well as their bottom line, we know that we have to move beyond knowing. The people in sales must be able to sell. Everyone in the process must be able to produce, to gather the right information, to make the best choices. Donald Kirkpatrick's (1998) four-level evaluation model reinforces this. Although Kirkpatrick states that the first two levels - Reaction and Learning are important evaluative measures for any type of training and development effort, he states that the real payoff for learning is at the third and fourth levels—Transfer and Results. Organizations must ask, "Did/

Will the employee use the learning? And, "Will it matter to the organization?" These two levels will yield the highest return on investment for an organization. Why can't the curriculum for managers be based on the organization's expectation of the manager? After all, if the organization is making good choices about what needs to be done and managers are tasked to do it, what better measure can there be to determine the value of a manager?

But the question is how can that happen? What vehicle can be used to provide this level of learning for managers in the workplace?

Real world projects done in real time that have implications for the successful completion of the company's strategic plan are an ideal vehicle for management education. We see these strategic management projects as an untapped, powerful learning vehicle to discover what competencies managers must exercise to add value.

The inclusion of an education team to facilitate management education on the job, grafts two worlds of curriculum together—the collegiate or corporate program of study and the "natural curriculum" that is the organizational learning done by those who work to fulfill the strategic plan of their organization. The presence of a team results in at least are two advantages.

The first advantage is that with a "neutral" person acting as a guide or "sounding board, the probability is lessened that a manager begins activity before his or her ability to do so is evaluated. The second advantage is that this evaluation can take place in a non-threatening environment. The evaluation is the result of an analysis between the manager and the team or team member. The benefit of all of this is that managers don't have to "pretend" that they know everything that is required to successfully complete the project so there is some control over the quality of the outcome.

Companies sometimes look to consultants to help them think through new strategies, especially when the company has determined that these strategies will help them remain competitive. Too often, when the consultants leave, the talent leaves with them because educating the managers to sustain the strategy and evaluate it over time is not part of the consultants' responsibility. Thus a niche exists for Universities—to make sure that managers, as they manage the implementation of strategies, through their projects, learn how to perform them successfully by understanding what tasks have to be accomplished, if they have the competencies to do the tasks, and if not, where and how they can become competent.

The projects that we are managing are "natural projects" in that they're required by the company's strategy. The projects are not set up for education purposes (as would be the case or simulation of traditional education). The projects are designated and authorized by the top management of the organization.

The objective of our approach is to affect the development of both the organization and the manager. The objectives for both have measurable outcomes. Success on a project is not complete until it can be shown that the manager has increased his or her ability to direct both future strategic projects and their own ability to solve the difficult tasks. They will have learned to "unpack" tasks and recognize the competencies they'll need to shore up. And, they will have learned to find people to help them.

The approach of teaching managers how to unbundled projects into tasks and acquiring competencies when needed is not a one-act play. We see it as leading to a dynamic change within an organization.

Based on the arrangements made with the organization, we see ourselves becoming familiar with new projects assigned to the managers in the program and helping them to repeat the process, perhaps with less help. There is a high chance that the next project will have tasks that will call for support and it may be that the next project will require some of the same tasks that the manager wasn't proficient in but became so while doing the first project. That is a savings. That is growth.

We also anticipate finding that there are new required institutional competencies caused by new technologies, change, downsizing, and new strategies—opportunities for a group of managers to become knowledgeable and for our managers to become proficient. It is possible that set of managers who are managing several concurrent projects can constitute the "class" at any moment in time, not based on the project but based on the need to acquire new competencies. The membership of this "class" is dynamic. Managers cycle in and out of the Two Worlds system.

REFERENCES

Cavaleri, S., & Fearon, D. (2000). Integrating organizational learning and business praxis: a case for intelligent project management. *The Learning Organization, 7*(5), 251-258.

Christensen, C.M., & Raynor, M. (2003). *The innovators solution: Creating and sustaining successful growth.* Boston: Harvard Business School.

David, F. (2004). *Strategic management: Concepts and cases.* Upper Saddle River, NJ: Prentice-Hall.

DiBella, A., & Nevis, C. (1998). *How organizations learn.* San Francisco: Jossey-Bass.

Garvin, D. (2000). *Learning in action: A guide to putting the learning organization to work.* Boston: Harvard Business Press.

Kirkpatrick, D. (1998). *Evaluating training programs.* San Francisco: Berrett-Koehler.

Knowles, M. (1980). *The modern practice of adult education: Andragogy versus pedagogy*. Englewood Cliffs: Prentice Hall.

Marquardt, M. (1999). *Action learning in action: Transforming problems and people for world-class organizational learning*. Palo Alto, CA: Davies-Black.

Raelin, J. (2000). *Work-based learning: The new frontier of management development*. Englewood Cliffs, NJ: Prentice-Hall.

Seijits, G.H., & Latham, G.P. (2005). Learning versus performance goals: When should each be used? *Academy of Management Executive, 19*(1), 124-131.

Tobin, D. (1998). *The knowledge-enabled organization: Moving from "training" to "learning" to meet business goals*. New York: AMACOM.

Wagner, S. (2001). Retention update: Fighting the war for talent with training: One year later. *Training & Development, 55*(8), 63-69.

Zemke, R., & Zemke, S. (1995). Adult learning: What do we know for sure? *Training, 6*(32), 31-40.

PART IV

A POTPOURRI OF
PROJECT-BASED PRACTICES AND PERSPECTIVES

CHAPTER 12

WORK EMBEDDED E-LEARNING

Paul Shrivastava

This chapter explores the use of technology to make training an integral part of work. In many work environments, workers do not have time to get training, yet they have short periods of down-time that could be effectively used for training. Pulling workers out of the work setting for training is time inefficient due to excessive set-up and restart activities. It also imparts knowledge in a noncontextual mode. Knowledge is imparted outside the context where it is to be used. This chapter proposes and illustrates work embedded learning systems. With the advent of telecommunications networks, technology integration, the Internet, and online collaboration technologies it is now feasible to build training right into work processes. This allows organizations to build a new, holistic, knowledge ecology of work, that actively supports the emerging dynamic knowledge needs of modern organizations.

INTRODUCTION

Knowledge organizations are seeking to develop learning applications that leverage technology to simultaneously improve worker productivity and accomplish worker training. They view training as an integral part of work, and try to find ways of making work a vehicle for learning. With the

Educating Managers through Real World Projects, 277–287
Copyright © 2005 by Information Age Publishing

advent of technologies that aid organizational integration, collaboration and transformation, a new set of innovative learning approaches are emerging.

A key challenge facing many organizations is to some how utilize the dead time in between tasks. Most organizational workflows are such that there are natural idle times for workers. These are "dead" time periods that get frittered away while workers wait for next task to begin. While some highly organized workers may find ways of occupying that idle time productively, the average worker simply wastes that time. In highly interdependent tasks, this waste can account for 20% to 30% of the work-day.

A related problem is that knowledge needed for performing tasks is sometimes not available to the person who needs it, even though this knowledge is available somewhere within the organization or with a co-worker. In the emerging knowledge organization we need to reconsider traditional ways of packaging knowledge and training workers (Hildreth & Kimble, 2004; Shrivastava, 1999; Sparks & Richardson, 1998; Wankel & DeFillippi, 2002; Wiig, 2004).

Historically, efficient utilization of worker time has been the domain of industrial engineers, time and motion specialists, and task design analysts. This was the essence of the "scientific management" movement in the first half of the 20th century. Organizational behavior scholars have also contributed by examining the motivational aspects of this productivity challenge. These approaches were fruitful when we were dealing largely with an industrial manufacturing economy. In the service economy of the latter half of the last century, the main sources of productivity enhancement were technological automation and information systems. That trend is now intensified. In this paper I explore the use of technologies that allow companies to fundamentally restructure work and knowledge and combine them in different ways to increase productivity.

TECHNOLOGIES OF INTEGRATION, COLLABORATION AND TRANSFORMATION

The recent development of "embedding technologies" allows organizations to reconfigure organizational knowledge in new and innovative ways. Knowledge can be embedded into organizational work processes at points where it has the most chance of being used effectively. This is made feasible by three specific technologies—technologies of integration, collaboration, and transformation.

Integration

This section reviews some key technological developments that now enable improvement of worker learning options and productivity. After decades of stand alone IT system, both government and private companies have started taking integration seriously. Technological integration has become a priority and new integration platforms have emerged rapidly. The President's Management Agenda (PMA) and the E-government Act of 2002 require "agencies to improve government performance through business focused collaboration and shared use of effective technologies." The Federal Enterprise Architecture (FEA) provides government organizations a common infrastructure to meet PMA requirements. It is the foundation technology that supports business process automation. It eliminates or consolidates redundant IT investments, business processes and technology assets. It seeks to identify common business functions across agencies. It integrates performance measurement with budget processes along key business lines.

An example of intense integration is the eArmy University program. IBM's technology for the eArmy University integrates components from Cognos, Fiberlink, Intel Online Services, Netegrity, Saba, Stalker, Blackboard, SmartThinking and Peoplesoft. Reference materials and professional journals are provided by the University of Georgia's Galileo system. This first stage of integrtion is now being pushed to another level with merger of the eArmyU with the National Guard's GuardNet and the Reserves' ARNet into a single unified system.

Collaboration

The Internet has vastly expanded possibilities of collaboration through tools such as email, bulletin boards, instant messaging, presence awareness, chat, application sharing, blogging, web conferencing, and online project management. The tools are easily and inexpensively available to all users. Companies have adopted them selectively as they find ways of making productive use of the tools. The main challenge has been finding ways of using tools without distracting people from their work. The integrated implementation of collaborative tools is reflected in the emerging change management initiatives, information communities, knowledge management, and communities of practice across organizations (Seeley-Brown & Duguid, 1991).

Transformation

Process transformation has been a high priority in businesses for the last decade. Business Process Engineering and Business Process Redesign were popularized in the 1990s. They spawned Business Process Outsourcing in the 2000s.

Business Process Redesign involves analysis and design of workflows and processes within and between organizations. It is the critical analysis and radical redesign of existing business processes to achieve breakthrough improvements in performance measures. IT technologies allow recombining process elements in new and innovative ways (Davenport & Short 1990; Grover et al., 1995).

Hammer (1990) proposes several principles of business process reengineering, including: (a) Organizing around outcomes, not tasks; (b) Having users of process outputs perform the process; (c) Subsuming information processing work into the work that produces the information; (d) Technologically centralizing geographically dispersed resources; (e) Linking parallel activities instead of integrating their results, (f) Put the decision point where the work is performed, and (g) Building control into the process. These principles can be implemented using information technologies that enable process transformations.

The combination of these technologies offers potent solutions for reconfiguring learning in organizations. Together they offer learning designs that can exploit work flow gaps to maximize worker productivity. Work embedded learning is one such approach to learning design (Davenport, 1993; King, 1994).

Work Embedded e-Learning Solutions

By designing organizational tasks, and embedding training as a natural part of work, companies can develop work embedded learning systems that provide just-in-time learning and also save training time. The goal of such learning systems is to systematically analyze work tasks and their knowledge requirements, and then to structure work, and learning to make the needed knowledge available to workers when they need it.

Work embedded learning systems use a variety of learning resources, activities, and materials. Information is chunked not in conventional sections, chapters and reports, but rather in small nuggets that elucidate specific work processes, and can be consumed in short durations of time, say ten or fifteen minutes. The keys to success in creating such systems are, the selection of the right work environment for embedding learning, use of interactive and multimedia online learning methodologies, and user friendliness of the system.

Mini Case Example

Day-Timers, Inc. (a business unit of the Acco division of Fortune Brands) is one of the largest producer and distributor of calendaring products. Its East Texas, PA plant makes stores, and markets calendars, refills, and associated goods. It operates a small sized Call Center with capacity of 200 seats. Call Center agents are typically low wage workers used as temporary staff during peak ordering seasons. For the calendar business the peak season is one a year in November and December. Day-Timers wanted to use home-based agents to handle incoming order calls. Home-based agents pool was considered to be better qualified and experienced than the traditional onsite call center workforce. These home-based workers had to be trained via distance learning on product knowledge, and the use of the order processing software. In this work environment a worker is idle if there is no incoming call. Idle times can last a few minutes to half hour or more.

Day-Timers, Inc. hired eSocrates, Inc., an e-learning company, to develop a training solution for its Call Center workers. The client wanted the training to be integrated with the order processing procedure and software application in a manner that idle times could be productively used for training. The training was designed to impart product knowledge and knowledge on operating the order processing software. It was designed as a blended solution with some face-to-face component and some Web-based training. In class component was mainly used to let the agents experience the products by touch and feel. Content was chunked into small pieces so that discrete learning could be accomplished in short periods.

The system consisted of a Learning Management System supported by a Content Database. The eSocrates LMS was used as the delivery platform. Training window and order processing windows remain open simultaneously on the agent's desktop. Agents can switch between them at will. During idle periods agents can learn about the products they are booking orders for or learn about specific functions of the ordering system. They can search for specific product information to answer customers' questions. In the first year 158 agents were trained using this system with great client satisfaction.

STEPS IN CREATING WORK EMBEDDED LEARNING SYSTEMS

While the concept of work embedded learning is intriguing, it is not equally suited to all work environments. Care must be exercised in selecting work areas for this type of learning and in designing the learning system. It should also be noted that there are workflow and organizational changes that accompany work embedded learning. Implementation of such learning systems involves Needs analysis to identify the tasks/work flows where embedded learning would be useful.

- Instructional Design to establish training methodology, learning objectives, and resolve issues of integration with work-flows (Wood & McQuarie, 1999).
- Work redesign to rationalize procedures and identify venues and opportunities for learning, and identify features and functions of the overall learning system.
- Development Training Content includes developing text, graphics, audio, and video content as needed.
- Establishing the Application, Technical Support involves programming the application—usually includes some customization of LMS to deliver mandatory and desirable features and functions.
- Implementing Organizational Changes.

BENEFITS AND COSTS OF WORK EMBEDDED LEARNING

Work embedded learning systems offer many advantages for companies. First, they provide Just-in-time knowledge to workers. Knowledge acquired at the point of work is more likely to be used. It also makes positive impact on performance. By engaging the worker continually it improves the level of skills and knowledge of workers and makes them more productive.

The main advantage and reason for adoption of work embedded learning is that it efficiently uses idle work time for training. It frees up conventional training time. This may have secondary savings in terms of saved travel and hotel costs associated with training.

By avoiding pulling workers out of production space and time for training purposes, work embedded learning saves setup and set down times. It may completely eliminate several setup cycles.

When delivered as Web-based training such learning can be accessed anytime from anywhere. The convenience of always-available learning encourages workers to access it during off hours, and whenever they need the knowledge.

Finally designing work embedded learning systems offer an opportunity for redesigning work flows in more logical and rational manners. This rationalization of work itself can lead to savings

But with all these benefits come challenges and costs. One important challenge is technological. Although (and perhaps because) there are numerous enabling technologies that can be used, the task of selecting the right technologies and integrating them is significant.

There are significant costs involved in building work embedded learning systems. Generally such systems are more expensive than other online training systems because they include an additional component of workflow changes.

A key barrier in implementing redesigned workflows is the natural organizational resistance to change. Embedding work with new knowledge opportunities requires changed behaviors on the job and changes in social relations in the workplace. It changes the performance levels of workers. It calls for new reward systems to acknowledge performance. All these are deeply rooted in organizations and pose formidable behavioral challenges.

Implementing Complete Solutions

Work embedded learning is a wave of the future. It calls for carefully thought-out and customized solutions. It works best if several technological and social conditions are kept in mind. First, a manager does not have to be a technologist to succeed. The technologies of integration, collaboration and transformation are easy to understand from a functional standpoint. They were designed for mass nontechnical clients and are user-friendly. The technological requirements of the user are an important factor in success of work embedded learning.

Work embedded learning is not a panacea for all organizational situations. These solutions work best in industries and tasks where immediate knowledge infusion makes a major performance difference. For example in maintenance situations (aircraft, auto, heavy equipment, etc.) a mechanic can often troubleshoot problems with much greater success rates if (s)he has hints or tips or detailed drawings, on what to look for. They are also appropriate in situations where there are high work interdependencies and workers have to wait for some tasks to occur for them to perform. For example, call center operators wait for calls, bank tellers wait for walk-in customers, and in assembly line work, workers may wait for a part or sub assembly to arrive, or a process to be completed before they can act.

Another requirement for success is that the project should include a comprehensive needs assessment, system design, development and implementation stages. Throughout these stages, teams of corporate professionals work with vendors to engage the organization in an interactive consultative process.

Teams focus on work redesign, knowledge management, instructional design, graphics design, multimedia design, and software development. This involves fundamental changes in which work and knowledge configured and relate to each other. Each of these sub projects could be lengthy, time consuming, and expensive. The importance of effective project management to coordinate the various sub projects cannot be over emphasized.

Once the development and implementation are accomplished, there is a need for training workers in the new system. Creating work embedded learning systems often means enterprise wide changes. The new procedures need to be articulated, codified and communicated to all employees.

Each step needs to be carefully documented and shared with clients. An organizational learning process should be evoked in the client organization, which allows the company to better understand its work processes and rationalize them.

Knowledge Management

This paper reported on a new approach to design of learning systems in organizations—referred to as work embedded learning. The goal of work embedded learning systems is to repackage knowledge required to do work, into work procedures themselves. The idea is simple but its design and implementation requires careful thought and analysis. Technologies enabling such work embedded learning are now becoming widely available. The challenge facing companies is to manage the comprehensive technological and organizational change processes that such systems entail. Embedding learning into work processes changes not only the nature of learning, but also work itself. This can be beneficial in terms of improved productivity and decreased down time.

The type of learning advocated in this paper, is a crucial aspect of overall organizational knowledge management. As organizations become increasingly knowledge driven, both workers and managers will need comprehensive knowledge management strategies. Management education and training would benefit by adopting a focused knowledge management framework that I refer to here as "knowledge ecology." This framework is responsive to rapidly expanding information technologies and knowledge work, and combines the *human intellectual capital and digital technological processes* that jointly enable knowledge work and knowledge value creation (Wiig, 2004).

Organizational knowledge processes deal with the creation, distribution, use and exchange of knowledge for purposes of value creation. They involve managing the intellectual capital of organizations. These processes are best understood with "ecology" and "ecosystems" metaphors. Performative organizational knowledge is a knowledge ecology—a system consisting of many sources, venues, forms and species of knowledge agents in a symbiotic relationship of productive exchange and value creation. The output of the knowledge ecology is both forms of knowledge that add value in the enterprise, and perform the work of the enterprise. Organizational knowledge and learning occur in these ecologies (Bateson, 2000).

To concretize this concept of knowledge ecology, let me expand it in the context of business education and training. On the education and training industry knowledge management represents the core work of organizations such as, colleges, universities, training consultants, corporate training programs, and corporate universities. It deals with the creation, interpretation, critique, and distribution of knowledge within communities. The knowledge ecology of management education includes systematized and structured relations among managers, scholars, consultants, students, authors, publishers, business organizations, industry experts, industry associations, university libraries, school administration, computer networks, the Internet/WWWeb, information data bases, and other knowledge sources and processes. The work place, training rooms and interaction between instructors and learners are at the core of this ecology. The performative function of this core is to create knowledgeable managers that can function effectively in the knowledge economy. The core is contextualized by environmental conditions characterized by institutional and social structures of business education. Boundaries between the core and its context are often fuzzy and changing, and to some extent definitional. The important point is to view these elements as part of a single organic ecosystem.

Traditional teaching/learning approaches of highly structured and polished lessons in preprogramed classes are too static for the digital economy environment. They are not conducive for improvisation in the learning process (Weick, 1997). Carefully prepackaged knowledge resources (books, articles, case study packages) sometimes become obsolete even as they are under preparation. For learning to be successful it must be plugged into the permanent and continually updating knowledge instruments and networks of the organizational knowledge ecosystem.

Most learners learn best when they are ready to learn and have need for the knowledge. This calls for a continual anytime anywhere learning approach. Thus, the knowledge ecology perspective sees business education programs as places to initiate learning processes that can extend over entire working life of the learner. The objective of the knowledge ecosystem is to create and maintain learners as strategic human resources that are capable of continually creating competitive advantage for their companies, through knowledge application.

The thick interdependencies and interconnectedness of businesses and knowledge resources in the digital economy calls for reconceptualizing classrooms as venues for building "learning communities" or communities of practice where learning and practice can occur simultaneously (Seeley-Brown & Duguid, 1991). Knowledge ecology framework views class rooms as learning communities that extend beyond the physical confines of the actual building in which they are located. Classes can become virtual electronic learning communities consisting of interconnected co-learners who pursue their intellectual interests in a networked environment. These communities can be as local as a single classroom, regional as a network of companies, or as global as a multinational listserv with members from every country.

This description of the knowledge ecology of management education for the digital economy is quite different from the practices of most business schools today. However, some schools, several corporate universities, and consulting firms are pioneering knowledge management by creating necessary knowledge infrastructure and support systems.

REFERENCES

Bateson, G. (2000). *Steps to an ecology of mind: Collected essays in anthropology, psychiatry, evolution, and epistemology.* Chicago: University of Chicago Press.

Davenport, T.H. (1993). *Process innovation.* Boston: Harvard Business School Press.

Davenport, T.H., & Short, J.E. (1990, Summer). The new industrial engineering: Information technology and business process redesign. *Sloan Management Review,* 11-27.Grover, V., Jeong, S.R., Kettinger, W.J., & Teng, J.T.C. (1995). The implementation of business process reengineering. *Journal of Management Information Systems, 12*(1), 109-144.

Hammer, M. (1990, July-August). Reengineering work: Don't automate, obliterate. *Harvard Business Review,* 104-112.

Hildreth, P.M., & Kimble, C. (2004). *Knowledge networks: Innovation through communities of practice.* Hershey, PA: Idea Group.

King, W.R. (1994). Process reengineering: The strategic dimensions. *Information Systems Management, 11*(2), 71-73.

Seeley-Brown, J., & Duguid, P. (1991). *Organizational learning and communities-of-practice: Toward a unified view of working, learning, and innovation.* The Institute of Management Science. Retrieved March 15, 2005 from http://www2.parc.com/ops/members/brown/papers/orglearning.html

Shrivastava, P. (1999, December). Management classroom as online learning community. *Journal of Management Education.*

Sparks, D., & Richardson, J. (1998). *Job-embedded training*. Oxford, OH: National Staff Development Council.

Wankel, C., & Defillippi, R. (Eds.). (2002). *Rethinking management education for the 21st century*. Greenwich, CT: Information Age Publishers.

Wood, F.H., & McQuarrie, F., Jr. (1999). On-the-job learning. *Journal of Staff Development, 20*(3), 10-13.

Wiig, K.M. (2004). *People-focused knowledge management : How effective decision making leads to corporate success*. Oxford: Elsevier.

Weick, K. (1997). The teaching experience as learning in public. In R. Andre & P. Frost (Eds.), *Researchers hooked on teaching*. Thousand Oaks, CA: Sage.

CHAPTER 13

PROBLEM-BASED LEARNING APPROACHES IN MANAGEMENT EDUCATION

Oon-Seng Tan

The new millennium with the unprecedented breakthroughs in knowledge and technology calls for a new wave of management education where learning how to learn, multiple ways of knowing, and integration of a diversity of information and disciplinary intelligence are important in dealing with real world problems. This chapter reveals why problem-based learning (PBL) is a holistic approach in management education and explains how real world problems should be used as the starting point and focus of learning. Although PBL has been used extensively in medical education and other disciplines, this chapter attempts to provide a fresh perspective of PBL innovation based on the author's extensive experience in many PBL trials and implementation projects. The pedagogical, psychological, and technological aspects of PBL are discussed. The chapter will also illustrates the design of problems, the PBL cycle, collaborative learning and blending of Internet communication technologies possibilities in PBL.

INTRODUCTION

Traditional education in most areas of knowledge including management was primarily about the pedagogy of making content knowledge "visible."

Educating Managers through Real World Projects, 289–308
Copyright © 2005 by Information Age Publishing
All rights of reproduction in any form reserved.

The concerns centered on enhancing clarity of explanations and elucidation of difficult terrains of well demarcated disciplinary knowledge. Improvements came about when learning in management education became more "active" and experiential. These developments in teaching methodologies can be characterized as making the teachers' thinking "visible," namely, the use approaches to support and model process skills, problem-solving skills and thinking skills in business and management exercises and case studies. The new millennium with the unprecedented breakthroughs in knowledge and technology calls for a new wave of management education where learning how to learn, multiple ways of knowing, and integration of a diversity of information and disciplinary intelligence are important in dealing with real world problems. I will describe this new wave as making the learner's thinking "visible." The challenge of management education is to design learning environments and processes where participants' ways of thinking and knowing is manifested in active, collaborative and self-regulated learning. This chapter reveals why problem-based learning (PBL) is a holistic approach in management education and explains how complex, real world problems should be used as the starting point and focus of learning.

NEW TECHNOLOGIES, NEW PARADIGMS AND REAL-WORLD PROBLEMS

Management educators need to ask not only the "how" questions but also the "why." There is a need to think in terms of 3Ps, namely, (i) Paradigms (What are our worldviews?), (ii) Philosophy (What are our beliefs?) and (iii) Practicality (What do we do?) (Tan, 2003). Our worldview must be both telescopic and helicopter in nature. By telescopic I mean understanding the past (where we came from and how we arrived at the present) and seeing into the future (intelligent extrapolation). We also need a helicopter view of things: rising above micro and fragmentary issues and having a big picture of things. We need the appropriate paradigms with the right worldviews and the right assumptions. Kuhn (1962) was probably the first to use the term *paradigm* through his work *The Structure of Scientific Revolution*. He was alluding to the existence of a conflict of worldviews where there was a need to shift our underlying assumptions about things.

As management educators, we operate with many assumptions. For example:

- What are our assumptions about knowledge on management and how it should be best transmitted (Tan, 2002a)?

- How do we look at knowledge and information today (Tan, 2002b)?
- Is management education primarily about dissemination of content knowledge often in separate disciplinary silos?
- How do management teachers view their interaction and that of their students with the knowledge milieu (Eraut, 1994)?
- What are our assumptions about adult student learning, participation and empowerment (Knowles, 1980)?
- What are our assumptions about how we should prepare our students for the future such as for lifelong learning (Knapper & Cropley, 1991)?

We live in a new millennium characterized by unprecedented breakthroughs in knowledge and technology. To cope with the changes in many aspects of life, we need to prepare management students with a different set of intelligences to function effectively in a new world. Traditional notions of the transmission of knowledge, skills and attitudes seem inadequate to address this need. There is an urgent need for educators to recognize the implications of these dynamic changes.

Management education in the 21st century is about dealing with new real-world problems. Effective learning approaches involve harnessing intelligences from within individuals, from groups of people and from the environment. Intelligence in the real world involves not only learning how to do things and actually doing them, but also the ability to deal with novelty as well as the capacity to adapt, select and shape our interactions with the environment (Sternberg, 1985, 1986, 1990). Problem-based learning (PBL) is about harnessing the kinds of intelligences needed in confronting real-world challenges: the ability to deal with novelty and complexity (Tan, 2004a).

The challenge is indeed for educators to design new learning milieus and curricula that really encourage motivation and independence so as to equip students with learning, thinking and problem-solving skills. Management education should involve:

- encouraging lifelong learning (learning throughout life);
- fostering life wide learning (transfer of learning across contexts and disciplines);
- assuming greater personal responsibility for one's learning;
- learning how to learn from multiple sources and resources;
- learning collaboratively;
- learning to adapt and to solve problems (i.e., to cope with change).

PROBLEM-BASED LEARNING (PBL) IN PROFESSIONAL
TRAINING AND MANAGEMENT

Problem-based learning (PBL) is an active-learning and learner-centered approach where unstructured problems are used as the starting point and anchor for the learning process. PBL is not just about problem-solving processes it is a pedagogy based in constructivism where realistic problems are used in conjunction with the design of a learning environment where self-directed learning, information mining, dialogue, and collaborative problem-solving are incorporated. In recent years, PBL has gained new momentum as a result of several developments. The first is the increasing demand for bridging the gap between theory and practice. The second factor is information accessibility and knowledge explosion resulting in new possibilities in the use of multidisciplinary problems. Thirdly, the emphasis on real-world competencies, such as skills in independent learning, collaborative learning, problem solving, and decision making, provides a strong rationale for adopting PBL. Fourthly, developments in learning, psychology, and pedagogy appear to support the use of inquiry and problem-based approaches (Tan, 2004b).

Beginning with medical education PBL has been one of the most popular curricula innovations in professional education (Baker, 2000; Bechtel, Davidhizar, & Bradshaw, 1999; Berkson, 1993; Bridges & Hallinger, 1995; Wilkerson & Gijselaers, 1996; Boud & Feletti, 1997; Savin-Baden, 2000; Tan et al., 2000). In nursing education, for example, prior knowledge was utilized in relation to the problem and was seen as beneficial as students became more confident and were able to use the knowledge gained for practice (Darvill, 2003). It has been found that by reflecting upon prior learning, students are able to analyze and synthesize the contextual information, acquire further knowledge and assimilate it into their existing knowledge base (Nelson et al., 2004). Previous research shows that PBL enhances flexibility in the use of knowledge base (Chung & Chow, 2004) through building on prior knowledge and connecting meaningfully to real life situations (Tan, 2003; Carder, Willingham, & Bibb, 2001). Breton (1999) found that students were also able to relate theory to practice and developed greater ability to remember and re-use what they have learnt in the case of PBL in accounting education. In their meta-analysis, Dochy Segers, Van den Bossche, and Gijbels (2003) showed that PBL has a significant effect on the knowledge application skills of students. Tan (2003, 2004a, 2004b, 2004c) explained that through PBL cycles students learn to connect information to prior knowledge, prior experience, theory, new facts and ideas, other people's perspectives and the real world context as such this develop their capacity to apply knowledge gained to a variety of problem situations. Management in the real world today often involves dealing with chaos and complexity (Bawden & Zuber-Skerritt, 2002) as such PBL is highly suitable for management education as it uses unstructured real world problems as the starting point and anchor of the learning process. Unlike case studies where content knowledge is usually presented first, PBL uses the ill-structured nature of problem scenarios to provide the stimuli for learners to identify the problem and their gaps in information and knowledge. Individual research and collaborative learning follows. As such, the PBL process captures action research processes but makes use of problems and the PBL cycle to develop problem-solving skills and problem-solving acumen. Previous studies suggest that PBL develops problem solving skills by enabling students to transfer the problem solving strategies that were modeled for them in PBL to a similar problem on a related topic (Pedersen & Liu, 2002). Tan and Lee (2004) observed that cognition, metacognition and self-regulation characterize effective PBL. Chung and Chow (2004) found that PBL promotes ability to apply appropriate metacognitive and reasoning strategies. In PBL students learn to critically question and draw their own conclusions (Nelson et al., 2004). Bechtel et al. (1999) found that PBL is helpful in developing proficiency in problem solving skills and overcoming the theory-practice gap. PBL also helps promote critical thinking (Cooke & Moyle, 2002). I also like to point out that PBL provides a learning environment where cognitive immersion happens. Traditional approaches and didactics are not able to provide for opportunities of learning where intuition and insights can occur.

As Tan (2003) noted PBL creates goal-direction. Goal mediation is also important PBL process (Tan, 2004c). Self-directed learners become proactive in achieving their goals, adapting their personal strategies according to the situational demands. According to Hmelo-Silver (2004) the more reflective learners become, the greater the likelihood that they were able to adapt their self-directed learning strategies. The strategies adopted interacted with students' previous learning knowledge, self-regulated strategies, self-efficacy and the features of the learning environment. Students were able to transfer hypothesis-driven strategies from problem solving into their self-directed learning as they planned their learning using their hypotheses. Tan and Lee (2004) highlighted the advantages of collaborative and communicative inquiry in PBL. Explaining one's ideas is important for productive collaboration and also serves to enhance learning (Chung & Chow, 2004). Evidences appear to support the usefulness of PBL in encouraging students learn to work as a group (Sharp & Primrose, 2003; Lee & Tan, 2004). Through group dynamics students learn to deal with dysfunctional aspects of a group and address them in a constructive manner (Sharp & Primrose, 2003), To become effective collaborators student as team members learn to establish a common ground, resolve discrepancies, negotiate group action and develop consensus. These tasks require leaning to dialogue, and transparency and openness in the exchange of ideas. These cognitive and metacognitive processes are important many aspects of management education.

PROBLEM-BASED LEARNING MODELS FOR MANAGEMENT EDUCATION

A PBL model is characterized by the following (Tan, 2003).

- The *problem* is the starting point of learning.
- The problem is usually a *real-world* management problem that appears unstructured.
- The problem calls for *multiple perspective and use of cross-disciplinary knowledge*.
- The problem challenges students' current knowledge, attitudes, and competencies, thus calling for identification of learning needs and *new areas of learning*.
- *Self-directed learning* is primary. Thus, students assume major responsibility for the acquisition of information and knowledge.
- *Harnessing of a variety of knowledge sources* and the use and evaluation of information resources are essential PBL processes.
- Learning is *collaborative, communicative and cooperative*. Group work, peer learning and peer teaching happen.
- Development of *inquiry and problem-solving skills* is as important as content knowledge acquisition for the solution of the problem. The management tutor thus facilitates and coaches through questioning and cognitive coaching.
- Closure in the PBL process includes *synthesis and integration* of learning.
- PBL also concludes with an *evaluation and review* of the learner's experience and the learning process.

Figure 13.1 illustrates the key components in a PBL model.

We will consider a simple PBL example in economics to illustrate these components and their characteristics. One of the typical topics in economics concerns the various types of business units. Students may be expected to explain the purposes and characteristics of units such as sole proprietorships, partnerships, private limited companies and public listed companies. Traditionally, a teacher would give a series of lectures beginning with one on sole proprietorship and moving on sequentially to the other types of registered businesses. However, a lecturer may choose to use a PBL approach by posing the following problem:

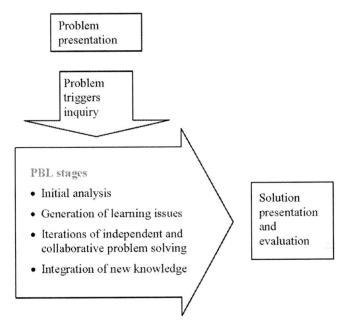

Figure 13.1.   Components of the PBL model.

- You and two of your friends would like to start a business to design
  Web pages for corporate clients. Amongst you there is a great deal
  of expertise in Web-based programming. Each of you agreed to put
  in $2,000 to start this business. How would you go about registering
  and setting up your business?

Thus, instead of having a didactic delivery and students passively copying
notes, students are now presented with a real-world problem scenario as
the starting point of learning. Learning thus begins with meeting a somewhat messy and unstructured problem. The problem triggers learning by
having students:

- define the problem;
- analyze the problem;
- generate ideas (and hypotheses);
- identify learning issues.

Students are usually given sufficient time to study the problem individually before they are formed into groups. They are encouraged to underline key words and jot down ideas and questions that come to their minds.

Students work in small groups (of 3-4 people) to discuss the problem scenario. They ask themselves questions, such as what they know from the problem presented, what they need to know and what ideas come to mind. They are expected to paraphrase the problem and come up with a problem statement to describe the scope of their engagement. Many questions will arise. In this case, some of the questions raised may be:

- What is the goal of our company?
- What must we know about the different kinds of business units?
- Should it be a partnership or limited company?
- What are the legal requirements?
- How do we go about registering the business?

Hence, instead of being told what partnership or limited company is and being presented with the sequence of planning and registering a business, the students now need to inquire, seek information from books and Web sites, and think about how to solve the problem. Apart from the economics perspective pertaining to types of business units, they also need to consider other perspectives, such as the legal aspects of registering a business and accounting requirements.

As the students deliberate on the problem, brainstorming and discussing collaboratively, they are expected to draw up their learning issues and objectives based on the questions raised. They then divide the work amongst themselves to seek the necessary information on their own. In a group discussion facilitated by their PBL tutor, the students refine their learning objectives into more pertinent questions that require the acquisition of deeper knowledge and insights important for their future professional practice. In this case, their learning issues and objectives may be stated in the form of questions such as the following:

- What are the various types of business units?
- What are the types of business units appropriate for the give purpose of the business?
- What are the advantages and disadvantages of a partnership versus a private limited company?
- What are the legal requirements associated with the registration of the business?

The questions raised provide the parameters and motivation for learning. The learning objectives are attained through self-directed learning and group discussions mediated by the tutor. Several meeting and learning sessions may follow depending on the structure of the PBL process. In a PBL course that I know, students were actually made to present a business proposal with actual forms from the registry of businesses and com-

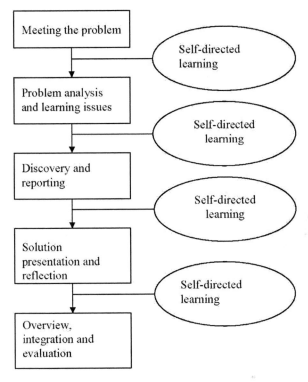

Figure 13.2.   The PBL process.

panies duly completed and submitted to the tutor. In the process, the students actively sought information about liabilities, tax policies and the advantages of the various types of businesses. They also went through the planning processes through active discussion and even interviewed people who were running businesses of their own.

At the closure, students contextualize and integrate their learning from presentations made by team members and peer groups. The tutor facilitates synthesis of the new knowledge and competencies acquired. The concluding session would also incorporate the students' reflection, review and evaluation of various aspects of the learning. Figure 13.2 provides a schema of a typical PBL process.

USE OF REAL-WORLD PROBLEMS AND PROBLEM DESIGN

The roots of problem design are real-world problems. It seems obvious and common sense that teachers in management education should be teaching students how to deal with the problems that business and management executives face in the business world and industry today. There is a need for students to be taught the problems of management that they will encounter in practice, including how to deal with new challenges where solutions have yet to be found. The management educator is expected to show management trainees how to handle situations in the real world. Yet, all too often the gap between theory and practice remains. It is interesting to consider the history of professional education. Universities were traditionally hubs of philosophies, deep thinking and inquiry. In the early days, many philosophers in the sciences were also scientists who made great discoveries of natural laws and principles and laid the foundations of the scientific approach and the rigors of inquiry. Developments in the arts, humanities and political and social sciences have similar beginnings in the universities where critical thinking, reasoning and appreciation made their mark. I am presenting an oversimplified picture here. It can be said, however, that professional education was more about apprenticeship. The training of engineers, architects, accountants, legal professionals, managers and so on had its beginnings in the apprenticeship form of learning. The apprentice learnt by seeing how experts solved real-world problems and subsequently taking up the problems themselves. When professional training was incorporated into higher education, the training process was meant to accelerate learning as well as inject multidisciplinary and deeper reasoning and inquiry. Real-world problem solving in the apprenticeship model was not meant to be replaced. There is thus the need to be cognizant of real-world problems and challenges in order to bring good problems into the curricula. The need for educators to design and bring good problems to their students means that they have to be constant learners themselves to be in touch with the challenges of society and industry.

According to Michael Hicks (1991), four things are implicit when we talk about a problem: (1) we recognize that there is a problem, (2) we do not know how to resolve the problem, (3) we want to resolve it, and (4) we perceive that we are able to find a solution. A problem presented to students in PBL should therefore evoke a recognition of the problem, an awareness of the existing gap in the students' knowledge, a willingness to resolve the problem and a perception that they can find a solution. In many cases, it also implies that they are able to implement the solution.

The following are some examples of the types of problem triggers and stimuli.

1. *Failure to Perform.*   A problem could be a malfunctioning management system. It could be something that is not working according to order. It could be a person's performance that falls short of expectation.

2. *Situations in Need of Immediate Attention or Improvement.*   There are many management problems in the world that are situations in need of immediate help and improvement, such as a strike, disasters, economic crisis, bankruptcy, etc. A course in logistic operations may have a problem scenario such as this:

    • The workers in a manufacturing plant are increasingly frustrated that the gains they have achieved at their plant are being frittered away in the distribution system. Some 30% of the cost of the product has been attributed to distribution and sales.

3. *Finding Better and New Ways to Do Things.*   Often, normal-functioning business operations and operation systems present a problem situation where we want to raise standards, improve quality or obtain better results. Many businesses have to continually improve their company image, create higher value and so on in order to survive. Similarly, companies often seek to improve their operation systems in terms of reducing cycle time, eliminating errors and so forth. Rather than teaching the subject matter and content, we could present relevant cases, data and information to students. The students' knowledge gaps will create the need for learning the content and at the same time stretch their creativity in applying the knowledge. For example, detailed reports of an anonymous company can be given, such as its annual report, balance sheet and profiles of its management team. The problem could be posed as follows:

    • ABC is a private limited company whose major products and services are as given in the portfolio and reports. It plans for public listing to raise funds of $100 million for international expansion. You and your team members are tasked by the management consultancy you work for to undertake feasibility studies and present reports and executive summaries based on the studies.

4. *Unexplained Management and Business Phenomena or Observations.*   It has been said that discovery is seeing what everybody has seen and thinking what nobody has thought of. Breakthroughs in knowledge are often a result of understanding observations. Problems can be presented in the form of a phenomenon or observations and students are required to seek explanations to these observations. In some cases, it could be problems where causes are actually unknown and current explanations lacking. For example, what is

meant by the new economy today from different data sets and observations.

5.   *Gaps in Information and Knowledge.*   We can also present the current state of knowledge or the state of the art in practice as a problem in terms of a gap in understanding. The lack of valid and reliable data and information can also be a problem situation. Sometimes habits, routines and practices are taken for granted. However, a junior high school student was concerned and asked: "Does microwave cooking with plastic-wrapped food pose any problem to health?" Such questions can be interesting problems.

6.   *Decision-making Problems.*   In the real world, decision making represents one of the most important forms of challenges. It often involves taking into account rational as well as emotive aspects of reasoning. Issues of policies, public opinions, human rights and ethics are examples that can be used in PBL curricula. Specific issues such as the rights of the minority, the rights of people with disabilities, abortion and euthanasia are often raised in the news. A newspaper cutting on a specific case or incident can be a problem trigger.

7.   *Need for New Design or Invention.*   Creative problems that lead to a new system design or an invention of a new service or process represent an important category of problems in the knowledge-based economy. Are there new ways of doing things? What are the possible consequences and impacts? Industries and businesses are always looking for new designs, inventions, new combinations, new products, new ways of branding and so on. Depending on the discipline and the relevance, a host of challenges pertaining to new service designs, new features or untried combinations are possible.

A problem should take into consideration the possible learning goals. Consider the simple example of the economics problem given earlier involving registering and setting up a business. Figure 13.3 illustrates the possible goals of the problem. Apart from acquiring content knowledge, including understanding the purposes and characteristics of sole proprietorships, partnerships, private limited companies and public listed companies, we also want students to take a multidisciplinary perspective where they would learn about setting up a business and apply their writing and communication skills in putting together a business plan and proposal.

Having established the goals of using PBL in your curriculum, the next step is to understand the characteristics of PBL participants, including their profile, prior knowledge, prior experience and their foundation

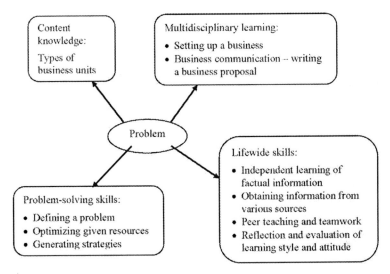

Figure 13.3.   Examples of the goals of a business problem

knowledge. Participants in management education often bring with them rich prior experience and knowledge, which can contribute much to the learning process. The nature and complexity of the problem posed will depend very much on the background and profile of the learners. As mentioned earlier, we need to prepare the mindset of students, who are only used to a more didactic mode of learning. We also have to ascertain that students have the basic and foundational knowledge needed to inquire and to understand the problem Productive inquiry cannot take place in a vacuum, and it is important to consider the appropriate level and type of problem to be used to make the most of the PBL experience (Tan, 2004a,b).

When selecting or designing a problem, several features of the problem have to be considered. These pertain to the problem characteristics, problem context, learning environment and resources, and problem presentation. The following are some key points to note.

- What is the real-world relevance of the problem?
- What is the curriculum relevance?
- What is the level of difficulty?
- What is the level of complexity?
- Is it an interdisciplinary problem?
- Does the problem call for integration of multiple disciplines (or topics)?

- How open is the problem (in terms of possible solutions)?
- Does it trigger curiosity?
- Will it motivate ownership?
- How can the problem stimulate collaborative inquiry?
- What kinds of independent learning can be incorporated?
- What is the extent of guidance needed for using the learning resources?
- Does the problem require further data collection?
- Will field work be incorporated?
- Will information gathering include interviews and experts' views?
- What is mode of problem presentation (problem scenario, detailed case write-up, video clips, audio news, role play, simulation, news-paper cuttings, journal reports)?

COLLABORATIVE LEARNING IN PBL APPROACHES

PBL provides an excellent opportunities for collaborative inquiry and learning. Bray and his colleagues (2000) described collaborative inquiry as a process in which people are engaged in "repeated episodes of reflec-tion and action" as they work in a group to "answer a question of impor-tance to them" (p. 6). According to the authors, collaborative inquiry involves:

- formation of a collaborative inquiry group;
- establishing conditions for group learning;
- acting on inquiry questions;
- making meaning by constructing knowledge.

In PBL classes, learning is done in small groups. Small group learning provides opportunities for students to be actively involved and engaged in interactive inquiry and group learning, with to aim to:

- gain a deeper understanding of the knowledge (content and pro-cess) being acquired;
- learn problem-solving processes;
- learn to benefit from team perspectives;
- develop interpersonal and communication skills;
- learn to be effective team contributors (Lee & Tan, 2004).

There are two strong arguments for collaborative learning:

- Collaboration as competence.
- Value of collaboration in higher cognitive and metacognitive processes.

Collaboration as competence includes inter- and intrapersonal skills and effective communication and social skills (Eraut, 1994). The ability to work in teams and collaborate effectively is critical for all professionals today. Globalization calls for effective communication across cultures and we need to learn to work with others for mutual benefit and the achievement of goals. Moreover, with increasing complexity and specialization, we need to share and optimize on the various strengths of people in a group.

In the PBL process, students learn that teamwork and collaboration are important for developing cognitive processes pertaining to scanning the environment, understanding the problem, gathering essential data and analyzing data, and elaborating on solutions. Dialogue is essential to ensure that we are not locked into our own limited or prejudiced perspectives. It is important for developing critical thinking and reflection. Small group teaching in PBL also helps to make students' thinking "visible" to tutors. In traditional teaching, the lecturers' job is to make their thinking visible to the students by being clear, systematic and organized. We have, however, neglected an equally important, if not more important, aspect of education, which is for students to make visible to us their thinking. Are they only able to regurgitate information or are they sufficiently analytical? Are they learning to connect information and ideas? Do they see things in systemic (big picture) and systematic ways? Through collaborative discussions, students learn to inquire and employ metacognitive processes.

BLENDING OF INTERNET COMMUNICATION TECHNOLOGIES IN PBL

Currently, many e-learning management systems, such as Blackboard, provide convenient tools and resources, such as announcements, course information, course documents, assignments, books, communication system, virtual classroom and discussion board. With rapid improvement, the tools and sequencing are becoming more flexible and user-friendly. This means that we will be able to customize the learning management system to suit a particular PBL program. Furthermore, problems can be easily presented in a variety of innovative ways, including text, hypertext, photographs, graphics and digital videos. A rich amount of data, Web sites and Internet links can also be conveniently incorporated.

To facilitate the PBL process, we suggest making the following information and resources available online:

- PBL homepage;
- Course objectives;
- Course structure;
- Portfolio of problem scenarios;
- PBL cycle and inquiry tools;
- Tutor's guide;
- Student's guide;
- Resources and links;
- Assessment criteria;
- Communication system.

The opportunities for PBL and e-learning integration abound considering what learning management systems and Web-based learning could offer. Since PBL involves immersion in the problem as well as the collection, connection and communication of information over an extended period of time, such learning management systems will support and facilitate the learning and communication process (Chen & Tan, 2002).

The effective integration of PBL models and e-learning appears to be a promising way to go in educational and training innovation. The creative combination of face-to-face mediation and technological mediation will characterize learning in the future. It would be unwise for educators to ignore the use of problems and the psychological and motivational benefits of PBL processes. In PBL, face-to-face interaction is important for learning the complexities and heuristics of thinking, problem solving and application through inquiry and discussion. It is difficult to structure and sequence such metacognitive learning. Perhaps artificial intelligence and more sophisticated multimedia delivery and interaction will assist in more domains of metacognitive learning in the future.

One serious consideration for e-learning program providers is to take the PBL approach and make the best of technology to facilitate the collaborative and problem-solving learning processes. By using problems as triggers for learning and interactivity, the potential of technology could perhaps be more fully harnessed.

Some of the underpinning principles of the use of PBL in e-learning are:

- Make use of the power of real-world problems to motivate learning;
- Design the learning environment such that it employs the global information network;
- Encourage the development of learning-to-learn processes, heuristics, and thinking skills;
- Emphasize problem solving and decision making rather than content learning;
- Provide for systems of engagement and collaboration;
- Provide opportunities for active application of knowledge and self-review;
- Optimize the use of flexible structures to support and sustain independence and interdependence;
- Develop evaluative and critical use of information sources.

CONCLUSION

Glasglow (1997) observed that most curricula tend to "focus on content coverage and exposing students to wide knowledge base ... the better models engaged students in problem scenarios that are similar to authentic real-world situations" (p. 13). He advised:

> Curricular planners and designers do not have to look any further than the real world, outside institutionalized education frameworks, to find curricular and pedagogical models for relevant learning applications. The bottom line here is that the world is an integrated, multidisciplinary, and interdisciplinary place. It is also filled with problems, projects, and challenges. Beginning to create curriculum that reflects this reality makes sense. (p. 14)

In designing problems, we have noted the need to establish our goals for using PBL. Once you have decided on your goals, you need to consider at which level you can introduce PBL into the management curriculum. One should be aware, however, that PBL is not a "one size fits all" methodology. It is more of a philosophy and approach that emphasizes the effective use of problems through an integrated approach of active and multidisciplinary learning. A review of the desired graduate profile of the program, the nature of the disciplines, disciplinary goals, assessment criteria, current resources and the profile of students is essential to bring about effective introduction of a PBL curriculum. With good planning, management support, resource allocation and staff development, PBL can become a predominant mode of learning supplemented by a range of good instructional methodologies.

REFERENCES

Baker, C.M. (2000). Problem-based learning for nursing integrating lessons from other disciplines with n experiences. *Journal of Professional Nursing, 16*(5), 258-266.

Bawden, R., & Zuber-Skerritt, O., (2002), The concept of process management. *The Learning Organisation, 9*(3), 132-138.

Bechtel, G.A., Davidhizar, R., & Bradshaw, M.J. (1999). Problem-based learning in a competency-based world. *Nurse Education Today, 19*, 182-187.

Breton, G. (1999). Some empirical evidence on the superiority of the problem-based learning (PBL) method. *Accounting Education, 8*(1), 1-12.

Berkson, L. (1993). PBL: Have the expectations been met? *Academic Medicine, 68*, 79-88.

Boud, D., & Feletti, G.I. (Eds.). (1997). *The challenge of problem-based learning* (2nd ed.). London: Kogan Page.

Bray, J., Lee, J., Smith, L., & Yorks, L. (2000). *Collaborative inquiry in practice. Action, reflection, and making meaning.* London: Sage.

Bridges, E.M., & Hallinger, P. (1995). *Implementing problem based learning in leadership development.* Eugene: ERIC Clearinghouse on Educational Management, University of Oregon.

Carder, L., Willingham, P., & Bibb, D. (2001). Case-based, problem-based learning information literacy for the real world. *Research Strategy, 18*(3), 181-190.

Chung, J.C.C., & Chow, S.M.K. (2004). Promoting student learning through a student-centered problem-based learning subject curriculum. *Innovation in Education & Teaching International, 41*(2), 157-1 68.

Chen, A.Y., & Tan, O.S. (2002). Towards a blended design for e-learning. *Centre for Development of Teaching and Learning Brief, 5*, 6-8.

Cooke, M., & Moyle, K. (2002). Students' evaluation of problem-based learning. *Nurse Education Today, 22*, 330-339.

Darvill, A. (2003). Testing the water—problem-based learning and the cultural dimension. *Nurse Education Today, 3*, 72-79.

Dochy, F., Segers, M., Van den Bossche, P., & Gijbels, D. (2003). Effects of problem-based learning: A meta analysis. *Learning and Instruction, 13*(5), 533-568.

Eraut, M. (1994). *Developing professional knowledge and competence.* London: Falmer Press.

Evans, J.B.T., Venn, S., & Feeney, A. (2002). Implicit and explicit processes in a hypothesis testing task. *British Journal of Psychology, 93*, 31–46.

Glasgow, N.A. (1997). *New curriculum for new times: A guide to student-centered, problem-based learning.* Thousand Oaks, CA: Corwin Press.

Hicks, M.J. (1991). *Problem solving in business and management: Hard, soft and creative approaches.* London: International Thomson Business Press.

Hmelo-Silver, C.E. (2004). Problem-based learning: What and how do students learn? *Education Psychology Review, 16*(3), 235-266.

Knapper, C.K., & Cropley, A.J. (Eds.). (1991). *Lifelong learning and higher education* (2nd ed.). London: Kogan Page.

Knowles, M.S. (1980). *The modern practice of adult education: From pedagogy to andragogy.* Chicago: Follett.

Kuhn, T.S. (1962). *The structure of scientific revolutions*. Chicago: University of Chicago Press.

Lee, M.G.C., & Tan, O.S. (2004). Collaboration, dialogue, and critical openness through problem-based learning processes. In O.S. Tan (Ed.), *Enhancing thinking through problem-based learning approaches: International perspectives* (pp. 133-144). Singapore: Thomson Learning.

Nelson, L., Sadler, L. & Surtees, G. (2004). Bringing problem-based learning to life using virtual reality. *Nurse Education Today, 3*, 1-6.

Pedersen, S., & Liu, M. (2002). The transfer of problem-solving skills from a problem-based learning environment: The effect of modelling an expert's cognitive processes. *Journal of Research on Technology in Education, 35*(2), 303-320.

Savin-Baden, M. (2000). *Problem-based learning in higher education: Untold stories*. Buckingham; Philadelphia, PA: Society for Research into Higher Education and Open University Press.

Sharp, D.M.M., & Primrose, C.S. (2003). The "virtual family": An evaluation of an innovative approach using problem-based learning to integrate curriculum themes in a nursing undergraduate programme. *Nurse Education Today, 23*, 219-225.

Sternberg, R.J. (1985). Approaches to intelligence. In S.F. Chipman, J.W. Segal, & R. Glaser (Eds.), *Thinking and learning skills, Vol. 2: Research and open questions*. Hillsdale, NJ: Erlbaum.

Sternberg, R.J. (1986). *Intelligence applied: Understanding and increasing your intellectual skills*. San Diego, CA: Harcourt Brace Jovanovich.

Sternberg, R.J. (1990). *Metaphors of mind: Conceptions of the nature of intelligence*. New York: Cambridge University Press.

Tan, O.S. (2002a). Project management in educational development: A Singapore experience. In M. Yorke, P. Martin, & C. Baume (Eds.), *Managing educational development projects: Maximising impact* (pp. 153-170). London: Kogan Page.

Tan, O.S. (2002b). Knowledge and participation reconsidered: Some implications for teaching and learning. *Academia, 1*, 3-4.

Tan, O.S. (2003). *Problem-based learning innovation: Using problems to power learning in the 21st century*. Singapore: Thomson Learning.

Tan, O.S. (Ed.) (2004a). *Enhancing thinking through problem-based learning approaches: International perspectives*. Singapore: Thomson Learning.

Tan, O.S. (2004b). Students' experiences in problem-based learning: Three blind mice episode or educational innovation. *Innovations in Education and Teaching International, 41*(2), 169-184.

Tan, O.S. (2004c). Cognition, metacognition, and problem-based learning. In O.S. Tan (Ed.), *Enhancing thinking through problem-based learning approaches: International perspectives* (pp. 1-16). Singapore: Thomson Learning.

Tan, O.S., & Lee, J. (2004). Project work through problem-based learning approach. In B.T. Ho, N.S. Jo-Ann, & A.S.C. Chang (Eds.), *Managing project work in schools: Issues and innovative practices* (pp. 174-184). Singapore: Prentice-Hall.

Tan, O.S., Little, P., Hee, S.Y., & Conway, J. (Eds.) (2000). *Problem-based learning: Educational innovation across disciplines*. Singapore: Temasek Centre for Problem-based Learning.

Wilkerson, L.A., & Gijselaers W.H. (Eds.). (1996). *Bringing problem-based learning to higher education: Theory and practice*. San Francisco: Jossey-Bass.

CHAPTER 14

BUSINESS PLAN COMPETITIONS

Vehicles for Learning Entrepreneurship

Malu Roldan, Asbjorn Osland, Mark V. Cannice, Michael Solt, and Burton V. Dean

Business plan competitions at 2 universities are described—one in its early stages is the Silicon Valley Business Plan Competition (SVBPC) at San Jose State University (SJSU) and the other is the well-established competition at the University of San Francisco (USF). Also provided are the learning outcomes from the Hewlett Packard Mobile Computing Grant Project (HPMCG). The New Venture Fair (NVF) at SJSU, held the semester before the SVBPC, fosters ideas for the SVBPC. One key to the success of the 2003 NVF was the involvement of the HPMCG student teams. In contrast to the beginning efforts at SJSU, the USF International Business Plan Competition is one of the nation's leading graduate university business plan competitions. Graduate students from many nations are invited to submit business plan proposals for participation. Lessons learned from the above are listed. As a learning vehicle for entrepreneurship, business plan competitions are hard to beat.

INTRODUCTION

Businessweek estimates that seventy college or university sponsored business plan competitions exist today, attracting some 3500 students worldwide (Merritt, 2004a,b). These competitions have proven to be excellent

Educating Managers through Real World Projects, 309–332
Copyright © 2005 by Information Age Publishing
All rights of reproduction in any form reserved.

venues for helping student entrepreneurs attract seed funding and crack the venture capitalist network. Half of the teams participating in UT Austin's MOOT CORP Competition—dubbed the "Super Bowl" of business plan competitions—launch their ventures yearly (University of Texas at Austin, 2003) and MIT claims that almost 80% of the ventures emerging from their contests over the past fifteen years are still in business (Merritt, 2004b).

Clearly, business plan competitions are impressive vehicles for inspiring innovation, spawning new businesses, and boosting university development. Small wonder then that the Moot Corp. Competition regularly hosts observers from other colleges and universities seeking to start competitions of their own (Sauer, 2003). Founded in 1983, Moot Corp. has developed into the world's foremost business plan competition. Directed by Dr. Gary Cadenhead, it continues to assemble interesting business plans from all over the world. Visiting with the various teams during the exposition evening held before the final competition is comparable to attending an elite entrepreneurial trade show. In *No Longer MOOT* (2002), Cadenhead describes, in a manner akin to an anthropological participant observer, how the competition survived and grew. It continues to offer M.B.A. students a risk-free venue to present their ideas and get feedback from venture capitalists, attorneys and others who are part of Austin's entrepreneurial system as well as professors and students from around the world. Dr. Cadenhead's book, *No Longer MOOT*, is an excellent guide and benchmark for other universities, such as The University of San Francisco and San Jose State University, that want to learn how to launch a business plan competition and seek a point of reference for comparison.

This chapter describes business plan competitions at two universities—one in its early stages is the Silicon Valley Business Plan Competition (SVBPC) at San Jose State University (SJSU) and the well-established International Business Plan Competition at The University of San Francisco (USF).

Aside from programmatic impacts and outcomes directly attributed to these competitions, we will also provide results from the assessment of learning outcomes from an interdisciplinary set of courses that participated in SJSU's competition, the Hewlett Packard Mobile Computing Grant Project (HPMCG). In particular, we will focus on impacts on ability of participants to work in cross-functional teams. We focus on these skills as the cross-pollination that occurs within such teams is generally recognized as a fertile substrate for innovation (Berlin, 2004; Bond et al., 2004; Fleming, 2004; Horne & Kristensen, 2004; Hull, 2004; Lin, 2004; Luthje, & Herstatt, 2004; Paramanathan et al., 2004).

Cross-functional and virtual teams are a well-studied phenomenon (Clark, Amudson, & Candy, 2002; DeSanctis, Wright, & Jiang, 2001; Legare, 2001; Kock, 2002; Sethi, Smith, & Park, 2002). Their design and effectiveness have been examined in settings as diverse as Strategic Planning (Andersen, 2004), financial services (Blazevic & Lievens, 2004; Rowe, 2004), the semiconductor industry (Schofield, & Gregory, 2004) and the Department of Defense (Sherman, 2004). Research suggests that interdisciplinary product development experiences provide strong preparation and relevant background for students about to enter the workforce (Darian & Coopersmith, 2001; Rothsteing, 2002).

In part due to the popularity and necessity of using cross-functional teams in industry, various academic accrediting bodies require teamwork, including engineering (Accreditation Board of Engineering and Technology, 2003; www.abet.org) and business (www.aacsb.edu). Numerous examples of teamwork in engineering education can be found (Feland, 2002; Feland & Fisher, 2002; McMahon & Lavelle, 1998; Anwar & Rothwell, 1997; Kiely, 1997; Wilson & Costlow, 1999). The importance of teamwork is also true for other fields such as Industrial Design, one of the disciplines participating in the SVBPC process.

Groups have been used in higher education for decades. As early as 1963, Dean demonstrated the benefits to students of using groups as an educational tool in an operations research graduate program. Anwar and Rothwell (1997) reported on the importance of team-based collaborative problem solving in an engineering technology class and concluded that the team process dramatically improved students' ability to work and problem solve. Colbeck, Campbell, and Bjorklund (2000) studied the implementation process and reported additional concerns such as the importance of: faculty guidance, students converging on a common goal, and managing diversity-related conflict. The authors concluded that group projects should be employed throughout the curriculum. As reported below, an independent evaluation of the HPMCG found that students in cross-functional teams, involved in business plan competitions, identify the ability to work in such diverse teams as one of the top take-aways from the experience.

The next section of this chapter provides an overview of business plan competition efforts at SJSU and USF. The remainder of the paper is organized as follows: descriptions of the events are provided; then a brief summary evaluation of some of the participants and attendees will be presented, as well as of the students involved in the HPMCG; and, finally, lessons learned from the SJSU events and the USF International Business Plan Competition, now in its fifth year, will be discussed.

BUSINESS PLAN COMPETITIONS: AN OVERVIEW

SJSU's Silicon Valley Business Plan Competition

During 2003 a team of faculty from the Colleges of Engineering, Humanities and Arts, and Business at SJSU and several Silicon Valley entrepreneurs and financial investors focused on new venture creation by students. Out of these discussions was formed the SVBPC held in June 2003 and the New Venture Fair (NVF) held on December 16, 2003. The two are intertwined in that one of the primary lessons learned from the 2003 SVBPC was that students needed more than one semester to ramp up from the ideation stage to a completed business plan. The NVF was intended to foster more ideas for the 2004 SVBPC. One key to the success of the NVF was the involvement of the HPMCG student teams that used cross-disciplinary Entrepreneurial Teams (E-Teams) to develop mobile computing applications. SJSU first began using E-Teams in the 2003 SVBPC (Osland et al., 2004). E-Teams are promoted by the National Collegiate Inventors and Innovators Alliance (www.nciia.org) and are composed of students engaged in innovation from various colleges within the university.

The SVBPC is in part modeled after the University of Pennsylvania's Wharton Business Plan Competition (www.whartonbpc.com/participants/phasei.html) that comprises three phases and a culminating event called the Venture Fair. Phase I is for idea generation while in Phase II the teams provide more detail in a business overview that focuses on issues that must be addressed before the business plan is developed. The best 25 Phase II teams then progress to Phase III where they present a business plan. The Venture Fair offers eight finalists the opportunity to present plans before a distinguished panel of judges and an audience of more than 200 venture capitalists, investment bankers, attorneys, business community leaders and students. At SJSU we chose to conduct the SVBPC in two phases: an ideation stage in the fall semester culminating in the NVF, in 2004 renamed the "Neat Ideas Fair," and the SVBPC the following semester (http://www.cob.sjsu.edu/svbpc/ & http://www.cob.sjsu.edu/svnif/).

USF's International Business Plan Competition

In contrast, the University of San Francisco (USF) International Business Plan Competition is one of the nation's leading graduate university business plan competitions. It is held each spring in San Francisco, California. Graduate students from many nations are invited to submit business plan proposals for participation. While total cash prizes for the competition total approximately $25,000, the real prize is the chance for students to offer a business proposal before leading Silicon Valley venture capitalists and chief executives. Judges from previous USF competitions have included venture capital partners (e.g., Benchmark Capital, Draper Fisher Jurvetson, Hummer Winblad Venture Partners, Garage Technology Ventures, Kleiner Perkins, and many more). The opportunity for exposure to these leading venture investors has made the USF contest one of the most competitive in the nation, with the 2004 contest receiving 150 graduate student applications from 100 universities (e.g., Cambridge, Harvard, Hong Kong University of Science and Technology, SJSU, University of North Carolina, USF, etc.) in 18 nations (e.g., Australia, China, India, Spain, United Kingdom, United States, etc.).

There are four phases in the USF competition: (1) initial proposal screening to determine the invited semifinalists, (2) trade show and elevator pitch (90 second) presentations, (3) semifinalist (15 minute) presentations, and (4) finalist (15 minute) presentations. Every team that passes the initial screen is invited to attend the competition and will at least compete in the elevator pitch and semifinal presentation events. Teams also are encouraged but not required to attend the optional warm-up/feedback round (1 hour). The five finalists chosen from the approximately 25 semifinalists present their proposals in the final round.

The judging criteria at the USF contest are those of a venture capitalist; simply, how likely are the judges to invest their fund's capital into the teams business? This decision is, of course, based on the likely success of the enterprise, its competitive advantage, growth and profit potential, relative risk, management team strength, payback or return on their investment, and exit strategy, among other factors.

The competition is primarily for growth-oriented enterprises, not small-businesses. This does not rule out traditional businesses, such as restaurants, retail, etc., but these businesses should be growth oriented. A business plan for an individual sandwich shop business would likely not be selected; however, one for a franchise lunch business might be.

For the presentation rounds, the judges make their assessment on the presentations alone. They will not have seen the proposals before. We are pleased that many of the teams that present have follow-up meetings with the venture investors and executives at the contest, and all of the teams, faculty and student organizers, and the audience learn much from the experience.

DETAILED DESCRIPTIONS OF THE SJSU COMPETITION

The 2003 SVBPC

The SVBPC was organized into four rounds: Proposed Venture Concepts, Marketing and Competitive Analyses, Financial Plans, and Complete Business Plans. Feedback was given to each submission for each round. During each round, faculty and external mentors worked with the student E-Teams. Our objective was to empower business, engineering, industrial design, and computer science students with the entrepreneurial skills to start businesses. A completed business plan was the main deliverable from the E-Teams process, with new venture creation the goal for the best plans. Assessment of this phase was reported at the 2004 NCIIA conference in San Jose, California (Dean, Osland, & Solt, 2004).

Coordination at SJSU proved a challenge. Dean's Project Management course was used as a structural coordinating mechanism. Dean (1986) teaches a method he calls project management of innovative startup firms (PMIS). He demonstrates that eight basic tasks exist in every startup, and that applying the critical path method to the activities in these tasks, along with corresponding precedence relations and activity durations, yields status reports on the startup firm, as well information that is useful in the startup's business plan. During Spring 2003, PMIS was applied in 13 E-Teams and in three startup firms in Silicon Valley.

The 2003 SVBPC was the output of the E-Team process. Student teams competed internally in three rounds. All the final round judges were active in entrepreneurship practice. The 2003 winners were Dr. Mohamed Aslam Ali and Ilya Ronnin, both SJSU MBA students, who won incubator space at the Environmental Business Cluster and the Software Business Cluster, respectively. Dr. Ali's business plan focused on converting automobile waste tires to activated carbon for use in water filters. He also won the eight-state business plan competition held in conjunction with the Minority Business Development Agency Youth Symposium on August 9, 2003 in Oakland, California. Dr. Ali reportedly has commitments for $5 million of the $6 million required to complete the project and incorporated his firm in 2004. Ilya and his partners developed a $30,000 software-driven add-on for machine tool lathes to do the work of computerized machine tools that cost $1 million or more new. However, they later abandoned the business as used equipment sold on E-Bay was reportedly priced too competitively for them to continue.

Many business plan competitions at major universities have reported the creation of new ventures, including what is considered the top competition, University of Texas at Austin's Moot Corp., as well as the University of Arizona, University of Oregon, University of Chicago, MIT and the University of Georgia (Ballon, 1998; Merritt, 2004a). With an output of one promising new venture, we consider the first SJSU SVBPC successful.

In May 2003 we asked the E-Teams for feedback—using a process roughly comparable to a course evaluation—to see if the process was leading toward the goal of new venture creation through effective business plan development. The challenges cited led faculty to conclude that the process be spread over an academic year. Hence, the NVF idea was born, which concluded with a campus-wide event held December 16, 2003.

The New Venture Fair

The NVF was formed as the kick-off event for the SVBPC to showcase innovation produced by SJSU students and faculty and to strengthen the connections between SJSU and the Silicon Valley entrepreneurship community. The NVF featured tables set up by exhibitors that were perused by an audience strolling through the NVF and enjoying refreshments; COMDEX (http://www.comdex.com) served as the model. The exhibits featured innovations created by SJSU students and faculty members and by Silicon Valley start-ups.

The NVF organizers had to create the infrastructure for an event unlike anything that SJSU had undertaken before. Web pages were key parts of the infrastructure put into place early in the process and were the main way that the organizers informed students, faculty, start-ups, service providers, sponsors, and the general public about the NVF.

The NVF became a seven-day-per-week activity for the organizers and was operated very much like a start-up, with all of the ups and downs that start-ups face. Many logistical issues had to be handled: venue, parking, catering, volunteer staff, media coverage, room set-up, audio-visual equipment, prizes, gift coupons, and securing a keynote speaker. Keynote speaker U.S. Congresswoman Zoe Lofgren, representing the San José district, personally visited each exhibit at the NVF.

Funding for the NVF was secured from the Silicon Valley Bank Foundation, Hummer Winblad Venture Partners, TechStock Ventures, the Silicon Valley Center for International Trade and Development, Fernandez & Associates LLP, and Fenwick & West LLP. Start-up companies that had exhibits at the NVF paid a small fee to help cover the expenses of the NVF. All of the NVF expenses were covered and a small surplus was generated. C&J Engineer of Hollister, California, donated a motorized scooter that became the Grand Prize, and Microsoft Corporation donated Xboxes that were given to the Elevator Pitch Contest winning team.

The biggest challenges facing the organizers were assuring participation in the NVF by SJSU student and faculty teams, Silicon Valley start-ups, and service providing organizations, and attracting an audience of students and faculty, Silicon Valley investors (i.e., angels and venture capitalists), and the general public. Within SJSU, top down and bottom up approaches were used. The organizers spoke at a Provosts' Deans Council meeting, at the University Chairs meeting, and at a College of Science Chairs meeting. Emails were sent directly to faculty members, a flyer was put in every faculty mailbox on campus, and flyers were distributed outside the Student Union and posted in classrooms across campus. Email messages were sent to SJSU alumni and the event was posted in the University Calendar of Events. An article about the NVF appeared in the campus newspaper two weeks before the NVF. Outside the SJSU campus, well over 5,000 emails were sent to constituencies of the Software Developer Forum, the Silicon Valley Association of Start-Up Entrepreneurs (SVASE), and the International Angel Investors. The eleven business incubators to whom San José is home were also contacted directly.

Arranging for exhibitors was a major task. More than 100 start-ups from local incubators were contacted. Faculty members in Biology, Business, Engineering, Environmental Sciences, Industrial Design and Hospitality Management were contacted directly about having student and/or faculty exhibits at the NVF. The organizers also worked with the DeAnza Community College Entrepreneur Boot Camp to have exhibits by its students. However, the largest set of internal exhibitors was from the HPMCG, as nine of the ten HPMCG teams exhibited their projects at the NVF. The faculty involved in this project (i.e., Roldan, Solt, and Engineering Professors Xiao Su and Weider Yu) were supportive of the NVF throughout the fall semester, and this led to the high level of participation by these teams. Notably, the Elevator Pitch Contest was won by an HPMCG team that was developing a wireless Tablet PC application for managing housekeeping activities in collaboration with management from Hotel Valencia in San Jose's Santana Row, a new, upscale shopping area.

The NVF included 16 exhibits by SJSU students and faculty. Nine were by HPMCG teams, four were by SJSU College of Engineering faculty and students, and one was by an SJSU student who wanted to start a Louisiana Bayou restaurant chain. Also, two exhibits were from the DeAnza Community College Entrepreneurship Boot Camp. Twenty-three startup companies from local incubators, including the two winners from the 2003 SVBPC, and five service providing organizations set up exhibits, including SJSU's Career Planning & Placement office, Masters in Biotechnology program, and the Entrepreneurial Society student club. Approximately 240 people attended the event. The NVF served as a successful springboard to prepare participants for the SVBPC, in the event that they chose to develop their business concepts into business plans.

2004 SVBPC

The final round of judging for the second annual SVBPC was held on June 25, 2004. Nineteen complete business plans were submitted, nine written by undergraduate teams and ten by MBA teams. College of Business faculty members initially screened these plans and selected seven plans for the final round. Of the recommended plans, one was written by an undergraduate team (the Hotel Valencia HPMCG project) and six by MBA teams.

By all accounts, the 2004 competition was improved over the previous year: one team who competed in both years affirmed this, and one judge stated that the quality of the SVBPC business plans and presentations compared favorably to those in the UC Berkeley competition in which he had also been a judge.

All of the finalists presented potentially viable businesses. Numerical Engines, Inc., (the winner) plans to "change the way we think, build, and deploy high-end computing systems, allowing customers to build high-end computer systems using commodity hardware in a unique way." Numerical-intensive software applications will be able to run 4 to 1,024 times faster, and hardware infrastructure will require 1/16th of the current cost with 1/4th of current annual operating expenses. Inovamar LLC (the runner-up) has assembled a team of experts possessing a rich heritage in the development of wireless solutions for physiological and medical vital signs monitoring. Inovamar LLC plans to capitalize on the large amount of technology development already completed by NASA and leverage this work in the development of commercial wireless medical monitoring technologies. (For details of the other finalists, see: http://www.cob.sjsu.edu/svbpc/.)

Lessons learned from the 2004 SVBPC include: (1) the SJSU student body contains many innovators and entrepreneurs, (2) the year-long schedule improved the quality and quantity of the submitted business plans, (3) getting students to write business plans on their own outside of course requirements was difficult (e.g., only one of ten HPMCG teams carried on their work after the NVF), (4) getting faculty and alumni involved in submitting business plans was a challenge, (5) undergraduate and graduate students needed separate competitions, and (6) echoing USF's experience, meeting potential investors and getting their feedback was more important to the finalists than prizes.

On deck for the future are the following: (1) revamping the NVF to be a Neat Ideas Fair that will focus more on creativity and innovation than on business plan writing, (2) working with the College of Business Alumni Association to increase alumni involvement in advising, mentoring, and business plan writing activities, (3) continuing efforts to increase participation by students, faculty, and alumni in non-College of Business parts of SJSU, and (4) hosting separate undergraduate and graduate BPCs.

HP Mobile Computing Grant E-teams

This section is based on a presentation at NCIIA's March 2004 conference (Roldan, Solt, & Su, 2004). A core multidisciplinary effort that fielded teams to the NVF and SVBPC was the HPMCG. It funded an E-Team project in which cross-functional teams of students developed mobile computing applications in partnership with local clients and entrepreneurs. The project brought together courses from Management Information Systems, Finance, and Computer Engineering. True to the University's metropolitan mission, the project participants sought to leverage the resources available in the greater Silicon Valley area to enrich the project learning environment. It took a Lead User approach to product development (Luthje & Herstatt, 2004)—involving context experts from partner organizations to develop requirements and test prototypes.

The project was supported by a $230,000 Applied Mobile Technology Solutions in Learning Environments grant from Hewlett Packard. The grant included equipment, installation, and student support which, along with a $50,000 matching grant from SJSU's Provost's office, provided mobile equipment to participating faculty, allowed for loans of devices to students for a semester, and supported the creation and staffing of a lab that would serve as the center of activity for the classes in the project. In the same time frame, Microsoft Corporation was launching its next generation server (Windows Server 2003) and developer products (Visual Studio.Net 2003) that incorporated the company's core platform for the development of applications for mobile devices (the Compact.Net Platform). Through participation in the Microsoft Developer Network Academic Alliance, the various departments involved were able to obtain the training, software, and support for the HPMCG student teams' development work. In addition, San Jose's SDForum (i.e., Software Development Forum) provided students in the classes with free student memberships. These memberships not only gave students access to the SDForum user groups and events but also made them eligible to pitch their ideas to local venture capitalists in project showcases organized by the forum.

Student teams were required to develop a business plan and a working prototype of a mobile application solution to a problem or need posed by their clients. Finance students had the primary task of developing the financial analysis for the business plan while computer engineering (CmpE) students had the primary task of developing the prototype. Because of their grounding in both technology and business matters, MIS students were given the task of coordinating team's efforts and acting as bridges to aid communication between the team members and balance out the team's skills. All students were expected to collaborate on the design of the prototype and writing the business plan.

Nine of the ten HPMCG teams participated in the NVF, presenting their prototypes on the Tablet PCs or PDAs used to develop them. Each team put together a poster board introducing its project and team, to serve as a backdrop for its exhibit at the NVF. Several teams also selected a member to participate in the elevator pitch competition, which was eventually won by one of the HPMCG teams. The projects exhibited in Fall 2003 included:

1. Two teams partnered with Hotel Valencia on a project to transform the hotel's system for tracking housekeeping and maintenance work from a paper-based one to a real-time, mobile, wirelessly connected system, one each on the TabletPC and the PocketPC platforms.

2. Two teams partnered with Camera Cinemas on a project to integrate handheld PocketPC devices into the movie viewing experience—via chat sessions, concession stand orders, etc.

3. McGraw-Hill partnered with a team to explore enhancements to their e-book offerings through the application of TabletPC technologies.

4. The Chair of the MIS department partnered with a team to develop a grading application that leveraged the inking capabilities of the Tablet PC.

5. The University's Parking Services Department partnered with a team to explore a solution to the university's parking crunch via a system for distributing information on space availability in various university parking lots.

6. A local entrepreneur, Paseman, partnered with a team to develop an online clearinghouse on the various events happening at any given time in the San Francisco Bay Area. His interest was eventually building an online resource to help individuals make decisions about which of the multitude of events to attend.

7. CmpE Professor Yu partnered with a team to develop a student information system providing access to general university information and student records via handheld devices.

8. An entrepreneur partnered with a team to build enhancements to an e-book markup application.

EVALUATION AND ASSESSMENT

Evaluating the NVF

Based on comments recorded by the participants and visitors, future planners of the NVF should consider suggestions such as the following:

1. The organizing team needs to be flexible and understanding in addition to being well organized.

2. The NVF principals should have a designated project office to facilitate coordination and communication; effective communication is crucial.

3. Attract more participation from VCs, angel investors, and service providers (e.g., law firms, accounting firms, etc.).

4. Provide a catalog with complete contact numbers/emails and more information about the exhibitors.

5. Send out maps and provide more signs to give directions to event hall.

6. Booths would be better than tables and the booths should have better visual aids.

7. Consider rotating the location (e.g., convention center).

8. More advertising on campus and off would make more people aware of the NVF.

9. Invite more CEOs to participate and speak.

In sum, the NVF exceeded the expectations of its organizers and the consensus of registrants and exhibitors was that it was useful and informative.

Evaluating the HPMCG

To assess the learning outcomes and guide future design for this novel class, we administered several questionnaires throughout the semester, including: (1) a pretest with items on student demographics, confidence with various skills involved in completing course requirements, civic engagement, technology knowledge, and expected use of mobile devices, (2) a pretest on course and team expectations, (3) peer review questionnaires administered twice over the semester assessed each students' perspective on how well he or she was performing on his/her team, how well his/her teammates were performing, and how well the team itself was performing, and (4) a post-test with items on confidence with various skills involved in completing course requirements, technology knowledge, and expected use of mobile devices. Additionally, as part of the HPMCG process, an independent evaluator interviewed students and clients about their experiences and learning outcomes in Spring 2004.

Fifty-three students completed the pretest and 43 completed the post-test. The questionnaire items and a chart summarizing the findings are provided in Figure 14.1. These results show that the cross-functional collaborative nature of the HPMCG classes helped students achieve the overall learning goals established for each of the linked courses, paralleling the roles that each team member played in his/her team. MIS and Finance

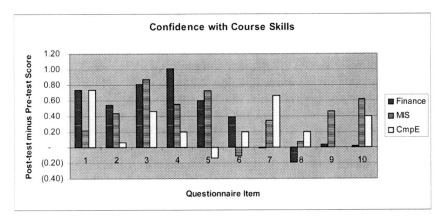

Questionnaire items corresponding to the X-axis in the chart:

1. I am confident that I can conduct access and assess the quality of materials necessary to conduct research on mobile technologies, industries and companies.

2. I am confident that I can conduct a thorough assessment of mobile technology's development and future prospects.

3. I am confident that I can conduct a thorough analysis of the application of mobile technologies in a specific business or non-profit organization.

4. I am confident that I can work with a team to develop a prototype of a mobile technology application that meets the requirements of a business or non-profit client.

5. I am confident that I can work with a team to analyze the feasibility of a mobile technology application.

6. I am confident that I can work with a team to assess the costs and benefits of deploying or commercializing a mobile computing application.

7. I am confident that I can quickly learn and integrate mobile computing tools into my daily activities – in and out of school.

8. I am confident that I can quickly learn and integrate mobile computing tools to coordinate meetings and activities with my teammates.

9. I am confident that I can work with a team to develop a mobile computing prototype and business case in a professional manner and deliver it on time.

10. I am confident that I can work with a team to present a mobile computing prototype and recommendations to a business audience in a concise, clear and professional manner.

Figure 14.1.   Questionnaire items and chart of changes between pre- and post-tests on course-specific skills.

students tended to gain the greatest confidence in their understanding of mobile technologies and their application in specific business settings (Items 1-4). The MIS and CmpE students reported the greatest gains in their confidence with the integration of mobile computing into their everyday lives (Items 7 & 8) and with skills associated with project management—delivering the project on time and presenting the team's work in a professional manner (Items 9 & 10).

The independent evaluation of the HPMCG (Kelley, 2004) identified the ability to work in a cross-functional team as the skill most likely to be mentioned by students as the most valuable learned in the project. This was a first time for most of the students to work directly with their peers in other disciplines and they struggled to overcome obstacles to communication and collaboration, learning valuable lessons in leadership and management in the process. Clients appreciated the collaboration with university students as well. They benefited from the students' enthusiasm and contrasting perspectives and from the exposure to leading edge technologies.

LESSONS LEARNED AT SJSU

Lessons Learned from the NVF

For a first effort, the NVF was very successful. The feedback from all sources has been very positive. Since the infrastructure for the event has been built, future NVFs should be even better. Also, repeat performances should be enhanced as the NVF's reputation grows throughout the region. Still, there are many lessons that have been learned from the initial efforts:

Earlier involvement by support structure.   Students from Dean's project management class were brought in to help manage some of the growing number of tasks surrounding the NVF, but they began their efforts late in the Fall Semester, and to get the full benefit of their efforts, these students need to be brought in much earlier in the process.

Timing of the NVF.   The NVF was held during Final Exam week, and getting the attention of students and faculty during this time was challenging. This date was selected so that the NVF could be held simultaneously with the Department of Industrial Design's student-project exhibition and because the number of student exhibitions would be maximized by holding an event at the end of the semester when class projects would be finished. Future NVFs will likely be held at a different time.

Strengthening the connection to Silicon Valley.   A "chicken and egg" situation exists for the start-up companies and investors: neither group will commit to coming without knowing that the other group has committed. In October, the International Angel Investors agreed to hold its December meeting on the SJSU campus at the conclusion of the NVF, and this was important in getting the attention of the start-up companies. However, the process of locking in the start-ups took longer than expected, so the necessary information about which start-ups would be exhibiting at the NVF was not transmitted early enough to the angel group for them to get a large number of their members to attend, and this was probably compounded by having the NVF so close to the holidays. More timely execution of getting start-ups and investors involved can solve this problem.

Lessons Learned from the HPMCG

As with all first attempts at a new class structure, the HPMCG team's first semester with the E-team structure was quite challenging—although not without its successes. Despite difficulties and through much effort, all teams completed projects that were impressive to most observers from the university and greater community, including attendees of the NVF, ICIS2003, and a final joint meeting of all classes in December. On average, clients gave teams a score of 9.2, out of a possible 10 points, when asked to rate the overall performance of the team. Below is a summary of some of the lessons and challenges to be addressed by the team in the second semester of the project.

Need to define MIS students' role more explicitly as that of project management. As the bridge between their business and technology teammates, MIS students play a role that is continually shifting and somewhat undefined. This is a very difficult position for an undergraduate to handle. To address this difficulty, students will be provided with more material on project management in the early part of the semester. MIS students will also be explicitly assigned to take on the role of project managers on their teams. To encourage team participation, all professors will be asked to include a team participation requirement as part of their grading schemes.

Aim to match classroom experiences more closely with field experiences. HPMCG students responded best to classroom situations that captured the applied and motivating nature of their real-world experiences with clients and their teams. Classroom experiences will be structured to minimize lecturing and have students working in breakout groups and then reporting on their analyses to the entire class. To this end, students will be encouraged to use their devices to support the research and analyses that the teams do in class. Additionally, students' experiences in the field will be used as case studies for class discussion.

Use formative evaluation extensively.   Given the high levels of uncertainty in a project-based class, where expectations from many constituents have to be balanced and creativity encouraged, conscious use of formative evaluation is useful for reducing ambiguity regarding student team goals and class requirements over the course of the semester. As teams present their prototypes, faculty members give them feedback on how close they are to the final class requirements –giving teams guidance on how to best match expectations and temper their creativity. Rather than receiving one final summative score on their work for the semester, teams are provided with interim scores that allow them to assess how well they are meeting course goals. The teams are then provided the opportunity to improve on these interim scores in future presentations of their work.

Set student expectations not only regarding course goals but also regarding uncertainty levels. Lastly, given that most of their undergraduate classes are highly structured, students tend to get frustrated with the high levels of uncertainty inherent in problem-based courses such as those in the HPMCG project. While this can be and will be addressed by the HPMCG team via an increase in course structure, it will also be necessary to point out that the uncertainty is a key element of life and work and essential to bringing an element of reality to such courses. Providing a setting where students can experience and work through their reactions to such uncertainty can help students develop valuable skills to take into the workplace, particularly in these times of high uncertainty and change in the business world and in the information technology industry.

Lessons Learned From the USF International BPC

The BPC hosted by USF has a longer history than the efforts at SJSU and its long-running success provides rich insights. University business plan competitions are becoming more and more prominent in the United States and around the world. These valuable and popular events integrate student learning with an exciting environment and provide real entrepreneurial opportunities through exposure to and feedback from professional investors and executives. However, there exist few resources or how-to manuals for university administrators and faculty who wish to launch a business plan competition at their own universities. In the process of organizing six business plan competitions over the last four years, the most recent two on a global scale, we at the University of San Francisco Entrepreneurship Program, have learned from our successes and mistakes. We are pleased to pass along what we know about the nuts and bolts of hosting a world-class competition (for details, go to the web page: http://www.usfca.edu/sobam/nvc/). Below are several points to consider when getting started.

Figure out the primary objective for hosting a business plan competition. Is the competition primarily meant to be a learning experience for your own students (graduate and/or undergraduate)? What about alumni? Do you envision your school becoming a regional, national, or global hub of entrepreneurship? In that case, you may wish to open your competition to participation by other universities. Your objective for hosting a competition drives the size, scope, cost, and time involved in putting together the event. Once chosen, however, that objective should be adaptable. For example, the USF competition was initially launched as a learning experience primarily for our undergraduate business majors, all of whom take a class in entrepreneurship and business plan development. However, we rapidly broadened our objective to encompass our graduate students and alumni and other local university graduate students. As we better recognized our Silicon Valley location as a global entrepreneurial hub, we further broadened our objective to establish USF as a recognized leader in entrepreneurship, and now attract participation from graduate student entrepreneurs from around the world. For example, in the 2004 USF International Business Plan Competition, more than 150 graduate student teams of entrepreneurs from more than 100 universities around the world applied to compete at USF.

What are the eligibility requirements?   Who can compete? The objective for your competition should drive this decision. Will the competition be only for your own current students? Will your alumni be able to compete? If so, is there a limit to the alumni eligibility (e.g., graduated in last 5 years)? Or, are you extending the invitation to others? Can students from other universities apply? Are you restricting this to other regional universities? For example, the Georgia Bowl Business Plan Competition is primarily for major Southeast universities. Can non-students be members of the entrepreneur team? If so, how can you be sure, that the team is actually founded and led by students? Can non-student team members present at the competition? We recommend—definitely not. We have noticed an increasing number of applications where the teams are essentially real businesses that have drafted a student-intern in order to qualify for a university business plan competition—essentially a shill. To maintain the collegiate and student nature of these events, it is critical to flush out these shills before they are inadvertently accepted to your competition. Will the student teams present business concepts or real businesses? How large can these businesses be if they already exist? USF limits its contestants to those having businesses with no more than $100,000 in annual revenue and $250,000 in equity capital—essentially seed-stage companies. Without specified limits, the competition may become unfair.

Who will organize the event—faculty and staff, or students?   This is a critical decision and is also driven by the underlying objective of your competition. There are competitions organized by all of the above at various schools. (For links to other business plan competitions open to outside student teams, please see http://www.usfca.edu/sobam/nvc/events.htm). However, at USF, a full-time faculty does most of the organization of the event with key MBA student assistance. Although it requires a great deal of time and commitment, this approach allows for continuity from year to year.

How much will it cost, and who's footing the bill?   Estimate about $10,000 per day for food and logistical costs (for approximately 25 teams). That is in addition to prize money, travel subsidies, marketing expenditures, and pre-event planning and staff. Thus, the total costs for a three-day event, including about $25,000 in cash prizes, will total about $75,000, not counting gratis faculty time. Thankfully, funding for entrepreneurial events is available from federal and foundation grants as well as from corporate and individual donors, so many of these costs can be offset by sponsorships.

Marketing the competition to participants.   In the 2003 USF International Business Plan Competition, 80 graduate student teams of entrepreneurs from universities in 10 countries applied to compete at USF. Most of the 26 semifinalist teams that presented their business plans at USF stated that the judges' panel was the primary attraction. The panel included 25 venture capitalist partners and eight CEOs. MIT contestant Tahsin Alam, the 2003 USF second-place winner for his company, Ferrate Solutions, commented, "The USF business plan competition stood apart in my mind for two reasons—one was its international nature, and the other was the exposure to venture capital firms."

Few other locations offer such access to venture capital; therefore, we emphasize that aspect in promoting our business plan competition to student entrepreneurs.

Feedback from participants.   According to data collected from 45 of the attending contestants, students' primary reasons for participating in a business plan competition were:

1.   Potential funding from investors closely followed by
2.   Feedback from investors and executives
3.   Overall learning experience and
4.   Prize money (at a fairly distant fourth place).

Clearly, this data is helpful when directing resources toward the planning and funding of a competition, as well as positioning a competition in the minds of potential student teams.

How did students find out about the USF competition? Our data showed that the best marketing media were the following (from most effective to least effective):

1. Posted paper announcements at their own university.
2. Word of mouth.
3. Web surfing/searching.
4. E-mail announcements at their own university.
5. Their own university's Web site.
6. Internet banner ads (*coming in a distant last*).

Naturally, our marketing communications plan for the USF 2004 Competition was modified based on the above feedback.

Identifying and recruiting top judges and sponsors.   We have found that excellent judges attract excellent contestants, and vice versa. Alumni contacts and university trustees are good pools for identifying potential judges, and this group may form the core of a strong judge's panel. However, ensuring enough premier judges to cover a three-day event generally entails going outside your school's current circle of supporters.

Develop a database of local potential judges (venture capitalists, chief executives, angel investors, entrepreneurs) and invite them to participate. Don't underestimate the power of a well-crafted letter of invitation on university letterhead, signed by the dean. Expect a 5% to 10% positive response rate, with some attrition likely as the contest draws nearer. So, take the number of judges you will need for all the sessions, subtract your core group from that, and multiply the remainder needed by 20. That's the number of new potential judges you should invite. Don't forget that this process also has the added benefit of expanding your university's local executive support group.

After one good competition, it will be much easier to recruit judges for subsequent events. Our data, from 15 of the judges at our 2003 competition, indicates that:

1. Approximately 95% would like to judge again.
2. Approximately 33% would consider sponsoring future events.
3. Approximately 33% would consider hiring an MBA intern.

Competitions are expensive, and most universities can't foot the entire bill. Therefore, organizational and government sponsorship is essential. To defray the cost, look for one or two key lead sponsors (often university alumni or trustees), and they will often help you recruit more. (The sponsors for USF's business plan competition are the U.S. Department of Education, Mike McGraw, CEO, Pacific Specialty Insurance, and Claudio Chiuchiarelli, Partner, Banyan Securities.) However, university support is usually necessary in the early stages of building a competition.

Selecting top teams.   So your marketing has proved successful, and competitors are lining up. This, of course, leaves you with the challenge of selecting from among dozens of strong entries. What makes a successful team? In the 2003 USF competition, teams made up of graduate engineering or science students along with MBA students fared much better overall. Nine of the top ten teams had this combination of engineering or science with MBA talent. (Complete 2003 competition results, including finalists, honorable mentions, and special prizes can be found at http://www.usfca.edu/sobam/nvc/business_plan_03.htm.) Naturally, having a first-round selection committee of investors as well as faculty makes the job easier, and also helps build core financial support for the event.

Details and more details.   Naturally, we have not covered all possible issues in organizing a business plan competition in this article (e.g., scouting out a good host hotel, arranging local transportation, helping international contestants with visa applications, etc.). We did hope to raise some issues that could be considered in your own planning. Have other specific questions about running your own business plan competition? Please e-mail Professor Mark Cannice at cannice@usfca.edu, or check out our site at http://www.BusinessPlanCompetition.org.

An excellent hands-on approach to developing and growing a business plan competition is provided by the MOOT CORP. Fellows Program, led by Dr. Gary Cadenhead, Director of the University of Texas MOOT CORP. Competition. Dr. Cadenhead's 2002 book, titled, *No Longer MOOT: The Premier New Venture Competition from Idea to Global Impact*, also offers a comprehensive history as well as instructions for developing a world-class business plan competition. Perhaps the best way to get a sense of a global business plan competition is to attend in person, and to get a sense of the event a short film of the 2003 USF competition can be seen at: http://www.usfca.edu/sobam/nvc/movie/movie2003.htm.

Success breeds success.   The success of the 2003 contest appeared to create more momentum the following year, when nearly twice the number of teams applied to compete, and the number of judges swelled by about 50%. This branding effect not only increases the scope and value of the event, but also minimizes some marketing costs, as word of mouth begins to spread the news.

BUSINESS PLAN COMPETITIONS AS
LEARNING VEHICLES FOR ENTREPRENEURSHIP

As a learning vehicle for entrepreneurship, business plan competitions are hard to beat. They require students to creatively develop new business ideas, assess the macro and industry environment, develop a sustainable business model, link their strategic objectives for their venture to financial forecasts, and hone their presentation skills as they practice to present their presentations in a pressure-packed contest before critical investors, entrepreneurs, executives, and faculty and students.

This real life laboratory is an excellent opportunity for students to integrate and practice their knowledge across a range of disciplines and skills. When students work jointly with others from varying disciplines, the entrepreneurial learning is dramatically further enhanced through co-teaching and learning within student teams made up of engineers, scientists, lawyers, and MBAs. The cost in time, effort, and dollars cannot be ignored in coordinating these events; however—as evidenced by the findings reported here from the evaluation of SJSU's HPMCG—the payoff in terms of student learning, and the creation of new opportunities for all of the participants, appear to be well worth the work.

REFERENCES

Accreditation Board of Engineering and Technology. (2003). *Criteria for accrediting engineering programs*. Retrieved March 15, 2005 from http://www.abet.org/images/Criteria/E001%2004-05%20EAC%20Criteria%2011-20-03.pdf

Andersen, T.J. (2004). Integrating decentralized strategy making and strategic planning processes in dynamic environments. *Journal of Management Studies, 41*(8), 1271-1299.

Anwar, S., & Rothwell, W. J. (1997). Implementing team-based collaborative problem solving in ET: A case study. *Journal of Engineering Technology, 14*, 34-38.

Ballon, M. (1998). Upstarts: University tournaments. *Inc.*, (December). Retrieved March 15, 2005, from http://www.inc.com/articles/1998/12/11699.html.

Berlin, C. (2004). Change management: Implementation of a process oriented management system based on business ideas and values in a high technology company. *Total Quality Management & Business Excellence, 15*(5-6), 569-592.

Blazevic, V., & Lievens, A. (2004). Learning during the new financial service innovation process—Antecedents and performance effects. *Journal of Business Research, 57*(4), 374-391.

Bond, E.U., Walker, B.A., Hutt, M.D., & Reingen, P.H. (2004). Reputational effectiveness in cross-functional working relationships. *Journal of Product Innovation Management, 21*(1), 44-60.

Cadenhead, G. (2002) *No longer MOOT: The premier new venture competition from idea to global impact*. Austin, TX: Remoir.

Clark, M., Amudson, S., & Candy, R. (2002). Cross-functional team decision-making and learning outcomes: A qualitative illustration. *Journal of Business and Management, 8*, 217-237.

Colbeck, C.L., Campbell, S.E., & Bjorklund, S.A. (2000). Grouping in the dark: What college students learn from group projects. *The Journal of Higher Education, 71*, 60-83.

Darian, J., & Coopersmith, L. (2001). Integrated marketing and operations team projects: Learning the importance of cross-functional cooperation. *Journal of Marketing Education, 23*, 128-136.

Dean, B.V. (1963). Group research as an educational tool. *Proceedings of the 3rd International Conference on Operational Research*, 471-489.

Dean, B.V. (1986). The project management approach in the "systematic management" of innovative startup firms. *Journal of Business Venturing, 1*, 149-160.

Dean, B., Osland, A., & Solt, M. (2004, March). Lessons Learned in a First Business Plan Competition at San Jose State University. *Proceedings of the NCIIA 8th Annual Meeting: Education That Works: Invention, Innovation, and Entrepreneurship in Practice*, San Jose, CA.

DeSanctis, G., Wright, M., & Jiang, L. (2001). Building a global learning community. *Communications of the ACM, 44*, 80-83.

Feland, J. M. (2002). Building teammates: bringing better team skills to design courses. *Proceedings of the American Society for Engineering Education Annual Conference*.

Feland, J.M., & Fisher, C. (2002). Cramming twenty pounds more into a sophomore design tool kit: Increasing curricular loads on design students and enjoying it! *Proceedings of the American Society of Mechanical Engineers International Mechanical Engineering Congress and Exposition*.

Fleming, L. (2004). Perfecting cross-pollination. *Harvard Business Review, 82*(9), 22.

Horne, A.K., & Kristensen, T.L. (2004). The development of MyContents, an enriched electronic tables of contents service. *Portal Libraries and the Academy, 4*(2), 205-218.

Hull, F.M. (2004). A composite model of product development effectiveness: Application to services. *IEEE Transactions on Engineering Management, 51*(2), 162-172.

Kelly, L. (2004). *Problem based learning through mobile technology: External evaluation report*. San Jose, CA: SJSU & HP Mobility Project, San Jose State University.

Kiely, T. (1997). Innovation congregations, *Technology Review, 97*, 54-61.

Kock, N. (2002, May). Managing with web-based IT in mind. *Communications of the ACM, 45*, 102-107.

Legare, T. (2001). How Hewlett-Packard used virtual cross-functional teams to deliver healthcare industry solutions. *Journal of Organizational Excellence, 20*, 29-38.

Lin, B.W. (2004). Original equipment manufacturers (OEM) manufacturing strategy for network innovation agility: The case of Taiwanese manufacturing networks. *International Journal of Production Research, 42*(5), 943-957.

Luthje, C., & Herstatt, C. (2004). The lead user method: An outline of empirical findings and issues for future research. *R & D Management, 34*(5), 553-568.

McMahon, C.S., & Lavelle, J.P. (1998). Implementation of cross-disciplinary teams of business and engineering students for quality improvement projects. *Journal of Education for Business, 73*, 150-157.

Merritt, J. (2004a, March 15). Will your plan win a price? B-school business-plan competitions can yield good feedback—and seed money. *Business Week*.

Merrit, J. (2004b, November 1). Big plans on campus: These entrepreneurs used business plan competitions to supercharge their companies. What they learned and what you can learn from them. *Business Week*.

Osland, A., Roldan, M., Solt, M., & Dean, B.V. (2004). Description and Assessment of a Business Plan Competition and New Venture Fair at San Jose State University. E-Teams and Business Plan Competitions as Vehicles for Learning About Entrepreneurship. *Proceedings of the 2004 ASEE Annual Conference and Exposition*, Salt Lake City, UT.

Paramanathan, S., Farruk, C., Phaal, R., & Probert, D. (2004) Implementing industrial sustainability: The research issues in technology management. *R & D Management, 34*(5), 527-537.

Roldan, M., Solt, M., & Su, X. (2004, March). Fostering creativity and collaboration via cross-functional education. *Proceedings of the NCIIA 8th Annual Meeting*, San Jose, CA.

Rothsteing, P. (2002). When worlds collide: Integrated development with business and design students. *Design Management Journal, 13*, 62-69.

Rowe, C. (2004). The effect of accounting report structure and team structure on performance in cross-functional teams. *Accounting Review, 79*(4), 1153-1180.

Sauer, P.J. (2003, September 1). How to win big and get ahead fast. *Inc.*

Schofield, M.E., & Gregory, M. (2004). The impact of uncertainty on product introduction in dispersed environments. *Proceedings of the Institution of Mechanical Engineers Part B—Journal of Engineering Manufacture, 218* (7), 749-763.

Sethi, R., Smith, D., & Park, C. (2002, August). How to kill a team's creativity. *Harvard Business Review, 80*, 16-17.

Sherman, J.D. (2004). Optimal modes and levels of integration, and the identification of cross-functional coordination deficiencies in concurrent engineering. *IEEE Transactions on Engineering Management, 51*(3), 268-278.

University of Texas at Austin. (2003, April 23). Super bowl of business plan competitions lures MBA entrepreneurs from around the world. *Ascribe Higher Education News Service*.

Wilson, R., & Costlow, T. (1999). Rethinking education, with an emphasis on teams. *Electronic Engineering Times*, (1050), 130-138.

CHAPTER 15

THE ROLE OF THE STUDENT IN PROJECT LEARNING

Timothy C. Johnston

This chapter discusses how a teacher can use clear student roles and responsibilities to manage successful real world projects. Real world projects are an
active learning approach in which teams of students pursue real world
objectives as part of an academic course of study. "Co-production" roles for
students help assure that students learn from participating in the project:
(1) ready learner, (2) coachee, (3) contributor, (4) team member, and (5)
academic scholar. Students can share responsibility for important managerial tasks: engage a client (80% student responsibility), set project objectives
(60%), take action (70%), report on results (100%), and assess performance
and be assessed (20%). With clear roles and responsibilities, students may be
better equipped to deal with the less-structured, self-directed, ambiguous
nature of projects, and to complete a project successfully. Finally, opportunities to expand course boundaries with real world contacts other than a
course project are discussed.

INTRODUCTION

Many students enjoy learning with real world projects, when the projects
are managed well. But some students hate team projects, and do not
enjoy the learning experience. Teachers enjoy teaching with real world
projects, although they find that projects take more work than more tradi-

tional teaching methods. When a project doesn't go well, it can be a disaster for everyone. What can a teacher do to improve the chances that a project will be a good learning (and teaching) experience? This chapter discusses how a teacher can use clear student roles and responsibilities to manage successful real world projects.

Real world projects are an active learning approach in which teams of students pursue real world objectives as part of an academic course of study. Projects are designed to give students some real world experience. Yet students are not paid and are not employed in an ongoing relationship with the client organization. The primary objective of a team project is to support academic learning, not to accomplish client objectives. What student roles assure that he or she learns from participating in the project? This chapter discusses five student roles that are especially relevant to learning with team projects.

Also, how do the responsibilities of student and teacher change as the teaching model shifts from a passive, teacher-centered approach to a team project that features active, student-centered learning? Clear responsibilities can help prepare students for their active roles in a team project. A well-defined project process can minimize the ambiguity inherent in real world projects, and help the teacher maintain his or her course workload at a manageable level. This chapter addresses this question by discussing the responsibilities of student, teacher, and client in the project process.

First, a real world project is defined to provide a context for this chapter in the literature. Next, student roles in the project learning process, including ready learner, coachee, contributor, team member, and academic scholar are discussed. Students who embrace these roles are better equipped to avoid the pitfalls of team projects. Third, the responsibilities of a student in the project process are presented as a percentage of the work involved. Students who understand their responsibilities expect to take an active role in managing the project process. Finally, opportunities to expand course boundaries with real world contacts other than a course project are discussed.

This chapter primarily cites literature in the management and marketing fields, and specifically research that relates to the pragmatic aspect of teaching with projects. The emphasis here is more on the management of the project learning process than on the theory behind project learning. Even so, the author relies heavily on his own published research and teaching experiences, and therefore this chapter is not meant to be a comprehensive review of the literature on teaching business students with project learning. Some research in learning theory is mentioned to give context, but an exhaustive inventory of research on experiential or active learning is beyond the scope of this chapter.

REAL WORLD PROJECT DEFINED

What is a real world project? There are countless variations of student projects. For the purpose of this chapter, a working definition of real world project includes the following:

1. A real world project involves "active learning" and places additional responsibilities on a student as compared to passive learning.

The stereotype of passive learning is to receive knowledge and information through lecture, note taking and reading. Student learning is assessed through exams to identify knowledge gains. The student's role is to take notes, read a textbook, and sit for examinations. In contrast, an active learning, student-centered approach features the student as creator of knowledge, multi-way communication between students, teacher and others, and more responsibility for the student to deliver outcomes. Students are not assessed simply for their accumulation of knowledge, but for their skills in using and applying knowledge.

Active or experiential learning is based on the belief that learning occurs when students participate actively with an experience, and then reflect on what they learned. Active learning approaches are based on the theory that learners construct knowledge actively from their experiences (Dewey, 1938; Kolb, 1984). Learners need to take an active role in selecting and organizing information, constructing hypotheses, making decisions, and reflecting on their experiences to generalize their new knowledge to other situations (Coombs & Elden, 2004; Frontczak & Kelley, 2000).

Many terms have been used to denote active learning teaching approaches in the management literature, including project-based learning (Rhodes & Garrick, 2003; Smith & Dodds, 1997), problem-based learning (Duch, Groh, & Allen, 2001; Gijselaer, 1996), just-in-time teaching (Bolton, 1999; Watson & Temkin, 2000), action learning (Marsick & O'Neil, 1999), experiential learning (Bobbitt, Kemp, & Mayo, 2000; Bridges, 1999), service learning (Johnston, 2000; Petkus, 2000), live cases (Kennedy, Lawton, & Walker, 2001; Elam & Spotts, 2004), co-operative learning (Siciliano, 2001) reflective practice (Schon, 1983; Ayas & Zeniuk, 2001), and the case method (Barnes et al., 1994). From learning theorists one can add collaborative inquiry (Bray et al., 2000), cognitive apprenticeship (Collins, 1991; Jarvela, 1995; Hendricks, 2001) and transformational learning (Mezirow, 1991).

The terms may have more in common than they have differences. Different academic disciplines use different terms for essentially similar concepts. Coombs and Elden (2004, p. 525) searched discipline-specific databases of academic journals and found the most hits for "case method" in business, "cooperative learning" in education and psychology, and "problem-based learning" in medicine. These approaches all involve giving students more responsibility for their own education, by asking students to solve problems, often with teammates. The goal of active learning is for students to better retain the knowledge, transfer it to other situations, and "learn how to learn" (Norman & Schmidt, 1992).

The purpose of this chapter is not to present the many benefits of project learning and other active learning methods. The basic premise that traditional classroom activities focus too much on knowledge acquisition and technical skill development is assumed. Experiential learning approaches are advocated for teaching higher order thinking skills, by getting students to develop and apply new knowledge and skills and reflect on this experience. It also has related "learning to learn" benefits which are themselves important outcomes, and cannot only help students learn the "academic" course content, but can better teach team building and teamwork, communication and listening skills, and critical thinking and problem solving (Gremler et al., 2000; Hernandez, 2002; Bigelow, 2004).

2.   A real world project addresses a "live" objective from the real world.

Pursuing a project with real objectives is perhaps the best way for students to have real world experiences in an academic course. The primary benefit of a project is a safe environment in which to test out theory-to-practice learning, and an "apprenticeship" in which to develop skills. Real management problems for student projects are abundant, and can be found in not-for-profit organizations (Kloppenborg & Baucus, 2004) and small businesses (Kennedy et al., 2001). Coming up in this chapter is a discussion of sources of real world problems. In defining real world, the key distinction is between current problems in the field and simulated or historic case problems with realistic attributes.

3.   This chapter focuses on a project as conducted by a team of students, who receive academic credit.

The discussion is limited to team projects performed by undergraduate students as a course requirement. There are many opportunities for individual students to participate in real world projects outside of a course, such as internships and co-operative education jobs. The author believes that student teams pursue the majority of projects. One reason is that students working in teams learn teamwork skills that may benefit them after graduation. Another more practical reason is that it is easier for a teacher to supervise one project team with four members that to supervise four individual projects.

When students complete projects as a course requirement, they receive academic credit. Students typically receive academic credit for mastering a body of knowledge in their discipline. Course projects are thereby distinguished from extracurricular projects and work experiences: projects achieve course learning objectives and fulfill course requirements.

In summary, projects can be used as an active learning approach in which teams of students pursue real world objectives as part of an academic course of study. In addition to enhanced learning, projects have other benefits to the students and teacher. Many recruiters consider student experiences in internships and part-time jobs to be better indicators of future job performance than classroom experiences (Barr & McNeilly, 2002). Recruiters, when told about student experiences with real world projects, may consider them the next best thing to work experience. Real projects free the teacher from the need to design a realistic "context" within which to pose academic problems (Sherwood, 2004). The teacher has no worries about keeping real world projects relevant, as is the case for reality-based learning (Smith & Van Doren, 2004). The question then is how to make projects rich and meaningful as teaching and learning experiences for both professors and students. Students can assume roles that are important to the success of project learning (Johnston, 2005a), and these roles are discussed next.

STUDENT ROLES IN PROJECT LEARNING

Project learning is not without challenges: student unhappiness with working in teams, student and teacher resentment of increased workload, lack of academic rigor, and ambiguity aversion of students (Pfaff & Huddleston, 2003). The problems of project learning can be traced to its unique features: projects with unique objectives and ambiguous tasks. These are both a blessing and a curse.

They are a blessing because student projects with unique objectives and ambiguous tasks provide exposure to the characteristics of real world, post-graduation work projects. They are a curse because unique, ambiguous projects can cause discomfort and a perception of increased workload for students whose expectations are based on traditional passive learning techniques. Clear roles can mitigate some of these problems. What follows is a discussion of the student roles in project learning of (1) ready learner, (2) coachee, (3) contributor, (4) team member, and (5) academic scholar, shown in Table 15.1.

Student as Ready Learner

A student is ready to learn in a real world project if he or she (1) is qualified to participate in a team project, and (2) has realistic expectations about the process. Students are not fully formed people, much less fully

Table 15.1.   Student Roles in Project Learning

Student Role	Definition
Ready learner	Hold realistic expectations; is qualified
Coachee	Apply concepts; seek help when needed
Contributor	Contribute to classmates' learning experience
Team member	Participate in and learn teamwork
Academic scholar	Learn the academic course content

functioning managers. One cannot expect students to be qualified to successfully complete a project. But some students are more qualified or ready than others to participate in project learning. Students should be relatively mature, use good judgment, be willing to negotiate, and be willing to "go the extra mile" to get the job done (Papamarcos, 2002). Students should also have a desire to gain experience or to serve a client as sufficient reward for their extra effort.

Students should bring some technical, interpersonal, communication or creative thinking skills to the project. They should be willing to subordinate their personal preferences to the decisions of the team, and be willing to compromise in order to achieve a group consensus. Students should be trustworthy in terms of their ability to represent the university to their client, and to keep client information confidential as needed.

A teacher may not have the power to accept or deny enrollment in a course based on a student's qualifications to undertake a project. However, a teacher may communicate the qualifications so that students who feel unqualified may choose to enroll after they acquire skills. Students who are strongly averse to pursing the project as described may self-select out of the course or take another course option. In addition to screening students, a teacher can use pre-qualification data to form balanced teams, with less-qualified students joined with more-qualified students.

Students also need to begin a project with realistic expectations about the process. Students must replace their "traditional" course expectations with an awareness of the characteristics of a project. Real world problems are inherently ambiguous have no obvious action plan and no right or wrong answer. Many traditional college students have "ambiguity aversion." They are used to passive classroom teaching methods in which the process and outcomes of learning are fairly clear in advance. Indeed, the opportunity to learn about the ambiguity of real world projects, and how to deal with it, is a benefit to students of doing projects.

The author has often received student satisfaction ratings of courses that feature real world projects in a bimodal distribution. Many students have rated a course with real world projects highly, while many any other students rated it very low: "You either love it or hate it." Dissatisfied students cite a number of factors, including bad experiences with their team, a bad client, unhappiness with the project process, and the unexpectedly high amount of effort needed to complete the course.

A teacher can reduce post-project student dissatisfaction by managing pre-project expectations. The teacher should clearly describe his or her teaching philosophy regarding groups early in the course (preferably before the add-drop deadline). For example, Crustinger et al. (2004) described to students the "transference" technique, which transfers "responsibility for work and performance from the faculty member to the student." Transference claims that a teacher "can instill in students self-motivating attitudes and behaviors and help them develop a strong sense of ownership of their academic pursuits."

Each student should know in advance that his or her initiative will determine the success of the project, that one's performance (and grade) is linked with one's teammates, that the project process will be ambiguous, that the project outcome has no right or wrong answer, and that the project will involve a client who is a potential "wild card" in the process. Despite the warning, some students will not thrive in a real world project environment and will give the course a low rating. Students find it difficult to have realistic expectations about something that they have never experienced, such as a real world project. Another reason for low ratings is that students knew what to expect, and didn't like it, but took the course because it was their only option to earn credit.

In summary, students should have the opportunity to self select, or be selected, to participate in a real world project based on their aptitudes and preferences. And students should be told up-front about the challenging features of a project, so that the reality of project learning will not clash violently with their expectations.

Student as Coachee

The role of the student in project learning is inextricably linked to the role of the teacher. Therefore, any discussion of student roles must also address teacher roles. A teacher can perform the roles of expert, formal authority, personal model, facilitator, delegator, and more in the classroom (Grasha, 1994).

The role of teacher as coach is associated with real world projects (Bolton, 1999). A coach inspires, models, guides, trains, challenges, sponsors, and helps the "coachee" succeed by increasing motivation, enhancing abilities, and providing support (Longenecker & Pinkel, 1997). O'Neil and Hopkins (2002) define the teacher as coach role as having three elements: building relationships; increasing students' self-discovery and self-knowledge through co-inquiry; and seeking to combine theory with practice via a pragmatic orientation (p. 404).

What is the role of the student as coachee in project learning? Based on the O'Neil and Hopkins model, the student as coachee role includes: willingness to be part of a relationship of dialogue with the teacher; willingness to pursue the project as a "co-inquirer" with the teacher; and willingness to apply learning to the real world project.

First, the student must seek instruction and advice on the project from the teacher. It is the student's responsibility to ask the teacher for help. The dialogue approach to teaching emphasizes the "interactive, cooperative, and relational aspects of teaching and learning" (Tiberius, 1986). Teacher and students must have an ongoing dialogue, especially since the design of the project may "emerge" over time, and the teacher only has periodic input. This is the basis for the "just-in-time" approach to teaching, where the teacher provides guidance at strategic intervals during the semester (Bolton, 1999).

Second, the students and teacher should approach the project as "co-inquirers." Co-inquiry was originally conceived as a process by which a researcher and participant jointly reveal knowledge. Teacher and students are co-inquirers because each project is unique and has no right or wrong answers. Teacher and students may contribute ideas, and draw different conclusions from the project experience and learn different things. The "co-inquiry" process requires that students shed their traditional roles of receivers of knowledge and teachers to avoid being transmitters of knowledge.

Finally, students must take responsibility for applying course content to the real world project. The students are most qualified to apply theories to their project because they are the "experts" on their team's client and needs. The process of bridging the gap between academic theory and real world application not only helps students to understand the theory, but also gives students a competence to apply theories to future problems. The teacher as coach facilitates this process. In summary, a student as coachee is ready to seek instruction and advice from the instructor as a "co-inquirer," and to apply academic course content to their client's needs and to project objectives.

The Student as Contributor

What about the extra work to the teacher associated with managing a class of team projects? Depending on the course format, there may be a lot to do. A teacher may become consumed with administering the course, at the expense of teaching. A teacher works harder when using experiential teaching techniques, such as project learning, than with passive methods. This is a robust research finding and is a given in this discussion.

One option is to delegate administrative overhead tasks to students. Classrooms are full of talented students. It stands to reason that a teacher who can harness the talent and energies of students to contribute to a course will create a better learning experience. It is a waste to not involve the talents of students in the learning process.

The author was motivated by this untapped pool of talent to involve his students in the "production" of learning. Cahn (2000) discussed "co-production" in the context of getting social services recipients to participate in the process by which they are served. Co-production relies on a non-monetary market in which each person's "time in service" is the currency. It begins with the belief that each person can provide a valuable service to someone else. The co-production concept is not limited to the not-for-profit context. Marketers have found that consumers can improve a product or service by participating in its production or delivery (Song & Adams, 1993).

The author has asked student teams to complete a "contribution" portion of their course grade (about 6% of the total grade). Although technically an assignment, the term "contribution" better described its purpose—to add value to everyone's learning experience (Johnston, 1996, pp. 6-7). For example, in marketing principles classes, student teams coordinated the logistics of a trade show, created flyers and cultivated publicity, and represented their clients to the public. In marketing research classes, students organized a conference, compiled project abstracts into a program, coordinated presentations, and presented their findings to the public in "poster" sessions. Students also helped their peers to learn the course subject matter, by publishing study guides and presenting review sessions. Essentially the entire class of students became a second client to each team, and each team found an opportunity to contribute to the needs of their classmates.

Students can also use the Internet to "add value" for their classmates. The author has engaged students in contributing to an online study guide for an e-commerce course (Johnston, 2002), using free, web-based "blog" software. The ability to publish work online enabled students to make contributions to the class, promoted peer learning, and encouraged quality work. Teachers have shied away from reaping the benefits of publishing student work online because of the effort needed to create and maintain class web pages. The blog method requires simple software, minimal training, and delegates the task of posting information to the students. Also, a course management system (e.g., BlackBoard) makes it relatively simple for a student to post documents and PowerPoint files to an online discussion board and make them available to all students, without the need to create a class blog.

In summary, students can contribute to the course by performing administrative overhead tasks, which by themselves can be valuable real world experiences. Students can help their peers learn course material. Students are motivated because the product of their efforts has real value to their peers, and will be displayed for everyone to see. By engaging students as contributors to the course, the teacher can harness student talents to improve the learning experience. The teacher can then focus more on teaching and less on administrative tasks.

Student as Team Member

Students may learn teamwork as an incidental by-product of the project process, or teamwork may be the subject of the academic course. Many of the "team learning" concepts discussed in this chapter were pioneered in organizational behavior courses in which teamwork was an important academic topic (Michaelsen et al., 2004).

The student and teacher share responsibility for developing effective teams. Researchers have criticized the notion that cohesive teams will form naturally (Deeter-Schmelz, Kennedy, & Ramsey, 2002) or that skills will necessarily transfer between student projects and real work teams (Ettington & Camp, 2002). Holmer (2001) suggested that students may learn "skilled incompetence" by participating in poorly designed team projects. Some researchers have called for teachers to reexamine their use of teams in courses because of serious pedagogical problems (McCorkle et al., 1999). Methods for forming teams and teaching teamwork are beyond the scope of this chapter (see Peterson, 2004; Williams, Beard, & Rymer, 1991; Siciliano, 2001; Wood, 2003; Stinson & Milter, 1996; Wilkerson & Gijselaers, 1996).

The best asset of a student is perhaps a good attitude toward working in a team. The individual student's role as team member should include a willingness to participate in the team, build up the team, and learn teamwork. "Free-riding" is one of the biggest problems in project learning (Joyce, 1999; Ashraf, 2004), and the ways that free-riding has been addressed are beyond the scope of this chapter. One strategy is for the teacher to stress the responsibility of each student to subordinate his or her preferences to the objectives of the team, and to work for the good of the team. There is no substitute for a team-player attitude, because mechanisms to control free-riding are imperfect and the controls themselves can be distracting. If students accept their team member roles, then free-riding controls become unnecessary.

Student as Academic Scholar

The student "scholar" role means that a student must learn the academic course content, and not just participate in a project for its own sake. How can the teacher assure that students are mastering the academic course content? One option is to combine the full range of academic content of a course with an additional project. The result can be a course workload that is far beyond the norm, which can cause resentment among students and burnout of the teacher.

Another option is to accept that students will learn a narrow, possible atypical set of skills and knowledge that are associated with their team project. Projects may contain unique objectives; hence students assigned to different projects may have very different learning experiences. The lack of standardization of project learning experiences is a potential drawback, especially when students are expected to master a defined domain of knowledge in a course.

A third option is to make learning the subject matter part of the student's role. Society is becoming more do-it-yourself (DIY) oriented. For example, people often prefer to make their own travel plans and place their own stock trades online. Computer networks have also contributed to the DIY trend in higher education. Students often prefer self-directed tasks to mediated tasks at school, such as paying fees, planning course schedules, and registering for classes. Course management software programs in particular (BlackBoard, WebCT, etc.) have encouraged self-directed learning in higher education. A teacher can set up a schedule of online assessments to encourage students to read and master broad subject matter, and hold them accountable for progress.

The author found that 90% of students in a study preferred online to pen-and-paper homework assessments (Johnston, 2004b). The students had experienced both online and pen-and-paper methods (in a previous course with the same teacher). Also, a large majority (86%) believed that their homework performance would be better with the online method than with the pen-and-paper method. The actual homework performance of students who used the online method was substantially similar to that of students who used the pen-and-paper method.

The online homework method provides important benefits to students. Students like to have control over the homework process. They like the capability of completing their homework at their convenience, and to work ahead of the class schedule. They like the ability to get immediate feedback, see their grades in the grade book, and return to view the assessment later. The online method automates the repetitive tasks that add little value to the teaching process. Moving these repetitive tasks outside of the class time period enables students and teacher to do more interesting things in the classroom, such as work on a project. Students' strong preference for online to pen-and-paper homework suggests a "hybrid" online/project learning course format.

Another option to ensure that students learn course content is to make it part of the team's role and keep the do-it-yourself tasks offline. Michaelsen and Black (1994) presented a DIY process for combining individual and team input into assessments. The author has used this method to encourage students to read and master academic subject matter, while using only a small percentage of class time. The author assigned a schedule of textbook chapter readings. On a chapter's due date, each student was asked to complete a brief pencil-and-paper quiz (10 multiple choice questions). After submitting his or her responses, each student met with his or her teammates and completed the quiz again, and together they submitted one team response.

Students usually resolved any uncertainties about the questions within the team, and occasionally "appealed" questions to the teacher. Both scores counted toward a student's grade, and the team's score usually matched or bested the individual scores. The team meeting showed the degree to which individual members had prepared, and the importance of everyone's input on important decisions. A student who failed to prepare risked receiving a low individual score and eventually a low peer evaluation.

The team-learning homework method gave students an opportunity to work together successfully as a team early on in the course. It also made expectations transparent and tangible. Another benefit is that it encouraged students to make progress on learning the subject matter, while spending the majority of their time on the team project. As with the online method, the unsecured nature of giving quizzes to teams can raise questions about the authenticity of the work and free-riding behavior. For both methods the author gave exams in a relatively secure classroom setting so that students could demonstrate their individual mastery of the course content.

Both the online and team-learning methods encouraged students to make progress on learning the subject matter, without taking much class time, and thereby freed up time to work on the team project. These approaches to teaching course content are consistent with the project learning philosophy of giving students more responsibility for, and control over, their learning.

In summary, a student as ready learner has considered his or her aptitudes and preferences, and chosen to fully accept the challenges of a real world project and the responsibility for its success. A student as coachee is ready to seek instruction and advice from the instructor as a "co-inquirer," and to apply academic course content to the real world project objectives.

A student as contributor is willing to contribute his or her talents to improve the learning experience of the class as a whole. A student as team member is willing to participate in the team, build up the team, and learn teamwork. And a student as academic scholar is willing to take responsibility for learning the course material.

Students who understand and accept these roles should be better equipped to deal with the less-structured, self-directed nature of projects, and to complete a project successfully. After discussing student roles in team projects, this chapter next presents a model for allocating specific project responsibilities to students.

STUDENT RESPONSIBILITIES IN THE PROJECT PROCESS

What are appropriate responsibilities of students and teacher in the project process? A teacher who clearly delineates a student's responsibilities in the project process may minimize the student's "ambiguity aversion." Another strategy is for the teacher to set the expectation that the student is responsible to deal with the ambiguity. Clear responsibilities prepare a student to expect a more active role than is typical in non-project courses. Bacon, Stewart, and Silver (1999) found that the clarity of instructions to the team positively affected student experiences. Well-defined responsibilities can also help the teacher maintain his or her workload and course overhead at a manageable level. In addition, teaching students explicitly about managing group work (group process and group task structuring) is beneficial. See Table 15.2 for the proportion of teacher, student, and client responsibility for each step in the project process.

This project model is not unique, but is typical, and the responsibility percentages for each role were derived mainly from the author's experience (Johnston, 2005b). The project steps are (1) set learning goals, (2) engage a client, (3) set project objectives, (4) implementation, (5) report results, and (6) assess performance. What follows is a discus-

Table 15.2.   Student, Teacher, and Client Responsibilities

Set learning goals	100% Teacher
Engage client	80% Student, 10% Teacher, 10%Client
Set objectives	60% Student, 10% Teacher, 30% Client
Implementation	70% Student, 10% Teacher, 20% Client
Report results	100% Student
Assess performance	20% Student, 70% Teacher, 10% Client

sion of each step, with suggestions for the proportion of responsibility that should be given to the student, teacher, and client. The bias of this chapter is to assign as much responsibility for the project as possible to the students.

For example, a learning goal in a marketing course may be for students to learn to "think like a marketer." This involves taking a dynamic, action-intervention mindset and applying a linear, step-by-step approach to an ambiguous problem. In doing so a student learns the logic of management, which involves analyzing seemingly chaotic information, diagnosing a problem, making a decision, and taking action. The project learning process is designed to foster theory-to-practice connections, and the student has the responsibility to make these connections within a framework designed by the teacher.

Set Learning Goals

A teacher typically has 100% of the responsibility to set the learning goals of a course of study. The project is generally one part of a course, which may in turn be part of a larger plan of study (e.g., a degree and major field). Learning goals are different from the project objectives, which will be discussed later. Learning goals are "metagoals" which refer to the reasons for doing a project rather than the outcomes of a project.

A teacher sets a learning goal for a project to link a real world problem or task with course subject matter topics. For example, the author defined learning goals for a marketing management course as "Upon completion of the course, each student should be able to do the following: (1) identify and describe the marketing strategy of an organization; (2) create and implement a promotion plan for an organization; (3) contribute to a team to solve problems in the pursuit of marketing opportunities; and (4) use proper communication techniques to talk to a business person" (Johnston, 1996).

With the exception of relatively rare self-directed courses, the student's role in setting learning goals for a course of study is limited. In setting learning goals, the teacher walks a fine line between setting tangible goals that tie the project to a domain of academic knowledge defined by the course, and letting students construct the particular objectives of each project that serve these goals as they emerge in the process. The more "constructivist" approach to letting students set project objectives is discussed later.

Engage a Project Client

Students may take 80% of the responsibility of engaging a client, which includes identifying a prospect, approaching and setting an appointment, interviewing and persuading a prospect, and obtaining a client engagement letter. By meeting with students and making the commitments embodied in the client letter, the client has perhaps 10% of the responsibility during the engagement process. The teacher also has about 10% of the responsibility, which involves reviewing the engagement letter and verifying that the client fits the recruiting guidelines.

In some cases the teacher should obtain the client. If the teacher has very specific project tasks in mind, then he or she could recruit a client who needs these tasks performed. If the teacher knows of a willing client who could provide multiple projects for a few student teams, then it would be simpler to use the teacher's contact than for students to recruit clients. Generally, students can obtain their own clients. The process of recruiting a client is itself a valuable real world experience, because students get to approach and persuade a prospective client to join the project.

The teacher can guide the students by providing general client selection guidelines and a deadline. For example, the author defined client selection criteria for a team project as follows: (1) Client location is convenient for team-client meetings; (2) Client product or service has appeal to the campus community, and the client would benefit by being promoted to the community; (3) Client product or service has some "sizzle" appeal to generate excitement between students and prospective customers, and community members would benefit by seeing the promotion; (4) Client contact person is an adult (not a student), and serves a managerial role and can make decisions to spend money and take action; (5) Client contact person is interested in and willing to spend time with students; and (6) Client product or service fits with the theme of the trade show (Johnston, 1996, p. 51).

The author has not allowed student teams to recruit other students or student organizations as clients. This is to encourage students to get out of their comfort zone and into the real world, and to prevent "fake" projects. This may not be a concern when the teacher is supervising a few teams.

The campus community can be a source of clients, again depending on the course topic. For example, the author has supervised projects with university departments. Most organizations, including profit, not-for-profit, and government, have "customers." They need to understand and communicate with their customers, and hence have market research and promotion needs. These needs can be translated into objectives for marketing projects. Most organizations have employees, and hence have personnel management issues. All organizations have a mission and a strategy, whether they realize it or not. Finding organizations with needs that dovetail with business course content is not difficult.

A successful recruiting process should yield a "client engagement letter" on the client's letterhead. The client should verify in the letter that he or she understands the client role and has realistic expectations for the project. It is good practice for the teacher to reply to the engagement letter on university letterhead. A letter adds a touch of formality to the assessment, provides an opportunity to state the commitments of the students and teacher to the project, and provides contact information to the client.

Determine Project Objectives

Students are mainly responsible, with about 60% of the responsibility for setting project objectives and tasks. The client has about 30% of the responsibility, to work with students to ensure that project objectives meet the needs of the organization. The teacher has about 10% of the responsibility for determining each project's objectives.

It has been said, "defining the problem is half of the solution." A successful real world project starts with objectives that are important to a client and achievable by students within an academic term. The teacher can simplify the process by clearly specifying the criteria for objectives, offering a menu from which students and client can choose objectives, or providing examples of objectives. When a teacher intervenes to modify proposed objectives it is usually to make them more focused and measurable. Students often submit objectives that are vague, far-reaching, and not practical to pursue.

The teacher can provide generic objectives that reinforce the course learning goals. The students and client can then decide how to apply the objectives to the client's needs, and how to implement an "action plan" and measure the results. For example, the author has defined a generic objective for a market research class as "perform a market survey." The students and clients then decided on specific objectives such as the market of interest (current customers, non-customers, target segments, etc.) and the information desired (customer satisfaction, product usage, customer perceptions about competitors, etc.). This approach yielded projects with objectives and tasks that were unique, yet aligned with the academic topics of a market research course (survey instrument development, sampling, data analysis, etc.).

The author defined a generic objective for a marketing principles class as "promote your client at a trade show." Tasks included interviewing the client, conducting a survey, creating a flyer, and developing and implementing a promotion plan. The role of students was to determine the promotion need of the client, craft the message and materials, and stage a "booth" at a trade show. Although teams started with "generic" objectives and tasks, they produced unique promotional efforts for their client and thereby had a unique learning experience.

In some situations, students can be an appropriate source of their own projects. Students in a marketing research course applied the principles of marketing research to the course itself, to identify what student "customers" wanted from the course (Bridges, 1999). Students in an organizational behavior (OB) course applied OB concepts to solve problems that students had within their work, school, or home groups (Miller, 2004). Entrepreneurship students raised funds and recruited members for student organizations (Daly, 2001).

For example, the author has taught students to sell items (of their choice) on eBay. By listing an auction a student can experience first-hand the issues that face all e-commerce merchants, such as choosing products, crafting offers and web pages, and receiving payments and fulfilling orders. Working with the eBay web site gives students two perspectives on the e-commerce customer interface—the perspective of a seller creating an auction for a good, and the perspective of a buyer of selling services from eBay (Johnston, 2003b). Each student learned from his or her unique experience as well as from observing the collected experiences of classmates.

Implementation

Students can be responsible for 70% of the implementation, clients 20%, and the teacher can have 10% of the responsibility. The students' role is to satisfy the client, so most of their interaction should be with the client and within the team. Depending on the scope of the project, the teacher may have infrequent or no direct contact with the client in the course of the project.

What is implementation? Implementation is the process of pursing the project objectives and tasks, and the outcomes of that pursuit (i.e., carrying out the action plan). Students generally have to meet as a team several times, and meet with the client a few times as well. Setting up meetings with a busy client and equally busy students is a challenge in itself and a useful real world experience. Teachers have found that allocating class time for some team meetings help to mitigate the scheduling problem and improve the team experience (Papamarcos, 2002; McKendall, 2000).

Although students are primarily responsible for implementation, the teacher has an important role to keep students on task. The teacher's role in general is to set interim deadlines, review drafts of work, and hold students accountable for progress. With any luck the student teams will be "self-managed" and the teacher will need to intervene only when asked for advice or to provide occasional discipline and motivation to stalled teams. The teacher also is responsible for teaching team management issues.

This brings up a related question: Should the teacher allow the student team to fail? Consider two types of failure—failure of project and failure of effort. If "project failure" is defined as failing to meet the project goals, then yes, the team should be allowed to fail. Students can reflect on an otherwise failed project and successfully learn what to do differently in the future.

Students who do not pursue the project (a failure of effort) and are not open to coaching (discussed later in this chapter) should see that the consequences of these behaviors are failure. Like an athlete, a student must be willing to experiment, reflect on outcomes, alter behaviors, and strive for improved performance (Bolton, 1999). For a teacher to intervene with a team of slackers and force them to perform or "rescue" the team would be doing the students a disservice.

Report on Results

Students have 100% of the responsibility to report on the results of their project. Assuming that students began the project with clear, measurable objectives, then reporting on the team's accomplishments is a fairly straightforward task. Often students produce a written report on a project. A written report format is universally understood and easy to handle for everyone involved.

Students can get focused on the report itself to the detriment of its contents, however. In addition, even real world written reports sometimes fail to find an audience. An option is to downplay the report and emphasize other "deliverables" instead, such as oral presentations, posters, models, etc. Students who display or present their work in a class or public forum can get instant feedback and recognition.

Using oral presentations, poster sessions, or trade show booths to report results also creates a hard deadline for students. Students cannot slip a presentation under the teacher's office door like a written report. Students can also present results to a wider audience, including client representatives, expert judges, and other students. In addition, students can learn a lot by viewing the work of their peers. For example, teachers have found the trade show format useful for integrating classes (Bobbitt et al., 2000) and teaching large classes (Taylor, 1998).

Assess Performance

The teacher is responsible for 70% of performance assessment; the student contributes 20%, and the client 10%. The teacher has most of the responsibility for assessing student performance on a project. The teacher's effort to assess student performance in a course with a project may be greater than in a course without a project. The teacher may need to assess the quality of work of several student teams who served unique clients.

Ultimately a student receives an individual course grade. Should a student receive an individual grade for his or her contribution to the team's performance? If the team members receive a common grade, how much should the grade count toward a student's individual course grade? Should students grade each other?

One option is to make the team project grade a small proportion of the individual course grade, but this can cause a problem when the team project work is a large proportion of the course work. McKendall (2000) said students should receive a team grade for the team output of a project, and to assign individual grades is to defeat the concept of teamwork. According to Kerr (1975) team work should have team rewards.

Student self-evaluation, peer evaluation, client evaluation, and teacher evaluation can provide valuable feedback to the student. A student may have some responsibility for evaluating his or her own performance. Self-evaluation can prompt students to reflect on their learning, and reflection is an important element of active learning (Ayas & Zenuik, 2001).

Students can experience the real world task of evaluating others by giving feedback to their peers. The prospect of receiving peer feedback can be a source of learning as well as an incentive to contribute to the team and a disincentive to free-riding behavior. Chen and Lou (2004) found that students saw peer evaluations as valuable if the evaluations were used to determine grades. Peer evaluations can be used to reduce intragroup conflict and remedy an uneven distribution of workload.

The results from research on student preferences regarding peer evaluations are mixed. Chapman and Van Auken Stuart (2001) found that "students were more likely to have positive attitudes about group work if they had instructors who ... used methods to evaluate individual performance within the group (e.g., peer evaluations)." Bacon, Stewart, and Silver (1999) found that the use of peer evaluations was negatively associated with student ratings of "good" team experiences.

Finally, the client has a role in evaluating how well the students served his or her needs in completing the project. Client feedback can be the "acid test" of the project's real world contribution. While this may seem like a lot of evaluations, the process is consistent with a real world "360 degree feedback" system (Lepsinger & Lucia, 1997).

In summary, a student shares responsibility for important managerial tasks in a real world project: engage a client (80% of the responsibility), set project objectives (60%), take action (70%), report on results (100%), and assess performance and be assessed (20%). The teacher has most of the balance of the responsibilities, with the client playing a supporting role. Clear responsibilities may minimize a student's "ambiguity aversion," and set the expectation that the student is responsible for dealing with the ambiguity. Students can expect a more active role than is typical in non-project courses, and the teacher can maintain his or her workload and course overhead at a manageable level. What follows is a discussion of how the project learning model can be extended beyond the boundaries of a single course.

LEARNING BEYOND CLASSROOM WALLS

The solution to real world problems is not always found within one "department" in an organization. The tools to address real world problems are not always found in one academic course, either. These multifaceted problems can give teachers the opportunity to teach an interdisciplinary approach to problem solving, and for projects to transcend the bounds of one course or one academic term.

For example, the Greenway Project was a "campus-wide" project that engaged students from a variety of academic programs in the support of a common goal to build a greenway (Johnston, 2004c). Students surveyed the route, prepared a preliminary engineering cost estimate, raised money, designed brochures and signage, and obtained publicity for events as course projects, internships, and extracurricular activities. The students contributed to a complex real world project that will ultimately make a significant and visible benefit to the community.

Project learning is ideal for teaching in an interdisciplinary team format. Dickens and Watkins (1999) discuss the process and goals of "action research," defined (in the tradition of Kurt Lewin) as "cross-functional teams who address deep-rooted organizational issues through recurring cycles of action and reflection." The role of cross-functional student teams can be viewed as assisting the client in "experimenting" with changes in the client organization, to study the results and suggest subsequent interventions (Coghlan, 2001).

Teachers have used projects in interdisciplinary settings, including entrepreneurship and marketing (Kennedy, Lawton & Walker, 2001), production and marketing (Darian & Coopersmith, 2001), marketing and bioresearch (McKeage et al., 1999), and marketing, principles of selling, and sales management (Bobbitt et al., 2000). Other teachers have used technology to develop team projects that transcend geographic boundaries, such as between students in the United States and Germany (Kaiser, Tullar, & McKowen, 2000).

Project learning would not fit with the goals of many courses, and it is "expensive" in many ways. It is more feasible in many situations for a teacher to use written and video cases, problems, and simulations to bring reality-based problem-solving experiences to students. For example, a teacher may use guest speakers or an executive-in-residence class, rather than a class project, to connect students and practitioners. Students are not going to learn teamwork or problem-solving from listening to a manager speak, but they can learn what employers want in employees, access a network for potential job opportunities, and inform their expectations with the realities of the working world. Teachers can also learn some new real world examples and up-to-date career advice for students (Johnston, 2004a).

As another example, the author used a case-like exercise to teach Brazilians and Americans about cross cultural negotiations. After the exercise, participants were more aware of culture and its effect on the negotiation process (Johnston, 2003a; Johnston & Burton, 2002). A realistic exercise provides "experience" at low cost. Although a negotiation exercise does not make one a veteran international negotiator, it may teach one to avoid a costly and embarrassing fundamental mistake. A person can become oriented to the cross-culture negotiation process without the risk of real consequences—costly business errors, damaged relations, or missed opportunities.

In summary, teachers are not limited to a course-length team project to bring real world experiences to students. Teachers can expand student-practitioner connections to transcend courses or disciplines, or create limited interactions within a classroom setting.

CONCLUSION

Real world projects are an active learning approach in which teams of students pursue real world objectives as part of an academic course of study. This chapter presented special "co-production" roles for students, to assure that students learn from participating in the project: (1) ready learner, (2) coachee, (3) contributor, (4) team member, and (5) academic scholar. Students who understand and accept these roles should be better equipped to deal with the less-structured, self-directed nature of projects, and to complete a project successfully.

This chapter presented a model for allocating student responsibilities in real world projects. Students can share responsibility for important managerial tasks: engage a client (80% student responsibility), set project objectives (60%), take action (70%), report on results (100%), and assess performance and be assessed (20%). The teacher has most of the balance of the responsibilities, with the client playing a supporting role. With clear responsibilities, students may be better equipped to deal with the ambiguity of a project. Students can expect a more active role than is typical in non-project courses, and the teacher can maintain his or her administrative workload at a manageable level.

Teaching with real world projects has benefits and challenges. The benefits are great, and a teacher can minimize the challenges and costs by defining clear roles and responsibilities in the project learning experience. A team project with well-defined roles and responsibilities can be good learning experience for students, teacher, and client. Future research can test more formally the hypotheses that clear student roles and responsibilities in project learning enhance student learning and satisfaction.

REFERENCES

Ashraf, M. (2004). A critical look at the use of group projects as a pedagogical tool. *Journal of Education for Business, 79*(4), 213-216.

Ayas, K., & Zeniuk, N. (2001). Project-based learning: Building communities of reflective practitioners. *Management Learning, 32*, 61-76.

Bacon, D.R. Stewart, K.A., & Silver, W.S. (1999). Lessons from the best and worst student team experiences: How a teacher can make the difference. *Journal of Management Education, 23*, 467-488.

Barnes, L.B., Christensen, C.R., & Hansen, A.J. (1994). *Teaching and the case method: Text, cases, and readings* (3rd ed.). Cambridge, MA: Harvard Business School Press.

Barr, T.F., & McNeilly, K.M. (2002). The value of students' classroom experiences from the eyes of the recruiter: Information, implications, and recommendations for marketing educators. *Journal of Marketing Education, 24*, 168-173.

Bigelow, J.D. (2004). Using problem-based learning to develop skills in solving unstructured problems. *Journal of Management Education, 28*, 591-609.

Bobbitt, L.M., Inks, S.A., Kemp, K.J., & Mayo, D.T. (2000, April). Integrating marketing courses to enhance team-based experiential learning. *Journal of Marketing Education, 22*, 15-24.

Bolton, M.K, (1999). The role of coaching in student teams: A "just-in-time" approach to learning. *Journal of Management Education, 23*, 233-250.

Bray, J.N., Lee, J., Smith, L.L., & Yorks, L. (2000). *Collaborative inquiry in practice: Action, reflection and meaning making.* Thousand Oaks, CA: Sage.

Bridges, E. (1999). Experiential learning and customer needs in the undergraduate marketing research course. *Journal of Marketing Education, 21,* 51-59.

Cahn, E.S. (2000). *No more throw-away people: The co-production imperative.* Washington, DC: Essential Books.

Chapman, K.J., & Stuart Van Auken (2001). Creating positive group project experiences: An examination of the role of the instructor on students' perceptions of group projects. *Journal of Marketing Education, 23,* 117-127.

Chen, Y., & Lou, H. (2004). Students' perceptions of peer evaluation: An expectancy perspective. *Journal of Education for Business, 79*(5), 275-280.

Coghlan, D. (2001). Insider action research projects: Implications for practising managers. *Management Learning, 32,* 49-60.

Collins, A. (1991). Cognitive apprenticeship: Making things visible. *American Educator, 15*(3), 6-11, 38-46.

Coombs, G., & Elden, M. (2004, October). Introduction to the Special Issue: Problem-based learning as social inquiry—PBL and management education. *Journal of Management Education, 28,* 523-535.

Crustinger, C.A., Pookulangara, S., Tran, G., & Duncan, K. (2004). Collaborative service learning: A winning proposition for industry and education. *Journal of Family and Consumer Sciences, 96*(3), 47-52.

Daly, S. (2001, December). Student-operated Internet businesses: True experiential learning in entrepreneurship and retail management. *Journal of Marketing Education, 23,* 204-215.

Darian, J.C., & Coopersmith, L. (2001). Integrated marketing and operations team projects: Learning the importance of cross-functional cooperation. *Journal of Marketing Education, 23,* 128-135.

Deeter-Schmelz, D.R., Kennedy, K.N., & Ramsey, R.P. (2002). Enriching our understanding of student team effectiveness. *Journal of Marketing Education, 24,* 114-124.

Dewey, J. (1938). *How we think.* Boston: D. C. Heath.

Dickens, L., & Watkins, K. (1999). Action research: Rethinking Lewin. *Management Learning, 30,* 127-140.

Duch, B.J., Groh, S.E., & Allen, D.E. (2001). Why problem-based learning: A case study of institutional change in undergraduate education. In B.J. Duch, S.E. Groh, & D.E. Allen (Eds.), *The power of problem-based learning: A practical "how to" for teaching undergraduate courses in any discipline* (pp. 3-12). Sterling, VA: Stylus Publishing.

Elam, E.L.R., & Spotts, H.E. (2004). Achieving marketing curriculum integration: A live case study approach. *Journal of Marketing Education, 26,* 50-65.

Ettington, D.R., & Camp, R.R. (2002). Facilitating transfer of skills between group projects and work teams. *Journal of Management Education, 26,* 356-379.

Frontczak, N.T., & Kelley, C.A. (2000). The editor's corner: Special Issue on experiential learning in marketing education. *Journal of Marketing Education, 22,* 3-4.

Gijselaers, W.H. (1996). Connecting problem-based practices with educational theory. In L. Wilkerson & W. H. Gijselaers (Eds.), *Bringing problem-based learn-*

ing to higher education: Theory and practice (pp. 13-22). San Francisco: Jossey-Bass.

Grasha, A.F. (1994). A matter of style: The teacher as expert, formal authority, personal model, facilitator, and delegator. *College Teaching, 42*, 142-149.

Gremler, D.D., Hoffman, K.D., Keaveney, S.M., & Wright, L.K. (2000). Experiential learning exercises in services marketing courses. *Journal of Marketing Education, 22*, 35-44.

Hendricks, C.C. (2001). Teaching causal reasoning through cognitive apprenticeship: What are results from situated learning? *Journal of Educational Research, 94*(5), 302-311.

Hernandez, S.A. (2002). Team learning in a marketing principles course: Cooperative structures that facilitate active learning and higher level thinking. *Journal of Marketing Education, 24*, 73-85.

Holmer, L.L. (2001). Will we teach leadership or skilled incompetence? The challenge of student project teams. *Journal of Management Education, 25*, 590-605.

Jarvela, S. (1995). Socioemotional aspects of student learning in a cognitive-apprenticeship environment. *Instructional science, 26*(6), 439-472.

Johnston, T.C. (1996). *Marketing management: The hands-on/team learning approach.* Knoxville, TN: Self published.

Johnston, T.C. (2000). The case for service learning in marketing education. *Marketing Management Association 2000 Educators' Conference Proceedings*, 16-18.

Johnston, T.C. (2002). Teaching with a weblog: How to post student work online. *Proceedings of the Academy of Educational Leadership*, 33-38.

Johnston, T.C. (2003a). International marketing role play negotiation: A case study of Brazil. *Journal of Business and Behavioral Sciences, 10*(1), 122-131.

Johnston, T.C. (2003b). Using eBay to teach e-commerce. *Proceedings of the American Society of Business and Behavioral Sciences, 10*(1), 700-706.

Johnston, T.C. (2004a). An executive in residence business course design. *Proceedings of the Academy of Educational Leadership*, 39-44.

Johnston, T.C. (2004b). Online homework assessments: Benefits and drawbacks for students. *Academy of Educational Leadership Journal, 8*(3), 29-41.

Johnston, T.C. (2004c). A Campus-wide teaching scheme: The Greenway Project. *Proceedings of the International Academy of Business and Public Administration Disciplines, 1*(2), paper #163.

Johnston, T.C. (2005a). Student roles in team learning. *Proceedings of the Teaching and Learning Conference*, Article #247.

Johnston, T.C. (2005b). A model of teacher, student, and client responsibilities in team projects. *Proceedings of the Teaching and Learning Conference*, Article #246.

Johnston, T.C., & Burton, J. (2002). Using a negotiation simulation to teach cross-culture skills. In S. Hall & M. Martinez (Eds.), *Proceedings of the American Society of Business and Behavioral Sciences Conference* (pp. 167-175).

Joyce, W.B. (1999). On the free-rider problem in cooperative learning. *Journal of Education for Business, 75*, 271-74.

Kaiser, P.R., Tullar, W.L., & McKowen, D. (2000). Student team projects by internet. *Business Communication Quarterly, 63*(4), 75-82.

Kennedy, E.J., Lawton, L., & Walker, E. (2001). The case for using live cases: Shifting the paradigm in marketing education. *Journal of Marketing Education, 23*, 145-151.

Kerr, S. (1975). On the folly of rewarding A while hoping for B. *Academy of Management Journal, 18*, 769-783.

Kloppenborg, T.J., & Baucus, M.S. (2004). Project management in local nonprofit organizations: Engaging students in problem-based learning. *Journal of Management Education, 28*, 610-629.

Kolb, D.A. (1984). *Experiential learning: Experience as a source of learning and development*. Englewood Cliffs, NJ: Prentice-Hall.

Lepsinger, R., & Lucia, A.D. (1997). *The art and science of 360 degree feedback*. San Francisco: Pfeiffer.

Longenecker, C.O., & Pinkel, G. (1997). Coaching to win at work. *Manage, 48*(2), 19-21.

Marsick, V., & O'Neil, J. (1999). The many faces of action learning. *Management Learning, 30*, 159-176.

McCorkle, D.E., Reardon, J., Alexander, J.F., Kling, N.D., Harris, R.C., & Iyer, R.V. (1999). Undergraduate marketing students, group projects, and teamwork: The good, the bad, and the ugly? *Journal of Marketing Education, 21*(2), 106-117.

McKeage, K., Skinner, D., Seymour, R.M., Donahue, D.W., & Christensen, T. (1999). Implementing an interdisciplinary marketing/engineering course project: Project format, preliminary evaluation, and critical factor review. *Journal of Marketing Education, 21*, 217-231.

McKendall, M. (2000). Teaching groups to become teams. *Journal of Education in Business, 75*, 277-282.

Mezirow, J. (1991). *Transformative dimensions of adult learning*. San Francisco: Jossey-Bass.

Michaelsen, L.K., & Black, R.H. (1994). Building learning teams: The key to harnessing the power of small groups in higher education. *Collaborative learning: A sourcebook for higher education* (Vol. 2). State College, PA: National Center for Teaching, Learning & Assessment. Retrieved March 16, 2005, from ftp://www.ntlf.com/ntlf/teamlearn.doc.

Michaelsen, L.K., Knight, A.B., & Fink, L.D. (Eds.). (2004). *Team-based learning: A transformative use of small groups in college teaching*. Sterling, VA: Stylus Publishing.

Miller, J.S. (2004). Problem-based learning in organizational behavior class: Solving students' real problems. *Journal of Management Education, 28*, 578-590.

Norman, G.R., & Schmidt, H.G. (1992). The psychological basis of problem based learning: A review of the evidence. *Academic Medicine, 67*, 557-565.

O'Neil, D.A., & Hopkins, M.M. (2002). The teacher as coach approach: Pedagogical choices for management educators. *Journal of Management Education, 26*, 402-414.

Papamarcos, S.D. (2002). The "next wave" in service learning: Integrative, team-based engagements with structural objectives. *Review of Business, 23*(2), 31-39.

Peterson, T.O. (2004). So you're thinking of trying problem based learning? Three critical success factors for implementation. *Journal of Management Education, 28*, 630-647.

Petkus, E., Jr. (2000). A theoretical and practical framework for service learning in marketing: Kolb's experiential learning cycle. *Journal of Marketing Education, 22*(1), 64-70.

Pfaff, E., & Huddleston, P. (2003). Does it matter if I hate teamwork? What impacts student attitudes toward teamwork. *Journal of Marketing Education, 25*, 37-45.

Rhodes, C., & Garrick, J. (2003). Project-based learning and the limits of corporate knowledge. *Journal of Management Education, 27*, 447-471.

Schon, D. (1983). *The reflective practitioner: How professionals think in action*. New York: Basic Books.

Sherwood, A.L. (2004). Problem-based learning in management education: A framework for designing context. *Journal of Management Education, 28*, 536-557.

Siciliano, J.I. (2001). How to incorporate cooperative learning principles in the classroom: It's more than just putting students in teams. *Journal of Management Education, 25*, 8-20.

Smith, B., & Dodds, R. (1997). *Developing managers through project-based learning*. Brookfield, VT: Gower.

Smith, L.W., & Van Doren, D.C. (2004). The reality-based learning method: A simple method for keeping teaching activities relevant and effective. *Journal of Marketing Education, 26*, 66-74.

Song, J.H., & Adams, C.R. (1993). Differentiation through customer involvement in production or delivery. *Journal of Consumer Marketing, 10*(2), 4-12.

Stinson, J.E., & Milter, R.G. (1996). Problem-based learning in business education: Curriculum design and implementation issues. In L. Wilkerson & W.H. Gijselaers (Eds.), *Bringing problem-based learning to higher education: Theory and practice* (pp. 33-42). San Francisco: Jossey-Bass.

Taylor, K.A. (1998). The marketing trade show: A new method for incorporating student projects in to large classes. *Journal of Marketing Education, 20*(3), 250-257.

Tiberius, R.G. (1986). Metaphors underlying the improvement of teaching and learning. *British Journal of Educational Technology, 17*, 144-156.

Watson, C., & Temkin, S. (2000), Just-in-time teaching: Balancing the competing demands of corporate American and academe in the delivery of management education. *Journal of Management Education, 24*, 763-778.

Wilkerson, L., & Gijselaers, W.H., (Eds.). (1996). *Bringing problem-based learning to higher education: Theory and practice*. San Francisco: Jossey-Bass.

Williams, D.L., Beard, J.D., & Rymer, J. (1991). Team projects: Achieving their full potential. *Journal of Marketing Education, 11*, 64-71.

Wood, C.M. (2003). The effects of creating psychological ownership among students in group projects. *Journal of Marketing Education, 25*, 240-249.

CHAPTER 16

ASSESSING PERFORMANCE IN PROJECTS FROM DIFFERENT ANGLES

Marjolein van Noort and A. Georges L. Romme

Students in higher education are increasingly confronted with learning environments in which they have to work together to analyze and solve complex problems of client organizations. In this chapter the authors describe three design propositions for assessing team and individual performance in project education. These propositions suggest to delegate part of the assessment to exploit the benefits of self- and peer assessment; provide feedback from different angles and stakeholders; and set clear and vivid assessment criteria to create a constructive friction between the skills students have initially and those expected at the end. These three propositions together constitute a general design philosophy for assessing student projects on authentic business problems. These propositions were tested in assessing student performance in projects done for external clients in an undergraduate Business Studies program. This pragmatic test showed positive results regarding the feasibility of the assessment system as well as its fairness and completeness. The different angles taken by academic staff, students and clients can therefore be effectively combined in assessing team and individual performance on projects.

INTRODUCTION

To facilitate the process of acquiring both problem-solving and team-related skills, students in higher education are increasingly confronted

Educating Managers through Real World Projects, 359–376

with complex learning environments in which they have to work together to solve a problem. An important objective for business educational programs is that students acquire the attitude and skills required in those environments. By learning to solve authentic business problems together with peers, students acquire team-related skills as well as the conceptual and procedural knowledge necessary to solve the kinds of problems they will encounter in their professional careers.

In this chapter three design propositions for assessing authentic business projects are described: delegate part of the assessment to exploit the benefits of self and peer assessment, provide feedback from different angles, and set clear and vivid assessment criteria to create a constructive friction between the skills students have initially and those expected at the end. These design propositions together constitute a general design philosophy for assessing student projects on authentic business problems. The assessment method presented is "empty" in the sense that, as long as the educational program is organized around projects, it can also be applied to other disciplines (e.g., engineering, psychology).

We tested the three design propositions in the undergraduate program in Business Studies at Tilburg University. The project assignments in this program involve an assessment approach that informs teaching staff about student progress and performance and provides the students with feedback regarding their work on the assignment. Moreover, students actively participate in the assessment procedure.

In this chapter we will first explore the issue of assessing complex problem-solving skills. Subsequently, project-based education is discussed. We then turn to several propositions for the design of an assessment system for performance in authentic projects. The next section shows how these propositions were applied to assessing performance on projects in an undergraduate program at Tilburg University. We also discuss how students, instructors and client-organizations evaluated this assessment approach.

ASSESSMENT

Assessment is typically defined as the testing methods used to measure the knowledge and skills level of students. However, Frederiksen (1984) argues that educators need a much broader conception of what testing is if they want to use test information to improve educational processes as well as want to reflect on educational goals. What exactly are those educational goals? Lengnick-Hall and Sanders (1997) identify three major goals:

1. *high levels of learning* (e.g., increased knowledge, skill, and understanding),

2. *high levels of change in, or intention to, change behavior* (e.g., application of new knowledge and skills), and

3. *highly positive reactions* (e.g., satisfaction with the educational program, the method of instruction, and the value of what was learned and intentions to recommend the educational program to others).

Dochy and McDowell (1997) argue that recent developments in western society, such as the increasing production of new scientific knowledge and the use of modern communication technology, have encouraged educators to implement new methods (like case-based and problem-based learning) that are directed toward producing highly knowledgeable individuals. These methods do also stress problem-solving skills, professional skills and learning in real-life contexts (Dochy, Segers, & Sluijsmans, 1999). This implies that the development of students into *reflective practitioners* is the ultimate goal of educational programs (Schön, 1987).

Birenbaum (1996) translates this goal into four competencies: cognitive competencies (such as problem solving, making informed judgements, oral and written expression), meta-cognitive competencies (self-reflection and self-evaluation), social competencies (leading discussions and conversations, persuading and working in groups) and affective dispositions (e.g., internal motivation, responsibility, self-efficacy, independence, flexibility and coping with frustrating situations).

Conventional assessment methods, such as multiple choice testing, reinforce a *testing culture* in which the more complex cognitive abilities are not tested (Frederiksen, 1984), but only the reproduction of knowledge is measured. Therefore, assessment should also aim to provide information about the ability of students to solve ill-structured problems, because most of the important problems that students face and will face in real life indeed are ill-structured. Birenbaum (1994) states that, at least rhetorically, a shift has taken place from this culture of testing to a so-called *assessment culture*, in which a strong emphasis is put on integrating assessment and instruction. Alternative assessment methods, such as self, peer and co-assessment (Dochy et al., 1999), group assignments, portfolios, overall-tests (Van Berkel & Bax, 2002), theory-based class activities (Fiet, 2000) and collaborative problem-solving tasks (Frederiksen, 1999) encourage active learning and reflecting by students upon their own work. Sambell, McDowell, and Brown (1997) argue that the use of alternative assessment methods leads to the integration of assessment, teaching and learning that involves students as active and informed participants. This involvement means that educators have to establish a student-approved system for assessment (Fiet, 2000). An exploratory study of student perceptions of the effects of assessment on learning and teaching by Sambell et al. (1997) suggests that assessment has a positive effect on student learning and is perceived to be "fair" when it answers to the following criteria: the assessment should

- relate to authentic tasks,
- represent reasonable tasks,
- be perceived to have long-term benefits,
- provide adequate feedback about students' progression, and
- reward genuine effort, rather than measuring "luck."

PROJECT-BASED EDUCATION

To engage in project-based education means that teaching staff becomes less the initiator of knowledge transfer and more the coach who has a facilitating role toward students. Because the problem the students have to solve determines the theoretical concepts to be used, a large part of the responsibility for the learning process is delegated to students.

Project education can be divided into design-oriented (know how) and problem-oriented (know why) education (Kjersdam & Enemark, 1999). Design-oriented project education deals with practical problems for which students, mostly in teams, have to formulate solutions on the basis of a synthesis of knowledge from several disciplines. Problem-oriented project education deals with the solution of theoretical problems by students through the use of any relevant knowledge regardless of the discipline the knowledge derives from. Kjersdam and Enemark (1999) suggest this makes project education multidisciplinary by nature. General themes and related projects connecting different subjects thus make up the curriculum; subject courses provide student learning with regard to the core elements of the subjects included and project work provides the opportunity to explore the application of the subjects in practice.

Romme (2003a) thus argues that the educational philosophy of project-based education implies that education is organized as an authentic organization. This idea provides an important bridge between educational practice and organizational theory. It suggests we can design and shape education as an organizational system, similar to any other organization out there. Designing education as an authentic organization implies that students and their instructors experience and create organizational roles, procedures, leadership, group dynamics and performance directly, rather than only studying these phenomena indirectly. In this respect, the lack of (opportunities for) firsthand experience in higher education typically leads to substitutes such as case teaching, games, simulations, and so forth: thus, students explore, study and "apply" ideas, concepts, theories and methods on the basis of substitute-experiences. Designing a class of students as an organizational system does not imply simulation (doing things "as if"), but setting up an organization that deliberately focuses on producing the kind of learning behavior that leads to the intended learning outcomes or products. Thus, the goal of this organization is to produce learning and the organization is structured, managed and monitored by means of tools, procedures and systems which are designed or chosen in view of the organization's goal.

An important implication of designing education as an organization is that task interdependencies between participants have to be substantial. Without task interdependency, the learning process will become largely individual (as in instruction-centered education) rather than social and organizational (Romme, 2003a). With task interdependencies, shared responsibilities can be created that will give rise to "organizational" processes, behavior and learning.

DESIGN PROPOSITIONS FOR ASSESSING PERFORMANCE IN PROJECT EDUCATION

We now turn to several design propositions for designing an assessment system for performance in authentic projects. Romme (2003b) describes the methodological nature of design propositions—that have descriptive as well as normative properties—in more detail.

Peer mentoring in the context of teamwork appears to provide a bridge between organizational and educational theory and practice (McDougall & Beattie, 1997). In this respect, Piaget (1970) emphasized the importance of social interactions among students, as an important resource for teaching and learning. He believed that for intellectual development, cooperation among peers is as important as the student's interaction with teachers. Discussion and cooperation among students can cause awareness of different points of view, and other students at similar cognitive levels can often help the student more than instructors to move away from deeply ingrained misconceptions and convictions (Piaget, 1970; Vygotski, 1978).

Thus, reciprocal teaching and peer mentoring produces significant learning benefits, compared to ways of teaching and mentoring by people of a higher hierarchical status (e.g., Bruffee, 1993; McDougall & Beattie, 1997). For example, students who are continually engaged in peer group discussions about their work in mathematics and science courses have been observed to perform significantly better than students who work largely isolated from one another outside class hours (Bruffee, 1993).

Dochy et al. (1999) argue "self and peer assessment are combined when students are assessing peers but the self is also included as a member of the group and must be assessed. This combination fosters reflection on the student's own learning process and learning activities compared to those of the other members in the group or class" (p. 340).

Peer review helps individuals within the group to learn about their team related skills (Lejk, Wyvill, & Farrow, 1996) and when combined with self-assessment allows a student to make comparisons between the reflection on his/her own learning process and those of the other members in the group (Dochy et al., 1999). In sum, the first design proposition is:

> *Design Proposition 1:*   When assessing individual and team performance in authentic projects, delegate part of the assessment in order to exploit the benefits of self and peer assessment.

In general, it is important to leave the assessment with the people best equipped to evaluate certain aspects of the performance being assessed. This idea sounds very straightforward. However, it's often the case that instructors assess the relevance and applicability of findings and recommendations with regard to a real life (business) problem. Having the owner of this problem assess the relevance of the findings would in all likelihood be more insightful and straightforward, in terms of direct feedback to both students and the instructor.

However, involving different types of assessors (e.g., academic supervisor, students, and the client-owner of the problem) in the assessment procedure can cause confusion: who is to assess which aspect? Therefore, it should be clear from the outset who is going to assess, what this person is going to assess and how 'rich' the feedback should be.

Regarding the richness of the feedback, there are two options. Formative assessments aim to improve learning while it is happening, in order to determine to what extent the students are realizing the objectives set by the educational program or by themselves (Topping, 1998). Summative assessment usually takes place at the end of the semester or academic year, and only indicates whether or not the student has mastered a subject. In sum, we propose the following design principle:

> *Design Proposition 2:*   In assessing performance in authentic business projects, provide formative and summative feedback from different angles to assess whether relevant concepts, theories and methods are applied correctly to understand and solve the client's problem.

In an educational setting, delegating without well-defined responsibilities and standards may lead nowhere. Recent work by Dougherty (2001) suggests that standardization is not only an important process in bureaucratically organized systems involving highly programmable activities, but also in organizations relying on innovative capabilities and work. In the latter organizations senior managers can generate specific, vivid standards that represent the practice overall in all local teams and communities of practice, and then oversee their ongoing enactment and re-enactment. These visible and achievable standards "are there leading the way, so to speak, helping to frame the kinds of actions people might take in their particular situations of practice" (Dougherty 2001, p. 629).

The purpose of setting standards and criteria is to create constructive friction between the competences and skills students have at the outset and those expected (e.g., when completing the course). In the case of too large friction—that is, a huge destructive gap between the initial competences and skills and what is expected—students feel overcharged and become confused and frustrated (Burns & Gentry, 1998).

The assessment criteria regarding performance in projects should therefore offer a clear sense of purpose. This purpose typically is dualistic, for example, involving the development of individual skills and knowledge as well as understanding and solving a real business problem. This type of purpose and assessment criteria secures the link between the educational program and (business) organizations. In this respect, real life issues of clients ensure the educational program stays outwardly focused and avoids students being 'sheltered' from real life (Fiet, 2000). To make this experience as real as possible, the client must participate in the assessment (as suggested in Proposition 2). In sum, this leads to the following proposition:

> *Design Proposition 3:*   When assessing performance in authentic projects, set clear and vivid assessment criteria to create a constructive friction between the competences and skills students have at the outset and those expected at the end.

PROJECT EDUCATION AT TILBURG UNIVERSITY

This section focuses on the assessment of authentic projects in the undergraduate Business Studies program at Tilburg University (Netherlands). This is a three-year program leading to a Bachelor of Science in Business Studies degree. It provides students the opportunity to develop knowledge and skills for a career in business organizations. To develop the ability to think and act effectively when working with people in business organizations, the program covers the standard business subjects such as marketing, organization, accounting and finance. In addition, this undergraduate program targets the development of skills in the area of project management, interpersonal communication, teamwork, research, planning, writing, reporting and entrepreneurship.

The educational approach in each semester involves a combination of several subject courses and a project for an external client-organization.

Similar to Aalborg University (Kjersdam & Enemark, 1999), each semester is organized around a single theme: subject courses require students to study the core elements of the subjects and the project work involves applying (some of) these subjects to practical issues. All the project work is done in teams of about five students; the same teams also deliver work on several team assignments in the subject courses—that also involve individual performance measurements (e.g., paper assignments or exams).

In the first year of the program the university acquires the client projects, but as of the first semester of the second year students are expected to do this themselves. This means that student teams engage in networking and acquisition activities; when a team has found an interested client, it collaborates with the client-organization to translate the client's needs and problems into project objectives. The team then draws on concepts, models and techniques of at least two different courses offered and any other source in order to complete the project assignment successfully.

The requirement that a project should involve the application of material from at least two subject courses has several implications. First, it enables student teams to match client needs with subject courses chosen from a list of subjects (e.g., the subjects in the current and previous semester). Second, this requirement implies that students have to explore the relationships between different subjects (e.g., marketing and accounting).

The search for authentic projects requires students to leave the classroom environment. This can be very beneficial to the learning process. In classroom settings in which the instructor lectures and students listen and interact with the instructor, students generally work alone, student participation tends to be passive and students tend to feel disconnected from the task and its meaning (Clearly, 1996). Going into the "real business world" gives the curriculum an outward focus with greater reference to the needs of future employers.

APPLYING AND TESTING THE DESIGN PROPOSITIONS

In this section we turn to the development and implementation of the assessment system in the undergraduate program outlined in the previous section. We developed a specific assessment system by applying and elaborating the general design propositions into a specific real system (summarized in Figure 16.1). The relationship between the three design propositions and the actual design is such that the latter must be congruent with the design propositions, but that other designs in other settings can also be developed. In this respect, the design propositions serve as heuristics in developing an assessment system that can be tested in practice.

The assessment system is developed in a particular semester in the undergraduate program outlined in the previous section: the first semes-

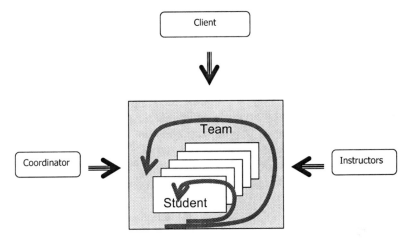

Figure 16.1.   Assessment from different angles.

ter of year two of the curriculum. In the winter semester of 2002-2003, we developed and pilot tested an assessment system in this semester. On the basis of the findings of this pilot test, the assessment system (with a few minor modifications) was subsequently also implemented in all other semesters.

The first semester of the second year of the Business Studies undergraduate program focuses on "business processes," the activities necessary to create value for consumers and buyers. The main subjects taught in this semester are operations management, consumer behavior and corporate finance. In addition, an introductory course in the philosophy of science outlines key philosophical ideas and concepts—such as induction and deduction—in order to help students understand the process of knowledge development. The integrating element of this semester is the project assignment in which student teams apply theories and methods to practice. More specifically, students are challenged to provide a tailor-made solution to an authentic business problem in the area of business processes. As we have described in the previous section, each student team is invited to acquire a client for their project assignment.

On the basis of the three design propositions described earlier, the following assessment system is developed. First, an academic staff member serves as the project coordinator of the project assignment. The project coordinator coaches each student team, with support from instructors of the subject courses regarding advanced issues. The project coordinator assesses the final report together with the client and instructors on the basis of a list of criteria for assessing the report (see Appendix A). The client is invited to assess the report with regard to one criterion only: the usefulness and relevance of the findings and recommendations. Depending on which subjects are applied, the project coordinator invites academic instructors of these subjects to participate in the assessment (focusing in this case on those criteria that relate to the application of their subject area).

Second, to assess the process by which the project comes about *and* the team-related skills, the students deliver both a midterm and a final self and peer assessment form. The midterm self and peer assessment is for formative purposes only, to get a feel of what self and peer assessment is about and to get an idea of what the current performance is. The assessment at the end of the semester is also used to derive individual grades from the team grade.

Third, the self and peer assessment process draws on eight criteria. Six criteria are standardized across all teams; program management and the project coordinator selected these criteria from an overview of peer assessment methods by Lejk et al. (1996). In addition, each team can propose two criteria also believed to be important for assessing individual performance in their team. These two additional criteria are formulated in a so-called team contract, an agreement between the members of the team that is developed and submitted in the first two weeks of the semester. Appendix B provides an overview of the criteria used, the assessment procedure and the algorithm adopted to differentiate team grades into individual grades.

Because the calculation and application of self and peer assessment scores involve a substantial amount of work, Tilburg University developed a web-based software program for the assessment procedure. The outcomes of the self and peer assessment procedure are, formally, not more than "recommendations" to the project coordinator. In particular cases—for example, when the standard deviation of the peer assessments regarding a certain student is high—the project coordinator will invite individual students or the whole team to a meeting to discuss the why and how of these results. These additional data then also serve as inputs to the final decision by the coordinator to differentiate the grade for the team report into individual grades.

Method

We collected qualitative data throughout the semester starting in September 2002 and completed in January 2003. The methods for collecting data included participant observation and interviews with students, instructors, and clients (cf. French & Bell, 1984).

One of the authors acted as the project coordinator of the project assignment in this semester. This role allowed her to directly observe students and instructors (and in a few cases also clients) while working on the projects or supervising student teams.

In the interviews with students a staged approach was employed (Sambell et al., 1997). In the early stages of the semester, semi-structured interviews with key groups of students were conducted, followed by interviews with individual students in which data obtained from the previous interviews are fed back in order to extend these data and deepen our understanding.

The interviews with clients and instructors were semi-structured, and were conducted after the semester ended.

Findings

The semi-structured group discussions with student teams showed that they are very positive about the opportunity to go "outside the classroom" and apply theories to practice. Students also thought that the requirement to deliver a team agreement early in the semester together with the peer assessment approach strongly prevent and reduce (potential) free riding in their teams. In the group interviews, most teams also referred to the experiences they had with an earlier project assignment (in the first year of the program) that was more restrictive:

> Last year we had to write a business plan according to a preset structure for a firm, so we didn't have the opportunity to kind of "zoom in" on certain aspects, because we were required to cover certain topics. With the current project we have more freedom to focus on certain topics.

Student teams were rather effective in finding client-organizations: 25 out of 28 student teams found their own client without any help from staff members. The remaining three teams either got a client via the project coordinator or were allowed to work on a university project.

Both the group and individual interviews point out that almost all students were very satisfied with the self and peer assessment approach. During the semester some students feel somewhat anxious about being assessed by their peers, but this anxiety has typically dissolved toward the end of the semester—also for students whose individual grades end up being lower than the team grade. In other words, the assessment process is being perceived as fair and students readily accept the outcomes regardless of whether these are negative or positive for their individual grade.

In general, the interviewed clients appreciated the professional attitude of students and the opportunity to engage with the research process and outcomes regarding a business issue of the client-organization. In most cases, clients also perceived the findings and recommendations by student teams as very useful. These findings were confirmed in their assessments of the project reports, as communicated directly to the project coordinator.

Some clients, in particular small firms, did not like the fact that student teams wrote reports in English (this is a requirement in the Business Studies program that is fully conducted in English). The representatives of these client-firms typically did not, or barely, understand English and therefore preferred a report in Dutch. These student teams therefore translated the final report (to the coordinator) into Dutch for the client. This extra work, evidently, was also a source of frustration for the students involved.

Instructors observed that the team agreements (between team members) and project contracts (with clients) facilitated a rather smooth process; most instructors attributed this to the formalized and transparent nature of both agreements—transparency arising from the fact that these agreements and contracts were communicated to all parties involved.

Depending on whether their subject was applied in a particular project, instructors were invited to co-assess the project report. In this respect, the instructors rated team reports with regard to research methods, literature review and other criteria pertaining to how their subject was applied in the project (see Appendix A). In general, instructors were quite happy with the quality of the reports they assessed, with some reports being of exceptional high quality and several others being insufficient (the latter had to be substantially rewritten). They were particularly surprised about how well student teams at this level (second year) were able to combine different research techniques (e.g., analyzing documents, conducting interviews with different parties, conducting surveys). According to one of the instructors:

> Compared with students in other programs taught by our faculty, for example those who are writing a Master's thesis, these second year undergraduate students are very creative in applying different research techniques.

One of the authors of this chapter served as project coordinator in this pilot semester. She was also quite positive about how assessing students from different angles affects student motivation and performance. A major drawback of including different stakeholders—peers, clients, instructors, and coordinator—in the assessment process is that the coordinator has to collect all inputs, compare these inputs, and draw up a final assessment form for each team report. This means the coordinator has to spend extra time on completing the assessment at the end of the semester. Significant time delays in getting this done arise from clients requiring several weeks to (internally) distribute, read, discuss and evaluate the report; this in itself signifies that the clients were willing to spend time on discussing and evaluating the findings and conclusions, but also generated substantial delays in giving feedback to students.

Another problem for the coordinator was that when teams were off campus doing field research she was unable to communicate directly with these teams. In this respect, teams had the discretion to contact the coordinator or instructors whenever they felt it was necessary. Toward the end of the semester, the coordinator observed that those teams that faced the most severe problems—either interpersonal issues within the team or issues related to the research process—had failed to get help from the coordinator or one of the instructors. As such, the coordinator as well as the instructors involved felt that the supervision of teams, also when they were off campus, could be organized in a somewhat more structured manner.

Implications

Overall, the findings regarding the design and application of the assessment approach were quite positive. The assessment system was subsequently applied and implemented in the project assignments in all other semesters in the undergraduate Business Studies program. Some minor modifications were introduced regarding the language of the team reports and the supervision process during the semester. In addition, we developed some additional guidelines for the project contract with clients, to create more awareness up-front of what was expected of them regarding the assessment process later on in the semester.

CONCLUDING REMARKS

In this chapter we described three design propositions for assessing team and individual performance in project education. These propositions suggest to delegate part of the assessment to exploit the benefits of self and peer assessment, provide feedback from different angles and stakeholders, and set clear and vivid assessment criteria to create a constructive friction between the skills students have initially and those expected at the end. These design propositions together constitute a general design philosophy for assessing student projects on authentic business problems.

The three design propositions can be applied and developed into a specific assessment system in many ways. One particular way to apply these propositions involved the assessment of performance on projects for external clients in an undergraduate Business Studies program. This pragmatic test showed positive results regarding the feasibility of the assessment system as well as its fairness and completeness. Thus, the different angles taken by academic staff, students and clients can be effectively combined in assessing team and individual performance on projects.

APPENDIX A: PROJECT REPORT CRITERIA

A. Research Questions
1. The main research question is formulated in an useful and measurable way
2. The sub-questions logically follow from the main research question

B. Method
1. The methods and techniques used to gather and analyse data are appropriate (in view of the research questions) and effectively used

C. Literature research
1. The literature used is relevant in view of the research questions
2. The amount of literature studied and applied is sufficient (at least 8 items)

D. Structure & readability
1. The report is logically structured
2. The report contains no writing or style errors (in grammar, word choice, or paragraph writing)

E. Conclusion
1. The conclusion provides an answer to the research questions
2. The conclusion shows the authors have correctly applied theories and methods to understand (and if possible, solve) the business issue at hand

F. Managerial relevance
1. The research report contains useful and practical recommendations for the client

G. Number of pages
1. The research report doesn't exceed 20 pages (excluding any appendices)

APPENDIX B: SELF & PEER ASSESSMENT

Write your own name and the names of the other members of your team in the spaces in the first row. Subsequently, assess yourself as well as each team member on all criteria by using a scale from –1 to 3, defined as follows:

- 3 for *better than most of the team in this respect*
- 2 for *about average for this team in this respect*
- 1 for *not as good as most of the team in this respect*
- 0 for *no help at all in this respect*
- -1 for *a hindrance to the team in this respect*

CRITERIA:	Your own name:	....	....	....	....
-- team criterion 1 --					
-- team criterion 2 --					
Participation in team meetings:					
Helping the group to function well as a team:					
Literature search and study:					
Data collection:					
Data analysis:					
Report writing:					

Comments:

- This is the form that students can print and use for formative purposes during the semester, to evaluate and discuss individual contributions to the team. The formal self and peer assessment done at the end of the semester is processed entirely via a web-based electronic system, in which the names of all students have been entered; thus, each student enter his/her quantitative assessments on a computer screen which gives the names of all the team's members (incl. own name) as well as the two criteria the team has added at the beginning of the semester.

- The form above involves six 'standard' criteria: two criteria refer to the contribution to team process and four others refer to the individual contribution to the team assignment and report. In other semesters in the program these criteria may be somewhat different, depending on the priorities set by program management and the project coordinator.

- The peer assessment scores are the basis for differentiating the team's grade into individual grades. The course coordinator may first want to check the validity of the peer assessment outcomes for certain students, or a whole team—for example, in view of the variance of certain scores for a particular student and qualitative data he has obtained during supervision meetings. Subsequently, the coordinator can differentiate team grades into individual grades by using an algorithm that draws on the following variables (adapted from: Lejk et al., 1996):

  - Individual Peer Assessment (IPA), calculated as the average score on the eight criteria given by the four peers of the individual.

  - Average Peer Assessment (APA), calculated as the average score on all criteria for all members of the team.

  - W: the percentage of the individual mark that is based directly on the team grade (W is 40, 50 or 60 % in the case of the Business Studies program at Tilburg University).

  - Grade for Team Report (GTR): on a scale from 1 to 10, 10 being the highest grade for the best performance possible).

The algorithm used involves two equations:

$$\text{PA factor} = W\% + (100 - W\%) \times \text{IPA/APA}$$

$$\text{Individual Grade} = \text{PA factor} \times \text{GTR}$$

- In the web-based self and peer assessment system, the course coordinator has access to all individual and team data; that is, he can see how an individual student assessed herself, how peers assessed each other, what the standard deviations are, and so forth. When all assessments have been entered into the system, each individual student has access to a table that compares the self-assessment scores with the average scores given by his/her peers per criterion.

REFERENCES

Birenbaum, M. (1994). Toward adaptive assessment—the student's angle. *Studies in Educational Evaluation, 20,* 239-255.

Birenbaum, M. (1996). Assessment 2000: Towards a pluralistic approach to assessment. M. Birenbaum & F. Dochy (Eds.), *Alternatives in assessment of achievement, learning processes and prior knowledge* (pp. 3-31). Boston: Kluwer Academic.

Bruffee, K.A. (1993). *Collaborative learning.* Baltimore, MD/London: John Hopkins University Press.

Burns, A.C., & Gentry, J.W. (1998). Motivating students to engage in experiential learning: A tension-to-learn theory. *Simulation & Gaming, 29,* 133-151.

Clearly, B.A. (1996). Relearning the learning process. *Quality Progress, 29*(4).

Dochy, F., & McDowell, L. (1997). Assessment as a tool for learning. *Studies in Educational Evaluation, 23,* 279-298.

Dochy, F., Segers, M., & Sluijsmans, D. (1999). The use of self-, peer and co-assessment in higher education: A review. *Studies in Higher Education, 24,* 331-350.

Dougherty, D. (2001). Reimagining the differentiation and integration of work for sustained product innovation. *Organization Science, 12,* 612-631.

Fiet, J. O. (2000). The pedagogical side of entrepreneurship theory. *Journal of Business Venturing, 16,* 101-117.

Frederiksen, C.H. (1999). Learning to reason through discourse in a problem-based learning group. *Discourse Processes, 27,* 135-160.

Frederiksen, N. (1984). The real test bias: Influences of testing on teaching and learning. *American Psychologist, 39,* 193-202.

French, W., & Bell, C. (1984). *Action research and organization development.* Englewood Cliffs, NJ: Prentice-Hall.

Kjersdam, F., & Enemark, S. (1999). *The Aalborg experiment: Project innovation in university education.* Aalborg: Aalborg University Press.

Lejk, M., Wyvill, M., & Farrow, S. (1996). A survey of methods of deriving individual grades from group assessments. *Assessment & Evaluation in Higher Education, 21,* 267-280.

Lengnick-Hall, C.A., & Sanders, M.M. (1997). Designing effective learning systems for management education: Student roles, requisite variety, and practicing what we teach. *Academy of Management Journal, 40,* 1334-1368.

McDougall, M., & Beattie, R.S. (1997). Peer mentoring at work: The nature and outcomes of non-hierarchical developmental relationships. *Management Learning, 28,* 423-438.

Piaget, J. (1970). *Science of education and the psychology of the child.* New York: Viking Press.

Romme, A.G.L. (2003a). Organizing education by drawing on organization studies. *Organization Studies, 24,* 697-720.

Romme, A.G.L. (2003b). Making a difference: Organization as design. *Organization Science, 14,* 558-573.

Sambell, K., McDowell, L., & Brown, S. (1997). But is it fair?: An exploratory study of student perceptions of the consequential validity of assessment. *Studies in Educational Evaluation, 23*, 349-371.

Schön, D.A. (1987). *Educating the reflective practitioner: Towards a new design for teaching and learning in the professions*. San Francisco: Jossey-Bass.

Topping, K. (1998). Peer assessment between students in colleges and universities. *Review of Educational Research, 68*, 249-276.

Van Berkel, H., & Bax, A. (2002). *Toetsen in het Hoger Onderwijs*, Houten: Bohn Stafleu van Loghum.

Vygotski, L. S. (1978). *Mind in society: The development of higher psychological processes*. Cambridge, MA: Harvard University Press.

ABOUT THE EDITORS

Charles Wankel is associate professor of management at St. John's University, New York. Dr. Wankel publishes and presents research on the use of information technologies in support of management education and development. He is the leading founder and director of scholarly virtual communities for management professors, currently directing eight with thousands of participants in more than 70 nations. He has taught in Lithuania at the Kaunas University of Technology (Fulbright Fellowship), University of Vilnius (United Nations Development Program and Soros Foundation funding). Recent invited lectures include 2005 Distinguished Speaker at the E-ducation without Border Conference, Abu Dhabi and 2004 keynote speaker at the Nippon Academy of Management, Tokyo. Corporate management development program development clients include McDonald's Corporation's Hamburger University and IBM Learning Services. Pro bono consulting assignments include re-engineering and total quality management programs for the Lithuanian National Postal Service. Email: wankelc@stjohns.edu

Robert DeFillippi is professor of management and director of the Center for Innovation and Change Leadership (www.ciclsuffolk.org) at Suffolk University Business School. Dr. DeFillippi publishes in leading U.S. and European journals on issues related to how knowledge creation and learning can be fostered through the effective organization and management of innovative and creative work-based projects. Dr. DeFillippi is associate editor for the *International Journal of Management Reviews* and serves on the editorial boards of *Management Learning*, *Journal of Organizational Behavior* and *Organization Management Journal*. He has served as guest editor for past issues of *Management Lear*ning (2001) and *Organiza-tion Studies* (2004) related to his work on project-based learning and project-based innovation respectively. Dr. DeFillippi was 2001-2002 chairperson for Management Education and Development for the Academy of Management and currently serves on the Management Education and Development Executive Board. He has received national recognition for his workshops on project-based learning and is a frequent speaker at international conferences on project learning and project organizations. Email: rdefilli@suffolk.edu

Printed in the United States
62157LVS00002B/12

9 781593 113704